A Racial Timeline: Stigmatization to Execution

(A Resource for Atkins Claims[1])

Edward Burns
Professor Emeritus
Binghamton University

---

[1]Updated April 18, 2020

A Racial Timeline: Stigmatization to Execution
Copyright © 2018 by Edward Burns

Data, Revisions and Suggestions

Death penalty data and data for intellectual disabilities are dynamic and time dependent. Exact data for the number of inmates on death row can change daily as can the number of executions, exonerations, Atkins claims, etc. Data for reconciling childhood intellectual disabilities with the death penalty is no less daunting. Many inmates have been on death row for years and some for decades. The appropriate frame of reference for evaluating mental retardation/intellectual disability data should begin with the developmental years and consider all data that is germane to intellectual functioning and adaptive behavior. Unfortunately, data are not always available, or appropriate, and extrapolating from any database is, at best, an approximation. To this end, an attempt will be made to update this resource yearly. Just as important, suggestions, corrections and additional data that are relevant will be much appreciated. My hope is that by collaboration we will develop a better understanding of how intellectual disability is best defined and refined for purposes of the Supreme Court's Atkins v. Virginia decision in 2002. Send thoughts, corrections, and suggestions to eburns@binghamtion.edu.

Preface

The purpose of this book is not to focus on intellectual disability or the death penalty, but how mental retardation/intellectual disability[2] is used to stigmatize and deprive children of educational opportunity, many of whom are black, and then to deny adults, many of whom are also black, lesser culpability for capital crimes as mandated by the Supreme Court in Atkins v. Virginia in 2002.[3] The hypocrisy for how mental retardation/intellectual disability for children and adults is used by States is great.

For many black children the mental retardation/intellectual disability category has been a ready solution, incorrect as it is, to explain the effects of segregation and discrimination. Likewise for adults, States routinely re-interpret and contort the definition of intellectual disability so that the task for identifying offenders who warrant lesser culpability is very much "discretionary, haphazard, and discriminatory."[4] The litany of strategies used to reject Atkins claims— life in prison rather than execution because of intellectual disability— includes cherry picking "credible" IQ scores, creating evidentiary criteria for denying claims (e.g., being able to drive a car), and requiring a determination intellectual deficiency before age 18, at the time of the crime, while on death row, or a Kafkaesque combination of these and other factors..

Just as States employed a variety of strategies to avoid desegregation following Brown v. Board of Education of Topeka, Kansas in 1954,[5] States have been no less creative in finding ways to deny claims by capital offenders because of intellectual disability. There is overwhelming evidence, based on the number of black defendants sentenced to death, executions, exonerations, the disproportionate use of mild intellectual disabilities to identify black children, discounting mild intellectual disabilities for black

---

[2]The terminology has changed from *mentally retarded* to *intellectual disability* as a result of Rosa's law in 2010
[3]Atkins v. Virginia, 536 U.S. 304 (2002)
[4]Furman v. Georgia, 408 U.S. 238, 1972
[5]Brown v. Board of Education, 347 U.S. 483

adult defendants, and all other aspects of death penalty jurisprudence (e.g., juror selection), that race plays an important role when States are required to grant lesser culpability for adults seeking Atkins relief.

The piecemeal approach used by the Supreme Court to direct some degree of constitutional compliance with *Atkins*, as shown by the rejection of the strict IQ cutoff used by Florida and the interpretation of adaptive behavior in Texas, does not reconcile the fact that States are simply unable to determine who should be provided lesser culpability under *Atkins*. Until States can provide a coherent and constitutional plan for determining lesser culpability because of intellectual disability, the death penalty for all offenders should be suspended. If not, there is a great probability that many offenders who warrant lesser culpability will be executed. Indeed, many offenders who deserved lesser culpability have been executed.

In 2017 the Supreme Court rejected the enhanced definition of adaptive behavior used to guide Texas courts when determining intellectual disability.[6] Earlier, in 2014, the Court rejected the bright line IQ score of 70 used by Florida to preclude the consideration of other evidence of intellectual disability when the death penalty was a sentencing option.[7] Nonetheless, in spite of these efforts to narrow the category of offenders warranting execution, prosecutors and courts have many other strategies for rejecting claimants seeking relief and to circumvent *Atkins*.

One overriding difficulty when addressing Atkins claims, in addition to the idiosyncratic interpretations of intellectual disability, is the racism inherent in every aspect of the death penalty. This deep-rooted racism has emerged from the lamentable history of lynchings, the effects of *de jure* and *de facto* segregation, and a justice system which, as noted in Brown v. Board of Education, "deprives these plaintiffs of the equal protection of the laws." For Linda Brown and the other children comprising the 1954 Supreme Court decision, school segregation was found to violate the Fourteenth Amendment; for many on

---

[6]Moore v. Texas, Supreme Court of the United States, March 28, 2017.
[7]Hall v. Florida, 572 U.S. ____ (2014)

death the justice system weighs heavily against a fair and race neutral determination of intellectual disability for those most deserving of the death penalty. In 2014 the "court held that the Eighth and Fourteenth Amendments forbid the execution of persons with intellectual disabilities." For black defendants the Fourteenth Amendment should offer protection "against conviction except upon proof beyond a reasonable doubt of every fact necessary to constitute the crime with which he is charged"[8] but race often intervenes involving issues from arrest to conviction.

The cornerstone of *Atkins* is the Eighth Amendment and the prohibition against "cruel and unusual punishments." If convicted of capital murder, the Eighth Amendment prohibiting the execution of the intellectually disabled, and the underlying belief that this Amendment protects "human dignity," is noteworthy more for eloquence than consequence. For many black defendants convicted of capital murder a re-interpretation of "equal protection" is used to ignore a prior determination of intellectual disability and the denial of educational opportunity.

For both children and adults IQ tests are bandied about but in a disingenuous and self-serving manner. Black children are stigmatized as intellectually disabled to rationalize (and dismiss) wretched educational and environmental circumstances, but adults seeking Atkins relief are found to be intellectually whole under the guise, of all things, the Eighth Amendment where the "cruel and unusual punishments" clause is used to permit rather than restrict executions. The Eighth Amendment is interpreted to require a heightened standard in Atkins claims by adhering to criteria for intellectual disability that are contrary to the history and purpose of the professional definitions of intellectual disability—and often contrary to common sense.

 Atkins v. Virginia highlights rather than solves the problem for determining intellectual disability in capital sentencing. Florida is a case in point. In August of 2017 the death row population of Florida was 365 and the average age slightly over 50 years. In 1980, when many of these inmates were of school age, the black

---

[8]Cage v. Louisiana, 498 U.S. 39 (1990)

school enrollment in Florida was 20.4 percent ,yet over 60 percent of the children classified as **educable mentally retarded** (EMR[9]) were black.[10] One explanation for this disproportionality was simply to meet the educational needs of black students; a less sanguine explanation is that many black children were classified as EMR because they were black—and thus deserving of an inferior education— just as many offenders receive the death penalty because they are black. Intellectual disability has different ends for black children and adults but the commonality for both is an invidious purpose, a much nuanced form of racial animus, and, for both, a very bad outcome.

In schools before *Brown* (and after) racism was transparent: black children were segregated because they were black. Following *Brown* EMR became a popular method for dealing with the effects of segregation by attributing poor school performance to intellectual disability. And, lo and behold, the solution for addressing the effects of prior segregation and discrimination was a more benevolent form of segregation but segregation nonetheless. The underlying racial intent for disproportionality in the intellectual disability category becomes apparent when considering the racial makeup in other disabilities that are less stigmatizing and segregative. Black children are mentally retarded/intellectually disabled when the solution is segregated classes and a second-rate curriculum (at best) but not having other disabilities when services are extensive, often more costly, more needed or less segregative—or, for adult Atkins claimants, when execution is a possible solution.

In more recent years racial disproportionality in classes for children with intellectual disabilities has decreased in Florida and nationwide. However, in 1998 when actual enrollment data for children in classes for the mentally retarded were collected in compliance with the Individuals with Disabilities Education Act, there were over 19,000 children identified as EMR in Florida and

---

[9]The traditional EMR category was referred to as EMH (Educable Mentally Handicapped) in Florida
[10]The total number of children classified as EMR was more than 18,500. 1980 Elementary and Secondary Schools Civil Rights Survey, State Summaries, Washington, D.C., 1982, ED#219478

of these children 50.1 percent were black in comparison to a black 6 to 21 population of 21.4 percent. In spite of the large number of black children identified as having mental retardation in 1998, Florida has found few black adults eligible for Atkins relief. The reasons for this are many and range from a strict interpretation of criteria for adults—and a not so strict interpretation for children—to the difficult-to-believe notion that when a defendant is able to assert the constitutional right not to be executed that this is an indication that the defendant is really not intellectually disabled.[11]

For black adults the reasons for the racial disproportionality on death row and for executions is hidden in the motive and intent of arresting officers, courts, prosecutors, and juries. This was not always so, as it was for children, when racism was open for all to see. During the Jim Crow era blacks comprised 88 percent of all lynchings and 97 percent of lynchings when the reason involved "rape" and "attempted rape" which were goto words for all manner of perceived slights. For black adults following the reinstatement of the death penalty in 1976, racial motive might have become less obvious, but invidious purpose and capital punishment are inextricably related. [12]

When stigmatization and an inferior education are educational possibilities, black children are readily considered intellectually deficient. When the death penalty is a sentencing possibility, States become incredibly racial conscious and readily ignore past and present intellectual disability criteria. Given that the death row population in the United States is 41.6 percent black according to an NAACP 2020 report[13] and because of the disproportionate identification (sometimes correct and often not)

---

[11]Goodin v. Mississippi, Supreme Court of Mississippi, No. 2010-CA-01762-SCT, December 13, 2012

[12]Espy, M. Watt, and John Ortiz Smykla. Executions in the United States, 1608-2002: The ESPY File . ICPSR08451-v5. Ann Arbor, MI: Inter-university Consortium for Political and Social Research

[13]Source: DEATH ROW U.S.A., A quarterly report by the Criminal Justice Project of the NAACP Legal Defense and Educational Fund, Inc., Deborah Fins, Esq. Consultant to the Criminal Justice Project NAACP Legal Defense and Educational Fund, Inc. at https://www.naacpldf.org/wp-content/uploads/DRUSAWinter2020.pdf

of many black children as having intellectual disabilities, a significant number of black adults on death row were either identified intellectually disabled as children, were regarded as intellectually disabled, or had IQ scores that would indicate as much. As will be shown, and as per the Americans with Disabilities Act, racism resulting in mental retardation/intellectual disability for children should not be used as a pretext to deny Atkins relief for an adult.

The most important evidence, a determination of intellectual disability when an offender was a child, is offhandedly dismissed in favor of a subjective interpretation of IQ scores and adaptive behavior by judge or jury who are often ill-equipped to decipher a maze of psychometric data and opposing, albeit predictable, interpretations of intellectual disability by experts. If there is one bright line for Atkins claims, this should be to give lesser culpability to all offenders who have been classified as intellectually disabled as a child, could or should have been so classified.

For every Atkins claim the first question to be answered is whether the offender has a record of intellectual disability. As the Supreme Court decided in 1998 in a case involving prisoner rights under the American with Disabilities Act (ADA) "the ADA unambiguously extends to state prison inmates."[14] For purposes of the ADA there is no Eighth Amendment standard for determining intellectual disability, or denying a previous determination of intellectual disability by judicial or legislative fiat, but the simple fact that someone who has a record of a disability cannot "be excluded from participation in or be denied the benefits of the services, programs, or activities of a public entity, or be subjected to discrimination by any such entity." Certainly a successful Atkins claim does result in a benefit assuming that life in prison is more beneficial than execution.

The next question to be answered in Atkins claims is whether an offender could or should have been identified as having an intellectual disability. A classification of a disability such as specific learning disability as a child does not necessarily mean

---

[14]Pennsylvania Dept. of Corrections v. Yeskey 524 U.S. 206, 211 (1998)

that the offender did not meet the criteria for intellectual disability. Likewise, not having been determined to have a disability before age of onset (age 18) was never intended to be an absolute standard for determining intellectual disability. There are a variety of reasons why "cognitive and behavioral impairment…make mentally retarded defendants less morally culpable" might have occurred after age 18. These include brain injury, Alzheimer's, dementia, the effects of addiction, the effects of prolonged time on death row or in isolation, and the various combinations of these and other factors.

When Freddie Lee Hall was in elementary school in the 1950s, not only was school segregation holding strong well after *Brown* in 1954, but inferior services were part and parcel of an inferior education for black children. The racism of providing an inferior education and limited or no services should not be used as a shield to suggest that there was no record of a disability for an adult. For Freddie Lee Hall his intellectual disability was finally recognized after almost 38 years on death row. Just as there are offenders who might not have received necessary services because of race, there are white offenders on death row who might not have been classified as having an intellectual disability because of race. In one county in Georgia in 1983 the white enrollment was 77 percent but only 18 percent of the children classified as educable mentally retarded were white.[15] This not only indicates that black children were routinely classified as EMR, correctly or incorrectly, but there very well might have been white children who should have been classified as EMR were it not for race.

The determination of mild Intellectual disability and the death penalty are ripe with racism. This has been the case for children "denied the opportunity of an education…made available to all on equal terms" as promised in Brown and for adults seeking Atkins relief. Hopefully, this book will provide some insight into the relationship between mild intellectual disability for children, and the many factors that should be considered when determining whether an adult offender is entitled to lesser culpability when a State seeks the death penalty.

[15]Georgia State Conference of Branches of NAACP v. State of Georgia, 775 F.2d 1403 (1985)

1. Protecting Human Dignity

"...among a capriciously selected random handful..."[16]

Freddie Lee Hall - 2016

The Supreme Court's Hall v. Florida decision in 2014[17] suggests that Freddie Lee Hall's death sentence, and almost four decades on death row beginning in 1978, was finally resolved but the Court made no such judgment concerning Hall's intellectual disability or ineligibility for the death penalty. The Court articulated a very specific, albeit overly simplistic rule that, "When a defendant's IQ test score falls within the test's acknowledged and inherent margin of error, the defendant must be able to present additional evidence of intellectual disability, including testimony regarding adaptive deficits." Rarely if ever does an Atkins claim center about a single IQ score and the "inherent margin of error" varies with a test's reliability. The upshot of this rule— grounded in the Eighth Amendment and the "cruel and unusual punishments" clause— was to exchange one IQ bright line (70) for one somewhat higher but just as strict, or even more so, for a bright-line of 75.

The IQ bright-line of 70 was a matter of interpretation by Florida and other States. Now the IQ bright-line is not open to interpretation but a score with a very specific reference point. Hall eventually prevailed in his Atkins claim—his death sentence was vacated in 2016—not because of the newly anointed bright-line of 75 but because "the unrefuted evidence in this case has consistently demonstrated that Hall meets the clinical and statutory definition of intellectual disability."[18]

The Supreme Court decided in 2014 that the IQ cutoff used by Florida for determining intellectual disability violated the 2002

---

[16]Furman v. Georgia, 408 U.S. 238, 1972
[17]Hall v. Florida, 572 U.S. ____ (2014)
[18]Hall v. Florida, SC10-1335, September 8, 2016

Atkins decision which prohibited the execution of the intellectually disabled (at the time, prior to Rosa's law, *mentally retarded*[19]). The Court did not conclude that Hall was intellectually disabled, or that he could not be executed, but that Florida could not use a strict IQ cutoff of 70 to prevent the consideration of other relevant evidence (viz., adaptive behavior). The decision to reject the strict cutoff was said to be "proper or humane" and consistent with the cruel and unusual punishment clause of the Eighth Amendment. In spite of the Court's good intentions, the decision does little if anything for undoing the cruel and unusual punishment caused by the misinterpretation of the professional definitions for determining intellectual disability. States are free to use a cutoff IQ score of 75 so that a score of 76 could result in the death penalty, disregard IQ scores for lacking credibility, dismiss relevant evidence of adaptive behavior, and essentially create a new definition of intellectual disability that meets a State's concept of an appropriate constitutional standard.

An added problem with the Supreme Court's 2014 decision is the impression that the strict bright-line rule used by Florida was absolute. As explained by the State of Florida in an answer brief in 2011 to the Supreme Court of Florida "in the abundance of caution, the Court will examine the Defendant's evidence proffered in support of the second (i.e., concurrent deficits in adaptive behavior) and third (i.e. onset of the condition before age 18) prongs of his mental retardation claim."[20] Florida acknowledged that as a matter of law the bright-line score of 70 precludes the consideration of adaptive behavior, but then considered adaptive behavior. The spin was then to herald Hall's "existence and interaction" while on death row as being the essential element of assessing adaptive behavior.

The Supreme Court has not been idle when dealing with the more glaring abuses of Atkins claims. More recently, in addition to the Hall decision, the Court rejected the Briseno factors used in Texas where finders of fact "might also focus upon in weighing evidence

---

[19]Public Law 111-256 enacted in 2010
[20]Hall v. Florida, Answer Brief of Appellee, CASE NO. SC10-1335, January, 2011.

as indicative of mental retardation or of a personality disorder." These "judicial standards" included a subjective analysis of "leadership" and "forethought, the ability to "respond coherently, rationally," and being able to "lie effectively.[21] Meeting the IQ prong of the definition of intellectual disability, as evidenced by the Briseno factors, is but one hurdle a defendant must overcome when proving—which a defendant must do—intellectual disability or, more accurately, a level of intellectual disability that would prohibit the death penalty.

The 2014 *Hall* decision gave the Supreme Court an opportunity to opine on "the Constitution's protection of human dignity" and "evolving standards of decency," by striking down the "rigid rule" that "creates an unacceptable risk that persons with intellectual disability will be executed, and thus is unconstitutional." What the Court seems to have established is a constitutional bright line for IQ, a score of 75, which can be just as pernicious and discriminatory as Florida's plain language interpretation of an IQ 70 in the determination of intellectual disability. The Court's decision solved, in part, Hall's problem whereby IQ precluded the admission of other relevant evidence. The Court decided that he must "have the opportunity to present evidence of his intellectual disability, including deficits in adaptive functioning over his lifetime." The Court acknowledged that a single IQ should not be considered "dispositive of a conjunctive and interrelated assessment." One consequence of the Court's decision was to establish an IQ score dispositive of intellectual disability that can be even less forgiving than the varied interpretations of an IQ cutoff of 70. As is the case in Oklahoma, "any" IQ score above 75 precludes a consideration of intellectual disability.

Apart from the declaration for human dignity, the Court ignored the incessant and often silly tactics used by States for denying Atkins claims by dismissing childhood intellectual disability, the fanciful notion that intellectual disability as a child and intellectual disability under the umbrella of the Eighth Amendment are different, the unabashed use of stereotypes to deny the existence

---

[21]In the Court Of Criminal Appeals of Texas, *Ex parte* Briseno, 135 S.W.3d 1, 3 (Tex. Crim. App. 2004)

of intellectual disability (e.g., the ability to read, to have a girlfriend, and the rather unbelievable ability to adapt to death row), reliance on anecdotal factors related to the crime (planning and forethought), or when the observations of prison officials are deemed more relevant than those of professionals. The list is long and inventive.

For Freddie Lee Hall, the Supreme Court of Florida did resolve the matter of his time on death row in 2016 when the court decided that Hall was intellectually disabled and not eligible for execution because of the 2002 *Atkins* decision. Between 2002 and Hall's resentencing to life in prison in 2016 Florida managed to re-interpret the definition of mental retardation/intellectual disabilities to create a variety of obstacles to thwart the identification of offenders who were not eligible for the death penalty including a bright-line IQ score of 70 and requiring a determination of mental retardation before and after age of onset (age 18).[22] The Supreme Court of Florida's decision in 2016 far surpassed the Supreme Court's Atkins decision by de-emphasizing an IQ bright line and placing appropriate emphasis on the determination of intellectual disability before age of onset rather than "present" levels as an adult or when on death row.

The Florida court seems to have recognized that the determination of intellectual disability "may not have a bright-line cutoff IQ test score" rather than simply establishing a higher cutoff as was done by the Supreme Court. While the Supreme Court has ignored the use of adaptive behavior to deny Atkins claims, the Florida court noted the practice of requiring evidence of deficits of adaptive behavior at the time of trial and while incarcerated. The court clarified that the "depth and breadth" of evaluations must be considered when determining deficits in adaptive and that a retrospective analysis (determining intellectual disability before age 18) could not be dismissed by focusing solely on present levels of adaptive behavior. The Florida court also explained, as

---

[22]Public Law 111-256 (Rosa's Law) was enacted in 2010 to change mental retardation to intellectual disabilities, and the reference of a children "having mental retardation" to "having intellectual disabilities." The rationale for the name change is that the term mentally retarded is "anachronistic, needlessly insensitive

few courts have been inclined to do, that the purpose of the age of onset criterion is to distinguish intellectual disability from other factors and was never intended to serve as a criterion for dismissing the circumstances necessitating lesser culpability in Atkins claims.

The Supreme Court of Florida has provided a glimmer of hope that a common-sense interpretation of intellectual disability, based on how the definition was and is conceptualized, can be used to identify offenders who meet the criteria for intellectual disability when the death penalty is sought. Freddie Lee Hall is no longer on death row, and time will tell how courts interpret the 2016 Supreme Court of Florida decision to provide lesser culpability to qualified offenders.

Finally, for Freddie Lee Hall, there is the matter of his various trials and sentencings. Now that Florida has decided that he is intellectually disabled, there is every reason to assume that he was intellectually disabled at the time of his trial. This underlies the reason for Atkins whereby a defendant has difficulty understanding and processing information, "engage in logical reasoning," and to assist counsel. In short, a determination of intellectual disability following trial might cast doubt on the fairness of the trial itself. When a determination of intellectual disability is undertaken following trial, a successful Atkins claim should question not only the fairness of the trial (e.g., "a persuasive showing of mitigation," and "typically" being a poor witness) but the defendant's actions following arrest such as "the possibility of false confessions." Most important, intellectual disability would likely diminish the defendant's ability to understand "the nature and cause of the accusation," developing a coherent understanding when "confronted with the witnesses against him" and for "obtaining witnesses in his favor."[23] Most importantly, intellectual disability would limit the defendant's ability to help counsel to "derive the overarching duty to advocate the defendant's cause and the more particular duties to consult with the defendant on important decisions."[24] A defendant who is

---

[23]The Sixth Amendment
[24]Strickland v. Washington, 466 U.S. 668 (1984)

intellectually disabled might not understand what is relevant evidence including the defendant's history or evidence relating to the crime itself.

The 2002 Atkins decision gave the task to States to determine how the constitutional ban on the execution of the mentally retarded/intellectually disabled should be achieved. This was similar to the task given States to end *de jure* school segregation "with all deliberate speed" in Brown II in 1955 which was interpreted by States to mean deliberate avoidance or all deliberate delay.[25] The 2014 Supreme Court decision was more about dismissing relevant evidence than IQ. On the one hand the Court acknowledged the error inherent in IQ tests; on the other hand the Court ignored the racism that has been long associated with IQ tests and gave constitutional weight to these often maligned tests or, more importantly, how these tests are interpreted.

Freddie Lee Hall's successful quest to avoid the death penalty via intellectual disabilities and *Atkins* is not without paradox. States have consistently and disproportionately classified and stigmatized black children as intellectually disabled but, often disingenuously, deny the existence of intellectual disability for black adults to prohibit the death penalty. What might seem to be a paradox is really consistent with what has always been done to undermine equal protection and due process for black children and adults.

Stigmatizing black children as intellectually inferior might be more subtle than Jim Crow laws (ranging from "colored" drinking fountains to voted discrimination) but just as invidious. For adults seeking Atkins relief the new found racial consciousness does not belie the underlying racially discriminatory intent. The source of racial invidious intent[26] in elusive but does include mostly white judges and prosecutors, juror selection, the ability of finders of fact to even remotely understand the intricacies of the criteria for

---

[25]Brown v. Board of Education, 349 U.S. 294 (1955)
[26]See Arlington Heights v. Metropolitan Housing Dev. Corp., 429 U.S. 252 (1977)

assessing intellectual disability, the failure to prioritize the importance of childhood intellectual disability, the thoughtless use of IQ without considering the racial implications, the use of stereotypes for determining intellectual disability, disproportionately seeking the death penalty based on the race of the victim, jury override, the disproportionate number of black inmates on death row, exonerations, and executions.

The Supreme Court's 2002 Atkins decision provided an important standard for requiring lesser culpability for intellectually disabled offenders; the Court's Hall decision in 2014 was consistent with the 1986 Wainwright and Ford decision that relevant evidence could not be precluded from consideration when determining insanity in death penalty cases. *Atkins*, as was *Ford*, was not about definitions but concerned due process. In Both cases States were given the task to determine how the prohibition against the execution of the insane and intellectually disabled should be enforced. In *Ford* the Court criticized procedures for determining insanity which were tainted by the lack of due process; in *Atkins* the Court cited the Eighth Amendment as requiring a fair process to determine mental retardation/intellectual disability (which did not include a strict cutoff of 70).

The Supreme Court never decided that Daryl Atkins was not mentally retarded, but only that he could not be executed if Florida decided that he was mentally retarded. The essential problem in *Ford* was a process that prevented the consideration of all relevant evidence; the problem in *Hall* was similar in that Florida used a strict IQ score cutoff of 70 to prevent the consideration of all relevant evidence (viz., adaptive behavior). This was not necessarily the only problem, or the most essential problem, but a problem that was easily addressed by raising the IQ cutoff from 70 to 75. This new standard was beneficial for Freddie Lee Hall and others with IQ scores in the 70 to 75 range because professionals have long encouraged the interpretation of an IQ by taking into account the margin of error. However, the margin of error is not a fixed amount but depends on the test and the test's reliability. At best, the five point margin of error is a ballpark estimate and certainly not an absolute standard (acknowledging that the Supreme Court has, indeed, created an absolute standard). Added to the degree of error in the much discussed "margin of error" is the fact, usually ignored, that the base score of 70 is completely arbitrary. States have used cutoff values higher and lower than 70. A state could change the definition so that the cutoff was 75 and the margin of error a confidence band from 70 to 80. Would professionals be angered if a State used a more liberal interpretation of IQ to ensure that someone who was intellectually disabled is not executed? If a State could raise the base IQ score, there is no reason why the base score could not be lowered to 65 or even 60.

One reason for not simply raising the cutoff to 75 in the professional definition, as was done by the Supreme Court, is that this could result in a substantial increase in the number of children classified as having mild intellectual disabilities. As it is the definition of intellectual disabilities is most often used in relation to the Individuals with Disabilities Education Act for providing special education services. According to 2016-2017 IDEA data[27] of the 6,048,882 children receiving services, 6.88 percent (416,295) are in the intellectual disabilities category. In 1998 this category comprised 610,978 students of whom 204,739 were black (33.5 percent). The reasons for the dramatic decrease in the mental retardation (then intellectual disability category) are many and include the problem of racial misclassification, using mental retardation/intellectual disability category as a reason for prior racism and lack of educational opportunity, and the availability of other categories that are less offensive and provide more appropriate educational services (for the most part). For example, the other health impairments category increased from 167,268 in 1998 to 934,020 in 2017, and the autism category increased from 34,386 in 1998 to 578,765 in 2017. This does not signify that a child who is placed in a category other than intellectual disability does not meet the criteria for intellectual disabilities. This becomes important for adults seeking Atkins relief when a State suggests that not having been identified as having mental retardation/intellectual disability as a child

---

[27]https://wwww2.ed.gov/programs/osepidea/618-data/static-tables/2016-2017/part-b/child-count-and-educational-environment/1617-bchildcountandedenvironment-1.xlsx

precludes a successful claim because of the age on onset prong of the definition (i.e., manifestation during the developmental period).

A definitional increase of the IQ cutoff to 75 would have serious racial implications. Although increasing the IQ cutoff to 75 would benefit many Atkins claimants, many of whom are black; this would also increase the number of black children who are stigmatized and inappropriately classified. Professional guidelines note that IQ scores should take into account the margin of error, or take into account the standard error of measurement by stipulating a 95 percent confidence level (which is actually 1.96 times the standard error of measurement). The Supreme Court simplified all this psychometric nitpicking and decided that a score of 75—the traditional IQ cutoff of 70 plus five points—was the required standard for interpreting IQ for Atkins claimants.

Alyin Bernard Ford

Before Freddie Lee Hall, and before the namesake of Atkins claims, Daryl Renard Atkins, there was Alyin Bernard Ford. The *Hall* decision to reject Florida's plain language interpretation of the statute (921.137) requiring an IQ score of 70 or below is in complete agreement with the Court's Ford v. Wainwright decision in 1986 in that relevant evidence should not be excluded from the inquiry that would bar execution.[28] The Court observed in *Ford* that "in all other proceedings leading to the execution of an accused, we have said that the factfinder must 'have before it all possible relevant information about the individual defendant whose fate it must determine." The *Hall* decision to reject the plain language interpretation of the definition of mental retardation (as cited in the statute) was in response to Florida's exclusion of relevant evidence in the form of adaptive behavior.

The rule in Florida at the time of Ford v. Wainwright was whether an offender "has the mental capacity to understand the nature of the death penalty and the reasons why it was imposed on him."

---

[28]Ford v. Wainwright, 477 U.S. 399 (1986)

This is a variation of the 19ᵗʰ century M'Naghten Rule (1843) where a defendant must prove an inability "to appreciate the nature and quality or the wrongfulness of his acts."[29] Whereas intellectual disability results in lesser capability because of the disability which has defined parameters (viz., IQ, adaptive behavior and age of onset), *Ford* requires the consideration of all relevant evidence because Florida, prior to *Ford,* used a flawed fact-finding procedure that prevented a "full and fair hearing." The three psychiatrists who interviewed Alyin Ford all reached different conclusions, as experts do, as to his type of insanity (psychosis with paranoia, psychotic, severe adaptational disorder) but all agreed that he did not meet the legal definition of insanity. The determination of insanity in Florida at the time was made by the Governor who decided whether "the convicted person has the mental capacity to understand the nature of the death penalty and the reasons why it was imposed upon him or her."[30] In Florida and elsewhere, insanity concerned the very specific ability to understand the death penalty and why it was being imposed and not hearing voices, delusions, a professional label such as psychosis, or any number of labels from the Diagnostic and Statistical Manual of Mental Disorders by the American Psychiatric Association (APA).

The Supreme Court announced in *Ford* that the constitution prohibited the execution of the insane and that States must offer a full and fair evidentiary hearing when considering a claim of insanity. Florida, before *Ford,* offered a hearing for insanity claims but one lacking in fairness and due process. In 1974, Alyin Bernard Ford, shot a policeman twice in the abdomen during a Fort Lauderdale, Red Lobster restaurant robbery. Ford, abandoned by his accomplices, attempted to flee in the officer's police car but returned to get the car keys from the wounded officer whereupon he shot the officer in the back of the head and then escaped in the officer's car. Ford was found mentally competent at the time of his offense, convicted of murder, and sentenced to death in Broward County, Florida. In 1981 the

---

[29]18 U.S. Code § 17 - Insanity defense
[30]Florida Statute 922.07 and Rule 3.811 Insanity at Time of Execution: Capital Cases

Governor signed Ford's first death warrant. In 1982 he began to have delusions about the "Klan," conspiracies, and a belief that family members were being held in another part of the prison. Ford believed he had control of the hostage situation, was able to appoint new justices to the Supreme Court, and referred to himself as Pope John Paul, III. He "sincerely believed that he would not be executed because he owned the prisons and could control the Governor through mind waves." A panel of three psychiatrists examined Ford for approximately 30 minutes and found various diagnoses, but all agreed that he understood his pending execution. The Governor, in 1984, signed Ford's second death warrant with no comment or explanation. The United States Court of Appeals decided in 1985 "that the Florida statute meets minimum standards required by procedural due process."[31]

In 1986, the Supreme Court recognized the difficulty in determining mental competency and that experts "disagree widely and frequently on what constitutes mental illness [and] on the appropriate diagnosis to be attached to given behavior and symptoms."[32] The Court declared the execution of the insane was prohibited by the Eighth Amendment "to protect the condemned from fear and pain without comfort of understanding, or to protect the dignity of society itself from the barbarity of exacting mindless vengeance." The Court faulted Florida, not the definition of mental illness, but for the "failure to include the prisoner in the truth-seeking process" and leaving the determination of mental competence entirely within the executive branch. No mention was made of what was relevant information or what definition of mental illness should or should not be used, but the Court was very clear that the factfinder must have all relevant information available.

The problem in *Ford* was that the executive branch was able to reject a claim of mental illness before Ford was allowed an opportunity to substantiate his claim. The Court was concerned with the procedures used in Florida for determining insanity which denied a fair evidentiary hearing, the ability to cross

---

[31]752 F2d 526 Ford v. L Wainwright
[32]477 U.S. 399, 1986

examine witnesses, and a process where "subordinates have been responsible for initiating every stage of the prosecution of the condemned, from arrest through sentencing." Following the Supreme Court's 1986 decision Florida developed procedures (Florida statute 922.07) involving evidence, due process and the role of the governor's office that met constitutional scrutiny for determining insanity. In 1989, with due process procedures in place, Ford was determined to be sane. He died of natural causes in 1991 at age 37 in his death row cell.

Daryl Renard Atkins

Before Freddie Lee Hall's successful Supreme Court appeal in 2014 which resulted in a less draconian interpretation of IQ, and the decision by Florida in 2016 that he was intellectually disabled, there was the unusual case of Atkins v. Virginia in 2002. In 1998, Daryl Renard Atkins was convicted of the 1996 robbery, abduction and killing of Eric Nesbitt, along with co-offender William Jones. A forensic psychologist reviewed his history, conducted interviews, administered the Wechsler Adult Intelligence Scale (WAIS), and concluded that he was "mildly mentally retarded." The sentencing jury determined that regardless of an IQ of 59 "the murder of Nesbitt had been outrageously or wantonly vile." His low IQ or "mild mental retardation" was not presented to the jury as a mitigating factor other than a reference to his "low intelligence" during closing arguments. There might be some justification to suspect a low IQ score obtained in conjunction with a claim of intellectual disability is the result of lack of motivation or outright malingering, but for Daryl Atkins expert testimony indicated that these were not factors.

The jury found that Atkins met both aggravating factors, a future danger to society (prior felony convictions) and an outrageously or wantonly vile act, and imposed a sentence of death. Atkins and Jones were not overly thoughtful in their criminality—both were recorded by video camera when Nesbit was forced to withdraw money from a drive-through ATM. While Atkins gave initial accounts of the murder and his own culpability, Jones gave no statement and eventually accepted a plea for first-degree murder and a sentence of life in prison in exchange for testimony against Atkins.

In 1999 the Supreme Court of Virginia set aside Atkins death sentence and remanded the case for a new penalty proceeding because the jury form did not properly instruct the jury to consider only a sentence of life in prison if neither of the aggravating factors were proven beyond a reasonable doubt. The court also made note of Atkins mental retardation, although mental retardation was not included in the jury instructions as a factor militating against the death penalty. As is usually the case the expert testimony concerning Atkins mental retardation "was in conflict." One expert found that Atkins was mild mentally retarded in conjunction with an antisocial personality disorder. A second expert concluded that Atkins, in spite of an IQ of 59, was "of at least average intelligence" based on his verbal behavior (he was able to use words such as *orchestra* and *parable*) and available school records suggested lack of motivation and concentration rather than mental retardation. The expert testified that there was no evidence that Atkins was "in the least bit mentally retarded" based on factors such as vocabulary, syntax and knowledge of historical facts. Other relevant evidence of intellectual disability was discounted because Atkins did not sound intellectually disabled.

All this mattered not because Virginia contended "that execution of a defendant who is mentally retarded does not contravene the practices that were condemned when the Bill of Rights was adopted or the evolving standards of decency." The sentencing jury found that neither his low IQ nor possible mental retardation warranted a sentence other than death. In 2000 the Supreme Court of Virginia affirmed Atkins death sentence. In his sentencing, the court acknowledged his low IQ but reasoned that "we are not willing to commute Atkins sentence of death to life imprisonment merely because of his IQ score." In spite of his IQ, and conflicting testimony of adaptive behavior, the deciding factor to affirm the death penalty was an insanity-type reasoning that his ability, as testified by both experts, "to appreciate the criminality of his conduct and understood that it was wrong to shoot and kill Eric Nesbitt."

In 2002, the United States Supreme Court intervened on Atkins behalf. The Court decided that mentally retarded defendants have lesser personal culpability, and capital punishment for the mentally retarded is "cruel and unusual punishments" prohibited by the Eighth Amendment.[33] The Circuit Court of York County Virginia was required to empanel a new jury for the sole purpose of determining whether or not Daryl Atkins was mentally retarded. This jury decided that he was not mentally retarded and the death sentence was reinstated. However, because the expert witness for the State did not "satisfy the statutory criteria in order to testify as an expert" (he was not expert in the standardized assessment of adaptive behavior), and because prejudicial information was given to the jury (they were told of a prior jury decision), another jury was directed by the Virginia Supreme Court in 2006 to determine whether Atkins was mentally retarded.[34]

In Virginia the determination of intellectual disability to preclude the death penalty is made during sentencing by either judge or jury and the defendant must prove "mental retardation by a preponderance of the evidence.[35]" If the defendant is found guilty and is also determined to be mentally retarded, the punishment is life in prison. If the jury is unable to agree on the penalty, the court is required to "impose a sentence of imprisonment for life."[36]

There is an element of illogic when a determination of intellectual disability is made after trial and conviction. In Virginia "after a defendant who has given notice of his or her intention to raise mental retardation as a bar to the death sentence is convicted of a capital felony and an advisory jury has returned a recommended sentence of death, the defendant may file a motion to determine whether the defendant has mental retardation."[37] If a determination of intellectual disability is made, this provides support for the contention, as expressed by the Supreme Court in

---

[33]Atkins v. Virginia, 536 U.S. 304 (2002)
[34]Atkins v. Virginia, Supreme Court of Virginia, 272 Va. 144, 2006
[35]Virginia Statute § 19.2-264.3:1.1
[36]Virginia Statute § 19.2-264.4
[37]Florida Statute, F.S. 921.137(4)

the 2002 Atkins's decision, that the defendant might have had limited ability to assist counsel or to serve as a witness. Although mental illness is distinct from intellectual disability, especially regarding specific criteria, intellectual disability can result in "reasonable cause to believe that the defendant may presently be suffering from a mental disease or defect rendering him mentally incompetent to the extent that he is unable to understand the nature and consequences of the proceedings against him or to assist properly in his defense."[38] A determination of intellectual disability during sentencing is also a determination that the fairness of the trial itself is suspect.

Before a jury could again consider Atkins mental retardation, an evidentiary hearing revealed that exculpatory evidence was suppressed from his first trial. Atkins accomplice was said to have been "coached" so the "version of the facts changed after the rehearsed and coached unrecorded reenactment of the murder." The alleged prosecutorial misconduct was found not to be misconduct by a disciplinary hearing in July of 2010 when a three-judge circuit court decided that Eileen Addison did not coach, manipulate or prompt "untruthful testimony."

In 2009, the Supreme Court of Virginia "had no confidence in the integrity of the judicial process and the jury verdict that resulted in Atkins sentence of death" and that the court's life sentence without parole was an act "already done" which could not be undone. Probably more from judicial exhaustion than anything else, the circuit court imposed a life sentence without parole for Daryl Atkins without considering the issue of mental retardation.

Several juries decided that Daryl Atkins was guilty and a jury found that he was not mentally retarded. However, his death sentence was reduced to life in prison because of alleged prosecutorial misconduct which was determined to be otherwise, Atkins v. Virginia became the standard for not executing the intellectually disabled. The foundation for an Atkins claims was

---

[38] 18 U.S. Code § 4241, Determination of mental competency to stand trial to undergo postrelease proceedings⊠11⊠So

shaky to begin with and then things went south. The lessons for determining mental retardation/intellectual disability learned in Virginia, for the most part, staid in Virginia.

Aside from the idea that the intellectually disabled should be less culpable and not subject to the death penalty, the devil is in the details. As aptly stated by the Supreme Court "To the extent there is serious disagreement about the execution of mentally retarded offenders, it is in determining which offenders are in fact retarded." Simply announcing that the execution of the mentally retarded is contrary to the Court's "narrowing jurisprudence, which seeks to ensure that only the most deserving of execution are put to death" and "evolving standards of decency," would do absolutely nothing without clear guidelines for determining intellectual disability in capital murder cases. As was the case with Freddie Lee Hall in 1999 before *Atkins*, his mental retardation, taken as a mitigating factor, did not outweigh the aggravating factors or reduce his degree of moral culpability. The Supreme Court of Florida heard testimony from mental health experts and "all discussed Hall's mental retardation and expressed an understanding of the standard for finding a defendant competent, which requires that he or she be able to understand the nature of the proceedings and to confer with counsel."[39] The court acknowledged that he was "probably somewhat retarded" but he was competent to be sentenced to death.

The Supreme Court did not provide guidelines for determining mental retardation such as when this issue should be decided, by whom, the standard of proof, childhood disability, interpreting multiple IQ scores, and the thorny matter of adaptive behavior. However, the Court did offer some direction by citing definitions by the American Association on Mental Retardation (or AAMR which became the American Association on Individuals with Developmental Disabilities (AAIDD) and the American Psychiatric Association (APA) in the form of Diagnostic and Statistical Manual (DSM) guidelines. As was done in Ford v. Wainwright regarding insanity, the Supreme Court left "the task of developing appropriate ways to enforce the constitutional restriction upon its

---

[39]Hall v. Florida, Supreme Court of Florida, No. 92,008, 1999

execution of sentences" to the State. As Florida learned in *Hall* in 2014 this task was not completely unfettered. States have adopted the professional definitions cited in *Atkins* in 2002 which is based on the professional definition first proposed in 1959 by Rick Heber and endorsed by the American Association on Mental Deficiency:[40]

> **Subaverage general intellectual functioning which originates during the developmental period and is associated with impairment in one or more of the following: (1) maturation, (2) learning, and (3) social adjustment.**

The 1959 definition placed heavy emphasis on IQ where "subaverage" specifically meant "performance which is greater than one Standard Deviation below the population mean of the age group involved on measures of general intellectual functioning." Given a standard deviation of 15 on the Wechsler (or 16 on the Stanford-Binet), one standard deviation below the mean is 85 (or 16), and "greater than one Standard Deviation below" a mean score of 100 is a score of 84 or 83. In other words, "subaverage general intellectual functioning" was a euphemism for IQ scores less than 85 (or less than 84 depending on the IQ test). The IQ cutoff of 85, following much criticism, was later lowered to 70. Of particular interest in the 1959 definition is "developmental period" which is frequently used by States as a rigid standard for denying Atkins claims. If there is no evidence of intellectual disability during the developmental period (or below age of onset), a State might argue that the claimant has not met this extremely important, but often misinterpreted prong of the definition.

The developmental period prong was first proposed "for practical purposes...and services to distinguish mental retardation from other disorders of human behavior." Although States and courts refer to three prongs, the definition always emphasized a "two-

---

[40]Heber, Rick, A Manual on Terminology and Classification in Mental Retardation, Monograph Supplement, American Journal of Mental Deficiency (2nd ed.), 1959 and 1961

dimensional classification system" comprised of "measured intelligence and adaptive behavior."[41]   Rather than using the developmental period as an absolute standard, a more reasonable approach is to recognize the possibility of intellectual disability for both children and adults as is done by Social Security. For adults prior history of intellectual disability, such as a record of disability before age 18, can provide useful information but age is not a requirement so that "The evidence about your current intellectual and adaptive functioning and about the history of your disorder demonstrates or supports the conclusion that the disorder began prior to your attainment of age 22."[42]

The 1959 definition was tweaked in 1961 by consolidating the elements of adaptive behavior:

> **Subaverage general intellectual functioning which originates during the developmental period and is associated with impairment in adaptive behavior.**

In 1973, the American Association on Mental Deficiency definition changed the intellectual functioning component from "subaverage" to "significantly subaverage" and, more importantly, the IQ cutoff was changed from greater than one standard deviation below the mean (viz., an IQ less than 85) to an IQ score that is at least two standard deviations below the mean or an IQ of 70 or lower. [43] The revised definition stipulated that

> **Mental retardation refers to significantly subaverage general intellectual functioning existing concurrently with deficits in adaptive**

---

[41]*Ibid.*

[42]See https://www.ssa.gov/disability/professionals/bluebook/12.00-MentalDisorders-Adult.htm

[43]See also Classification in Mental Retardation, Editor: Herbert, J, Grossman, American Association on Mental deficiency, Washington, D.C., 1983, p. 198
https://law.resource.org/pub/us/cfr/ibr/001/aamd.classification.1973.pdf

> **behavior and manifested during the developmental period.**

The seemingly harmless addition of "concurrently" can be a useful tool for States to disallow an Atkins claim by interpreting this to mean "current" or "present." This semantic sleight-of-hand allows a State to skewer the interpretation of intellectual disability by accepting and/or rejecting IQ scores or creating unlikely criteria of intellectual disability (e.g., being able to adapt to death). Stephen Greenspan and Harvey N. Switzky explained that "This latter change, while seemingly minor, has been interpreted by some commentators as suggesting a shift away from viewing adaptive behavior as a necessary outgrowth of low intelligence, toward seeing it as something separate and orthogonal from intelligence, akin in some ways to a personality axis in a multiaxial classification system." The intended meaning of *concurrently* was further explained as "indicating that it is associated or exists concurrently with low intelligence" (p. 23).[44] This is clearly stated in the 2000 APA definition which refers to "significantly subaverage general intellectual functioning (Criterion A) that is **accompanied** by significant limitations in adaptive functioning" (bold type has been added).

In *Atkins* in 2002 the Supreme Court cited two definitions, both based on the 1959/61 and 1973 definitions of mental retardation. The 1992 AAMR definition states

> ***Mental retardation*** **refers to substantial limitations in present functioning. It is characterized by significantly subaverage intellectual functioning, existing concurrently with related limitations in two or more of the following applicable adaptive skill areas: communication, self-care, home living, social skills, community use, self-direction, health and safety, functional academics, leisure, and**

---

[44]Forty-Four Years of AAMR Manuals, <u>What is Mental Retardation</u>, edited by Harvey N. Switzky and Stephen Greenspan, Washington, D.C., American Association on Mental Deficiency, 2006

**work. Mental retardation manifests before age
18.**

The similar lawyer-friendly Diagnostic Statistical Manual-IV (DSM-IV) definition offers that

> **The essential feature of Mental Retardation is
> significantly subaverage general intellectual
> functioning (Criterion A) that is accompanied
> by significant limitations in adaptive
> functioning in at least two of the following skill
> areas: communication, self-care, home living,
> social/ interpersonal skills, use of community
> resources, self-direction, functional academic
> skills, work, leisure, health, and safety
> (Criterion B). The onset must occur before age
> 18 years (Criterion C).**

The original definition of mental retardation was intended for children to provide a sensible method for overcoming the deficiencies of IQ assessment alone. Prior to the inclusion of adaptive behavior in 1959 a single IQ score could determine whether a child was labeled mentally retarded or not. Even after the change to include adaptive behavior and age of onset, IQ has and often is the primary consideration in the determination of intellectual disability in spite of the fact that many factors (e.g., educational opportunity, socio-economic factors, and motivation) can impact a child's score on a test. The ability of a child to adapt to his or her environment, to succeed in school, to thrive socially and develop independent living skills is far more important than a score on a test. For this reason adaptive behavior was and is an important prong of the definition to offset overreliance on IQ alone.

By taking into account various benchmarks such as language development, motor skills, and social behavior, the likelihood is lessened that a low IQ score arising from environment will result in an erroneous determination of mental retardation. The problem occurs when this initial rationale for adaptive behavior for children is used with adults and adult behavior. For example, an offender might have legitimately met the IQ and adaptive behavior requirements for intellectual disability as a child, but a court or jury decides, often based on little more than stereotype, that for an adult seeking Atkins relief virtually any adult skill can be used to preclude a determination of intellectual disability. By the same token, if a defendant has a history of impairment in adaptive behavior, IQ can be used to discount these limitations by either requiring IQ data before age of onset (age 18), after age of onset, before and after age of onset, or by requiring all IQ scores below a certain cutoff such as 75. The options for denying an Atkins claim are many.

The substantive focus of the definition of mental retardation by the Supreme Court's in *Atkins* was to provide a mechanism for determining lesser culpability. The Court cited "diminished capacities to understand and process information, to communicate, to abstract from mistakes and learn from experience, to engage in logical reasoning, to control impulses, and to understand others' reactions" and to "control their conduct based upon that information," provide persuasive mitigation, assist counsel, serve as a credible witness, or show remorse. The Court did not prohibit capital punishment based on a label but factors the Court believed to be associated with defendants who deserve lesser culpability. Denying relief for a defendant who was brain injured, but who exhibited all the characteristics of someone deserving lesser culpability, is semantic nitpicking. For someone who was brain-injured, had dementia or an IDEA disability classification such as specific learning disability, emotional disturbance, autism or other health impairment, who met all the substantive factors cited by the Supreme Court for those who deserve lesser culpability, denying an Atkins claim because the label was something other than mental retardation/intellectual disability is contrary to the reasons cited by the Court for lesser culpability.

A label should not be the basis for denying Atkins relief. As a child, a defendant might have had met all the criteria for intellectual disability but a different label was used to meet the needs of the child, the school or the parents. Specific learning disabilities is frequently used to provide services to children who could otherwise be identified as mild intellectually disabled, emotionally disturbed, ADHD, etc. A school district might be disinclined to use the intellectual disability category except for children with clearly demonstrated cognitive and adaptive deficits (e.g., children with moderate and profound cognitive deficits). By definition, a child with a specific learning disability "does not include learning problems that are primarily the result of visual, hearing, or motor disabilities, of mental retardation, of emotional disturbance, or of environmental, cultural, or economic disadvantage."[45] Nonetheless, every categorization is, to some extent, subjective which is sometimes beneficial (as when an onerous label is avoided) and sometimes not. For a black child a clear history of "environmental, cultural, or economic disadvantage" is used to preclude a determination of specific learning disability but when intellectual disability provides a simple method for explaining educational needs. Sometimes subjective is good and sometimes not.

Although there are discrete disabilities for the provision of special education under IDEA, the regulations for IDEA make a distinction between disability data collection and the provision of services which meet the needs of the child and not the label:

> **The Act does not require children to be identified with a particular disability category for purposes of the delivery of special education and related services. In other words, while the Act requires that the Department collect aggregate data on children's disabilities, it does not require that particular children be labeled with particular disabilities for purposes of service delivery, since a child's entitlement under the Act is to FAPE and not to a particular disability label.[46]**

---

[45]34 § 300.8(c)(10) Child with a disability.

[46]Comments and discussion for the 2004 IDEA regulations, Federal Register /Vol. 71, No. 156 /Monday, August 14, 2006 /Rules and Regulations 46737

To illustrate the subjective character of disabilities a State can elect to use the broad term *developmental delay* for children aged three to nine "as measured by appropriate diagnostic instruments and procedures, in one or more of the following areas: physical development, cognitive development, communication development, social or emotional development, or adaptive development."[47] To understand how an Atkins claimant's needs were met as a child, not only must the defendant's school records, test scores, reports, etc. be carefully examined but also school policy for identifying children, the racial makeup of the school and racial disproportionality in the various disabilities,, how special education categories were defined by the school and/or district and by whom. This is not an exhaustive list of all the factors that should be examined.

A defendant like Freddie Lee Hall might not have been provided special services because a separate and inferior education for black children was the norm. When Hall was in grade school in the 1950s providing special services to the likes of Freddie Lee Hall would have been considered throwing good money after bad. Before Hall was finally determined to have mental retardation in 2016 Florida turned a blind eye to the racism that prevented the State from providing appropriate services to Hall as a child but then used the lack of services to suggest that Hall never had mental retardation. All this was happening when the State realized that disproportionally labeling children as having educable mental retardation provided a ready explanation for poor educational performance—an explanation not tainted by prior racism, discrimination and denial of educational opportunity.

The essence of the lesser culpability requirement is not IQ, adaptive behavior or a stereotype of what an individual identified as having an intellectual disability can accomplish but the substantive elements of lesser culpability (diminished capacities, assist counsel, serve as a witness, etc.) cited by the Supreme Court. The definition cited in *Atkins* was designed for children, readily used by States to disproportionately identify black children as

---

[47] 34 § 300.8(b) Child with a disability

having mental retardation/intellectual disabilities, readily accepted as the standard in Atkins claims, but then re-interpreted by using IQ scores "as final and conclusive evidence of a defendant's intellectual capacity" (when convenient), by interpreting adaptive behavior in a way never envisioned by professionals, and using the age of onset criterion to reject a claim of intellectual disability.

The definition for intellectual disabilities provided in the regulations for the Individuals with Disabilities Education Amendments is a barebones version of the basic definition first created in 1959 with no explication of subaverage general intellectual functioning or adaptive behavior. The intent seems to have been to allow States considerable latitude when assigning children to this category. On the one hand this provided States with greater opportunity to meet individual needs; on the other hand porous definitional criteria also provided greater opportunity for misclassification. Of note is that the IDEA definition is used to identify the vast majority of children having intellectual disabilities:[48]

> **Mental retardation means significantly subaverage general intellectual functioning, existing concurrently with deficits in adaptive behavior and manifested during the developmental period that adversely affects a child's educational performance.**

The above 2004 definition is the same as the 1973 American Association on Mental Deficiency definition used for Public Law 94-142 (Education for All Handicapped Children Act from 1975 and referred to as EAHCA or simply EHA). In the IDEA and EAHCA definitions there are four elements: 1) significantly general subaverage intellectual function, 2) deficits in adaptive, 3) manifested during the developmental period, and 4) an adverse effect on educational performance. This last requirement emphasizes the importance of educational performance when determining an intellectual disability. For example, no matter IQ score, if a child's educational performance is not affected there

---

[48]34 § 300.8[c][6]) Child with a disability

could be no classification under the special education law. Educational performance is generally cited as one of the elements of adaptive behavior ("functional academics" or "functional academic skills") but educational performance is a dimension unto itself because intellectual performance and deficits in adaptive behavior must affect educational performance to result in an intellectual disability determination as per the 1975 P.L. 94-142 special education law and the more recent 2004 Public Law 108-446.

In Justice Alito's dissent in *Hall* in 2014, he observed that raising the definition of intellectual disability to "constitutional significance" could create a problem when the definition is changed. He cites the APA definitional change of mental retardation in DSM-IV to that used in DSM-5 where the new definition "discards" the standard significantly subaverage intellectual functioning and "fundamentally alters the first prong of the longstanding, two-pronged definition of intellectual disability that was embraced by *Atkins* and has been adopted by most States." The DSM-5 definition of intellectual disability has reprioritized the prongs for a disability by providing a more expansive definition of intellectual functioning: "Deficits in intellectual functions, such as reasoning, problem solving, planning, abstract thinking, judgment, academic learning, and learning from experience, confirmed by both clinical assessment and individualized, standardized intelligence testing."

Also unique to the DSM-5 definition, the severity of the disability (mild, moderate, severe, profound) is determined by adaptive behavior rather than IQ. The explanation for this is "the various levels of severity are defined on the basis of adaptive functioning and not IQ scores because it is adaptive functioning that determines the level of supports required. Moreover, IQ measures are less valid in the lower end of the IQ range."[49] Interestingly, these "less valid" IQ scores are the very IQ scores used to make life and death decision in Atkins claims.

---

[49]Diagnostic and Statistical Manual of Mental Disorders, Fifth edition, 2013

Both professional definitions can be highly nuanced, and neither is easily amenable to bright-line interpretation, but another important consideration is the role of experts when determining intellectual disability. Contrary to the notion provided by professional groups/lawyers that "the clinical judgment of an experienced mental retardation professional is essential in assuring accuracy in the interpretation of test results,"[50] for children identified as having intellectual disabilities, the determination is made by a group of qualified professionals and the parent of the child.[51] The qualified group of professionals consists of the parents, a regular classroom teacher, a special education teacher, a representative of the public agency, "an individual who can interpret the Instructional implications of evaluation results," other individuals with special expertise, and when appropriate, the child.[52] The determination of intellectual disability for children is not the result of a single test score or made by one individual. When determining a disability the collective expertise of the various qualified professionals is of utmost importance. This is not the case when intellectual disability is determined by judge or jury in an Atkins claim—in spite of the guidance provided by experts where professionals, using the same criteria, somehow manage to reach different professional conclusions depending on whether the professional represents the defense or State.

Relevant data for a child is gathered as part of the referral for special education often includes developmental information, school records and reports, teacher evaluations, samples of classroom work, an analysis of oral reading, a speech and language evaluation, reports from other school personnel (e.g., social worker), standardized tests performance (often over years), State competency evaluations, standardized assessments of adaptive behavior, an individually administered test of intelligence, a

---

[50]Hall v. Thaler, Brief of the American Association on Intellectual And Developmental Disabilities (AAIDD) and The Arc of The United States as Amici Curiae In Support of Petitioner, In the Supreme Court of the United States, No. 10-37, August 5, 2010
[51]Regulations for Public Law 108-446, 34 §300.306(c) Determination of eligibility
[52]Regulations for Public Law 108-446, 34 §300.321 IEP Team

report of the full and individual evaluation, an Individualized Education Program (IEP) report, consideration of environmental and cultural factors, and assessments in all other areas that might be relevant (e.g., motor skills, vision and hearing assessments, communication skills). The rules for determining a disability also require public agencies to "Draw upon information from a variety of sources, including aptitude and achievement tests, parent input, and teacher recommendations, as well as information about the child's physical condition, social or cultural background, and adaptive behavior" to "ensure that information obtained from all of these sources is documented and carefully considered."[53]

The purpose for determining intellectual disability, or any disability for that matter, for children is to determine whether or not a child needs specialized instruction. The rather extensive regulations regarding the identification of a disability, assessment, procedural safeguards, the development of an individualized educational program, and placement in the least restrictive environment is far from perfect but the regulatory framework provides the foundation for a free and appropriate public education. Even with these guidelines, misclassification is possible, especially when a disability such as mild intellectual disability provides an opportunity to stigmatize and segregate under the guise of benevolence. When poor educational performance can be traced to environment, often caused by discrimination and segregation, mild intellectual disability provides an alternate reality to explain the effects of discriminatory and segregative causes.

For Atkins claims States have relied on the same definition used for children but with few, or idiosyncratic guidelines at best. The basic elements of the definition are re-interpreted to create a standard disability that benefits the State for denying claims rather than providing a fair mechanism for determining intellectual disability. States could define intellectual disability differently (as suggested in *Atkins*) but virtually all States rely on the professional definitions. The Supreme Court explained that

---

[53]Regulations for Public Law 108-446, 34 §300.306(c) Determination of eligibility

"the professional community's teachings are of particular help in this case, where no alternative definition of intellectual disability is presented and where this Court and the States have placed substantial reliance on the expertise of the medical profession." Many States, dissatisfied with the professional criteria, which ignore the circumstances and the heinousness of the crime, have expanded the definition to include the ability to plan a crime, avoid detection, etc.

Of the 340 prisoners on death row in Florida (as of November, 2019) 128 (126 males and 2 females) or 37.6 percent were black. In 1998 of the 38,086 children classified as having mental retardation in Florida 50.1 percent were black.[54] In 1998, prior to the 2002 Atkins decision, black children in Florida were routinely and disproportionately identified as having mental retardation—50.1 percent of more than 38,086 children. The disproportionate categorization of black children as having intellectual disabilities is consistent with the evolution of segregation and discrimination where segregative intent is not abandoned but simply evolved into something more sophisticated; the fact that many Atkins claims fail, especially in Florida, has the same segregative and discriminatory roots.

The dual approach for determining intellectual disabilities, interpreting the same definition differently for children and adults, is never explained by States but this differential approach to racism is achieved in many possible ways. The general rationale is to cite the Supreme Court's *Atkins* decision which gave the task for enforcing the prohibition against the execution of the intellectually disabled to States. Unfortunately, there was little guidance as to how this task should be accomplished. In 2004 the Court of Criminal Appeals of Texas decided that the real task was to "define that level and degree of mental retardation at which a consensus of Texas citizens would agree that a person should be exempted from the death penalty." The Supreme Court left the task to the States, and Texas seemed to believe that "a consensus of Texas citizens" was the most appropriate standard for enforcing *Atkins.* The Supreme Court never considered the creative and

---

[54]IDEA 22nd Annual Report

unrelenting efforts, very much like the efforts to thwart school desegregation following *Brown* in 1954, to undermine *Atkins*...and, one might add, very successful efforts.

States have acknowledged the basic definition of intellectual disabilities for Atkins claims, but have used the prongs as a series of hurdles to thwart and/or prevent successful claims. The Supreme Court required Florida to abandon the "plain language" interpretation of Florida statute 921.137 where significantly subaverage general intellectual functioning is defined as "two or more standard deviations from the mean" (or a score of 70 or less). Because a determination of intellectual disability requires low IQ and deficits in adaptive behavior, if the first prong was not met using the strict 70 IQ cutoff there was no need to consider the second prong (adaptive behavior). The Supreme Court decided this strict cutoff "bars consideration of evidence that must be considered in determining whether a defendant in a capital case has intellectual disability. Florida's rule is invalid under the Constitution's Cruel and Unusual Punishments Clause."

In Florida, for the many children classified as having an intellectual disability, contrary to Florida's "plain language" interpretation of the statute for adult Atkins claimants, a less rigorous interpretation of the IQ prong is readily used. In a 1996 Florida Bureau of Exceptional Education and Student Services technical assistance paper the use of the standard error of measurement is "treated as information one has about a test to be considered by the examiner and/or eligibility committee in determining the presence or not of a disability or giftedness" and "because of the greater weight that is placed on scores obtained on tests of intelligence, it is strongly recommended that appropriate confidence levels be provided to the reader of the psychological report."[55] In other words for children, IQ should be interpreted in conjunction with the estimated error associated with IQ scores. The Florida technical report for interpreting IQ scores is far more accurate, statistically speaking, than the various arguments advocating a strict IQ cutoff of 70 or even 75 (the Supreme Courts

---

[55]Technical Assistance Paper, Standard Error of Measurement (SEm). February, 1996 (#309159)

2014 *Hall* standard). Florida's constitutional misstep before *Hall* in 2014 was not the statute but the interpretation of the statute by the Supreme Court of Florida. This is another example of how intellectual disability is dismissed for Atkins claimants but readily accepted for a disproportionate number of black children.

For Atkins claims a pivotal problem is not only determining who is intellectually disabled, as noted by the Supreme Court in *Atkins*, but who will determine intellectual disability. The task was given to the States, just as it was for the determination of insanity in *Ford*, but a task that was not left unfettered. Contrary to the professional opinion that only professionals can interpret professional criteria for intellectual disability, in Atkins claims the determination must undergo an adversarial test so that all relevant evidence for and against a determination of intellectual disability can be presented.

In Florida a court appoints two experts to evaluate the defendant and, at sentencing, the court considers all the evidence and expert testimony offered by the defense and prosecution. If the court decides that defendant is intellectually disabled by a showing of clear and convincing evidence, a death sentence may not be imposed. In California, upon request by the defendant, the court conducts a hearing prior to trial without a jury and "the defendant's request for a court hearing prior to trial shall constitute a waiver of a jury hearing on the issue of intellectual disability." If the defendant has not requested a court hearing, a jury hearing is conducted following a finding of guilt with special circumstances." If this jury is unable to reach a unanimous decision that the defendant has an intellectual disability, a second jury is empanelled to consider the sole issue of intellectual disability.[56]

The mere mention by a court that a defendant is intellectually disabled, as was the case for Freddie Lee Hall when the trial court observed that Hall "has been mentally retarded all his life," is not a legal determination of intellectual disability. The legal determination of intellectual disability requires the finder of fact

---

[56]See California Penal Code § 1376

to weigh all relevant evidence offered by the State and defense to either refute or support a finding of intellectual disability. The task for determining intellectual disability for children is difficult to say the least, and even more difficult for an adult. Disentangling limited educational opportunity and overall pervasive racial discrimination from a fair assessment of the criteria for intellectual disability might be a task beyond the reach of most judges or juries. Then there is the conundrum for counsel when a defendant rejects a claim of intellectual disability when there is evidence to the contrary. The complexity of the task for determining intellectual disability increases with increasing age and this complexity is further confounded when simplistic bright lines are added to the mix.

One flaw of the clinical definition of intellectual disability, in the context of the judicial process, is the failure to acknowledge the ability of the State to rebut both IQ and adaptive behavior. No matter the offender's IQ score, no matter whether the cutoff is 70 or 75 (or 65 or 80), the State can rebut IQ score validity…and considering the validity of IQ this is not much of a task. A strict interpretation of the professional definition would require the defense to simply show deficits in "communication, self-care, home living, social skills, community use, self-direction, health and safety, functional academics, leisure, and work." For example, the defense could offer poor grades in school as evidence of a deficit in functional academics, but the State could then provide evidence that a defendant does not have deficits as shown by ability to complete a General Equivalency Diploma (GED) program. The defense shows that an IQ is within the prescribed range (75 or less), but the State rebuts this evidence by showing other IQ scores above 75. The clinical definition is further flawed by the contention intellectual disability is a "condition that can only be appropriately diagnosed by professionals." This suggests unanimity among professionals concerning criteria for intellectual disability a finding that is belied by the diametrically opposing assessments of intellectual disability by defense and prosecution experts.

The Supreme Court recognized the importance of experts in Ford in 1986 by noting the essential task "of selecting and using the experts responsible for producing that 'evidence' be conducive to the formation of neutral, sound, and professional judgments as to the prisoner's ability to comprehend the nature of the penalty. Fidelity to these principles is the solemn obligation of a civilized society." Yet, the Court understood that "clinical judgment" was not mechanistic but required cross-examination that "would contribute markedly to the process of seeking truth in sanity disputes by bringing to light the bases for each expert's beliefs, the precise factors underlying those beliefs, any history of error or caprice of the examiner, any personal bias with respect to the issue of capital punishment, the expert's degree of certainty about his or her own conclusions, and the precise meaning of ambiguous words used in the report." Exactly how this "comprehensive assessment and the application of clinical judgment" is incorporated in the determination of intellectual disability by the finder of fact is difficult to discern when experts disagree. Professional groups seem to believe there are limitations concerning cross-examination and that the factfinder cannot "hunt and peck among adaptive deficits, unfettered by the specific diagnostic criteria."[57] Unfortunately, there is a tendency of both defense and prosecution to "hunt and peck."

Michael Bies

The deference given to professional definitions of intellectual disability by the Supreme Court is counterbalanced by the need for a fair judicial proceeding to determine intellectual disability. Michael Bies was sentenced to death for the attempted rape, kidnapping and murder of a ten-year-old Aaron Raines in an abandoned building in Cincinnati in May, 1992. Following the Atkins decision, before Ohio could determine whether Michael Bies was mentally retarded, the U.S. District Court and the Court Appeals for the Sixth Circuit concluded that this question had already been decided when Bies' mental retardation was considered as a mitigating factor and double jeopardy prevented further reconsideration.[58]

---

[57]Wilson V. Thaler, *Amicus Curiae* Brief of American Association on Intellectual and Developmental Disabilities in Support of Petitioner

At that time, as per Penry v. Lynaugh in 1989,[59] States were allowed to sentence a mentally retarded defendant to death providing that mitigating (including testimony from a clinical psychologist that Bies was mild mentally retarded and had an IQ of 68 to 69) and aggravating factors were considered. Other reports indicated an IQ as low as 60.[60] The jury did *consider* mental retardation as a mitigating factor and decided these factors were outweighed by the aggravating factors. The jury recommended death and that was the sentence given to Bies by the court. The Ohio Supreme Court affirmed his sentence in 1996.

In Bobby v. Bies, in 2008, the Supreme Court decided that "Recourse first to Ohio's courts is what this Court envisioned in remitting to the States responsibility for implementing *Atkins*. The State acknowledges that Bies is entitled to such recourse, but rightly seeks a full and fair opportunity to contest his plea under the *Atkins* and *Lott* precedents."[61] The Supreme Court faulted the federal courts for treating a mitigating factor to derail "a state trial court proceeding "designed to determine whether Bies ha[s] a successful *Atkins* claim." The State must have an opportunity, as does the defense, to present and contest evidence. Most important, a unilateral decision by professionals when determining intellectual disability is not a fair process. This adversarial aspect of Atkins claims is unlike a determination of intellectual disability for children which is designed to be a collaboration (and sometimes not) between the parent and school to provide appropriate services (i.e., a special educational program via an IEP provided in the least restrictive environment)

The Ohio Supreme Court did not *determine* that Bies was mentally retarded but that his "personality disorder and mild to borderline mental retardation merit some weight in mitigation." The Supreme Court did not interpret this *consideration* of mental retardation as a *determination* of mental retardation. The Court

---

[58]Bies v. Bagley, 519 F. 3d 324
[59]492 U. S. 302 (1989)
[60]See Bies v. Sheldon, United States Court of Appeals, Sixth Circuit, Nos. 12–3431, 12–3457, December 12, 2014
[61]Bobby v. Bies, 556 U.S. 825 (2009)

believed that before *Atkins* there was less "incentive to contest" mental retardation because a judge or jury might believe that mental retardation "may enhance the likelihood that the aggravating factor of future dangerousness will be found by the jury." As a result, precluding a full hearing to determine mental retardation, and not merely claiming mental retardation as a mitigating factor "would not advance the equitable administration of the law." Simply rendering an opinion that intellectual disability might be a mitigating factor that a defendant is mentally retarded, as was done for Bies in 1996, is not equivalent to a determination of mental retardation. In terms of mitigation, simply citing a low IQ score, say 85 less, could be used to suggest that intellectual disability might be an argument for mitigation although an IQ score of 85 would certainly not meet the current professional definition guideline for subaverage general intellectual functioning. If the IQ used in an Atkins claim was determined before the cutoff was changed from one to two standard deviations below the mean (which will vary by State), an IQ of 85 might not only indicate mitigation but also a score that met the guideline for intellectual disability when the defendant was a child.

The Supreme Court reasoned that mental retardation as a mitigating factor and mental retardation under *Atkins* were discrete issues.[62] The Court decided that double jeopardy did not apply to Bies.[63]
The United States Court of Appeals for the Sixth Circuit then questioned the validity of Bies' interrogation and the various tactics used because

> **Even without knowledge of the medical reports concerning Bies' diminished mental capacity, the detectives observed behavior over the span of their twenty-four hour interrogation that should have led them to question Bies' mental capacity. Under the circumstances, the officers' uninhibited use of leading questions, off-the-**

---

[62]*Ibid.*
[63]*Ibid.*

> **record "fact-feeding," failure to adequately**
> **explain Bies' Miranda rights, and alleged**
> **failure to re-advise Bies of his rights after long**
> **breaks in questioning heighten the risk that**
> **Bies' confession was false or coerced, and call**
> **into question the admissibility of his custodial**
> **statements.[64]**

In 2010 Bies was "medically diagnosed and judicially determined to be a mentally retarded individual," his death sentence vacated, and he was sentenced to life with the possibility of parole after 30 years.[65]

The result of Bies' successful Atkins claim required a re-consideration of evidence of whether he could "knowingly and intelligently waive his Miranda rights" and for interrogators to utilize "appropriate interrogation techniques in order to ensure the admissibility of custodial statements." Citing Bies' IQ of 60 and adaptive skills "comparable to those of a ten-year old," the U.S. Court of Appeals, in 2014, decided that the State committed a Brady (John Leo Brady had been convicted of murder[66]) violation by not providing the defense with all available evidence which "included a substantial collection of tips, leads, and witness statements relating to other individuals who had been investigated for the murder." Specifically, the State did not reveal that an accomplice (Charles D. Boblit) had confessed to the murder. For Bies, Freddie Lee Hall and others who were determined to have intellectual disability after trial, there is no way to know the extent intellectual disability impacted prior statements (e.g., a false confession), ability to assist counsel, etc.

The court also had doubts about Bies' confession which was sometimes recorded and sometimes not and then cited the Supreme Court's warning that "defendants with intellectual disability are particularly prone to give false confessions." In an

---

[64]See Bies v. Sheldon, United States Court of Appeals, Sixth Circuit, Nos. 12–3431, 12–3457, December 12, 2014
[65]Bies v. Sheldon, United States Court of Appeals, Sixth Circuit, December 12, 2014
[66]Brady v. Maryland, 373 U.S. 83 (1963)

unusually descriptive analysis of his trial the court observed that "considering the evidence collectively, it is painfully clear that the result of the trial would likely have been different had the suppressed evidence been disclosed to the defense."

As a result of his interrogation and the suppression of evidence favorable to Bies the appellate court agreed that Bies should have a new trial. In November of 2015 Bies accepted a plea to voluntary manslaughter, attempted rape, kidnapping and aggravated burglary and was sentenced to 35 years with 23 years already served and he will remain in prison until 2027.

For Freddie Lee Hall, who was found to be intellectually disabled many years after trial, not only would a resentencing to life in prison be necessary (which was done), but potential errors at the time of trial would also require reevaluation and possibly new trial. If the State eventually decides that an offender on death row is intellectually disabled, there is no reason not to assume that the problems associated with elements of arrest, trial and sentencing were not tainted by someone who might not have been able to assist counsel, was a poor witness, and unable to understand due process and related rights.

Don William Davis

The definition of intellectual disability provides useful guidance but does not address the specific issue of whether a defendant warrants lesser culpability because of factors involving race or, for Don William Davis, reverse racism. For Don William Davis race, reverse racism, intellectual disability and other disabilities all come into play. Davis, white, was scheduled for execution on April 17, 2017 for the 1990 murder of 62 year-old Jane Martha Daniels of Rogers, Arkansas. [67] One argument offered by the defense was that Davis was ADHD and received medication as a child.

---

[67]Arkansas Code 2015, Title 5, §5-4-618

Although he knew the difference between right and wrong, his impulsivity might result in his not understanding the rightness or wrongness of a behavior and consequences. Davis was not allowed to file an Atkins claim because of the procedural rule prohibiting a "second or successive habeas petition" (in April of 2002) after the Atkins decision in June 0f 2002.

When Davis was in the primary grades (he was born in 1962), his IQ cited at a mental competency hearing included scores of 69 (Peabody Picture Vocabulary Test), 94 on the WISC when he was nine, and an IQ score of 77 when he was 12. These scores should be considered in the context of the racial climate in Arkansas and the educational advantages offered white students. If Davis were black, there is no reason not to speculate that his IQ of 77 might have been in the low 60's (referring to the much referenced black white IQ discrepancy of 15 points). During this time period black children with IQ scores in the 70s would be more than eligible for EMR placement but not so for white children.

Today ADHD is often associated with the other health impairment and the dramatic increase in the number of children in this disability category. For Davis his impulsivity, coupled with educational needs should have suggested that, were it not for his race, he might well have been identified as educable mentally retarded. There is no question that race and the determination of disability in Arkansas were related when Davis was a child. In a 1980 Office of Civil Rights report the black student enrollment in Arkansas was 22.5 percent, 51 percent of the EMR students were black, yet only 13.8 percent of the students identified as having specific learning disabilities were black.[68] The Supreme Court observed in *Atkins* that the mentally retarded are "less morally culpable" because of "diminished ability to understand and process information, to learn from experience, to engage in logical reasoning, or to control impulses." Attention deficit hyperactivity disorder (ADHD) is not synonymous with impulsivity or, more importantly, a level of impulsivity that would prevent the understanding the wrongfulness of behavior. An expert witness

---

[68]1980 Elementary and Secondary Schools Civil Rights Survey, State Summaries, Projected Data, Washington, D.C., 1982, ED#219478

testified that he would have understood the criminality of his behavior. For Davis a distinction must be made between a *disability classification* and a *disability classification that is race related*. Would Davis had been classified as EMR as a child? If he were black, had control issues, educational problems and an IQ of 77, very likely.

For Davis the State focused on ADHD more as a Ford claim which centered on whether Davis could understand wrongfulness of his behavior and not the criteria cited by the Supreme Court for warranting less culpability such as "controlling impulses" and how ADHD might impact processing. The disability categorization for Davis was complicated by the distinct possibility that as a child, if he were black, a determination of EMR would not have been out of the question. No matter his distinct disability categorization and IQ scores, Davis' mitigating evidence was insufficient to prevent his death sentence. For Davis mitigation should have considered the racial climate in his school system, how and why children received different disability classifications, and what special education services were provided. For example, a not uncommon practice is to group children with a variety of disorders into a single class so that the curriculum provided to all children attending the class would be the same no matter the special education designation. Davis might not have been labeled EMR but was treated and regarded as so by curriculum and placement. Although Davis' claim of diminished capacity was not successful, a stay was granted immediately before his April execution date based on an Eighth Amendment appeal that the lethal injection protocol used in Arkansas was cruel and unusual punishment.

In 2012 the Arkansas Supreme Court ruled that the death penalty law was unconstitutional because of the power given to the Department of Corrections rather than the legislature for determining the drug protocol for executions. In 2013 Arkansas legislature provided added guidelines for the drug protocol for executions, and in 2015 the Arkansas Supreme Court ruled that the law was constitutional. In 2016 the Arkansas court decided that the drug protocol did not violate the constitution although the availability of the necessary drugs may hinder an immediate resumption of executions in Arkansas. In April of 2017 the execution protocol was deemed appropriate resulting in the executions of Ledell Lee (April 17), Jack Jones (April 24), Marcel Williams (April 24) and Kenneth Williams (April 27). For Davis, who had been served his last meal, his execution was stayed. In March of 2018 this stay was lifted but no execution date was given. In July of 2018 he attempted suicide. As of May 2019 he remains on death row. After a series of four executions in Arkansas in 2017 (there were none from November of 2005 with the execution of Eric Nance to the execution of Ledell Lee in April of 2017), Much of the recent delay has centered about whether the drug protocol (midazolam) was sufficient for making the condemned inmate unaware of the effects of the subsequent lethal drugs (viz., potassium chloride).

Shawn Ryan Grell

Having objective criteria for determining intellectual disability is necessary because of the possibility that the heinousness of a murder can influence a fair rendering of an Atkins claim; [69] that is, the heinousness of a murder can increase the perceived culpability no matter what was decided by the Supreme Court. In Arizona, in 1999, Shawn Ryan Grell murdered his two-year old daughter, Kristen, by pouring gasoline over the small child and setting her on fire. In 2001 he was found guilty of first-degree murder and sentenced to death. In 2005, an Atkins hearing found that he had not proved mental retardation by clear and convincing evidence.

Between 1981 and 1989 Grell had taken seven IQ tests of which the lowest and highest were discarded based on what reasoning we know not. The five IQ scores reported were 72, 67, 69, 70, and 65. Grell was in special classes as a child but the State argued that "we should not rely on testimony from school employees or the school records diagnosing Grell with a "mental disability" or "mental handicap" because these were merely educational diagnoses that might not have considered adaptive skills." This is

---

[69]Arizona v. Shawn Ryan Grell, Supreme Court of Arizona, *En Banc*, No. CR–09–0199–AP, January 09, 2013

silly in that the definition of mental retardation at the time relied on the traditional three prongs (IQ, adaptive behavior, and age of onset) that have been the basis of virtually all determinations of mental retardation/intellectual disability. As a matter of fact, the adaptive behavior prong was developed especially for children, and if this prong is misinterpreted, the misinterpretation will more likely occur when used with adults.

The State experts believed that Grell's adaptive deficits were not sufficiently low for a determination of mental retardation. The State reasoned that the term used to describe his disability as a child was more important than the reasons for the classification. Apparently, although the criteria for placing Grell in special education centered about the criteria used for mental retardation, the State believed the criteria were less important than the label "mental disability" which was used instead of "mental retardation." No matter the classification, the State contended that Grell's adaptive behavior was "slightly below average." In a bizarre interpretation of average "one of Grell's special education teachers confirmed that although Grell showed some adaptive skills—such as good communication and good eye contact—his skills were 'good' only by comparison to the adaptive skills of similarly disabled students, but not when compared to non-disabled children." The State's concept of "average" was far below "average."

The Supreme Court of Arizona was able to do the difficult thing yet the right thing. The court gave considerable weight to the identification of mental retardation of Grell as a child and his record of mental retardation, and upheld his Atkins claim: *"We are fully aware* of the horrific nature of this crime and the devastation it has brought upon Kristen's family. But given the recognition under our Constitution that defendants with mental retardation are less morally culpable for their crimes, we conclude that under the Supreme Court's ruling in Atkins, Grell is ineligible for execution. We therefore vacate the trial court's death sentence and impose a sentence of natural life in prison."

2. Freddie Lee Hall - 1978

"It would appear that the trial judge did not understand the nature of mental retardation."[70]

Karol Lea Hurst

Freddie Lee Hall's many years on Florida's death row began on June 27, 1978 following his conviction for the separate murders of a 22-year- old housewife, seven months pregnant, on February 21, 1978 in Sumpter County, and, shortly thereafter, the murder of Deputy Sheriff Lonnie Coburn at a convenience store in Hernando County. The murder of Sheriff Coburn was later reduced to second degree murder because of insufficient evidence to prove premeditation.[71] Karol Lea Hurst was abducted by Hall, and accomplice Mack Ruffin, as she left a Pantry Pride grocery store in Leesburg, Florida. Hall and Ruffin drove Mrs. Hurst to a secluded area, raped her, and then Hall decided that she should be killed to prevent identification. Mack Ruffin, who participated in the murder, stated that he and Hall raped Mrs. Hurst but that he had wanted to "simply leave her, bound and gagged, in the woods. Mrs. Hurst begged them to spare her life and wrote them a check for $20,000, payable to 'John Doe.' Petitioner refused to accept the check; whereupon, Hall pistol-whipped Mrs. Hurst and, while she was lying face down on the ground, shot her in the back of the head."[72] According to Hall, Ruffin had "beat, sexually assaulted, and shot Mrs. Hurst."[73] The trial was moved from Sumter County, Florida to Palatka in Putnam County where he was sentenced to death on June 27, 1978.

In 1993 the Supreme Court of Florida recognized that there was a degree of uncertainty as to who actually shot Ms. Hurst so that

---

[70]Hall v. Florida, Supreme Court of Florida, 614 So. 2d 473, 1993, Barkett, C.J., dissenting
[71]Hall v. State, Supreme Court of Florida, 403 So.2d 1319 (1981)
[72]Ruffin v. Dugger, 848 F.2d 1512, 1988, United States Court of Appeals, Eleventh Circuit
[73]Hall v. State, Supreme Court of Florida, 403 So. 2d 1321 (1981)

"even if Hall did not fire the shot that killed the victim, he was a willing if not predominant participant in the other acts. The totality of the circumstances shows this murder to have been committed in a cold, calculated, and premeditated manner."[74]

Following the murder of Ms. Hurst later that day, Hall and Ruffin were seen at a Shop and Go store, the Sheriff's office was called, and shortly thereafter Deputy Sheriff Lonnie Coburn was found shot to death behind the store. A scant four months later, in June of 1978, Hall and Mack Ruffin were convicted of capital murder and sentenced to death. In 1988 the Court of Appeals decided because non-statutory mitigating factors were not considered in sentencing, a constitutional error was committed and Ruffin was re-sentenced to life while Hall's appeals were considered and summarily rejected.

The primary mitigating factor asserted by Hall during his original sentencing was not mental retardation,[75] but that a "capital felony was committed while the defendant was under the influence of extreme mental or emotional disturbance" and "the capacity of the defendant to appreciate the criminality of his conduct or to conform his conduct to the requirements of law was substantially impaired" because of "smoking dope and drinking."

In 1981, the Supreme Court of Florida found Hall was, if not directly responsible for the murders, an "aider or abettor" to both crimes. In 1982 the governor signed Hall's first death warrant but on appeal the case was remanded to consider his absence from the courtroom and ineffective assistance of counsel. All trial errors were found harmless and the governor signed a second death warrant and Hall's execution for September 20, 1988.

In 1989 the case was remanded for resentencing because a Hitchcock error had occurred which involved the failure to consider non-statutory factors.[76] The Supreme Court of Florida

---

[74]Hall v. State, Supreme Court of Florida, 614 So. 2d 473 (1993)
[75]The terms *mental retardation* and *intellectual disability will* be used in reference to the time when the term was actually used.
[76]James Ernest Hitchcock had been sentence to death in Florida for the strangulation murder of 13-year-old Cynthia Driggers in 1976. At the

ordered a resentencing because the trial court did not consider non-statutory mitigating factors such as horrendous childhood abuse, "limited intelligence, organic brain damage, extreme impairment of personality integration, psychotic disorganization, and possible schizophrenia." In addition, the court also noted a variety of non-statutory environmental factors including "Hall's sixteen brothers and sisters paint a stark portrait of a childhood filled with abject poverty, constant violence, and unbearable brutality. Born the sixteenth of seventeen children to a mother and father who fought ceaselessly with shotguns, knives, or whatever weapons were available, Hall's childhood was marked by an existence which can only be described as pitiful." This resentencing resulted in a jury vote of 8 to 4 for death.

In 1991, the trial court acknowledged that Hall was "mentally retarded" but gave this mitigating factor "unquantifiable weight" because of Hall's deliberation and planning. Mental retardation as mitigation, however, could have contrary results. As explained by the Supreme Court in *Atkins* "mental retardation as a mitigating factor can be a two-edged sword that may enhance the likelihood that the aggravating factor of future dangerousness will be found by the jury."

An evaluation of Hall revealed that "counselors described him as being mentally retarded and having a mental age well below his chronological age, he was classified as 4F and rejected for military service because of poor mental and intellectual functioning."[77] For the court, in spite of various IQ scores between 60 and 80, a horrible family environment, academic difficulties, his ability to "formulate a plan" seemed contrary to what would be expected of someone mentally retarded. This reasoning is exactly what the ADA Title II attempted to prohibit where a "public entity's

---

time the Florida statute (921.141) required that mitigating factors listed in the statute could only be considered and not other relevant non-statutory factors such as "family background and his capacity for rehabilitation." Following the Supreme Court's remand, Hitchcock was re-sentenced to death on three more occasions by votes of 7 to 5, 12 to 0, and 10 to 2.[76] As of April 2017 Hitchcock has continued to appeal his death sentence as he begins his fifth decade on death row.

[77]See Hall v. Florida, Application for stay of execution, 1988

determination that a person poses a direct threat to the health or safety of others may not be based on generalizations or stereotypes about the effects of a particular disability."

According to the Florida court Hall's "behavior at the time of the crimes for which he stands convicted, as well as some of the statements that he made previously. . . would belie the fact of his severe psychosis and mental retardation. Nothing of which the experts testified could explain how a psychotic, mentally-retarded, brain-damaged, learning-disabled, speech-impaired person could formulate a plan whereby a car was stolen and a convenience store was robbed" and "this Court believes that the evidence of the experts, for whatever reason or reasons, is exaggerated to some extent."[78] This is the essence of the Texas Briseno factors (now prohibited by the Supreme Court in 2017[79]) which highlighted crime-related behavior (e.g., stealing, robbery) to discount not only IQ, no matter how low, but all other behavior that might militate against the death penalty.

In 2008 the Supreme Court of Florida explained how "experts also agreed that the planning of the murder and cover-up" were "inconsistent with a finding" of mental retardation."[80] In other words, the definition of mental retardation to require low IQ, deficits in adaptive behavior and occurring before the age of onset is nullified if an offender exhibits the ability to plan and cover-up a capital offense.

No matter whether Hall was mentally retarded, or might have been mentally retarded, or in spite of school records showing that he should have been classified as mentally retarded, he was again sentenced to death in 1991 which was affirmed by the Supreme Court of Florida in 1993.[81] The court interpreted the underlying issue of mental retardation as that of competency to be sentenced to death: "All discussed Hall's mental retardation and expressed an understanding of the standard for finding a defendant

---

[78]See Judge Pariente's concurring opinion in Hall v. Florida, 109 So. 3d 704, 2012
[79]Moore v. Texas, Supreme Court of the United States, March 28, 2017
[80]Phillips v. State, 984 So. 2d 503 (Fla. 2008)
[81]Hall v. Florida, Supreme Court of Florida, 614 So. 2d 473, 1993

competent, which requires that he or she be able to understand the nature of the proceedings and to confer with counsel." In this respect, the issue is not mental retardation, in and of itself, but rather whether mental retardation results in competency for sentencing. By this interpretation the criteria for mental retardation/intellectual disability are secondary to a determination of competency similar to that used for an insanity plea.

Judge Rosemary Barkett, in her 1993 dissenting opinion which predated the Supreme Court's 2002 *Atkins* decision, opined that the death penalty for mentally retarded defendants was unconstitutional. She explained that "because a mentally retarded person such as Freddie Lee Hall has a lessened ability to determine right from wrong and to appreciate the consequences of his behavior, imposition of the death penalty is excessive in relation to the crime committed." She also asserted that executing the mentally retarded is disproportionate "and while a tragic childhood and mental retardation do not 'excuse' later criminal behavior, they do reflect on an individual's culpability." She also favored a narrowing of the law so "that the death penalty be reserved for the most heinous of crimes and the most culpable of murderers." Justice Barkett described Hall as having "an IQ of 60; he suffers from organic brain damage, chronic psychosis, a speech impediment, and a learning disability; he is functionally illiterate; and he has a short-term memory equivalent to that of a first grader." She also noted that Hall's teachers in elementary school believed that he was mentally retarded and the trial judge thought that Hall had been mentally retarded all his life.[82]

In 1993 the Supreme Court of Florida affirmed Freddie Lee Hall's death sentence. Justice Barkett believed that Freddie Lee Hall was mentally retarded and "executing the mentally retarded violates the state constitution. Consequently, I would remand Hall's case for imposition of a sentence of life imprisonment." In contrast to Justice Barkett's opinion, the majority believed "The aggravators clearly outweigh the mitigating evidence, and this cruel, cold-

---

[82]Hall v. Florida, 109 So. 3d 704; 201

blooded murder clearly falls within the class of killings for which the death penalty is properly imposed."

In 1997 an evidentiary hearing was held to consider Hall's appeal and in 1999 the Supreme Court of Florida again denied his claims and had no qualms for "allowing the death penalty for an incompetent or mentally retarded person."[83] In 2004, Hall filed an Atkins claim which resulted in a 2009 evidentiary hearing. As was the case in previous rulings, the Florida court found that the language of the statute required an IQ score of 70 or below, and because the statue did not use the term "approximate" or standard error of measurement, and because a defendant must meet all three prongs of the definition (including an IQ score of 70 or below), failure to meet the first prong precluded consideration of other evidence.. The court did not consider adaptive behavior, school records suggesting mental retardation as a young child, his assessment of intellectual ability by the army, or the various statements by family members and expert witnesses for the defense.

Florida, like most States following *Atkins* in 2002, set about developing legislation to meet the Atkins standard which prohibited the death penalty for mentally retarded offenders. Florida statute 921.137 used the professional definition as the basis for defining mental retardation as "significantly subaverage general intellectual functioning existing concurrently with deficits in adaptive behavior and manifested during the period from conception to age 18." The Florida statute requires the court to appoint two experts to evaluate the defendant's mental retardation. At the final sentencing hearing, without a jury, the court then considers "the findings of any other expert which is offered by the state or the defense on the issue of whether the defendant has mental retardation" using the "clear and convincing" evidence standard. After considering all expert testimony offered by the State and defense, and using the higher clear and convincing evidence standard, the court determines whether or not the defendant is mentally retarded. If the

---

[83]Hall v. Florida, Supreme Court of Florida, No. 92,008, July 1, 1999.

defendant is determined to be mentally retarded, the death sentence may not be given.

For Hall mental retardation was considered and acknowledged by the court prior to his Atkins claim as a mitigating factor, but for Hall the aggravating factors outweighed the mitigating factors. Hall's prior mental retardation, as suggested by teachers, and deficits in adaptive behavior were not considered because his various IQ scores (76, 79, 80, 73, 69, 71, and 72)—an IQ of 69 was not considered because it "lacked critical detail and information"—and therefore did not provide evidence of a sufficiently low IQ.

In 2014 the Supreme Court decided that the strict cutoff of 70 used by Florida for considering other evidence was unconstitutional while, at the same time, tacitly approving a strict cutoff of 75.[84] The Court did not say that Hall could not be executed, or that Hall was mentally retarded (although the Court strongly suggested that other evidence relevant to Hall's Atkins claim existed, especially regarding environmental factors), but that Florida must consider other evidence relating to intellectual disability.

The Supreme Court was certainly moved by mitigating factors on the part of Hall. The Court believed that there was other evidence relating to an intellectual disability such that Hall "presented substantial and unchallenged evidence of intellectual disability. School records indicated that his teachers identified him on numerous occasions as '[m]entally retarded.'" The Court then elaborated on these deficits by observing "Hall's upbringing appeared to make his deficits in adaptive functioning all the more severe" and reports by siblings indicated delayed development in speech, language, and walking. This developmental data, albeit anecdotal, was an essential element when the professional definition of mental retardation was first proposed in 1959. Testimony revealed that Hall's mental retardation did not result in sympathy "but rather caused much scorn to befall him," he was "constantly beaten for mistakes or for "simple mistakes."

---

[84]Hall v. Florida, 572 U.S. ____ (2014)

From a procedural standpoint for Atkins claims following the 2014 Supreme Court Hall decision, Florida need only consider all the evidence and then find that he is not intellectually disabled; or because the Supreme Court, in oral arguments, seems to have agreed with defense counsel that an IQ cutoff of 75 is constitutional, a single score above 75 could be used to end the inquiry (as can be done in Oklahoma); or that a single IQ test scone above 75 as part of a screening procedure could be used to end an Atkins inquiry; or that an Atkins claimant does not have deficits in adaptive behavior; or that both IQ scores and deficits in adaptive behavior do not comport with an intellectual disability; or adaptive strengths outweigh his deficits; or the claimant no longer has deficits in adaptive behavior based on his death row behavior(a strange but true strategy); or the intellectual disability was not manifested before age 18. In the end, the Florida Supreme Court, and not "the" Supreme Court decided that Hall was, in fact, intellectually disabled.

Timothy Stuart Ring

Death penalty calculus is more often mystery than science. Who should decide Atkins claims: judge or jury? Who should decide factors that preclude the death penalty in Atkins claims: judge, jury or experts? When should a determination of intellectual disability be made: before trial, before sentencing, or during sentencing? And what happens when there is evidence of some degree of intellectual disability, coupled with a lack of unanimity among jurors, but the death penalty is imposed nonetheless? In this regard, the Florida death penalty was under attack in 2016 because of a Supreme Court ruling in 2002. The Supreme Court required in 2002, in Ring v. Arizona, that a jury must decide the aggravating factor(s) required for the imposition of the death penalty. Florida ignored this interpretation of the constitution, "the Sixth Amendment right to a jury trial in capital prosecutions," [85] for 14 years before the Supreme Court of Florida intervened in 2016 in Hurst v. Florida.

---

[85]Ring v. Arizona, 536 U.S. 584 (2002)

Timothy Stuart Ring was sentenced to death for the 1994 murder of Wells Fargo armored van driver John Magoch in Glendale, Arizona. Because of a lack of evidence that Ring actually murdered Magoch, or even participated in the crime, the jury acquitted Ring of premeditated murder (by a 6 to 6 vote) but convicted him of felony murder because evidence showed that he received proceeds from the robbery. Based on the jury felony murder conviction, Ring should have been sentenced to life in prison but the trial judge, after considering aggravating and mitigating factors, decided that Ring warranted the death penalty. Upon review the Supreme Court explained that the Sixth Amendment (and a more nuanced interpretation of the Eighth Amendment) requires a jury to decide the necessary aggravating factors for a death sentence.[86]

The requirement in *Ring* is not as obvious as one would think. In Supreme Court oral arguments for Hurst (in October of 2015) Florida contended that although the law (*Ring*) required a jury to find an aggravating factor to justify the imposition of the death penalty, even if the jury recommends life during sentencing (by a 7 to 5 or even 12 to 0 vote), if the jury found a defendant guilty of capital murder who had a previous felony, this would be tantamount to a finding of an aggravating factor by the jury (although the logic here is not all that straightforward). According to Florida, this was implicit in the guilty verdict during the guilt phase even though the jury did not find a specific aggravating factor during sentencing (or at least an aggravating factor that was known). Florida was not alone in how *Ring* was interpreted. In Alabama, Ring is more suggestion than mandate as when juries voted for life for Arthur Jones (11 to 1), Henry Hays (7 to 5), Steven Thompson (10 to 2), Anthony Johnson (9 to 3), Willie McNair (8 to 4), and John Parker (10-2) but all were sentenced to death.

Joseph Robert Spaziano

---

[86]*Ibid.*

The reasoning behind the singular importance of the jury fact-finding process is best understood when the rationale for jury override is examined—at least with respect to Joseph Robert Spaziano. "Crazy Joe" was sentenced to death in 1976 for the torture, murder and mutilation of 18 year-old Laura Lynn Harberts (a second victim was unidentified) in Altamonte Springs, Florida. Spaziano, who was not intellectually disabled, illustrates how the heinousness of an offender's crime and subsequent behavior can cloud sentencing when the weighing of aggravators and mitigators are confounded by judicial interpretation.

Spaziano's capture was facilitated by bragging about the murders and showing others the corpses at a dump site where he had taken the victims. The jury recommended life in prison which was rejected by the judge because "the homicide was especially heinous and atrocious and that the defendant had been convicted previously of felonies involving the use or threat of violence to the person." In 1981 the Supreme Court of Florida remanded the case for resentencing because the trial court had used information from a confidential report that the defense did not have an opportunity to review or refute. The report contained formation that Spaziano was "a suspect in four homicides and three bombings, was a member of the 'Outlaws' gang, had been convicted of rape and sentenced to State prison, had been charged with forcible carnal knowledge, rape, and false imprisonment for another incident (but allegedly escaped prosecution because of harassment and threats towards the victim by gang members), and had been convicted of other nonviolent felony and misdemeanor offenses."[87] The reasoning for judicial override was based on information not available to the defense and was therefore unconstitutional as determined by the Supreme Court in 1977 in Gardner v. Florida.[88] In 1973 James A. Gardner assaulted and murdered his wife, Bertha Mae Gardner, in Citrus County, Florida, and was sentenced to death in 1974. The jury recommended life but the trial court, relying in part on

---

[87]Spaziano v. State of Florida, Supreme Court of Florida, 393 So. 2d 1119, January 8, 1981
[88]Gardner v. Florida, 430 U.S. 349 (1977)

confidential information not available to the defense, imposed the death sentence.

In Spaziano v. Florida, in 1984, the Supreme Court found that a judge override of a sentence of life in prison by the jury in favor of the death penalty was entirely constitutional because "the fact that the majority of jurisdictions with capital sentencing statutes give the life-or-death decision to the jury does not establish that contemporary standards of fairness and decency are offended by the jury override. The Eighth Amendment is not violated every time a State reaches a conclusion different from a majority of its sisters over how best to administer its criminal laws."[89] According to the Court the Sixth Amendment does not guarantee that a jury must decide the appropriate punishment. After surviving several death warrants, the Supreme Court of Florida agreed with a lower court that newly discovered evidence required a new trial.[90] In 1998 he pleaded guilty to second-degree murder and received a sentence of time served. Alas, he was also serving a life sentence for a 1974 rape conviction (sexual battery) of a 16-year-old in Orange County. For the 74-year-old Spaziano (born September 12, 1945) his sentence will likely end with his death at the DeSoto Annex where he is incarcerated.

Timothy Lee Hurst

The year 2016 was a busy one for the Supreme Court of Florida regarding the death penalty statute. Not only was the court considering what to do with Freddie Lee Hall's Atkins claim but the court was facing other constitutional issues relating to the advisory vote by jurors in death penalty cases, the controversial problem of judicial override, weighing of aggravating and mitigating factors, and determining whether the Supreme Court's 2014 Hall decision applied to all death row offenders, or only some, and then whether every death row offender should be re-sentenced because of Timothy Lee Hurst.

---

[89]468 U.S. 447, 1984
[90]State v. Spaziano, 692 So. 2d 174 (1997)

Hurst was convicted for the 1998 stabbing (using a box cutter) and murder of assistant manager Cynthia Harrison at a Popeye restaurant during a robbery in Escambia County, Florida. In 2000 Hurst was sentenced to death by an 11 to 1 vote. The jury was not swayed by his age (19 at the time) and evidence of mental retardation. In 2002 the Supreme Court of Florida found that "In toto, any error as to defendant's family background was harmless. The death penalty was not a disproportionate sentence in light of the heinous, atrocious, and cruel nature of the crime, and the negligible mitigation."[91] Florida statute required the jury to provide an advisory sentence so that "after hearing all the evidence, the jury shall deliberate and render an advisory sentence to the court" and "Notwithstanding the recommendation of a majority of the jury, the court, after weighing the aggravating and mitigating circumstances, shall enter a sentence of life imprisonment or death."[92]

At Hurst's first evidentiary hearing, in 2007, his Atkins claim was denied because of testimony that he did not have adaptive impairments. In 2009 the Supreme Court of Florida dismissed his guilt phase claims but believed that Hurst's counsel did not present all available information relating to mental retardation (e.g., low IQ, and a history of special education) during the penalty phase and the case was remanded for a new penalty phase.

During the second penalty phase in 2012 the trial court followed the 7 to 5 jury recommendation and Hurst was sentenced to death.[93] In his 2013 appeal Hurst was found to have a WAIS-IV IQ of 69. An earlier IQ testing resulted in scores of 76 and 78. The court refused to hold an evidentiary hearing on the issue of mental retardation but allowed a review of all evidence of "borderline intelligence" as a mitigating factor. Two expert witnesses opined that Hurst was mentally retarded and met the criteria defining mental retardation: low IQ, deficits in adaptive behavior, and onset before age 18. The evidence for denying his claim had little to do with IQ or deficits in adaptive behavior but centered about

---

[91]Hurst v. Florida, Supreme Court of Florida, 819 So. 2d 689 (2002)
[92]921.141 (now changed)
[93]Timothy Lee Hurst v. State of Florida, Supreme Court of Florida, No. SC12-1947, May 1, 2014 and October 14, 2016

his ability to plan, avoid detection, conceal, and work (exactly what had been done in Texas). Because of Hurst's actions around the time of the crime, his ability to acquire a driver's license, to recount events, give directions, recall telephone numbers, conceal his involvement, etc., the trial court decided Hurst was not mentally retarded as per IQ, adaptive behavior and age of onset criteria cited in Florida statute.

The jury for Hurst was required to determine whether sufficient aggravating circumstances existed, whether mitigating circumstances outweighed aggravating circumstances, and then render an advisory decision whether the defendant should be sentenced to life in prison or death.[94] Exactly which aggravating factors were considered by the jury is not known and that is the essence of the Sixth Amendment violation. The jury was instructed that it could recommend death if "at least one aggravating circumstance beyond a reasonable doubt" was found but there was no requirement to maintain a record of which aggravating factors were actually found. Assuming that the jury did find at least one aggravating factor, and then weighed mitigating and aggravating factor(s), the 7 to 5 vote indicated that five jurors were less than "beyond" in their reasonable doubt. The jury vote did not run afoul of the Sixth Amendment but rather the possibility existed that the trial court rather than jury found the specific facts which warranted execution. In other words the aggravating factor(s) found by the trial court might have been different than the aggravating factors found by the jury.

For Hurst, the trial court (not the jury) reported two aggravating factors: the murder was especially heinous, atrocious or cruel, and committed during a robbery. Judge and jury may have found identical aggravating or they might have not. If the court's aggravating factors differed from those of the jury, the court was the ultimate finder of fact and not the jury. More importantly, the role of the jury in Florida was advisory and a death sentence must be based "on a jury's verdict, not a judge's factfinding." The court also found three statutory mitigating factors including 1) no significant history of prior criminal activity, 2) the age of the

---

[94]Florida Statute, Criminal Procedure and Corrections, 921.141

defendant, and 3) factors in the defendant's background that would weigh against imposition of the death penalty (i.e., limited intellectual capacity). The Supreme Court found Florida's sentencing scheme unconstitutional because Hurst's death sentence might have been based on the judge's factfinding and not that of the jury.[95] On October 14, 2016 the Supreme Court of Florida decided that a jury, not the trial court, must unanimously agree that there is a least one aggravating factor, that the factor(s) warrant the death penalty, and the aggravating factors outweigh mitigating factors.[96]

The mathematics for weighing aggravating and mitigating factors is more mystery than science. For Hurst, two aggravators of great weight apparently outweighed three mitigating factors of moderate weight thereby allowing the trial court imposed the death penalty. If an Atkins claimant is somewhat short of meeting the intellectual disability standard, there must be a modicum of credible evidence to suggest intellectual disability. In view of evidence of intellectual disability and the Supreme Court's belief in *Hall i*n 2014 that "protecting even those convicted of heinous crimes, the Eighth Amendment reaffirms the duty of the government to respect the dignity of all persons," reducing evidence of intellectual disability to a factor of moderate weight seems inconsistent with the Supreme Court's with the Court's concept of "human dignity."

Florida statute 921.141 now requires that a jury (given that the defendant has not waived his right to a jury sentencing) unanimously finds at least one aggravating factor *beyond a reasonable doubt*, and then unanimously determines that the sentence should be death. If the jury recommends life in prison without the possibility of parole, the court must follow this recommendation. Following the jury decision, the court can impose a sentence of life in prison without parole.

---

[95]Hurst v. Florida, 577 ___ U.S. 2016 (January 12)
[96]See https://www.scribd.com/document/327590297/Hurst-v-Florida-Florida-Supreme-Court-Ruling-Released-on-October-14-2016#from_embed

In January of 2016 the Supreme Court decided Florida's sentencing scheme, which required the judge alone to find the existence of an aggravating circumstance, is therefore unconstitutional."[97] The court further held that the Sixth and Eighth Amendments were violated in Hurst's sentencing and that the jury must unanimously find "the existence of any aggravating factor, the jury must also unanimously find that the aggravating factors are sufficient for the imposition of death and unanimously find that the aggravating factors outweigh the mitigation before a sentence of death may be considered by the judge."[98] The Supreme Court of Florida decided that "in order for a death sentence to be imposed, the jury's recommendation for death must be unanimous" (and not the 10 to 0 vote specified by the Florida legislature. If the jury recommends life without parole, that is the sentence that the trial court must impose. In March of 2017 the Governor of Florida signed into law a revised statute, consistent with the Supreme Court of Florida's ruling, requiring a unanimous jury vote for the death penalty.

A jury vote of 7 to 5 is flimsy democracy for imposing the death penalty which was acknowledged by *Ring* and subsequent decisions. These various statutory and judicial revisions did not help Thomas Harrison Provenzano who believed he was Jesus Christ. He apparently understood why he was being tried, his trial, and his pending execution. Following a 7 to 5 advisory jury vote, the same as for Hurst, Provenzano was sentenced to death for the 1984 murder of Deputy Sheriff William Arnie Wilkerson. Deputy Sheriff Harry Dalton and Correctional Officer Mark Parker also died from complications following Provenzano's court house attack. Today, Provenzano would have been resentenced, and possibly given life in prison if recent changes in Florida's law death penalty statute and the Supreme Court of Florida's 2016 decision were applicable.[99] No matter this hypothetical, Provenzano was executed by lethal injection in June of 2000.

---

[97]Hurst v. Florida, 577 ___ U.S. 2016 (January 12)
[98]Hurst v. Florida, Supreme Court of Florida, No. SC12-1947, October 14, 2016
[99]Hurst v. Florida, 136 S.Ct. 616 (2016)

Mark James Asay

The Supreme Court's Hall decision leaves no doubt that the Court believed Florida's use of a strict IQ cutoff "disregards established medical practice" and fails to protect "the integrity of the trial process for individuals who face a special risk of wrongful execution.'" The result of this constitutional violation is that "Florida's law contravenes our Nation's commitment to dignity and its duty to teach human decency as the mark of a civilized world." There seems to be a clear constitutional standard for not executing the intellectually disabled, but maybe a standard that is more porous than would appear.

Mark James Asay, a white supremacist, was sentenced to death in 1988 by a 9 to 3 advisory vote for the 1987 "cold, calculated and premeditated" murder of Robert Lee Booker and Robert McDowell, both black. The trial court found the aggravating factors necessary for a death penalty, which may or may not have been the same as those found by the jury, and followed the jury recommendation and imposed the death penalty. He was scheduled for execution on March 17, 2016 but the Supreme Court of Florida granted Asay a stay on March 2, 2016 because of the *Hurst* decision and before the changes to Florida death penalty statute. The jury vote and the jury process would all be unconstitutional under current law and judicial decision in Florida. However, jury unanimity does not necessarily apply retroactively.

The ultimate question is whether jury unanimity is a rule change or a watershed decision. After all, others have been executed using the same procedural guidelines, developed before the *Hurst* decision, as were used to sentence Asay to death. In most instances, a simple rule change cannot result in relief based on a decision before the rule was changed. The reason for this is to achieve finality to the judicial process and acknowledge that a good-faith effort (the rule prior to change) was fundamentally fair. A watershed rule addresses a fundamental issue of fairness that must be applied to all cases no matter when decided. Roper v. Simmons, decided in 2005, prohibits execution for murder committed before the age of 18,[100] and Atkins v. Virginia (2002), are both used retroactively. Freddie Lee Hall was determined to be intellectually disabled in 2016, some 30 years after the murder of Karol Lea Hurst in 1978.

According to the Supreme Court in Teague v. Lane not every judicial decision is a watershed rule that alters "our understanding of the bedrock procedural elements that must be found to vitiate the fairness of a particular conviction."[101] To reach the level needed for retroactivity, the decision in question must propose a new rule that either is substantive in nature, or is a "watershed" rule that enhances the fundamental fairness of a criminal procedure.

In December of 2016 the Supreme Court of Florida decided that the Hurst decision did not apply to decisions made prior to Ring (June 24, 2002). The reasoning for this was that, after a very detailed review of the matter of retroactivity as applied to the Supreme Court's *Hurst* decision, "Granting collateral relief would have a strong impact upon the administration of justice. Courts would be forced to reexamine previously final and fully adjudicated cases. Moreover, courts would be faced in many cases with the problem of making difficult and time-consuming factual determinations based on stale records. We believe that a court's time and energy would be better spent in handling its current caseload."[102] The court acknowledged that "in death cases, this Court has taken care to ensure all necessary constitutional protections are in place before one forfeits his or her life, and the purpose of the new rule weighs in favor of applying Hurst v. Florida retroactively to Asay." However, the court decided that *Hurst* should not be applied retroactively to Asay where his death sentence was issued before *Ring*.

No white offender had ever been executed in Florida for killing a black but this was not to be for Mark Asay.[103] He was executed by lethal injection on August 24, 2017 using an experimental drug

---

[100]543 U.S. 551 (2005)
[101]Teague v. Lane, 489 U.S. 288 (1989)
[102]Asay v. Florida, Supreme Court of Florida, No. SC16-223, December 22, 2016
[103]*Ibid.*

(the anesthetic etomidate in addition to two other drugs to cause paralysis and stop his heart).

Lucious Boyd and Others

For Florida the *Hurst* decision has resulted in a bevy of rulings involving the retroactivity of the new rule that jury must be the ultimate decision-maker. Lucious Boyd, born March 22, 1959, was sentenced to death for the December 1998 murder of Dawnia Dacosta near Interstate 95 in Deerfield, Florida. The jury unanimously recommended death which the trial court imposed on June 21, 2002, shortly before Ring was decided on June 24, 2002. The unanimous vote does not explicate exactly what aggravating factors were found by the jury as required by *Ring*. Boyd remains on death row because of the three month gap between his sentencing (June 21) and *Ring* (June 24) in 2002.

John Steven Huggins, on the other hand, was first sentenced to death in 1999 for the first-degree murder of Carla Larson on June 10, 1997. Because of a Brady violation involving the suppression of evidence he was retried and on July 26, 2002 the jury voted 9 to 3 for an advisory sentence of death which the trial court issued on September 19, 2002. *Ring* did not apply to the Boyd who awaits an execution date (although he was received at the Union Correctional Institution on June 25, 2002 one day after the June 24 Ring bright line). Huggins would seem to have a more promising *Ring* outlook because his death sentence was given two days after *Ring* in spite of the fact that the trial court issued a special verdict interrogatories form which required the specification of specific aggravators and the number of jurors who did not reach this finding beyond a reasonable doubt.

For all defendants seeking Hurst relief the date of Ring is the ultimate factor and not the jury vote. For example a jury vote of 11-1 occurring after Ring would probably result in a reversal or remand for a new penalty phase (as was the case Harrel Braddy) but not a jury decision before Ring when the vote was 7-5 (Paul Alfred Brown).[104]

The reasons for jury override are many and always given for a reason, legitimate or not. As noted in the dissent in *Asay*, in addition to the difficult issue of unanimity, this does not mean that there is some high moral standard associated with the jury fact-finding process when race can be an intervening factor. Matthew Marshall, black, was sentenced to death in 1989 for the murder of another prisoner in 1988. The trial court overruled the recommendation of life in prison (by a 12-0 jury vote) to death. To complicate the now the impermissible judicial override in Florida are the bizarre and racist reasons given by some jurors for voting for life in prison, including "some jurors announced during the guilt phase that they were going to vote for a guilty verdict and a life sentence because they wanted Marshall to return to prison to kill more black inmates."[105]

The Florida Senate did not, until Hurst, repeal judicial override but required at least a jury vote of 10-2 for imposing the death penalty (March 7, 2016, HB 7101). This was negated in October of that year following Hurst v. Florida. The Bill to amend the death penalty statute in the Florida House revealed that of the 296 decisions reported where the jury recommended death (or the trial court exercised judicial override), of these death sentences 40 involved a vote of 7-5, 52 a vote of 8-4 and 71 (the most common vote) a vote of 9-3. All of these cases would have resulted in life without parole based on the 2016 revised Florida statute. Unanimity (a vote of 12 to 0) was reached in 70 cases (71 percent).[106] For sentencing prior to June 24, 2002 (Ring v. Arizona), Hurst does not apply. Of the 296 cases, as of February 10, 2017, there were 383 inmates on Florida's death row and 211 became final after *Ring* June 24, 2002.[107] A Hurst claim does not

---

[104]See Death Penalty Information Center, https://deathpenaltyinfo.org/Hurst_Cases_Reviewed
[105]Marshall v. State, Supreme Court of Florida, No.SC00-1186, June 12, 2003
[106]House of Representatives Staff Analysis, Bill #: HB 527, document date February 21, 2017. https://www.flsenate.gov/Session/Bill/2017/527/Analyses/h00 527c.JDC.PDF
[107]Florida Senate, Bill Analysis and Impact Statement, SB280, Sentencing

automatically vacate a death sentence. If the defendant has waived a sentencing proceeding, a Hurst claim is invalidated. Following a Hurst claim, a harmless error review is required to determine if the death sentence should be vacated and a new sentencing undertaken.

For successful Hurst claims the error associated with the non-unanimous jury vote is a difficult obstacle for the State to overcome and the likely outcome is life in prison as was the case for William Gregory. He was sentenced to death for the shotgun murder of Skyler Dawn Meekins and Daniel Arthur Dyer in 2007 near Flagler Beach, Florida. The advisory jury vote was 7 to 5. Following *Hurst* his death sentenced was vacated and on December 4, 2017 the prosecution, after considering the wishes of the family of the victims, decided not to pursue a new sentencing phase. Gregory was then sentenced to two life terms without the possibility of parole.

Raymond Bright was sentenced to death for the 2008 murders (using a hammer) of Derrick King and Randall Brown in Jacksonville, Florida. The jury advisory vote was 8 to 4. In September of 2017 a jury unanimously voted for death after a hearing that took into consideration evidence relating to his childhood and mental health. In December Judge Russell Healey followed the jury recommendation and the 63 year-old Bright was re-sentenced to death.

Michael Lee Marsh II

The Supreme Court seems to have solved some problems for courts when weighing aggravating and mitigating factors but not so for Kansas where the weighing of factors is less than straightforward for a State that rarely executed offenders. Michael Lee Marsh II shot, stabbed and slashed the throat of Marry Anne Pusch and then set fire to her home resulting in the death of her 19-month old daughter in 1996. The trial court found three aggravating factors: "1) Marsh knowingly or purposely killed or

---

for Capital Felonies, February 3, 2017

created a great risk of death to more than one person; (2) he committed the crime in order to avoid or prevent a lawful arrest or prosecution; and (3) he committed the crime in an especially heinous, atrocious or cruel manner." He was given the death penalty but a new trial was ordered because relevant evidence was impermissibly excluded from trial, and because of questions concerning the constitutionality of the Kansas death penalty statute which states that "If, by unanimous vote, the jury finds beyond a reasonable doubt that one or more of the aggravating circumstances enumerated in K.S.A. 21-4625 and amendments thereto exist and, further, that the existence of such aggravating circumstances is not outweighed by any mitigating circumstances which are found to exist, the defendant shall be sentenced to death; otherwise, the defendant shall be sentenced as provided by law."

The Kansas statute is more a riddle than question because of the hypothetical possibility that aggravating and mitigating factors are equal ("equipoise"). The probability aggravating and mitigating factors would be exactly equal is unlikely (as discussed in a 2004 Marsh dissent), the equipoise question is less a real constitutional issue than a pretextual means to contravene the death penalty. In 2004 the Supreme Court of Kansas decided that the equipoise possibility invalidated Marsh's jury instructions which directed that a "tie" went to the State.[108]

There have been no executions in Kansas since the double hanging of George York and James Latham in June of 1965. Although Kansas has 10 inmates sentenced to death (three of whom are black in contrast to a 6.2 percent black/African American population), Kansas does not have a "death row" and inmates sentenced to death are held in administrative segregation. In addition to California, Kansas is one of the few States which seems to have an awareness of the American Disabilities Act, especially in light of Yeskey v. Pennsylvania,[109] by specifying that "the defendant's counsel or the warden of the correctional institution

---

[108]State of Kansas v. Michael Lee Marsh II, 278 Kan. 520 (2004), 102 P.3d 445
[109]Pennsylvania Dept. of Corrections v. Yeskey, 524 U.S. 206 (1998)

or sheriff having custody of the defendant may request a determination by the court of whether the defendant is a person with intellectual disability."[110] If the court finds there is sufficient evidence, the court then conducts a hearing to determine whether or not the defendant has an intellectual disability.

The judicial sentiment in Kansas is certainly not to execute. In 2004 the Kansas Supreme Court ruled that the death penalty was unconstitutional and 2006 the Supreme Court found otherwise in Kansas v. Marsh. In a decision rendered by Justice Thomas the Court ruled that when aggravating and mitigating factors are in equipoise the death penalty may be imposed; that is, the death penalty may be imposed in Kansas when the State proves beyond a reasonable doubt that the mitigating factors do not outweigh aggravating factors albeit they are equal.[111] The Court explained that the Kansas statute does not favor the death penalty because the State must prove aggravating factors exist beyond a reasonable doubt and there is not a constitutional requirement for weighing aggravating and mitigating circumstances. After remand from the Supreme Court, the Kansas Supreme Court ordered a new trial. Marsh eventually accepted a guilty plea to two counts of first degree murder and was sentenced to two consecutive life terms.

The considerable concern for explicating the relationship between aggravating and mitigating factors in Kansas is in contrast to the Ford-like interpretation of intellectual disability in Atkins claims. The judicial sentiment in Kansas is not to execute but how the definition of intellectual disability was modified is unusual. The definition of intellectual disability includes IQ testing, taking into account the standard error of measurement and adaptive behavior. Age of onset is not mentioned in the statute (76-12b01). The Kansas statutes also direct that "significantly subaverage general intellectual functioning, as defined by K.S.A. 76-12b01, and amendments thereto, to an extent substantially impairs one's capacity to appreciate the criminality of one's conduct or to conform one's conduct to the requirements of law."[112] The

---

[110]Kansas Statute Kan. Stat. Ann. Sect. § 21-6622 (2014)
[111]Kansas v. Michael Marsh II, 548 U. S. 163 (2006)

wording of the statute seems to suggest that no matter the determination of intellectual disability, the death penalty would be permissible if the defendant was able to appreciate the criminality of his or her conduct. Likewise, limited intellectual disability as a mitigating factor could be minimized if the defendant also was able to appreciate the criminality of his or her conduct. The M'Naghten rule seems to chase after *Atkins*...and sometimes catches.

Added to the complex weighing of aggravating and mitigating factors is not only the heinous of the crime but the extent of that heinousness. A crime can be so brutal that a judge or jury might give weight to that factor above all other mitigating considerations, singularly or collectively. This can make diminished intellectual capacity as a mitigating factor irrelevant. More important, the possibility that the heinousness is given such weight that following conviction a determination of intellectual disability by the same court or jury must be suspect.

For Hall, murdering a pregnant 22 year old woman and a police officer might evoke a belief that the combined weight of statutory or non-statutory mitigating factors would never outweigh the aggravators. There were seven aggravators found at Hall's resentencing (three were found during his original sentencing): 1) previous conviction of violent felony 2) under sentence of imprisonment; 3) committed during the commission of kidnapping and sexual battery; 4) committed for pecuniary gain; 5) heinous, atrocious, or cruel; 6) cold, calculated, and premeditated; 7) committed to avoid or prevent arrest.

The fundamental problem when determining intellectual disability, when the heinousness of the crime is an overwhelming factor, is the underlying purpose of *Atkins*; that is, there must be some objective method for determining intellectual disability which precludes the imposition of the death penalty regardless of the heinousness of the crime. When there is no objective method for determining intellectual disability, determining if a defendant is ineligible for execution because of intellectual disability can be a

---

[112]Kansas Statutes Annotated, 21-6622(h)

difficult task when the murder involved a 22 year-old pregnant woman or the many other murders that were seemingly callus, calculated and, if there is a death penalty, deserving of this ultimate sentence.

Willie B. Miller

Nothing illustrates the distinction between a simple rule change and a watershed rule than IQ. Florida adopted a strict IQ cutoff of 70 in 2001 but according to the Supreme Court of Florida in 2001 an IQ below 70 prior to the statute was not bound by this requirement. Is this a simple rule change to be applied to all cases following the May 27, 2014 Hall decision, or a watershed rule that requires a reconsideration of all unsuccessful Atkins claims where a strict cutoff was used? Justice Alito noted this possibility in his *Hall* dissent when he observed that "because the views of professional associations often change, tying Eighth Amendment law to these views will lead to instability and continue to fuel protracted litigation."

Willie B. Miller was sentenced to death for the murder of security guard James Wallace during a robbery of the Jung Lee grocery store in Jacksonville, Florida in 1993. Following a jury recommendation of 12 to 0 for the death penalty, Miller was resentenced to death a second time in 2001. One expert reported an IQ of 64 but also observed that Miller had "street sense" and a letter written by Miller "was indicative of a higher level of function in that the letter further reflected a coherent, concrete thought process." Basically, as is often done, the ultimate reason for dismissing IQ and other indices of impairment in adaptive behavior was that Miller "knew right from wrong." His conclusion was that Miller "was malingering in order to avoid responsibility." The Supreme Court of Florida acknowledged that he was mentally retarded on March 20, 2001 but this section of the statute "does not apply to a defendant who was sentenced to death before June 12, 2001."[113] Because Florida's statute prohibiting the death

---

[113]Florida statute 921.137(8)

penalty (section 921.137) was proscriptive and not retroactive," Miller did "not come within the statute's purview."[114]

To further discount Miller's claim of mental retardation, in addition to the claim that the statute was not retrospective, was to simply announce that he had not met the statutory definition of mental retardation: "Even if this Court were to hold that the new statute should be retroactive, it cannot grant the relief Miller asks for because he has met none of the statute's requirements. Regardless of failing to meet the statute's notice requirements, the evidence introduced at resentencing did not meet the statutory definition of 'mental retardation'." This decision was reversed in 2004 when the circuit court decided that Miller did meet the criteria for mental retardation. In 2005 the Supreme Court of Florida re-sentenced Miller to life in prison without the possibility of parole for 25 years.[115]

This re-sentencing did not resolve the issue of whether the IQ cutoff of 75, decided by the Supreme Court, was prospective or retroactive. This might actually be a minor technicality when multiple IQ scores are considered, some above the new cutoff of 75, and the ability of the State to dismiss low IQ scores, no matter how low, because of perceived malingering or simply because one or more IQ scores were not credible for vague or poorly defined reasons.

Dean Kilgore

In that the Supreme Court of Florida decided *Hurst* was not retroactive for Mark James Asay, the court then determined whether Hall was retroactive for Dean Kilgore. In 1990 Kilgore

---

[114]Miller v. Florida, Supreme Court of Florida, CASE NO. SC01-837, Answer Brief of Appellee (State of Florida), December 1, 2001.
[115]Miller v. Florida, Supreme Court of Florida, 913 So. 2d 597; 2005 Fla. Decided September 15

was sentenced to death for the murder of another inmate, Emerson Robert Jackson (using a shank), at the Polk Correctional Institution in Polk City, Florida in 1989. At the time of the murder he was serving two life sentences for murder and kidnapping in 1978. In 1994, following a resentencing, the jury recommended death by a vote of 9 to 3 which was the sentence given by the court.

Upon appeal following Atkins in 2002 an evidentiary hearing was held in 2007 to resolve his claim of intellectual disability.[116] Kilgore had been given the WAIS on six occasions which resulted in IQ scores of 76 (in 1989), 84, 67 (in 1994), 75, 74 and 85 (in 2006).   Evidence of adaptive behavior was presented by defense and prosecution, each explaining that Kilgore did (defense) or did not have mental retardation. In 2008 the Florida court concluded that Kilgore's scores, with the exception of the score of 67, were all above the cutoff of 70, and therefore adaptive behavior and age of onset were not considered. A 2008 evidentiary hearing did not consider evidence of adaptive behavior because "Kilgore did not show subaverage general intellectual functioning, it would not consider the other two prongs of Florida's intellectual disability test."

An interesting hypothetical involving Kilgore's scores is the fact that they were all above 70 with the exception of a score of 67. The concept underlying the SEM and IQ scores for the purposes of the death penalty is not to preclude the concept of a bright line of 70 but rather to consider IQ scores up to 75, given a SEM of 5, that could be as low as 70. What if someone had multiple IQ scores, say as a result of 100 hypothetical IQ testings (obviously impossible but this is a hypothetical about SEM theory), and all scores were between 70 and 75 and the mean score 72.5? The best estimate of the person's "true score" would be 72.5 a score clearly above 70. In this hypothetical there would be absolutely no basis for assuming that the person's "true score" was 70 yet in this situation fact (100 scores above 70) would be trumped by

---

[116]Kilgore v. Florida, United States Court of Appeals for the Eleventh District, Case: 13-11825, 11/16/2015

theory (a single score of 75 could be as low as 70 when considering the SEM).

The existence of multiple IQ scores and how these scores would impact the estimate of a person's "true" IQ score is most often ignored. Justice Alito was correct when he commented "The Court never explains why its criticisms of the uncertainty resulting from the use of a *single* IQ score apply when a defendant consistently scores above 70 on *multiple* tests. Contrary to the Court's evident assumption, the well-accepted view is that multiple consistent scores establish a much higher degree of confidence." [117]

There is something disingenuous to treat IQ scores as if an IQ of 75 represented 75 points and one merely subtracts 5 from 75 to produce something that is meaningful and absolute. An IQ represents the number of standard deviations a score is above or below the mean with reference to the normal curve such that there is no such thing as an *IQ point.* Everything about IQ scores is relative. An IQ above 80 might indicate intellectual disability because that is how the State might have used IQ to classify a defendant as a child or as an adult during incarceration. Also suggested in Justice Alito's dissent, given two IQ scores, the higher score is probably more believable than the lower score. His reasoning, explained in a footnote where the suggestion is made that one can fake a low but not a high IQ score. But this too is relative. Factors such as malingering, motivation, the examiner, the circumstances, age at time of testing, the type of test, etc. can all play a role in test performance. A low IQ as a child might well be more relevant than an IQ as an adult but not if there were some intervening event such as brain injury. To make a distinction between scores of 65 and 75 is trivial in that, qualitatively speaking, both scores are low.

For Kilgore, after considering his various IQ scores, the Supreme Court of Florida denied his Atkins claim in 2010, as did the United States District Court for the Middle District of Florida. The Supreme Court decided *Hall* in 2014 and the prohibition against a strict IQ cutoff of 70 and, as a result, Kilgore renewed his Atkins

---

[117]Hall v. Florida, 572 U.S. ____ (2014)

claim. On November 16, 2015 the United States Court of Appeals for the Eleventh District determined that *Hall* in 2014 did not apply retroactively to Kilgore's 2010 Atkins claim. The reason for denying retroactivity was that the court believed that *Hall* provided a procedural change to the rule enunciated in *Atkins* rather than the creation of a new rule with a substantive constitutional restriction. The reasoning for not applying retroactivity to Kilgore was that "To retroactively apply this kind of new procedural rule to the final determination of a state court appeal would impose the very uncertainty and costs on the states that Teague warned against – discouraging the states from rigorously developing and following their intellectual disability law, decreasing the importance of finality and its effect on deterrence given the ever-changing nature of our understanding of intellectual disability."[118]

Even if retroactivity had been applied to Kilgore, the interpretation of the six IQ scores cited above have an average score above 75 which is the cutoff announced by the Supreme Court. Florida could cite Kilgore's average score or even discount his IQ of 67 which would result in an even higher IQ average. Or the court could mimic Oklahoma's approach and discount his claim because one of his scores is above 75 (actually two IQ scores). Finally, rather than a strict cutoff of 70, Florida could have simply "considered" all his scores, adaptive behavior and age of onset and then denied his Atkins claim.

The court of appeals explained that "The Florida Supreme Court's determination was neither contrary to nor an unreasonable application of clearly established Supreme Court law." The appellate court also noted that because there were four dissenting justices in *Hall,* the IQ cutoff of 75 "was not clearly established in the Court's existing precedent." As a result the court asserted that Florida did not violate *Atkins* when Kilgore was found not to be mentally retarded in 2010 because the *Hall* decision was not a new rule of substantive constitutional importance that warranted retroactive consideration. [119]

---

[118]*Ibid.*
[119]*Ibid.*

Part of the logic for not applying retroactivity to Kilgore makes sense, but a large part is based on a misunderstanding of the primary reasoning underlying *Atkins*. True, changing the IQ cutoff is a simple rule change and probably a minor one at that. After all, death penalty jurisprudence should not be changed every time a professional group decides to raise or low the IQ standard or to change the standard in a variety of other ways. Far more important than the IQ cutoff is why the Supreme Court rejected the strict IQ cutoff of 70 used by Florida. The problem recognized by the Court transcended the triviality of IQ points and was directed at the use of a strict cutoff to preclude the consideration of relevant evidence (i.e., adaptive behavior). The need for judicial finality should not undermine the need for a fair determination of intellectual disability. The *Kilgore* decision is not simply about a procedural guideline and whether raising the IQ cutoff from 70 to 75 warrants watershed status, but more about the consideration of relevant evidence as was the case in Ford v. Wainwright in 1986. In *Ford* the Florida statute was used to preclude relevant evidence, cross-examination and due process. For Dean Kilgore the question of retroactivity is no longer relevant. He died January 11, 2018 of natural causes (Florida Inmate mortality page[120]).

In *Hall* the Supreme Court acknowledged the Florida statute was not inconsistent with Atkins: "On its face this statute could be interpreted consistently with *Atkins* and with the conclusions this Court reaches in the instant case. Nothing in the statute precludes Florida from taking into account the IQ test's standard error of measurement, and as discussed below, there is evidence that Florida's Legislature intended to include the measurement error in the calculation." Florida courts could have said that Hall has had a variety of IQ assessments, some within the standard error of measurement (scores of 75 or lower) and some above, and then considered these data and evidence of adaptive behavior and data relating to age of onset. The Hall decision addressed exactly what was decided in *Ford* that a defendant must have a fair opportunity to present all relevant evidence (and the ability for cross-examination, etc.).

---

[120]http://www.dc.state.fl.us/pub/mortality/year.html?year=2018

A Reconsideration of 2014 Hall

In September of 2016 the Supreme Court of Florida reconsidered the meaning of the Supreme Court's 2014 Hall decision. After almost 40 years on death row, Freddie Lee Hall now resides at the Charlotte Correctional Institution where he is serving the remainder of his life sentence. Hall's resentencing to life in prison came about on September 8, 2016 when the Supreme Court of Florida vacated his death sentence and remanded his case for a sentence of life in prison. The Florida court rectified three elements of the States' very flawed Atkins process: First, the court acknowledge, as stated by the Supreme Court in 2014, that "It is not sound to view a single factor as dispositive of a conjunctive and interrelated assessment."[121] Second, the court discounted the idea that current adaptive function in prison is the only data relevant to adaptive behavior and that a retrospective analysis is entirely proper (i.e., an analysis of adaptive behavior before age of onset). Third, the court, unlike most other courts evaluating Atkins claims, understood that "the prohibition against executing the intellectually disabled is based, in part, on their culpability at the time the crimes were committed."

Lesser culpability is not about a label *intellectual disability*, but the recognition that specific deficiencies, explicated by the Supreme Court in *Atkins,* warrant lesser culpability including diminished capacity to understand others, process information, to think logically, control impulses, falsely confess, assist counsel, and showing remorse. Nothing is more probative of these deficiencies than a history of intellectual disability, especially by qualified professionals when the defendant was a child to determine intellectual deficiencies. The success of a State to develop independent and adaptive skills by providing an "appropriate" education does not undo the determination of intellectual disability, no matter whether right or wrong. In all likelihood, these skills do not include how to not falsely confess to a crime, to assist counsel or to show remorse when serving as a witness.

---

[121]Freddie Lee Hall v. State of Florida, SC10-1335, September 8, 2016

Learning to read or to become a productive citizen does not diminish possible thinking or behavior that would warrant lesser culpability as outlined in *Atkins*.

The Florida court in 2016 also explained that "The reason that defendants claiming intellectual disability must demonstrate its onset prior to adulthood is to differentiate them from those who have suffered brain damage in adulthood that rendered them incompetent but not intellectually disabled." Florida might be the first State to recognize that age of onset was never intended to preclude a determination of intellectual disability. Finally, the Florida court rejected the idea that manifestation before age of onset required a specific IQ test because "The State's argument that a proper IQ test prior to the age of 18 is the only valid evidence to establish this prong is unjustifiable and would effectively preclude a finding of intellectual disability in most people born prior to a certain era."[122]

In response to the Supreme Court decision in *Hall* in 2014, the Florida court contended that Hall's claim of intellectual should be subjected to a "full adversarial proceeding." The Supreme Court of Florida in 2016 chided the State because of "the fact that the State has chosen not to avail itself of prior opportunities is not a sufficient reason to expend further resources to continue to litigate this issue." Another evidentiary hearing was not held and the Supreme Court of Florida reversed his denial of relief, vacated Hall's death sentence and remanded "for imposition of a life sentence.

Between this new interpretation of the concept of intellectual disability in 2016 by the Supreme Court of Florida, and the requirement for unanimity by jurors, aside from the matter of retroactivity, Florida has begun to develop sensible guidelines for the processing of Atkins claims—maybe not for all claims such as those of Mark James Asay and Dean Kilgore—but Florida courts are becoming more introspective and less categorical...maybe, hopefully. In any case, this seems to be the direction of the Supreme Court of Florida.

---

[122] *Ibid.*

Karu Gene White

In *Kilgore,* in 2015, the United States Court of Appeals found that *Hall* in 2016 was not subject to retroactivity (as outlined by the Supreme Court in Teague v. Lane) because the rule articulated in *Hall* did not address a question that would "vitiate the fairness of a particular conviction."[123] Atkins v. Virginia, itself, is a watershed rule in that a State is prohibited from executing someone who is intellectually disabled. Watershed rule or not, Atkins protection depends on how intellectual disability is defined. What is retroactive in one State (or in one court) is not necessarily retroactive in another.

Although only three people have been executed in Kentucky since 1976,[124] one defendant sought Atkins relief in a rather important yet odd way. Karu Gene White, born in 1958, was sentenced to death for the robbery/murder of three elderly store owners in Haddix, Kentucky with accomplices Tommy Bowling and Charles Fisher.[125] Only White, in 1980, received the death sentence.[126] In October of 2016, the Supreme Court of Kentucky evaluated White's IQ in relation to the standard created by the Supreme Court in *Hall* in 2014. For the Kentucky court "the obvious question" was "How, if at all, does the sea change in Hall affect the claim of Karu Gene White, the Appellant in this case?" In Florida, for Dean Kilgore, the United States Court of Appeals decided that *Hall* retroactivity did not apply.[127] The Supreme Courts of Florida and Kentucky thought otherwise.

---

[123]Teague v. Lane, 489 U.S. 288 (1989)

[124]the last was Marco Allen Chapman in 2008 for the murders of Chelbi (age 7) and Cody Marksberry (age 6) in 2002

[125]White v. Commonwealth of Kentucky, Supreme Court of Kentucky, On Appeal from Powell Circuit Court v. Honorable, John David Caudill, Judge, NO. 79-CR-00024, October 20, 2016.

[126]White v. Commonwealth of Kentucky, Supreme Court of Kentucky 2013-SCX-000791-MR, October 20, 2016

[127]Kilgore v. Florida, United States Court of Appeals for the Eleventh District, Case: 13-11825, 11/16/2015

In October of 2016 the Supreme Court of Kentucky explained that because "We are dealing here with a U.S. Supreme Court directive that not only proscribes intellectually disabled people from being put to death, but defines the manner in which the mental deficiencies of offenders must be evaluated. Therefore, Hall must be retroactively applied." This might suggest that Kentucky used a bright-line of 70 to evaluate White and that now his IQ must be reconsidered in light of Hall. In fact there is only one IQ for White which is a score of 81 reported in 1980. Using American Psychological Association guidelines, the court explained that "a person's score would likely differ by five points, plus or minus, with 95% confidence. Using that confidence range, Appellant's true IQ based on the score obtained in 1980 of 81 would likely result in an IQ of 76 to 86—some six points above the cutoff of 70." For the Kentucky Supreme Court retroactivity applies but more as a hypothetical because White did not have an IQ of 75 or below, and more importantly, a determination concerning his intellectual ability was never made.

Frank A. Walls

Frank A. Walls was first sentenced to life in prison following a unanimous jury recommendation for the 1987 murder of Edward Alger and a recommendation of death by a 7-5 vote for the murder of Ann Peterson in Okaloosa County, Florida.[128] Before his trial three experts testified that he was competent to stand trial and two said he was not. The conviction for the first trial was reversed in 1991 because of illegally obtained evidence. A new trial resulted in the same sentence for the murder of Alger (life) and Peterson (death) in 1992 which was affirmed in 1994. In 2007, following an evidentiary hearing for an Atkins claim, the court found his IQ of 72 was above the strict bright line of 70 used at the time which was affirmed by the Florida Supreme Court in 2008.

In 2015, for Walls, the circuit court did not give retroactive status to *Hall* but did offer that the procedural history... at least implicitly

---

[128]Frank A. Walls v. State of Florida, Florida Supreme Court, No. SC15–1449, decided: October 20, 2016.

gives retroactive application to Hall." Walls' relief was denied, not because of *Hall* and retroactivity, but because of the age of onset criterion. He had IQ scores of 102 at age 12 and 101 at age 14 thereby precluding the use of IQ scores following age 18 (72 at age 23 and 74 at age 40). In October of 2016, one month after the court's re-conceptualization of *Hall* in September of 2016, the Supreme Court of Florida opined "that Hall warrants retroactive application as a development of fundamental significance that places beyond the State of Florida the power to impose a certain sentence—the sentence of death for individuals within a broader range of IQ scores than before." The court explained that at the prior evidentiary hearing Walls "did not receive the type of holistic review to which he is now entitled. Also, Walls' prior hearing was conducted under standards he could not meet because he did not have an IQ score below 70—a fact which may have affected his presentation of evidence at the hearing."

Walls was granted relief because of the retroactivity of *Hall* and because his prior evidentiary hearing was based on the former strict IQ cutoff of 70 used by Florida. If Walls' Atkins claim is successful, via a Hall "holistic" interpretation, he will be spared the death penalty. Frank Walls has been on death row since 1987 and there is no reason to believe that appeals will not go on for some time.

3. More Theory, Less Fact

"...an individual's intellectual functioning cannot be reduced to a single numerical score."[129]

Donald William Dufour

Along the way, when deciding *Hall,* the Supreme Court managed to ignore all criticisms of IQ testing by giving constitutional standing to IQ tests by way of the standard error of measurement (SEM). For the Court theory became fact and an IQ score of 75 (70 plus the standard error of measurement of 5) became the constitutional standard for mild intellectual disabilities with nary a thought to the complexities and criticisms of IQ testing and not a word about the history of IQ testing and racism.

For Atkins claims, there is a great possibility that the finder of fact might be oblivious to the intricacies of clinical definitions of intellectual disabilities or give differential weight to evidence presented, and slog through expert opinion. In 1982 Donald Dufour had murdered at least five people in Mississippi (where he was sentenced in 1983 for the murder of Earl Peeples) and Florida. For the murder of Zack Miller in Florida he was sentenced to death by a unanimous vote and was sentenced to death in Mississippi for the stabbing and murder of Earl Peeples in 1982 in Jackson, Mississippi. The Florida court found no mitigating factors and four aggravating factors: 1) a previous capital felony conviction; 2) a murder committed during an armed robbery; (3) a murder to prevent arrest; 4) a calculated and premeditated murder with no justification.[130] Of the 16 issues raised by Dufour on appeal in 2005 all but one were denied. The court did find that there was insufficient evidence to show that the purpose of the murder was to avoid arrest, but found that the three remaining aggravating factors sufficient for the imposition of the death penalty.[131]

---

[129]Hall v. Florida, 572 U.S. ____ (2014)
[130]Dufour v. Florida, February 3, 2011, Supreme Court of Florida, No. SC09-262

In 2003, following an evidentiary hearing in 2002, the trial court denied claims of ineffective assistance of counsel, a determination of organic brain damage, and the failure of Florida to preserve evidence. In 2005 the Supreme Court of Florida rejected Dufour's claim that an appropriate evaluation "would have revealed mitigating factors of brain injury, mental illness, borderline to mentally retarded I.Q., and sexual abuse."[132] The court also rejected Dufour's contention that the Florida death penalty statute was unconstitutional under *Ring* in 2002 because the judge and not the jury made the ultimate decision for death. This flaw in the State's death penalty statute was eventually found unconstitutional by the Supreme Court in *Hurst* in 2016.

Dufour then made an Atkins claim where two defense experts said that he was mentally retarded and two prosecution experts said that he was not.[133] The State experts cited IQ scores of 62 and 74, and one defense expert indicated that his IQ was 67. These experts believed that "Dufour did not appear to be making his best effort, due to either malingering or illness," and the fact that he received a GED indicated he did not have impaired adaptive behavior. The court found that he did not show, by clear and convincing evidence, that he was mentally retarded.

The circuit court found irregularities with the scoring of IQ cited by the defense, the IQ scores of the State were less than persuasive, but that each had some credibility. The circuit court then used the SEM band of confidence, which is often used by practitioners to interpret individual test scores, to show that Dufour's IQ was not in the mental retardation range in spite of two scores of 62 and 67. The use of the SEM involved first putting the strict IQ cutoff on hold, and then selecting Dufour's IQ of 67 to show that the "band of confidence" (five points below and above 67) of 62 to 72 had an upper range above the Florida IQ cutoff of 70. This statistical twist provided the reasoning for the court to show that the strict IQ cutoff of 70 was not really all that strict. If

---

[131]Dufour v. Florida, Supreme Court of Florida, 905 So. 2d 42 (2005)
[132]*Ibid.*
[133]Dufour v. Florida, February 3, 2011

someone received an IQ score of 67, the best estimate of their "true" score, if such a creature exists, is a score of 67. The SEM indicates that there could be error in every score (and there usually is). If Dufour could somehow be tested repeatedly, most of his scores— 95 percent of these hypothetical scores from repeated testings—given a SEM of 2.5, could be (and not "would be") between 62 and 72 given a base score of 67. Nonetheless, given a score of 67, the probability is far greater that his true score will be 70 or less rather than greater than 70.

Aside from selecting an IQ score of 67 ("approximately halfway between" available scores), the State was not completely at fault for using the SEM to establish a band of confidence. This, after all, is how the SEM is usually used for interpreting test scores and not to establish cutoff points. Florida's error was using the SEM to show that a score of 67 could be above 70 as shown by the band of confidence of 62 to 72. The upper range of the band of confidence demonstrated to the circuit court there was no clear and convincing evidence that Dufour was mentally retarded. According to the court's logic, Dufour would need a base score of 64 to be below the strict cutoff and thus provide clear and convincing evidence. The Supreme Court of Florida found it odd that the State would use the SEM to evaluate his "middle" score of 67, but rejected the use of the strict cutoff of 70 and the SEM (or a score of 75 or below as supported by the Supreme Court).

The Supreme Court of Florida found that the court had misinterpreted the SEM, not from a statistical standpoint, but because the State used the SEM to show that Dufour was not mentally retarded, while at the same time claiming that a strict cutoff of IQ, sans SEM, was the plain language of the statute for interpreting IQ. The court determined the "legal error" of the circuit court, the misapplication of the SEM, was not harmless and this might have affected the determination that his IQ did not indicate mental retardation. All of this mattered not because in 2011 the Florida Supreme Court also found that Dufour did not meet the criteria to show that he had deficits in adaptive behavior

Unlike *Hall* prior to 2014, the evidentiary hearing for Dufour did include an analysis of adaptive behavior so that the IQ prong was not used to bar relevant evidence.[134]   The Supreme Court of Florida decided that Dufour was not mentally retarded, but not without a strong dissent which questioned the majority decision by suggesting that other factors were an integral part for determining mental retardation such as poor school performance and environment. On November, 1, 2011 Dufour died of natural causes in the Union Correctional Institution near Raiford, Florida.

Griggs v. Duke Power Company

For death penalty jurisprudence the Supreme Court has placed considerable emphasis on test reliability and the standard error or measurement, a derivative of a test's calculated reliability. Test reliability provides a basic requirement for establishing a test's meaningfulness. However, test validity is what makes a test meaningful. If a test is not reliable, it cannot be valid; if a test is reliable and not valid, it is worthless. A test must have the basic element of reliability and then measure what the test purports to measure (or validity). The emphasis on the SEM in Atkins claims provides a bit of sleight of hand to endorse an IQ test's validity. With the complete emphasis on reliability, the meaningfulness of a test is ignored.

There was a point in time when the Supreme Court did place emphasis on what IQ tests measure rather than test reliability and the SEM. When all is said and done, the essential question about IQ tests is not reliability (of which the SEM is a direct reflection) but rather what a test measures or test validity. In the 1960s, at the Dan River Steam Station owned by the Duke Power Company in Draper, North Carolina (near Eden, N.C.), 13 black employees initiated a class action suit (by Willie S. Griggs and others) against the company. Within the company, there were five departments 1) Operations, 2) Maintenance, 3) Laboratory and Test, 4) Coal Handling, and 5) Labor.[135] All black workers employed by the Dan River plant were in Labor department "where the highest paying

---

[134]Dufour v. Florida, February 3, 2011, Supreme Court of Florida, No. SC09-262
[135]Griggs v. Duke Power Co., 401 U.S. 424 (1971)

jobs paid less than the lowest paying jobs in the other four 'operating' departments in which only whites were employed."[136] In 1964, Title VII of the Civil Rights Act seemed to offer black employees protection from practices that discriminated based on race. Not to be outdone by Congress, the Dan River plant initiated a new requirement on the date (July 2, 1965) that the Civil Rights Act went into effect: a requirement for promotion was to pass two professionally constructed tests (a test of general intelligence and a test to assess mechanical comprehension).
In *Griggs* the Duke Power Company did not intend, so said the company, for the requirements to discriminate against black employees but to improve the quality of the workforce. The position of Duke was that segregation was an unfortunate by-product of the legitimate need to improve quality. The Supreme Court cited data showing that 58% of white test takers passed these types of tests in comparison to 6 percent of black test takers.

Before the Supreme Court's decision in 1971 the appellate court surmised in 1970 that "plaintiffs would apparently concede that if Duke adopted its educational and testing requirements with a genuine business purpose and without intent to discriminate against future Negro employees, such requirements would not be invalidated merely because of Negroes' cultural and educational disadvantages due to past discrimination."[137] The reasoning by Duke was that if a test is adopted with no intent to discriminate, the fact that the test measured, in part, past discrimination and educational segregation, is not a basis for claiming discriminatory harm.

The Supreme Court dealt with the messy and highly subjective problem of intent by circumventing the question entirely: "We do not suggest that either the District Court or the Court of Appeals erred in examining the employer's intent; but good intent or absence of discriminatory intent does not redeem employment procedures or testing mechanisms that operate as 'built-in headwinds' for minority groups and are unrelated to measuring

---

[136]*Ibid.*

[137]Willie S. Griggs et al., Appellants v. Duke Power Company, a corporation, Appellee, 420 F.2d 1225 (1970)

job capability." Ignoring the fact that the test requirements adopted by Duke occurred in close proximity to Brown in 1954 and Brown II in 1955 and implemented on the day the 1964 Civil Rights Act went into effect, the Supreme Court focused on the requirements and not the intent for adopting the requirements: "The facts of this case demonstrate the inadequacy of broad and general testing devices as well as the infirmity of using diplomas or degrees as fixed measures of capability. History is filled with examples of men and women who rendered highly effective performance without the conventional badges of accomplishment in terms of certificates, diplomas, or degrees. Diplomas and tests are useful servants, but Congress has mandated the commonsense proposition that they are not to become masters of reality." In point of fact, IQ tests are often the masters of reality where IQ test scores are used without a thought given the underlying racism, or the fiction that an IQ point has some inherent meaning other than a reference to the normal probability curve.

The Supreme Court's final word in *Griggs* was that testing could be useful but "What Congress has commanded is that any tests used must measure the person for the job and not the person in the abstract." The Court decided that the ultimate issue was about fair labor practices under the Civil Rights Act. The Court's position was that the better test performance by whites "would appear to be directly traceable to race. Basic intelligence must have the means of articulation to manifest itself fairly in a testing process. Because they are Negroes, petitioners have long received inferior education in segregated schools, and this Court expressly recognized these differences in Gaston County v. United States, 395 U.S. 285 (1969). There, because of the inferior education received by Negroes in North Carolina, this Court barred the institution of a literacy test for voter registration on the ground that the test would abridge the right to vote indirectly on account of race." For black Atkins claimants, there is no way to calculate the impact of prior discrimination and lack of educational opportunity on IQ performance. Nonetheless, in that IQ is pivotal to Atkins claims every estimate of a black offender's intelligence is suspect.

In *Griggs* the Court was aware that segregation impacted scores no matter the type of test given. Every test used in schools measures intelligence to some degree, and there is no denying that individualized intelligence tests such as the Stanford-Binet and Wechsler tests have been expertly designed and standardized although probably not re-standardized as often as should be because of financial factors. Testing, after all, is a business and there are cost factors with every test re-standardization.

Intelligence tests measure a variety of idiosyncratic intellectual skills including but not limited to verbal analogies, vocabulary, picture completion, block design and the ever-motivating digit span. These various subtests are given great scientific gravitas although most were based on Terman's assessment procedures used in the early 1900's and tasks selected during the development of the Alpha and Beta testing during World War I. In addition to cognitive ability IQ tests also measure education, motivation, environment, socio-economic (lack of jobs, lack of money, lack of health care, lack of just about everything there is to be a lack of) and cultural factors (in addition to the random type of error reflected by reliability). The basis for *Griggs* was that test performance influenced by discrimination and segregation cannot be used to preclude opportunity. Intelligence tests, no matter how expertly developed and administered, do not transcend prior and existing discriminatory intent. This was also the rationale for *Brown* in 1954 when the Court declared that segregation deprives children of equal educational opportunity. In this regard the efforts to maintain segregation by States, vestiges of segregation, or the tactics to further a segregative agenda, have been unrelenting and matched by the brazen and often preposterous interpretation of intellectual disability to deny Atkins claims.

Intelligence tests can be used, as was the case in *Griggs,* to both deny educational opportunity for children (in *Brown* in 1954) and then used by States to sanction execution for adults by ignoring childhood data, re-interpreting IQ scores, re-conceptualizing the adaptive behavior prong of the professional definition of intellectual disability, using a strict cutoff or including whatever scores or data are useful for denying Atkins relief.

The Supreme Court left the interpretation of IQ, the problem of interpreting a variety of IQ tests, and the determination of intellectual disability to the States to unravel. Of the three elements of the definition of mental retardation used by Florida (subaverage general intellectual functioning, adaptive functioning and age of onset before 18), Florida interpreted the "plain language" of the Florida statute (921.137) to indicate an IQ score must be "two or more standard deviations below the mean." Although an offender must have an IQ score of 70 or below before adaptive behavior is   considered, the mathematics of this bright line are more fuzzy than bright. Would Freddie Lee Hall need one score of 70 or lower, or possibly two scores of 70 or lower, or 51% of scores of 70 or lower, an average IQ score of 70 or below, a median score 75 or less to meet the IQ prong of the definition according to the absolute bright-line rule of 70 used in Florida at the time? Added to this confusion is the credibility of IQ scores given before a capital murder, scores obtained when seeking Atkins relief before, during or after trial, and scores obtained after many years on death row. For Freddie Lee Hall and others in a similar situation, the fact that he was not tested as a child because of racism is used to show that he never had an intellectual disability and therefore could be executed as an adult (because of racism). Racism is more often about justification of invidious intent than logical explanation.

Complicating the bright-line rule, in addition to the mathematics of interpreting IQ scores, are questions of malingering and the age of onset prong of the definition. Common sense would indicate that IQ scores, especially on individualized tests such as the WISC and WAIS obtained before a capital crime, would be less likely susceptible to malingering than IQ tests given as part of an Atkins claim after age 18. Florida dealt with this common-sense approach to IQ scores by illogical assertion that the most relevant scores were those given as an adult or even on death row...an interpretation undone by the 2016 Supreme Court of Florida.

David Eugene Johnston

David Eugene Johnston's death sentence provides some insight for resolving IQ scores below and above 70. Johnston was sentenced in death for the 1983 murder of 84-year-old Mary Hammond in Orlando, Florida. As a child Johnston received an IQ of 57 on the Stanford-Binet and a 65 on the WISC at age 12. As part of his Atkins evidentiary hearing, Johnston was found to have a full scale IQ of 84. The expert for the State "discounted these earlier scores because the test administrators placed a caveat in their notes indicating 'that this was not an accurate assessment of his functioning because of behavioral and emotional issues, and that he was actually performing or was functioning at a higher level.'"[138] Because the lower IQ scores were dismissed, and his adult IQ score was above the strict 70 threshold and *the* new 75 cutoff, adaptive behavior was not assessed.

A diagnostic insight by the State's expert was "that Johnston told him he was mentally retarded, which is not typical of a person who is truly mentally retarded, and stated that he thought Johnston knew that being found mentally retarded would help his 'legal predicament.'" The expert contended that because Johnston's IQ scores were caused by something other than mental retardation, this indicated that mental retardation was not manifested before age 18. By this interpretation, the cause of performance that would warrant a classification of intellectual disability could be anything from environment to a disability other than intellectual disability so that all Atkins claims would fail if causation—something impossible to prove—was a primary consideration. More specifically, there is not a fourth element to the definition of intellectual disability where the cause of subaverage general intellectual functioning, adaptive behavior and age of onset must be shown. The cause of intellectual disability could be environment, genetics, an intricate combination of nature/nurture but the ultimate question is whether professional criteria for identifying mild intellectual disability warrants lesser culpability.

Whether a person who is legitimately intellectually disabled, whatever that is, would be "typically" aware of his/her intellectual

---

[138]Johnston v. Florida, Supreme Court of Florida, 960 So. 2d 757, 2006

disability was not explored, nor was Johnston's low IQ scores and educational performance as a child. Even if his low IQ score were the result of something other than intellectual disability, classification as having an intellectual disability would have created a record of a disability under the ADA. The reason for testing Johnston must have been the result of perceived educational needs although Johnson, born in 1957, might not have been identified as having mental retardation because of a lack of services or the fact that he was white.

In 2006, following an Atkins evidentiary hearing for Johnston in 2005, the Supreme Court of Florida was more than ready to use the standard error of measurement by stating that "Concerning the 95% confidence interval typically involved in IQ testing, Dr. Blandino testified that a score of 84 falls decisively in the 80-88 range, solidly in the borderline to low average intellectual functioning range." But then the court added a new twist to the definition so that "No matter how poor a person's adaptive functioning is, a person cannot be mentally retarded if he scores in the non-mentally retarded range" which gives supremacy to IQ tests as the all-important arbiter of determining mental retardation/intellectual disability. After having spent approximately 25 years on death row, Johnston died of natural causes in 2010.

Much has been misconstrued about IQ in Atkins claims, including efforts to explain what has been misconstrued. Justice Kennedy observed in the Court's majority opinion in *Hall* that "Florida seeks to execute a man because he scored a 71 instead of 70 on an IQ test. Florida is one of just a few States to have this rigid rule. Florida's rule misconstrues the Court's statements in *Atkins* that intellectual disability is characterized by an IQ of 'approximately 70.'" This is inaccurate in that Florida wanted to execute Freddie Lee Hall because he murdered or participated in the murder of 22 year-old Karol Lea Hurst. More specifically, the suggestion that the decision to execute Hall was the result of a single IQ point is also inaccurate. As explained by Justice Alito (joined by Justices Scalia and Thomas) in a well-reasoned dissent from the majority decision in 2014 "Florida's statute imposes no limit on the number of IQ scores that a defendant may introduce, so the Court is simply wrong to analyze the Florida system as one that views a single IQ score above 70 as 'final and conclusive evidence' that a defendant does not suffer from subaverage intellectual functioning."

Justice Kennedy might have mischaracterized the problem in that Hall had seven IQ scores with an average score of slightly greater than 74 and three scores over 75. As suggested in *Hall*, Florida could have "considered" his various IQ scores, then considered his adaptive behavior, and then determined his intellectual status. Unlike Oklahoma where any score above 75 ends an Atkins inquiry, Florida could have denied his claim based on adaptive behavior (a prong easily muddled by conflicting evidence). As a matter of fact, if all of Hall's IQ scores were below 70 or below 65, Florida could have been on solid constitutional ground by **considering** all scores, no matter how high or low, **considering** other relevant evidence, and then denying his claim. Of course the easiest path for Florida to deny his Atkins claims was to embrace the Supreme Court's sanctioned 75 IQ cutoff and then reject Hall's claim because of one or more scores above 75.

What would appear to be a straightforward cutoff of 75, endorsed by the Supreme Court, is riddled with possible exceptions that may or may not meet constitutional muster. Arizona mentions an IQ cutoff in prescreening but an Atkins claim can be denied if all IQ scores are above, in the final analysis, 70. In Arizona not only must all scores be above 70, but a claim can be denied if a score is above 75. Arizona appears to use a cutoff of 75 but the ultimate decision is based on all IQ scores and the possibilities are many.

Unlike other States, Arizona anticipates the consideration of multiple IQ scores. If the State seeks the death penalty, a prescreening is conducted to determine the defendant's IQ. If the defendant receives an IQ higher than 75 by the "prescreening psychological expert," the State can continue to seek the death penalty although the defendant can raise intellectual disability during the penalty phase of the proceedings. This prescreening via a single IQ test can preclude the consideration of other available IQ scores, especially those obtained before age of onset. If the defendant's IQ is 75 or less, "the trial court, within ten days of receiving the written report, shall order the state and the defendant to each nominate three experts in intellectual disabilities, or jointly nominate a single expert in intellectual disabilities." The trial court then selects one expert nominated by the defendant, one nominated by the State, and, if appropriate, one selected by the trial court. None of these experts can be involved in the prescreening evaluation.[139]

Following the prescreening evaluation, the defendant and State provide the experts with all records, and the defendant is then examined to determine the existence of an intellectual disability. Within 20 days of receiving all the reports and information, each expert examines the defendant and then within 15 days "using current community, nationally and culturally accepted physical, developmental, psychological and intelligence testing procedures." There does not seem to be much concern for the administration of the same test within a short period of time...a potential problem with many Atkins claims. Following this round of intellectual testing, the experts submit a written report.

If "all" the IQ scores found by experts are above 70, the State can pursue the death penalty. On this point the statute is not clear. All the experts could decide that the defendant has an intellectual disability but all the IQ scores are above 70 (but 75 or less) which would mean that the actual determination of intellectual disability is secondary to IQ scores. Even more confusing is how this is interpreted in view of the 75 point cutoff in Florida. Arizona could have argued that the SEM was taken into account via prescreening or when scores were above 70. To this end there is little doubt that the Arizona consideration of IQ might be confusing and possibly inconsistent with *Hall*. The statute clearly requires that "the court in determining the intelligence quotient shall take into account the margin of error for the test administered" and therefore seems to meet the primary mandate in *Hall* to consider the margin of error (sort of).[140]

---

[139]2005 Arizona Revised Statutes - Revised Statutes §13-703.02 Mental evaluations of capital defendants; hearing; appeal; definitions: https://law.justia.com/codes/arizona/2005/title13/00703-02.html
[140]*Ibid.*

Within thirty days after all the expert reports have been received, the trial court holds a hearing to determine intellectual disability. The defendant has the burden of showing an intellectual disability by *clear and convincing evidence*. At this hearing a rebuttable presumption is established if the defendant has an IQ of 65 or lower in which case the burden shifts to the State to prove mental retardation. Exactly what would or should be done if two IQ scores are 65 and 66 or a similar combination is not known. Finally, "the court's finding does not prevent the defendant from introducing evidence of the defendant's intellectual disability or diminished mental capacity at the penalty phase of the sentencing proceeding." Arizona places considerable emphasis on IQ testing conducted once the State has decided to seek the death penalty. No mention is made of childhood mental retardation, age of onset, or relevant IQ scores obtained during childhood, before age of onset, or prior to the capital murder.

Patrick Dwayne Murphy

A higher IQ cutoff is not necessarily a less restrictive cutoff; a higher cutoff does not necessarily achieve some lofty constitutional purpose. In 1999, Patrick Dwayne Murphy murdered and mutilated George Jacobs with accomplice Billy Jack Long. An initial claim was that Oklahoma did not have jurisdiction over his case because the murder occurred within "Indian country." His trial for murder and conviction in a State rather than Federal court was based on this tidbit of geography: Murphy was found to have committed the murder in non-Indian country because "100 % of the surface and 11/12ths of the minerals to the tract of land adjacent to and directly east of the crime scene is wholly unrestricted property, owned by non-Indians; and the remaining 1/12th mineral interest appears to be a restricted interest retained by Indian heirs of a Creek allottee."

After considering the complexity of where the murder occurred, the Oklahoma appellate court found in 2005 that Murphy "had provided sufficient evidence to raise a face question on the issue of mental retardation, thereby warranting a trial on that claim." Murphy's Atkins claim was based on an abbreviated IQ score of less than 70. Two other IQ scores of 80 and 82 were above the 75 IQ score cutoff required in Oklahoma. In Oklahoma, to initiate an Atkins hearing, the defendant must make a threshold showing of not just an IQ score of 75 or below but no IQ score above 75. As per the Supreme Court, the Oklahoma statute does consider the SEM so that "In determining the intelligence quotient, the standard measurement of error for the test administrated shall be taken into account."[141] The reasoning for this draconian interpretation of IQ—ending a claim if "any" score is above 75—is the belief that a defendant can fake a lower but not a higher IQ score; that is, a high score is more important for determining intellectual disability than a low IQ score. This suggests that given IQ score of 76 and all other scores 75 or lower, the higher score must be credible and the lower scores "faked." In 2015 the Eastern District Court of Oklahoma affirmed the trial court and the Oklahoma Court of Criminal Appeals' decision that Murphy was not mentally retarded.

Murphy was not mentally retarded in Oklahoma but could be in Oklahoma in Federal court. In 2017 the United States Court of Appeals for the Tenth Circuit decided that he was tried in the wrong court.[142] The Circuit court decided that the Oklahoma courts were in error and Murphy should have been tried in Federal court. Oklahoma has appealed this decision and the case will be heard by the Supreme Court to determine whether an Oklahoma or the Federal has jurisdiction involving the Muscogee (Creek) Nation reservation and whether or not the Muscogee Nation had been disestablished. This decision has important consequences for Oklahoma including tribal taxes, tax exemptions and the enhanced responsibility for the Federal government to prosecute crimes. If Murphy is tried again in Federal court where executing someone with an intellectual disability is prohibited but defining who is intellectually disabled is not explained.[143]

---

[141]Oklahoma Statute §21-701.10b

[142]Patrick Dwayne Murphy v. Muscogee Creek Nation Seminole Nation of Oklahoma United Keetoowah Band of Cherokee Indians In Oklahoma., United States Court of Appeals, Tenth Circuit. Nos. 07-7068, Decided: August 08, 2017

[143]18 USC §3596(c). Implementation of a sentence of death

The constitutionality of the Oklahoma statue to disallow a claim when "any" IQ score is above 75 on an individually administered test of intelligence such as the WAIS has support from the defense of Freddie Lee Hall. In oral arguments for *Hall* Justice Alito asked defense counsel "In your view, does the Constitution establish a State to establish any hard cutoff? Let's say 76. Can it do that?" The response was that "States like Mississippi and Oklahoma that, in fact, establish a cutoff of 75, in our view, is constitutional..."[144]

Rather than attempting to establish a bright-line as was done in Oklahoma, the Supreme Court might have explained that professionals have acknowledged that IQ scores have an error component and that experts have generally considered the error to be about five points, an IQ cutoff score of about 75 is a best guess or guestimate, often times, generally speaking. But this was not to be because the Court apparently needed a statistical basis— maybe any basis— for a cutoff of 75 and this is where the constitutional standard gets murky, misconstrued, and confusing for all. The basis for rejecting Florida's plain language cutoff of 70, yet apparently accepting Oklahoma's even more rigid cutoff of 75, had nothing to do with test validity and what IQ tests measure but entirely about test reliability and the standard error of measurement or SEM.

The decision by the Supreme Court's "independent assessment that an individual with an IQ test score 'between 70 and 75 or lower,' may show intellectual disability by presenting additional evidence regarding difficulties in adaptive functioning." Can a State simply take into account the SEM rather than using an error margin of 5 regardless of the actual SEM of a test? Must a State use a SEM associated with a confidence level of 95 percent or could a confidence level of 90 percent level be used? Apparently, in spite of the 75 cutoff, a State use this cutoff to impose a strict standard so that "any" score above 75 would preclude the consideration of additional evidence as is the case in Oklahoma.

---

[144]Hall v. Florida, Oral Arguments, March 3, 2014. https://www.c-span.org/video/transcript/?id=53812

The SEM is a very useful measurement device, part of the very interesting theory of reliability, but never has a statistic been so misinterpreted in the name of theory. The SEM is less science than story; sometimes a good story, sometimes not, but an interesting story nonetheless. In the never-ending quest to establish a simple bright-line for all to follow, both Florida and Supreme Court needed an underlying rationale. Florida rested its case on the "plain language" interpretation of IQ scores to support the use of a bright line of 70; the Supreme Court sought a statistical basis for its bright line of 75.

Florida's pre-*Hall* position was that if there was no IQ score of 70 or below, there is no Atkins claim. Florida's bright-line position dismisses many score possibilities as when one IQ score is below 70 and five scores above 75, or one score of 69 and one of 71, etc. The Supreme Court reasoned that intellectual ability cannot be reduced to a single number, and that IQ should be interpreted as range. The Court referred (in *Hall 2014*) to a SEM of 2.16 for the WAIS-IV and a SEM of 2.3 for the Stanford-Binet-5. For the WISC-IV, given a reliability of .9793 (a high level of reliability) the SEM of 2.16 is calculated by

$$\textbf{SEM} = \textbf{Standard Deviation}\sqrt{1 - \textit{Reliability}}$$

Or

$$\textbf{SEM} = \textbf{15}\sqrt{1 - .9793} = \textbf{2.16}$$

If a State used an error component of one SEM, given a value of 2.16, the IQ range would be 73 to 77 for a score of 75. However, the Court wasn't referring to a SEM of 2.16 but rather an estimate of the error associated with IQ tests based on clinical experience, with a little help from the SEM used in days gone by, and the academic-sounding confidence levels. On this note, if State and defense used a modicum of perspicacity, defense would opt for the less reliable test (which would increase the SEM) and the State would want the most reliable test (which would decrease the

SEM). Related to this is the fact that older versions of IQ tests often have lower reliability and therefore larger SEMs.

Contrary to the Supreme Court's interpretation of the SEM "as a statistical fact," when applied to individual scores, the SEM is very much theory. The theory is that the SEM, based on a group reliability statistic, can be applied to individual scores. If an individual received a score of 75 on an IQ test, a SEM of 2.16 can be used to show that, if this individual were tested repeatedly (say 100 times) 68 percent of these scores would probably be (all things being equal) between 73 and 77 (or 72.84 to 77.16 (75 ±2.16) assuming that, among other things, the hypothetical scores were normally distributed. Obviously one SEM does not suggest that a score of 75 would fall into the 70 or below range.

For academics a commonly used level of "significance" is the 95 percent confidence level (often cited as the .05 level in research studies). Based on the normal curve, 95 percent of scores—assuming a normal distribution—will be between -1.96 and +1.96 standard deviations. For the 95 percent confidence level the SEM is multiplied by 1.96 (the normal curve value for the 95 percent confidence level) which results in a value of 2.16 X 1.96 or 4.23. [145] Rounding 1.96 to 2, the 95 percent confidence level, when the SEM is 2.16, is 4.32 or 4. For an IQ score of 75 the result is a range of scores of 71 and 79 (75±4.23). Here too, when the SEM is 4, a score of 75 does not fall into the 70 or below range. In addition, the application of the SEM across all possible scores could less that accurate because the score variance might be quite small for one individual, especially with someone with very low scores, or quite high because of examiner error, motivation, health, etc.

All of this indicates that the appropriate error of margin for a 95 percent confidence level when the SEM is 2.16 should be 4 so that a score of 74 would be exactly at the cutoff and a score of 75 outside of the 95 percent confidence range. According to Terman in 1916 a score below 70 (not "at" 70) was definite feeble-minded

---

[145]Using -1.96 to +1.96 standard deviations rather than 2 is equivalent to a probability range of .0455 rather than 5 percent and would account for 95.45 percent of scores rather than 95 percent.

and scores between 70 and 80 indicated border-line deficiency (p. 79).[146]

As a matter of fact, fact can collide with theory. The probability, given one IQ score between 70 and 75, that this score could be as low as 70 is not an unreasonable possibility. However, this is rarely the case and a defendant might have numerous IQ scores above 70. With each score above 70, the probability increases that this person's "true score" is truly above 70. If a person was (hypothetically) tested 100 times and ever score was between 71 and 75, to say that a SEM of 5 indicates this person's "true score" could be as low as 70 would be contrary to fact; that fact being that all data suggests that the "true score" is above 70. For this hypothetical 100 test administrations to the same individual the best estimate of this person's true score would be the average of these 100 hypothetical IQ scores. More importantly, although the SEM is interesting theory, it is theory nonetheless. The obvious hypothetical nature of the SEM is further confounded by different tests, different standardizations, different examiners, different factors, different motivational influences, and then throw in the whole question of the determination of reliability, reliability for particular age groups, etc.

The reason for using 5 as the estimate of the SEM for all IQ tests has a twofold basis. The first is simply that 5 is what professionals believe to be the best estimate of error based on experience and common sense with a nod toward data such as the actual determination of the statistical SEM. The second reason is the assumption that all tests have a SEM of 2.5 and that doubling this will produce a SEM that will include 95 percent of a person's hypothetical scores on a test. Obviously the SEM is not 2.5 for all tests. The SEM is based on a group reliability statistic for a specific standardization groups or subgroups.

The actual SEM, when calculated using the standard deviation and test reliability, is statistical and not a qualitative concept. For the

---

[146]Terman, L. M. The Measurement of Intelligence an Explanation of and a Complete Guide for the Use of the Stanford Revision and Extension of the Binet-Simon Intelligence Scale, Riverside Press: Cambridge, Massachusetts, 1916, p. 91.

normal curve a score (referred to as a ***z score***) between -1.96 and +1.96 on the normal curve includes 95 percent of scores. The high tail plus the low tail (thus the name "two-tailed test") includes 5 percent of scores. Hypothetically, if the SEM is 2.5 (a big *if*), and is multiplied by 2, (who can remember 1.96), the result will show that 95 percent of a person's hypothetical scores will be in the range of 65 to 75 given a score of 70.

In that the Supreme Court has emphasized the importance of life and that the death penalty should be reserved for the most deserving, one can only wonder why the Court chose the .95 percent confidence level rather than the 99 percent confidence level. For the 99 percent confidence level, .5 percent of the scores will be higher than 2.58 (the normal curve equivalent) and .5 percent of scores lower than -2.58. For the normal curve equivalent, 99 percent of scores will be between -2.58 and +2.58 standard deviations below and above the mean.

When the normal curve value 2.58 is multiplied by the estimated SEM of 2.5, the result is 6.45 so that 99 percent of scores will be between 63.55 and 76.45 give a score of 70 (or 63 and 77). Based on the admittedly shaky statistical reasoning for use of the normal curve and the 2.5 estimate of the SEM, and given that preference for life over death by the Supreme Court, at the very least the upper limit for including IQ scores should be greater than 75...possibly 78 or even as high as 80.   For example, the 99.9 percent confidence level corresponds to **z score**s between -3.291 and +3.291 or IQ scores between 62 and 78.

Terman did not use statistics for the distribution of IQ scores (viz., the standard deviation, reliability and SEM) but he was acutely aware of the normality of IQ which he referred to as "remarkably symmetrical" (p. 66)[147] However, he believed "The number of mentally defective individuals in a population will depend upon the standard arbitrarily set up as to what constitutes mental deficiency" (p. 67)." [148]

---

[147]Terman, L. M. The Measurement of Intelligence an Explanation of and a Complete Guide for the Use of the Stanford Revision and Extension of the Binet-Simon Intelligence Scale, Riverside Press: Cambridge, Massachusetts, 1916, p. 91.

The statistical rationale for the SEM is more afterthought than science. In 1983 the classification manual for the American Association for the American Association on Mental Deficiency explains that "The maximum specified IQ is not to be taken as an exact value, but as a commonly accepted guideline. It is true that legislation, the courts, and service agencies often employ exact IQ values to determine eligibility for services, but the consistent point of view of AAMD and of professionals serving mentally retarded populations is that clinical assessment must be flexible" so that "the recommended ceiling may be extended up through IQ 75, particularly in school settings where intellectual performance is a prerequisite for success and special educational assistance may be required."[149] This does indicate that the 75 IQ ceiling is "particularly" important for children because of the need of "special education," but this does suggest that the 75 ceiling is less important for adults and Atkins claimants.

Rather than using a SEM of 4 as a bright line, the Court decided on an error value of 5 , not so much based on a purely statistical justification, but because this has been the value generally used. Specifically, the Court cited the DSM-III which provided that "Since any measurement is fallible, an IQ score is generally thought to involve an error of measurement of approximately five points; hence, an IQ of 70 is considered to represent a band or zone of 65 to 75. Treating the IQ with some flexibility permits the inclusion in the Mental Retardation category of individuals with IQs somewhat higher than 70 who truly need special education or other programs. It also permits exclusion from the diagnosis of those with IQs somewhat lower than 70 if the clinical judgment is that there are no significant deficits or impairment in adaptive functioning."[150] The key words in this clarification, and all

---

[148]Terman, L. M. The Measurement of Intelligence an Explanation of and a Complete Guide for the Use of the Stanford Revision and Extension of the Binet-Simon Intelligence Scale, Riverside Press: Cambridge, Massachusetts, 1916, p. 91.
[149]Classification in Mental Retardation, Editor: Herbert, J, Grossman, American Association on Mental Deficiency, Washington, D.C., 1983, pp. 22-23.
[150]Diagnostic and Statistical Manual of Mental Disorders (Third Edition),

professional definitions, are "approximately" and "flexibility." For a child who exhibited extensive deficits in adaptive behavior and an IQ of 76 or 77 would result in the denial of services if an inflexible ceiling IQ value of 75 were used.

When the above concept of an IQ score is interpreted as an approximation, the application to Atkins claims precludes all IQ bright lines whether 70 or 75. As for children, there could be a claimant with an IQ of 75 or below 70 who did not have deficits in adaptive behavior and no indication of intellectual disability in childhood or as an adult. As a matter of fact, States routinely disregard IQ scores of 75 or lower for this very reason. On the other hand, a child or adult could have an IQ above 75 but still meet the criteria for identification as having an intellectual disability.

All this seems fairly clear: the Supreme Court cited one version of the WAIS where the overall reliability was 2.16 with a SEM of 4 points and then decided that 5 was an appropriate standard because a professional group thought that a SEM of 5 was "generally" better (apparently). The problem is that there are various versions of the WAIS and the Wechsler Intelligence Scale for Children or WISC. For each test not only are there different types of reliability statistics (e.g., internal consistency, test-retest, split-half, etc.), different tests (WISC, WAIS, Stanford-Binet), different standardization versions, different overall reliability statistics, different reliability statistics for different test components and age groups(e.g., Full Scale IQ, Verbal IQ, Performance IQ), and the very relevant but usually not considered reliability statistics for specific groups such as for the general prison population, those on death row, etc..

As a test becomes more reliable, the SEM decreases. The WISC was released in 1949 and not re-standardized until 1974 (the WISC-R). There are Atkins claimants who were tested using the 1949 version. For this test the WISC manual reported a Full Scale IQ reliability for the 7 1/2 age group as .92, the SEM as 4.25, and the

---

95 percent confidence level would be ±8 or 8.33. If these data were used as part of an Atkins claims, the confidence band would be from 62 to 78 and citing a SEM of 5 and a 95 percent confidence level would be incorrect. Although the Supreme Court has established a cutoff of 75 defense counsel would be remiss by not showing why a higher IQ cutoff would be statistically appropriate depending on the test, the standardization version of the test, the type of reliability statistic used, and age group reliability statistics.

The 1983 the classification manual for mental retardation indicated that "if a person obtains IQ 70 on a particular test that has a standard error of 4, the chances are 2 to 1 that the 'true' IQ on that test is between 66 and 74, 95 to 5 (.05 level of confidence) that the true score is between 62 and 78, and 99 to 1 (.01 level of confidence) that the true score is between 60 and 80."[151] Incidentally, for a SEM of 4, the corresponding reliability (given a standard deviation of 15) is approximately .93—a bit on the low side. For a defendant who was given an IQ test when the professional interpretation of the 95 percent band upper limit was 78, restricting IQ scores to 75 or less to meet the IQ prong of the definition would be contrary to professional guidance and how tests were used at the time.

As bemoaned by Justice Alito in *Atkins*, "because of these factual errors and ambiguities, it is unclear to me whether the Court concludes that a defendant is constitutionally entitled to introduce non-test evidence of intellectual disability (1) whenever his score is 75 or lower, on the mistaken understanding that the SEM for most tests is 5; (2) when the 66% confidence interval (using one SEM) includes a score of 70 [the Justice probably meant the 68% confidence level]; or (3) when the 95% confidence interval (using two SEMs) includes a score of 70. In my view, none of these approaches is defensible."

When Freddie Lee Hall was in elementary school, the professional IQ cutoff was 85. Applying the error value of 5 to this cutoff would

---

[151]Classification in Mental Retardation, Editor: Herbert, J, Grossman, American Association on Mental Deficiency, Washington, D.C., 1983, p. 198

result in and upper IQ cutoff of 90. For all defendants having IQ evaluated as a child where the 85 cutoff was used, and used even it shouldn't had been, an argument could be made that IQ scores as high as 90 should be considered. This seems excessively high, and if a child were classified as mentally retarded/intellectually disabled based on a score in the 80s, this would be a travesty. Travesty or not, if a defendant had been so classified, it does not make a difference what the IQ score was because the classification is a *fait accompli*. A child must live with the consequences of this classification as a child; a State should also accept (and live with) the classification as an adult.

The reasoning for the popularity of the 95 percent confidence level is more about convenience than science. The 95 percent this confidence level is not too low, not too high, and is a nice even number that seems to be a common meeting ground for all manner of research. No great science here. The 95 percent level of significance (or .05) was not ordained on high but was discussed as early as 1925 by Ronald Fisher as a matter of "convenience" so that "The value for which P =·.05, or 1 in 20, is or nearly 2; it is convenient to take this point as a limit in judging whether a deviation is to be considered significant or not."[152] As was already said, for death penalty purposes a higher confidence level (viz., the 99 percent or even 99.9 percent) is consistent with the Court's belief that the death penalty should be for a narrow category of offenders and not subject to an index based on convenience.

The various statistical peregrinations can be distracting and maybe the Supreme Court decided that there were statistics, and then too much statistics, and opted to forgo a purely statistical explanation and simply adopted a margin of error of 5 points come hell or high water. In *Hall* the "Court agrees with the medical experts that when a defendant's IQ test score falls within the test's acknowledged and inherent margin of error, the defendant must be able to present additional evidence of intellectual disability, including testimony regarding adaptive

---

[152]Ronald A. Fisher, Statistical methods for Researchers, Chapter III, Oliver & Boyd, London: 1925.

deficits." The devil is in the details and exactly what that "acknowledged and inherent margin of error" is less than obvious.

Justice Kagan: *a tale of tails*

The Court is incorrect to suggest that only scores within the margin of error of 65 to 75 should allow for consideration of adaptive behavior. This would imply that scores below 65 would fail to satisfy the IQ prong which, of course, is nonsense. To make statistical sense out of the error guestimate of five points requires some backtracking. First, assume that the error component is 5 for the 95 percent confidence level and the SEM is 2.5. When the IQ score is 70, based on the normal curve, 47.5 percent of the scores from a series of hypothetical repeated testings will be between 70 and 75 and 47.5 percent of the scores between 65 and 70. In other words, 47.5+47.5 percent of scores, or 95 percent, will be between 65 and 75 (and 5 percent at the extreme tails of the distribution). This is the case for hypothetical test scores so the result may or may not apply to a specific individual's score, much less the IQ score of an Atkins claimant, or even more confusing, many IQ scores from many different tests administered at many different times, to defendants of unknown motivation.

Justice Kagan was intrigued by the 95 percent confidence level and asked in oral arguments why the 100 percent confidence level shouldn't be used in that "we're putting somebody to death" or a less stringent level of confidence such as 80 percent in that the burden of proof is on the defendant. A 100 percent confidence level would mean that all IQ scores would be considered when examining the IQ prong of the definition (which is not that bad of an idea). The mention of the 80 percent confidence level indicates some level of confusion. Justice Kagan seems to have meant that a more inclusive confidence level should be used such as the 99 percent which would expand the band of confidence to include scores above 75. A less stringent confidence (e.g. 80 percent) level would lower the margin of error but not necessarily the cutoff. For example, given a SEM of 2.5, the 80 percent confidence level is associated with normal curve scores of -1.282 to +1.282. In other words, 80 percent of scores are between -1.282 and +1.282 scores on the normal curve. Multiplying 2.5 by 1.282 results in an 80 percent confidence level score of 3.205 which is lower than 4.32 (calculated by 2.16 X 2). A less stringent confidence level when applied to the SEM results in a smaller band of confidence which for an Atkins defendant. The 68 percent level is the SEM X 1 or 2.5 X 1 = 2.5). At the 50 percent confidence level, the normal curve value (**z score**) is .674 and the margin of error is reduced to 2.5 X .674 or 1.685 (or 2 when rounded).

Justice Kagan's question concerning confidence levels is really directed at the importance of individualization during sentencing because any IQ cutoff precludes individual consideration "Because we have this whole line of cases that says when it comes to meting out the death penalty, we actually do individualized consideration, and we allow people to make their best case about why they're not eligible for the death penalty. And essentially what your cutoff does is it stops that in its tracks, as to a person who may or may not even have a true IQ of over 70, and let alone it stops people in their tracks who may not be mentally who may be mentally retarded."[153]

The Court has cited the 95 percent confidence level to support, more or less, the cutoff of 75 but with an unintentional accompanying result. In statistical research the 95 percent confidence level is often a threshold value for determining statistical significance but this is no less arbitrary than an IQ cutoff of 70. If the requirement is to simply incorporate the SEM when interpreting IQ scores, one SEM could be used which would result in a 68 percent confidence level. This seems consistent with the Supreme Court's requirement for "considering an IQ tests Standard Error of Measurement (SEM)." The SEM is what the Court refers to as an IQ test score "acknowledged and inherent margin of error" so that the defendant must be able to present additional evidence of intellectual disability, including testimony regarding adaptive deficits. Using a cutoff other than the 95

---

[153]Hall v. Florida, Oral Arguments, March 3, 2014. https://www.c-span.org/video/transcript/?id=53812

percent level, and a SEM other than 2.5, would entail **considering** the SEM but fall well short of the IQ cutoff of 75. A higher confidence level increases the band of confidence surrounding a given test score thereby ensuring that an IQ score that truly represents mild intellectual disability is not discounted. Confidence in confidence levels depends entirely on our confidence in the reliability statistic being used and the overall confidence in any IQ cutoff is far from compelling.

In Atkins claims the concern is not the percent of scores between 65 and 75 but the percent of scores 75 or less. Therefore, for the 95 percent confidence level, the normal curve value is not 2 (or 1.96) but 1.65; that is, for the normal curve 95 percent of scores are above -1.65 standard deviations and 5 percent below. A two-tailed test indicates 5 percent of scores are below -1.96 and 5 percent above 1.96 (and conversely 95 percent of scores between -1.96 and +1.96). For Atkins claims a one-tailed test applies. The pivotal question is not scores between 65 and 75 but the percent of scores at or below -1.65. Thus, 1.65 X 2.5 results in a value of 4.125 so that 95 percent of hypothetical scores are below 74.125 (or 7 4). If the SEM of 2.16 is used, the resulting margin of error for a one-tailed test is 1.65 X 2.16 or 3.564. No matter how parsed statistically the margin of error, statistically speaking, should be 4 and not 5. All of the above might be little more than statistical nitpicking but the lesson to be learned is that when applied to Atkins claims the SEM is far from fact or science.

Rather than bothering with the statistical realities of confidence levels, the arbitrariness of a score of 70, different reliability coefficients, and different SEM values, the Supreme Court settled on a cutoff of 75 to tidy up all these loose ends. The Court needed to address the use of IQ to preclude consideration of adaptive behavior, and did so by establishing a bright line of 75 much like an age cutoff is used to prohibit the death penalty for offenders under the age of 18. Professionals have been reluctant to raise the IQ cutoff to 75 because would be even greater disproportionality in the classification of black children as having intellectual disabilities; but not so the Supreme Court where the new bright line of 75 can be just as rigid as Florida's now unconstitutional bright line of 70.

The basis for the Supreme Court's belief that a margin of error of five points is appropriate for interpreting a base IQ score of 70 is not unreasonable and not inconsistent with what professionals have been recommending, in one form or another, for decades. What is flawed is the suggested accuracy of the cutoff of 75. There seems to be a belief this higher cutoff (as opposed to Florida's strict cutoff of 70) somehow eliminates error and that scores above this are not to be trusted, or that scores obtained as a child when above 75 are irrelevant (as when the IQ cutoff was 85).

Dutifully citing the IQ standard of 70 or 75 does not relinquish a State from a fair determination of intellectual disability, and that determination does not end with *Atkins*. In California assessment data for prisoners includes low cognitive functioning which is "usually shown" not just by IQ scores but adaptive needs (e.g., requiring prompts for self-care and victimization concerns). Inmates with IQ scores above 75 could be included in the Developmental Disability Program (DDP) with poor adaptive skills.[154] Rather than focusing entirely on stereotypes to establish adaptive skills (e.g., driving a car with a manual transmission no less), California examines behaviors relevant to intellectual ability that are helpful for identifying inmate needs. For example, an inmate may lack judgment and fail "to understand the consequences of their actions, may exhibit poor self-care skills relating to hygiene, organization, eating habits," and "the DDP inmates "may have difficulty advocating for themselves."

The reality of the newly sanctioned cutoff of 75 is that the base IQ 70 is completely arbitrary to begin with and adding five points to this score does not change this fundamental fact. Professionals are not likely to change the cutoff from 70 to 75 but are content with 70 ±5 points. To actually increase the cutoff from 70 to 75 would result in a large increase in the number of children, especially black children, identified as having intellectual disabilities—which is exactly what happened when the IQ cutoff was set at 85 in 1959. Professionals can live with the reality that a score of 71 or 76 is *about* 71 or 76; the Supreme Court has

---

[154]Clark v. California Remedial Plan

decided that a score of 75 cannot preclude the admission of relevant evidence of adaptive deficits. On the other hand, after considering all the vagaries of IQ testing, validity, reliability, standardizations, racism, confidence levels, an IQ of 76 can accomplish exactly what an IQ of 75 was able to accomplish before Hall v. Florida in 2014 and that is the preclusion of relevant data and allow the imposition of the death penalty. Maybe the best solution is to select a cutoff, if a cutoff must be had, to a high enough level to warrant consideration of relevant data.

The history of the magic cutoff of "70 or below" is inconsistent with the history of IQ testing where Terman in 1916 suggested that a score "Below 70" indicated "Definite feeble-mindedness." Wechsler in 1958 stated that score of "69 and below" fell into the "Defective" classification (p. 42).[155] In 1983 Grossman offered no absolute bright line but that "significantly subaverage is defined as an IQ of 70 or *below* on standardized measures of intelligence. This upper limit is intended as a guideline; it could *be* extended upward through IQ 75 or more, depending on the reliability of the intelligence test used.[156] He further clarified the less than absolute nature of an IQ cutoff by offering that mild mental retardation includes IQ scores in the range of 50 to 55 to approximately 70 (p. 13). No bright line here. Using a standard error of measurement of 5 by declaring that IQ scores as high a 75 could indicate intellectual disability because of error inherent in testing could mean that a score of 75 could suggest that a score as low as 70 might be the person's "true score". The problem with this reasoning, a problem recognized by professionals, is that a score of 70 may or may not indicate intellectual disability; that is, this possibility is predicated on the assumption that an IQ score of 70 is determinative of intellectual disability.

---

[155]Wechsler, David. The Measurement and Appraisal of Adult Intelligence (4th Ed.), The Williams and Wilkins Co, Baltimore, 1958, pp. 38-44.
[156]See also Classification in Mental Retardation, Editor: Herbert, J, Grossman, American Association on Mental deficiency, Washington, D.C., 1983, p. 198
https://law.resource.org/pub/us/cfr/ibr/001/aamd.classification.1973.pdf

If there is a threshold measure for IQ, that measure should begin with a prior determination of intellectual disability as a child and all corresponding evidence/data relating to that finding. If there has been no prior determination of intellectual disability, the more difficult task is whether there should have been a determination of intellectual disability (as for Freddie Lee Hall in the 1950s). The importance of a prior determination of intellectual disability cannot be overemphasized. For an adult seeking Atkins relief, the difficult task is to determine if a defendant warrants lesser culpability when there is no evidence of intellectual disability as a child.

All of these matters relating to the SEM, the underlying theory, different SEM values, two- and one-tailed tests, reliability, different tests, the administration of multiple tests often given over many years, racial disproportionality in testing, outright racial bias, defendant motivation, etc. might seem to be nitpicking over a point or two, but a judge or jury should be aware of the reality testing and the SEM. This is a difficult task, and maybe a task that borders on the impossible. But sentencing a defendant to death is no less a difficult task and no one would ever suggest that relevant information should be withheld because it is difficult to understand or, in the case of the SEM, somewhat messy.   In addition, every expert should be able to opine on the statistical issues of the SEM, the statistical history and meaning of IQ scores, racial bias, the intricacies of the SEM, the history of IQ in the determination of mental retardation/intellectual disabilities, etc. After all, experts should be experts.

Justice Alito: "true IQ"

The idea of "true IQ" is more than a misnomer but when you deal with a quirky concept expect quirkiness. The SEM is often used to bracket a person's true score such as by saying that a person's "true score" is between 65 and 75. What is actually meant is that a person's "best score" is probably between 65 and 75, all things being equal, ignoring the hypothetical nature of what the SEM represents, and ignoring different tests, different SEMs, etc. The iffy nature of the SEM is then used to define a cutoff score of 70.

Justice Alito in his dissenting opinion in Hall concluded that "To blindly import a five-point margin of error when we know as a matter of fact that the relevant SEM is 2.16 amounts to requiring consideration of more than *two* SEMs—an approach that finds no support in *Atkins* or anywhere else." What the Court seems to have blindly imported is a SEM of 2.5 and then used the 95 percent confidence level is generate a margin of error of 5 (2.5 X 2 or 2.5 X 1.96).

There is something called a "true score" in the SEM world but it is not the type of truth as in "a true score representing intelligence," or an ultimate truth from on high, but rather a "true score" is more on the order of a likely "best" score. As a matter of fact a "true score" can be very untruthful. For example, testing how far cabbages can be thrown might be reliable but hardly a valid measure of overall cognitive ability. In the testing business "true score" is purely theory and an estimate of what a person's average score would be given repeated testings or something akin to this. For each of these repeated testings there would be some random error and the "true score" represents an average or best score. In that this type of hypothetical testing cannot be done, the SEM provides an estimate of the range of scores which theoretically bracket a person's score. The problem is that the SEM is based on a group reliability statistic and will not apply to all individuals. If the SEM (or approximately two SEMs) is 5, for a score of 70 most scores, theoretically, would be between 65 and 75. That is, on the average, for most, maybe, depending on the group, depending on all kinds of things. For one individual there might be very little variance among scores and thus a smaller SEM, and for another individual just the opposite might occur. If a group does have less opportunity to develop cognitive skills because of environment, socio-economic factors, death row, and, of course, racism, the resulting statistics might be anything but normal. Consider an extreme and unlikely scenario was tested 100 times and received of 75 on each testing. The standard deviation for these scores would be o and the SEM 0 so that the person's "true," "best," or "average" score would be 75.

The Supreme Court was very aware of "true scores" in 2014 in Atkins and explained that "The SEM allows clinicians to calculate a range within which one may say an individual's true IQ score lies." There is actually a method that can be used to calculate true scores or, more accurately, *estimated true scores*. As shown below, this adjustment results in a slight regression toward the mean based on the test's reliability.

$$\overline{X} + r_{xx}(X - \overline{X}) = \textbf{Estimated True Score}$$

Given a mean score of 100, and a reliability of .95, and a score of 75, the estimated *true score* would be

$$\textbf{100 + .95(75-100) = 76.25 or 76}$$

As seen by the above formula the "true score" has nothing to do with "truth" but is a nod toward test error by considering the test's reliability. The Supreme Court stated, in Hall in 2014, that "Florida's approach treats IQ test scores as conclusive and ignores the fact that an IQ score might not reflect "true" IQ because of errors in measurement." For an obtained of 75 the estimated "true score" of 76.25 would be above the 75 score cutoff. Crazy business this SEM stuff! A calculated "true score" (see above) can show that the cutoff of 75 which is intended to identify a person's *true score* is, well, not exactly truthful.

Decimals are not used when reporting IQ scores unless you are a prosecutor showing that an obtained score is above 75. For example, for a score of 75 and a reliability of .97, the estimated *true score* would be 75.75. A score of 75.44 could be rounded to 75 while a score of 75.45 could be rounded to 76. Not only can a single score result in death, but a decimal can have the same result. Given a test with perfect reliability, the best estimate of the person's *true score* would be the obtained score in that there would be no error. On the other hand, for a test with a reliability of 0, the best estimate of the *true score* would be 100 (or the mean score of the test). Does this mean that for an IQ score of 75, where the reliability is .97, a *true score* calculation of 75.75 or 76 is above the Supreme Court's bright-line cutoff of 75? Could a prosecutor assert that the Court's attention to *true scores* should be pursued in the name of accuracy so that an obtained score of 75 should be transformed to a an estimated true score of 76 (if the reliability so warranted)? Unfortunately after the consideration of the calculation of *true scores* the Court did not opine on how to treat the rounding of decimals (or reliability and validity, multiple IQ scores, different IQ scores and most everything relevant to the interpretation of IQ).

As said before the *true score* is not necessarily evidence of the truthfulness of a test but an estimate—a very theoretical estimate—of the person's most likely score (aka "true score") when taking into account the reliability of the test. The SEM is an estimate of where most scores would occur given a large number of hypothetical testings. At the very least, considering the unique defendants in capital cases, there should be concern when States disregard adaptive behavior and age of onset no matter the SEM and the arbitrary cutoff. In essence, IQ is never determinative of intellectual disability but should be broadly interpreted so that relevant evidence regarding adaptive behavior and age of onset is considered, and the possibility of intellectual disability after age of onset because criteria for intellectual disability (viz., IQ and adaptive behavior would warrant lesser culpability).

All this business about *true scores*, estimates, etc. might seem unnecessary because in the real world theory is used as a pretext to develop a constitutional bright-line cutoff score of 75. An accurate interpretation of the SEM really doesn't matter, and psychometric theory is secondary to the Supreme Court's pronouncement that 75 is the new IQ cutoff. A court could adopt a different standard as was the case in California where the role of IQ is downplayed when considering Atkins claims. Exactly how the Supreme Court would view a State that took the standard error of measurement into account which resulted in a cutoff of 74 or less is not known. This possibility is mentioned by Justice Alito in his dissent in *Hall* in 2014 where the majority opinion noted an average SEM of 2.16 which would correspond to 95 percent confidence value of 4 and a corresponding cutoff value of 74 but then went on to ordain a cutoff of 75. As can be seen from the various interpretations and ambiguities associated with the SEM, accuracy is relative and the very meaning of the SEM can vary.

Gregory Lott

What seems like a complete disavowal of a cutoff of 70, replaced by a new cutoff of 75, is not as complete as one might expect. There are options. In Ohio "there is a rebuttable presumption that a defendant is not mentally retarded if his or her IQ is above 70."[157] The prevailing hypothesis is that a defendant is not intellectually disabled and therefore must prove that he/she is. This would seemingly allow for the consideration of IQ scores above 70, 75 or even 80 which is not a bad idea at all.

Gregory Lott, black, was sentenced to death in 1987 in Ohio for the 1986 murder of 82-year old John McGrath in a Cleveland suburb. The defense claimed that Lott's 1986 IQ of 72 was correct (taking into account the 5 point margin of error). Other evidence revealed IQ scores of 77-81, 83-91, 87-97 and a 1984 full scale IQ of 86. As with all Atkins claims the only real requirement is to *consider* other relevant evidence. The ultimate reason for rejecting intellectual disability might be that a score is below 70 but the constitutional violation seems to occur when the State does not consider other evidence even though this evidence might support a claim of intellectual disability. In spite of one IQ of 72, experts testified that he was not mentally retarded and his Atkins claim was denied. In 2014 but Governor granted a temporary reprieve to consider the drug protocol for execution. Lott's execution date was scheduled for March 12, 2020 by Governor Mike DeWine so that the lethal injection protocol could be modified (specifically the use of midazolam which was an inadequate sedative) as mandated by District Court judge Michael Merz.

Elroy Chester

The IQ bright-line of 75 for IQ tests was far from a simple task in Texas for a single test administration can produce more than a single IQ score. Most Atkins claims are mired in IQ scores from childhood, group IQ scores (as opposed to the individualized tests

---

[157]The State of Ohio v. Lott, 97 Ohio St.3d 303 (2002)

such as the Wechsler scales), nonverbal IQ tests, tests administered as part of previous incarcerations, IQ tests completed by professionals for the State and defense, and then there are a variety of subscores. For Atkins claims attention is given to Full Scale IQ scores but for tests such as the Wechsler Adult Intelligence Scale there are also Verbal and Performance IQ subscores. This adds another element of obfuscation to the interpretation of scores because a defendant could have a performance score above 75, a verbal score below 75, a full scale score somewhere in between, or some other combination that dances about the bright-line of 75. For the WAIS-IV (2008) modifications there are now four subscales: verbal comprehension, perceptual reasoning, working memory and processing speed. All these possibilities certainly did not help Elroy Chester who was black.

Chester's rampage occurred in 1998, in Jefferson County, Texas when he burglarized the home of Kim Ryman Deleon, raped her two daughters (age 14 and 16) and then murdered fireman Willie Ryman III, the uncle of the two girls, with a single shot as he entered the back door. He then fled, but not before attempting to murder Ryman's girlfriend who was waiting in a car. After confessing "to a host of other horrific crimes," four previous murders (including the murder of 87 year old Etta May Stallings during a robbery), Chester pleaded guilty to capital murder and was sentenced to death.[158]

Texas has further complicated this matter by deciding to consider multiple cutoff scores. Instead of using a Full Scale IQ score a Texas court decided that a determination of mental retardation requires scores on not only Full Scale IQ below 70 but also scores on Performance IQ below 70 and Verbal IQ below 70. Update this to the current cutoff of 75 and the requirement is not simply one IQ score at or below 75 but three subtest scores, three bands of confidence, and three "true" scores!

---

[158]Court of Criminal Appeals of Texas, AP-75,037, Ex parte Elroy Chester, Applicant, Application for a Writ of Habeas Corpus, 2007; Chester v. Thaler, United State Court of Appeals for the Fifth Circuit, January 3, 2012

Chester's IQ scores were 69 at age 7, 59 at age 12, 77 at age 13, and 69 at age 18. The Texas trial court observed that these IQ tests "would not adequately account for cultural, regional, or other types of factors that may have influenced the applicant's test results." This suggests that "cultural" factors are permissible for evaluating a child's poor school performance, declaring the child intellectually deficiency, and then providing a segregated education but not when considering the death penalty. The implication is that IQ tests are readily accepted for children to explain poor educational performance as a result of intellectual disability; for adults seeking Atkins relief there is a great need to take into account cultural bias in the standardized assessment of IQ.

The trial court then offered an interpretation that would substantially lower the required cutoff for mental retardation by saying "that the Texas education system requires that, in order for a student to be classified as mentally retarded, his or her test results must be below 70 for both verbal and performance scores, not only the full scale score."[159] What the court created was a classification scenario that went far beyond the normal curve. The IQ criterion was no longer one IQ test but rather performance on three scores: verbal, performance and full scale IQ, performance which must take into account the correlation between these various scores. The effect of this is to reduce the number of those below -2 standard deviations as the inter-correlations between these scores decreases. [160]

In 1977 on the WISC-R Chester received a verbal score of 77, a performance score of 69 and a full scale score of 69. In 1983, also on the WISC-R, he received a verbal IQ score of 70, a performance IQ score of 87, and a full scale IQ of 77. Chester's IQ verbal and

---

[159]*Ibid.*

[160]§ 89.1040. Eligibility Criteria (c)(5)(A) According to Texas Commissioner of Education and State Board of Education Rules (Texas Administrative Code) the criterion for determining significantly subaverage intellectual functioning is measurement by "a standardized, individually administered test of cognitive ability in which the overall test score is at least two standard deviations below the mean, when taking into consideration the standard error of measurement of the test."

performance IQ score difference (8 points) is mild in comparison to Jorge Junior Vidal's scores in California. Vidal was sentenced to death in California for the 2001 torture, sodomy and murder of Eric Jones, 17, with special circumstances. Vidal had been given various WISC and WAIS IQ tests and there was a consistent pattern that verbal IQ was far below performance IQ. In 1980 when he was 11 years old his verbal IQ was 59, performance IQ 109 and his full scale IQ 81. The State believed that the full scale score was the best predictor of IQ (a full scale score is more reliable than a part score); while the defense reasoned that his verbal deficit was tantamount to mental retardation. The trial court claimed that verbal IQ was of particular importance because it touched on matters underlying *Atkins* such as the ability to reason, appreciate, premeditate and foresight. This is quite true. On the other hand, verbal IQ is also based on verbal experiences which could suggest that English as a second language, environment, etc. could have impacted verbal IQ.

In 2005 the Court of Appeals disagreed and believed that full scale IQ was the standard, but this was overturned by the Supreme Court of California in 2007 because the statutory task for determining general intellectual functioning is not subject to an absolute rule such that full scale IQ is always the determining factor: "The question of how best to measure intellectual functioning in a given case is thus one of fact to be resolved in each case on the evidence, not by appellate promulgation of a new legal rule."[161]

For Chester in Texas requiring full scale, performance and verbal IQ scores below 70 added a new interpretation of IQ in death penalty cases. No matter Chester's IQ scores, especially his highly relevant low IQ scores as a child, the Texas Department of Criminal Justice had already determined Chester was mentally retarded. When he was 18 he was placed in the Mentally Retarded Offenders Program (MROP) based on his IQ scores, a score of 57 on the Vineland Adaptive Behavior Scales, interviews, and a 30 day observation period. The Court of Criminal Appeals of Texas

---

[161]People v. Superior Court (Vidal), Supreme Court of California, S134901, April 12, 2007

decided that Chester met the IQ criterion for mental retardation but not that of adaptive behavior. The 2007 Texas appellate decision regarded Chester's Vineland score of 57 and placement in the MROP as "persuasive" but this evidence was insufficient to reverse the judgment of the trial court "so long as the findings are supported by the trial record."[162]

Texas ignored the data and decided that he had a "specific learning disability" which was proof that he was not mentally retarded. By definition, someone with a specific intellectual disability does not have an intellectual disability.[163] As is often the case, the specific learning disability can have racial implications. A black child, especially when Chester was in school, might be classified as mentally retarded rather than having a specific learning disability but just the opposite when seeking Atkins relief. According to the Office of Civil Rights survey in 1980 (Chester was born in 1969) the black enrollment in Texas was 14.4 percent but the percentage of black children identified as EMR was 35.4 percent. Conversely, 17.7 percent of children having specific learning disabilities were black, but 50 percent of white children had this less onerous label.[164]

The data indicated that Chester could have or should have been classified as mentally retarded as a child but specific learning disability was used to explain his various educational deficiencies. To this end the regulations specify that a child cannot be classified as having a disability because of lack of instruction in reading or math or limited English proficiency.[165] There was testimony that

---

[162]Chester, 2007, 2012

[163]see 34 CFR § 300.8[c][10]

[164]1980 Elementary and Secondary Schools Civil Rights Survey, State Summaries, Washington, D.C., 1982, ED#219478. For Atkins claims the most relevant data concerning race and participation in programs for the educable mentally retarded pertain to racial categorization when the claimant was a child. Often these data are not available. The first systematic collection of data (rather than survey data) began with the 1998 child count data which was designed to "provide more information on the issue of potential minority overrepresentation among children receiving special education services." These data are found in the Twenty-Second Annual Report to Congress on the Implementation of the Individuals with Disabilities Education Act, Appendix A.

Chester was categorized as having a specific learning disability as a matter of school practice and not based on whether he actually had a specific learning disability or whether he had met the criteria for mental retardation. In a 2007 petition to the Supreme Court for certiorari, Chester's special education teacher testified that the Texas, Port Arthur school district "did not classify a child as mentally retarded so long as the child could be managed behaviorally within his home school's special education program" and "it was common for schools to label mentally retarded children 'learning disabled,' both to avoid the stigma of being retarded and to avoid the costs of special programs." The definition of specific learning disabilities explicitly states that a child's specific disabilities cannot be the result of mental retardation but this has never dissuaded schools from using this disability category to classify children no matter the data.

For Chester "the court found that the specifics of the various crimes to which the applicant confessed, including the use of masks and gloves, his practice of cutting exterior phone lines before entering homes to burglarize, and his deliberate targeting of victims like Cheryl DeLeon and his brother-in-law Albert Bolden, showed persuasively that the applicant was capable of forethought, planning, and complex execution of purpose."[166]

The appellate court decided in 2007 that Chester did not show by clear and convincing evidence that he was mentally retarded because "expert testimony stated that Chester could communicate clearly, understood current, topical matters, and understood his current legal situation." The court also found that his "criminal spree demonstrated the ability to plan, avoid detection, and lie." Concerning testimony about his mental retardation, the court decided "that the family had an incentive to lie," the defendant's expert "testimony was not credible" and evidence in general was "unpersuasive."

---

[165]34 CFR § 300.306 Determination of eligibility.
[166]1980 Elementary and Secondary Schools Civil Rights Survey, State Summaries,

Elroy Chester was executed by lethal injection in June of 2013 two days shy of his 44ᵗʰ birthday. The school district probably attempted to meet Chester's learning needs as a child by de-emphasizing stigmatization and possibly even providing a more inclusive education, but this good deed also provided, in part, a definitional basis for denying his Atkins claim because of the specific learning disability label even when there was sufficient data to support a determination of mental retardation.

Michael Dewayne Smith

In Hall the Supreme Court required the consideration of IQ scores of 75 or less but this seemingly absolute cutoff is not as absolute as one might think as shown by Oklahoma's strict interpretation of an IQ cutoff of 75. In Oklahoma the statute for Atkins requires taking into account the standard error of measurement, and recognizes IQ scores of 75 or less as required by the Supreme Court, but "in no event shall a defendant who has received an intelligence quotient of seventy-six (76) or above on any individually administered, scientifically recognized, standardized intelligence quotient test administered by a licensed psychiatrist or psychologist, be considered mentally retarded and, thus, shall not be subject to any proceedings under this section."[167] Florida could have adopted the Oklahoma guideline and summarily rejected Hall's Atkins claim because three of his IQ scores were above 75 while, at least according the defense in March 3, 2014 oral arguments for *Hall*, this would have been constitutional.

The Supreme Court suggested in *Hall* that raising the IQ cutoff to 75 will allow defendants the opportunity to present relevant evidence of intellectual disability. Contrary to this over-simplistic interpretation of IQ cutoff, Oklahoma illustrates how a cutoff of 75 can actually prevent the admission of relevant evidence. In Oklahoma the defendant must first give notice when filing an Atkins claim 90 days before arraignment that contains sufficient

---

[167]Oklahoma Statutes, §21-701.10b, Death sentence prohibited for defendants who were mentally retarded prior to age 18 - Sentencing proceedings

evidence to give a good faith belief of mental retardation. Next, the District Court conducts an evidentiary hearing whereupon the burden is on the defendant to prove mental retardation by clear and convincing evidence. The defendant can request, before sentencing, a jury determination of mental retardation where the burden is on the defendant to prove mental retardation by a preponderance of the evidence. If the jury is not unanimous in deciding that the defendant is mentally retarded, the jury can consider evidence of mental retardation as a mitigating factor. [168] Requiring jury unanimity for a determination of mental retardation seems an overly high standard which would result in the execution of some offenders who would otherwise be identified as having lesser culpability as envisioned by the Supreme Court.

Michael Dewayne Smith, a member of the Oklahoma City "Oak Grove Posse," was sentenced to death in 2003 for the 2002 murders of Janet Moore (reported to be a "snitch") and Sarath "Babu" Pulluru a store clerk who was shot repeatedly during the course of a robbery on the same morning that Moore was murdered. Both Moore and Pulluru were not the intended victims. Smith had one IQ assessment in 2001 before the murder when he was 18 which resulted in a WAIS-R IQ of 76, and two IQ scores, following the murders, of 79 on the WAIS-III in 2003 and 71 on the WAIS-IV in 2009.[169] Because Smith did not raise an Atkins claim at trial or for post-conviction relief, his application was not "timely" which he attributed to ineffective counsel.

A bright-line to dismiss an Atkins claim if "any" score is above 75 is contrary to the *Ford* mandate that the task should be to admit all relevant evidence. If a defendant had ten scores below 75 and one above 75, rejecting an Atkins claim because of this finding would hardly be a fair consideration of all the evidence. An average score could be used or somehow weighting scores in terms of importance. For example, an IQ score at age 7 might be far more relevant than a score obtained as part of an Atkins claim. In most situations, nothing is more relevant than a determination

---

[168]*Ibid.*
[169]See CR 8; 281 P.3d 1283; 2012 Okla.

of IQ as a child, yet a bright-line of "any" score above 75, or any determination involving IQ which limits an Atkins claim, is contrary to the ADA and common sense. If a defendant was brain-injured after age of onset, or dementia coupled with an iffy cognitive history, might make a childhood IQ completely irrelevant and an adult IQ score of utmost importance. There are many reasons why IQ scores would decrease over time which including mental illness, dementia, brain-injury, time in isolation, etc. To this extent extricating the motivation to perform well on an IQ test might be impossible to understand or take into account.

The Oklahoma Court of Criminal Appeals of Oklahoma (OCCA) dismissed Smith's Atkins claim because it "fails under the express language" of the Oklahoma Statute by the fact that two scores were 76 or above.[170] More specifically, the OCCA held the 76 cutoff was not subject to adjustment for the SEM because "the Legislature has implicitly determined that any scores of 76 or above are in a range whose lower error-adjusted limit will always be above the threshold score of 70."   Smith's counsel was not dissuaded and attempted to show that IQ scores of 76 and 79 might actually be lower.

When IQ scores were adjusted downward for the so-called "Flynn effect" (by lowing an IQ score by .3 points for every year since the test was standardized) Smith's scores were actually in the 64 to 79 range. This concept is based on the assumption that as a result of a conglomeration of studies involving many different tests, standardized at different times, a .3 IQ decrease per year applies to all individuals over a period time. This also assumes that over that same period of time an individual (and more importantly, the standardization group) would make no cognitive gains. In addition, the Flynn effect also ignores the fact that IQ refers to the normal curve. How adjusting scores would apply to prisoners, much less Atkins claimants is anybody's guess. The OCCA dismissed the downward adjustment of scores because "the Flynn Effect, whatever its validity, is not a relevant consideration in the mental retardation determination for capital defendants."

---

[170]Smith v. Oklahoma, CR 24; 245 P.3d 1233 (2010)

In the end, for Smith who is black, one IQ point, as trivial as it is, might well be the difference between life and death. Smith is currently on death row and his prospects are not promising. Oklahoma voters approved a measure that prevents State courts from declaring the death penalty cruel and unusual punishment within the framework of the U.S. Constitution. The measure was approved by a 66.4 percent majority in November of 2016 (State Question 776). Oklahoma voters seem to support the death penalty, and the IQ cutoff for Atkins claims is rigid, the State has not had an execution since that of Charles Frederick Warner on January 1, 2015 for the rape and murder of an 11 month old baby. The delay in executions has also been enhanced by the difficulty involved in obtaining drugs for lethal injection and the proposed (March, 2018) use of nitrogen gas for executions. Alternatives to lethal injection have also included re-introducing the electric chair (Tennessee) and firing squads (Utah).

Juan Lizcano

The EMR/mild mental retardation/mild intellectual disability does serve a purpose and that purpose is not necessarily in the best interests of either a child or an Atkins claimant. For a child, especially a black child, the mild intellectual disability category exonerates school and society from all sins associated with segregation and discrimination, before and after *Brown*, and explains poor educational performance as something entirely within the child. For an Atkins claimant intellectual disability provides an opportunity for courts to wallow in the Eighth Amendment and the "dignity of man" while giving lip service to the complex history of the purpose guidelines for determining intellectual disability. An IQ score is often a major factor when determining whether or not a child or an adult has an intellectual disability. For a black child the racial problems associated with IQ are legion but often ignored. On the other hand, for adults, factors that might have depressed an IQ score as a child are disingenuously embraced.

An Atkins defense can attempt to show that out of date norms (viz., the "Flynn effect") requires that IQ scores should be adjusted downward; a prosecutor can just as easily suggest that an IQ of 62 should be adjusted upward. Juan Lizcano was convicted in 2005 for the murder of police officer Brian Jackson and was sentenced to death in 2007. The Texas Court of Criminal Appeals, in 2010, decided he met the first prong of the definition of mental retardation, but then decided that "the jury's conclusion that the appellant was not mentally retarded is not so against the great weight and preponderance of the evidence as to be manifestly unjust."[171] In 2011 the Supreme Court denied his certiorari petition. What is interesting about Lizcano's Atkins claim is the approach by Texas to adjust his relatively low IQ scores upward.

Various testings for Lizcano revealed scores of 62, 60, 48, 69, and 53. The State suggested that because Hispanics score approximately 7.5 (one-half a standard deviation) below whites, adding 7.5 points to each score would raise his actual scores substantially to 69.5, 67.5, 55.5, 76.5, and 60.5. The math used by the Texas Court of Criminal Appeals 2010 decision is not always clear, but the point is that by adjusting the scores upward by 7.5 points, the cultural bias in IQ tests is diminished. In addition, in a twist for how the SEM of five points is used, the prosecution also believed that five additional points should be added to scores thereby raising the scores to 74.5, 72.5, 60.5, 81.5, and 65.5. The court disregarded this upward interpretation of scores, and the peculiar use of the SEM, and decided that he met the first prong of the definition. However, the strengths in his adaptive behavior cited by the prosecution included Lizcano's ability to make weekly car payments, knowing how many hours he worked, and that he "kept a neat and orderly cell and did not have any problems with his hygiene."[172] Juan Lizcano was not classified as mentally retarded as a child but his environmental and educational circumstances were less than ideal. His sixth grade teacher reported the "primitive nature" of his school environment, his very slow learning in comparison to others, and that he "graduated" from the sixth grade at age 15. As of March 27, 2019

---

[171]Juan Lizcano v. The State of Texas, Court of Criminal Appeals of Texas, AP-75,879, May 5, 2010.

[172]Lizcano v. State of Texas, Court of Criminal Appeals of Texas, Appeal from Case F05-59563-QS of the 282nd Judicial District Court of Dallas County, May 5, 2010

Lizcano remains on death row. However, in March of 2019 the Dallas News[173] reported Dallas County district attorney stated that he thought Lizcano's death sentenced should be reduced to life in prison because of problems of how Texas determines intellectual disability as articulated by the Supreme Court (see Moore v. Texas[174]).

For black claimants an upward adjustment of IQ would virtually eliminate all Atkins claims. Research, such as it is, has shown that black test takers score approximately one standard deviation (15 points) lower than white test takers on IQ. In Arthur Jensen's much cited article relating to race and intelligence he stated that "The basic data are well known: on average, Negroes test about 1 standard deviation (15 IQ points) below the average of the white population in IQ, and this finding is fairly uniform across the 81 different tests of intellectual ability…".[175] Considering *de jure* and *de facto* segregation, environment, educational opportunity and socio-economic factors, the difference between black and white IQ scores is not surprising.

An upward adjustment of a score of 61 would result in an adjusted score above the now sanctioned IQ cutoff of 76. In essence this could increase the cutoff of 70 to 85 (the 1959 IQ cutoff) or from 75 to 90. Adjusting the IQ scores of black Atkins claimants would deny the essential character of the ADA and previous State actions, based on race, to classify a child as having an intellectual disability. All of this might come under the category of *apologetic racism* so that past racial misdeeds are recognized but, for the sake of the Eighth Amendment no less, these past decisions that resulted in stigmatization, segregation and denial of educational opportunity, are deemed incorrect with the realization that IQ is but a score on a test and subject to cultural bias. When execution

---

[173]https://www.dallasnews.com/news/crime/2019/03/19/intellectually-disabled-man-murdered-dallas-cop-shouldnt-executed-da-says-juan-lizcano-brian-jackson-john-creuzot-craig-watkins
[174]Moore v. Texas, Supreme Court of the United States, March 28, 2017
[175]Arthur R. Jensen, How Much Can We Boost IQ and Scholastic Achievement? *Harvard Educational Review,* Vol. 39, No. 1, Winter 1969, pages 1-123.

is at stake, the racism of IQ testing is readily acknowledged; for children, just as readily ignored.

When making a decision to place a child in special education, even though cultural factors should be taken into account, IQ scores are often prioritized. A State stigmatizes a child, denies the child educational opportunity and provides an inferior education, and then asserts many years later that this needs to be taken into the context of providing necessary services and not as an indication of real intellectual disability. Paradoxically, the Eighth Amendment is not used to prevent cruel and unusual punishment but to feign allegiance to a strict interpretation of IQ, adaptive behavior and age of onset that can then be used to avoid the Supreme Court's 2002 "narrowing jurisprudence, which seeks to ensure that only the most deserving of execution are put to death, an exclusion for the mentally retarded is appropriate."

When making a decision to place a child in special education, even though cultural factors should be taken into account, IQ scores are often prioritized. A State stigmatizes a child, denies the child educational opportunity and provides an inferior education, and then asserts many years later that all of this was a mistake. Paradoxically, the Eighth Amendment is not used to prevent cruel and unusual punishment but to feign allegiance to a strict interpretation of IQ, adaptive behavior and age of onset that can then be used to avoid the Supreme Court's 2002 "narrowing jurisprudence, which seeks to ensure that only the most deserving of execution are put to death, an exclusion for the mentally retarded is appropriate."

The dangers associated with changing scores, either by lowering or raising scores, are several. First, the idea that there are "IQ points" which have some inherent meaning, so that adding or subtracting points somehow indicates less or more intelligence, is a fiction. The scores generated by IQ tests, certainly for recognized individualized standardized tests, as previously discussed, represent the degree to which a raw score deviates from the mean score with reference to the standard deviation and the normal curve. Second, the Code of Fair Testing Practices (2004)[176] States that test users should "follow established procedures for administering tests in a standardized manner." This concept seems to have escaped those who wish to lower a standardized IQ score based on when the test was standardized.

If a score is changed following a nonstandardized protocol, the result is no longer a "standardized score." Exactly what an adjusted IQ score means is difficult to say, but the score no longer indicates the number of standard deviations a score is above or below the mean based on the specific test used and the underlying standardization sample. This does not mean factors that limit the interpretation of test results (such as when a test was standardized) should not be taken into account. The Code cautions test users to "Interpret the meaning of the test results, taking into account the nature of the content, norms or comparison groups, other technical evidence, and benefits and limitations of test results."

Willie James Hodges

In 2001, Willie James Hodges, black, murdered Patricia Belanger (and was a suspect in two other murders in Alabama and Ohio) in Pensacola, Florida. The jury recommended death by a vote of 10 to 2 in March of 2008.[177] Hodges was given the Wechsler Intelligence Scale for Children (WISC) in fifth and seventh grades and received scores of 66, was in special education, and dropped out of school in the eighth grade. This evidence, his record of mental retardation and the very probative IQ of 66 in elementary school, should have been sufficient to substantiate an Atkins claim.

As an adult, Hodges received an IQ score of 62 and scores of 69 and 65 by the State's expert. One explanation for the low IQ scores was not inaccuracy but "research" showing that black test takers score lower than whites because of cultural factors. This

---

[176]The Code of Fair Test Practices was developed by a joint committee which included the American Educational Research Association, the American Psychological Association (APA), and the National Association of School Psychologists.
[177]Hodges v. State of Florida, Supreme Court of Florida, No. SC09-468, December 2, 2010

was not used to reject IQ scores entirely but to explain why someone might have been determined to have mental retardation as a child and to call attention to the importance of proving deficits in adaptive behavior as an adult. The Supreme Court of Florida decided that because Hodges "could follow the track of thinking in questions, clearly respond to the questions, provide additional information if he thought his answers to the specific question was not adequate to get his point across. He very clearly comprehended everything that was going on in this proceeding and behaved in a most appropriate and responsive fashion." What the Supreme Court of Florida did, as other States have done, was to create a new definition of intellectual disability based on a subjective analysis of behavior that transcended the professional definition. How did the Supreme Court of Florida determine that "he very clearly comprehended everything"? Whatever the court did, it was more relevant than IQ scores, the definitional elements of adaptive behavior, and a previous determination of mental retardation by a Florida school district as a child (assuming that is why Hodges was in special education).

The Florida Supreme Court agreed with the trial court in 2010 "that rather than clearly and convincingly showing deficits in adaptive functioning, the totality of the evidence established that Hodges had 'virtually no deficits in adaptive behavior'." The court concluded that Hodges had proved the subaverage intellectual functioning prong of the definition by clear and convincing evidence but not the adaptive functioning prong. The relief brought by the new 75 cutoff sanctioned by the Supreme Court will not help Hodges. The Supreme Court of Florida acknowledged that he met the intellectual functioning (IQ) prong of the definition and, for that matter, his scores could have been below 50 but IQ was irrelevant. An even more important tactic used by Florida was to not consider a previous determination of mental retardation because the second prong (deficits in adaptive behavior) had not been met as an adult. At the time when Hodges was a child, in about 1971, the professional definition of mental retardation required an IQ score below 85 and not 70 and deficits in adaptive e behavior. Hodges IQ was almost 20 points below this standard and there seems little doubt that mental retardation would have been the disability identified to receive special education services.

Hodges was sentenced to death in 2008 and the Supreme Court mandated that the jury and not the trial court must decide the aggravating factors. Because the vote for death was 10 to 2 the Florida Supreme Court decided that this "Ring error" was not harmless and upheld his conviction (and rejected all of his claims relating to effectiveness of counsel, DNA evidence, etc) but remanded for a new death penalty phase.[178]

George Ochoa

The most probative IQ scores are those obtained before the capital crime, and even more importantly, as a child when malingering is less likely. Oklahoma has decided that the most relevant facts are those showing mental retardation at the time of murder and that a defendant who is determined not to be mentally retarded at the time of the murder (or maybe trial) was never actually mentally retarded in the first place. The good news for a defendant previously identified as intellectually disabled is that his/her intellectual disability is no more; the bad news is that this State anointed intellectual wholeness will result in execution.

In 1993 George Ochoa and an accomplice burglarized the home of Francisco Morales and his wife in Oklahoma City, Oklahoma. During the course of the burglary Morales and his wife were shot repeatedly and both died. Ochoa was sentenced to death in 1996. In 2005 a jury decided that Ochoa did not prove that he was mentally retarded by a preponderance of the evidence. Ochoa's defense strategy rested on the claim that mental retardation was a "fluid concept" and that an Atkins claimant could outgrow mental retardation. Thus, he could have been mentally retarded at the time of the murders but not at the time of the trial in 1996 when his IQ scores were somewhat higher. The Oklahoma Court of

---

[178]Hodges v. Florida, Supreme Court of Florida, No. SC14-878, March 16, 2017, http://www.floridasupremecourt.org/decisions/2017/sc14-878.pdf

Criminal Appeals countered with an even more novel theory that Ochoa's ability to read and write was evidence that he was not really retarded because "while we do not dispute that a mentally retarded person can learn and develop skills, that ability is limited and the ability to learn and to adaptively function suggests the individual was likely not mentally retarded in the first place but fell into that borderline range or classification due to environmental or other factors which affected present ability."[179]

Age of onset is not a complicated concept. The idea is that showing intellectual disability before age 18 is useful for making a determination of intellectual disability—but this should not exclude Atkins relief for someone meeting the two primary criteria for intellectual disability after age 18. Oklahoma managed to complicate age of onset by conceptualizing a pseudo-scientific theory which was referred to as a Temporal Focus of Mental Retardation Determination. This intriguing idea necessitated a finding that the defendant "is" mentally retarded at the time of trial, as opposed to whether he "was" mentally retarded at the time of the murder. The Oklahoma court reasoned that the "ability to learn" indicates someone who was classified as having mental retardation but who was not really mentally retarded at all.[180]

The United States Court of Appeals, in 2012 concluded, that "mental retardation is a static condition—and that those who at the time of the mental retardation trial are not mentally retarded, never were mentally retarded." [181] In Oklahoma, a "record" of a disability does not apply nor does the ADA. For all those children who were tested and placed in special education classes because of mental retardation, and who later sought Atkins relief, would come to learn, following an unsuccessful Atkins claim, that they never were mentally retarded. If a determination that a defendant was not really mentally retarded as a child but provided an educational program and segregated placement commensurate with someone who was mentally retarded, the effects of this State

---

[179]Ochoa v. Workman, United States Court of Appeals, 10th District, January 18, 2012
[180]*Ibid.*
[181]Ochoa v. Oklahoma, 136 P.3d 661 (2006) and Ochoa v. Workman, United States Court of Appeals, 10th District, January 18, 2012

action, no matter the intended benevolence, should not be undone by the State when the defendant is an adult. This was not so for George Ochoa. His request for a term of life in prison was rejected by the Oklahoma Pardon and Parole Board in November of 2012 and in December he was executed by lethal injection.

Walter Alexander Sorto

A useful technique by States for dismissing Atkins claims is to suppress potentially relevant data by declaring that there is not a "reasonable likelihood" that a claim of intellectual disability will be successful. What the Supreme Court did not consider was the often peculiar nature of evidence (and the various courts as well). Not only is there IQ and adaptive behavior data, but there is the question of what exactly is "threshold" data, when the data was presented, what court the data were presented to, whether there is a "reasonable" or "substantial" need for additional data gathering, and whether the evidence was exhausted or unexhausted. Even though an IQ might indicate intellectual disability, a higher court might not consider this data because of limitations as to what the court could review. In many States procedure is more important than a fair determination of intellectual disability.

 Walter Alexander Sorto was sentenced to death in 2003 for the 2002 murder of Maria Rangel, age 38, and Roxana Capulin, age 24, in Houston, Texas. Edgardo Rafael Cubas was also sentenced to death in conjunction with these (and other) murders. Eduardo Navarro, a 15 year-old juvenile, received a 13 year sentence in 2004 for his participation as the getaway driver for Sorto and Cubas.

Sorto had an IQ of 66 on the Test of Nonverbal Intelligence which would indicate at least a threshold level of mental retardation. However, Texas law seems to place emphasis on full scale IQ scores. According to the appellate court "the state denied Sorto the resources necessary to obtain full-scale IQ testing and then refused to review his claim on the merits because he had not obtained a full-scale IQ score." In 2013 the district granted funds for IQ testing which revealed a score of 63 on the WAIS-III in 2013, and childhood deficits in adaptive behavior. A clinical psychologist found that his IQ test scores indicated mental retardation. The Texas court of criminal appeals did not and offered that Sorto "'failed to make a threshold presentation of evidence that, if true, is sufficient to show that no rational factfinder would fail to find that he is mentally retarded.'" Exactly why funding was provided for addition testing by the District Court is not clear in that these data were not considered because the court "could only review the record that was presented to the state court and thus was constrained 'from considering the results of Dr. Martinez's testing,' even though those results constituted 'compelling' evidence of intellectual disability." Even more unusual, additional funding to assess Sorto's adaptive behavior could not be given because this would only result in more data that could not be considered. Much of the argument centers about whether Sorto's evidence was exhausted which would leave most completely exhausted.[182]

The United States Court of Appeals believed that the evidence presented by Sorto was "significantly different and stronger evidentiary posture than the claim presented before the state court" and his claim was therefore "unexhausted" and the exhaustion requirement excused.[183] The Court of Appeals vacated "dismissal of Sorto's Atkins claim so that the District Court can reevaluate the claim taking into account the excusal of the exhaustion requirement and any additional evidence Sorto may present if further funding is granted." In 2018 this opinion was withdrawn upon appeal by the director of the Texas Department of Criminal Justice. In March of 2018[184] the case was remanded to the District Court in light of the Supreme Court's ruling that the legal standard for necessary funding for investigative purposes should be "reasonable" and "not substantial."[185] Sorto remains on death as of December, 2019.

---

[182]More about exhaustion of remedies at 28 U.S. Code § 2254 - State custody; remedies in Federal courts
[183]*Ibid.*
[184]Sorto v. Davis, 881 F.3d 933 (5th Cir. 2018)
[185]Ayestas v. Davis, 584 U. S. ___ (2018)

4. Proof and Consequences

"The accused, during a criminal prosecution, has at stake interests of immense importance..."[186]

Warren Lee Hill: two kinds of error

Warren Hill was serving a life sentence for the unprovoked murder of his girlfriend Myra Wright in 1985. In 1990 he beat a sleeping inmate, Joseph Handspike, to death with a nail-studded 2x6 board at the Lee Correctional Institution (Lee State Prison) in Leesburg, Georgia. Hill had no last words and, following a prayer, was executed on January 27, 2015 at 7:55 p.m. Hill's claim of mental retardation was sometimes persuasive and, in the final analysis, not.

In 1997 a Georgia Superior Court believed there was sufficient evidence to warrant a determination of mental retardation for Hill. In May of 2002 an evidentiary hearing by the Georgia Superior Court found that he did not prove mental retardation. In November of 2002, following *Atkins* 2002, the Superior Court vacated its decision so that Hill's mental retardation could be determined by the *preponderance of the evidence* standard.

In 2002 the Georgia court decided that Hill met the first prong of the definition of mental retardation, but not the second. His IQ scores were between 72 and 77 (later adjusted to 70 and 74), and a score of 74 on the Peabody Picture Vocabulary Test in the second grade. The defense for Hill provided a weak case for deficits in adaptive behavior and a showing of mental retardation during childhood which was confounded by a lack of academic performance and placement information. Whether Hill's schooling was in a completely segregated school, and the type of services provided or available, was never considered. In the 1960s, when Hill attended school, segregation was thriving in Georgia long after the 1954 Brown decision. As a matter of fact, in a 2007 report, 35 school districts in Georgia were declared unitary

---

[186]In re Winship, 397 U.S. 358 (1970)

and 74 districts were under court jurisdiction.[187] The Hart County School District cited in the District Court's 2007 Hill decision had yet to be declared unitary and had been under court order since 1969.[188]

Hill's defense "abandoned their efforts to obtain certain school records after making repeated requests when they were informed that no further records existed." This oversight and "newly discovered records" would not have changed the outcome and "would have been merely cumulative of other evidence of Hill's mental slowness, including the testimony of his psychiatrist, and, therefore, trial counsel's failure to obtain the additional records did not result in prejudice to Hill."[189] Because of his work history, military background, social life, "weak but sufficient writing skills", etc., Hill did not meet the impairment in adaptive behavior prong of the definition *beyond a reasonable doubt.*

The importance of avoiding cruel and unusual punishment is highlighted by the Supreme Court's belief that there is "no legitimate penological purpose is served by executing a person with intellectual disability" and "to do so contravenes the Eighth Amendment, for to impose the harshest of punishments on an intellectually disabled person violates his or her inherent dignity as a human being." This suggests that the Court would endeavor to err on the side of not executing someone who was incorrectly identified as having an intellectual disability rather than incorrectly executing an offender was truly intellectually disabled.

In 2010 a three-judge panel for the Court of Appeals explained that "Georgia holds that it is far better to erroneously execute a mentally retarded person than to erroneously impose a life sentence on one not mentally retarded."[190] The appellate court

---

[187]Georgia Advisory Committee to the United States Commission on Civil Rights, 2007
[188]Hill v. Hall, CIVIL United States District Court for the Middle District of Georgia, ACTION NO.: 1:04-CV-151 (WLS), 2007
[189]Hill v. Hall, United States District Court for the Middle District of Georgia, ACTION NO.: 1:04-CV-151 (WLS), 2007
[190]Hill v. Schofield, United States Court of Appeals for the Eleventh Circuit, June 18, 2010

panel decided that "The reasoning of the Georgia Supreme Court is contrary to the command of Atkins because the reasonable doubt standard, as applied to claims of mental retardation, necessarily will result in the deaths of mentally retarded individuals." This panel reasoned that "plainly, that standard is not an 'appropriate way' to vindicate a mentally retarded offender's constitutional right not to be put to death."[191] The panel noted "that the reasonable doubt standard ensures the execution of individuals who are nonetheless part of the national consensus" (of individuals who fall within the class of those identified as intellectually disabled which include, profound, severe, moderate and profound intellectual disabilities).

The decision by the appellate panel was not the final decision. In 2011 the entire Court of Appeals disagreed with the panel and decided that the *beyond a reasonable doubt* standard was constitutional as mandated by the Antiterrorism and Effective Death Penalty Act of 1996 and required the Georgia appellate court to "leave the Georgia Supreme Court decision alone -- even if the federal court believed it incorrect or unwise."[192] The full appellate court decided otherwise in 2011 and concluded that Hill was no longer mentally retarded or at least not sufficiently mentally retarded not to be executed.[193] His petition to the Supreme Court was denied on October 7, 2013. In Georgia, Hill was mentally retarded by the *preponderance of the evidence*, probably not mentally retarded by a *clear and convincing standard*, and not mentally retarded by a *beyond a reasonable doubt standard.*

Atkins in 2002 and *Hall* in 2014 underscore the importance of the Eighth Amendment and why the Constitution is offended when a person with an intellectual disability is executed. The heightened standard used by Georgia confuses the consequence of wrongful conviction in death penalty cases, where the State must prove guilt, and proving mental retardation by the same heightened standard. Wrongful conviction resulting in execution is a more

---

[191]Hill v. Schofield, United States Court of Appeals for the Eleventh Circuit, June 18, 2010
[192]Hill v. Humphrey, 662 F.3d 1335 (2011)
[193]Hill v. Humphrey, 662 F.3d 1335 (2011)

serious consequence (by most but certainly not all) than allowing someone who is guilty to go free, at least if the sanctity of life is a real consideration. In Atkins claims the consequence should dictate the burden of proof standard. If failure to prove intellectual disability can result in execution, the burden of proof standard should be a preponderance of the evidence so that the importance of life rather than execution is the primary consideration.

Applying Georgia's standard of proof, assuming that an IQ cutoff of 75 applies to a *preponderance of the evidence* standard, *clear and convincing evidence* standard would seem to apply to a cutoff of 70, and *beyond a reasonable doubt* standard to something below 70. In short, a more stringent evidentiary standard to determine intellectual disability compromises the purpose underlying a cutoff score of 75. That is, if the *beyond a reasonable standard* is constitutional to prove an intellectual disability, a cutoff of 75 using the *beyond a reasonable doubt* standard must somehow be different than when using a cutoff of 75 and a *preponderance of the evidence* standard. Somewhere in this mix of standards and cutoffs human dignity dwells.

For criminal cases the error to be avoided is the conviction of an innocent person. When a standard other than a *preponderance of evidence* is used in Atkins claims, the consequence of the burden of proof is ignored. The underlying rationale for the high burden of proof in criminal cases is the consequence of wrongful conviction. The same reasoning should be used in Atkins claims; that is, the error to be avoided is incorrectly determining that an intellectually disabled defendant does not warrant lesser culpability (given the null hypothesis that the defendant is not intellectually disabled).

Statistical terminology, when applied to legal matters, is more suggestive than definitive, but can provide some insight into the underlying logic of confidence levels and burden of proof, especially when applied to Atkins claims. In contrast to the supposed immutable character of statistics, a statistical analysis involves *samples* and *sample sizes* while, in the judicial, world of guilt and innocence the only relevant sample is the defendant. The reasoning in Atkins claims is the opposite of that in determining guilt and sentencing for capital murder. Because a defendant is presumed not to be intellectually disabled (the "null hypothesis"), the defendant must prove intellectual disability (by varying standards of proof, depending on the State).

The terminology for statistical decisions is often phrased in terms of Type I and Type II errors. A Type I error occurs when an innocent defendant is found guilty and the null hypothesis of innocence is rejected. A Type I error is also referred to as a **false positive** when the verdict is positive and guilt is incorrectly found. A Type II error occurs when a guilty defendant is found innocent; that is, the defendant is found innocent (a negative determination) when the defendant is actually guilty (**false negative**). Because the first type of error is considered more serious in criminal cases (by the Supreme Court[194]), the State must prove that a defendant is guilty by a high standard (although "high" can be variously interpreted). The essential task of avoiding Type I errors in criminal cases comports with the understanding that convicting an innocent defendant of capital murder is a more serious consequence (depriving a defendant of life and liberty) than finding a guilty defendant innocent. The following table shows the relationship between error and the "truth." Because the "truth" may never be known, the type of error committed is always a matter of probability.

The "truth"	Consequence	
	Acquittal	Guilty
Defendant is Innocent	Correct Decision	Type I Error
Defendant is Guilty	Type II Error	Correct Decision

For an Atkins claim a Type I error is finding the claimant who is not intellectually disabled (which is the presumption) to be intellectually disabled. This is tantamount to rejecting the null hypothesis that the defendant is not intellectually disabled when incorrectly concluding that the defendant is. In a death penalty trial a Type I error is finding an innocent person (the presumption) guilty; in an Atkins claim a Type I error is incorrectly finding someone intellectually disabled (the

---

[194]In re Winship 397 U.S. 358 (1970)

presumption) who is not. The consequences for incorrectly rejecting innocence (Type I error) in death penalty cases (which can result in execution) and incorrectly rejecting a claim of intellectual disability (accepting the null hypothesis when incorrect or Type II error) are completely opposite.

In guilt/innocence decision making incorrectly convicting an innocent person should be avoided and thus not incorrectly deprive someone of life and liberty; likewise, incorrectly finding a person not intellectually disabled should be avoided for exactly the same reason that the result (consequence) can be execution. The consequence of an incorrect decision should dictate the appropriate burden of proof. For criminal liability the burden of proof is *beyond a reasonable doubt*; for Atkins claim, to avoid the execution of someone who is intellectually disabled, the burden of proof should be a *preponderance of the evidence* standard. Using the lower standard of proof for Atkins claims will increase the likelihood that someone with an intellectual disability will not be executed. As shown below for Atkins claims the focus and consequence of a Type II error is of primary importance because the result can be execution.

The "truth"	Atkins Claim	
	Unsuccessful	**Successful**
No Intellectual Disability	Correct Decision	Type I Error
Intellectual Disability	Type II Error	Correct Decision

The type of error committed can be controlled, to some extent, by the confidence level for statistical decision making and the standard of proof for criminal liability. For statistical decision making a researcher might select the 95 percent confidence level so that the correct decision will be made 95 percent of the time (more or less). A more demanding standard could be used such as the 99 percent confidence level or even the 99.9 percent confidence level. Increasing the statistical criterion from 95 percent to 99 percent (increasing the IQ cutoff value) in Atkins claims will increase the likelihood of a Type I error, and more who are not intellectually disabled will be so determined, but also increase the task for proving intellectual disability.[195] If the 70 rather than 75 IQ cutoff is used, more persons with an intellectual disability will be denied relief.

The analogy between statistical and judicial decision is limited. The *preponderance* standard means more than 50 percent but exactly how much more, or more importantly, how a court or jury conceptualizes **how much more** is less than clear. Attaching a numerical value to beyond a reasonable doubt is even more problematic. In theory the probability for a correct decision in criminal cases should be quite high...maybe 90 percent, more likely 95 percent, or even 99 percent. The problem is how these numerical values are conceptualized by judge, jury and lawyers. Courts are likely to suggest a qualitative rather than quantitative approach as was done by the Massachusetts Supreme Judicial Court when requiring the following instruction:[196]

> **The burden is on the Commonwealth to prove beyond a reasonable doubt that the defendant is guilty of the charge(s) made against him (her).**
>
> **What is proof beyond a reasonable doubt? The term is often used and probably pretty well understood, though it is not easily defined. Proof beyond a reasonable doubt does not mean proof beyond all possible doubt, for everything in the lives of human beings is open to some possible or imaginary doubt. A charge is proved beyond a reasonable doubt if, after you have compared and considered all of the evidence, you have in your minds an abiding conviction, to a moral certainty, that the charge is true. When we refer to moral certainty, we mean the highest degree of certainty possible**

---

[195]As a side note discussions for reducing Type II errors often speak of "increasing sample size" which simply emphasizes the primary difference between statistics and death penalty jurisprudence: statistics is about sampling; the death penalty is about individualization.-
[196]Commonwealth v. Gerald Russell, 470 Mass. 464, Supreme Judicial Court of Massachusetts, Essex, January 26, 2015

in matters relating to human affairs -- based solely on the evidence that has been put before you in this case.

I have told you that every person is presumed to be innocent until he or she is proved guilty, and that the burden of proof is on the prosecutor. If you evaluate all the evidence and you still have a reasonable doubt remaining, the defendant is entitled to the benefit of that doubt and must be acquitted. It is not enough for the Commonwealth to establish a probability, even a strong probability, that the defendant is more likely to be guilty than not guilty. That is not enough. Instead, the evidence must convince you of the defendant's guilt to a reasonable and moral certainty; a certainty that convinces your understanding and satisfies your reason and judgment as jurors who are sworn to act conscientiously on the evidence.

This is what we mean by proof beyond a reasonable doubt.

For Massachusetts Supreme Judicial Court not "even a strong probability" is sufficient for a guilty verdict. In statistics the touchstone is a *significant* probability such as the 95 percent confidence level but the problem is the difficult task of equating something more than a "strong probability" with a significant probability. For criminal liability the standard is beyond a reasonable doubt; that is, a jury must be extremely confident, confident to a moral certainty that a defendant is guilty. Of course, the only way to ensure that an innocent defendant will not be found guilty is to set the probability error at 100 percent which would result in no defendant ever being convicted and thus no real need for judges, lawyers or juries.

Statistical analogies only go so far as is the case when attempting to define the standard of proof as a probability. The *preponderance of the evidence* standard requires something more than 50 percent, but 50 percent of what is vague. The ability for a juror or jury to actually calculate a metric for evidence is unlikely. One juror might conceptualize the *preponderance* standard as more than 50 percent of the evidence, a second juror might believe that the percent refers to 65 percent confidence, and a third might make a decision totally unrelated to court instructions, much less confidence levels.

The *preponderance* standard is difficult to define, as are the higher standards. At the other end of the burden of proof continuum the *beyond a reasonable doubt* standard is certainly much higher than 50 percent but not 100 percent. A probability of 95 percent is often mentioned but this precision is troubled by interpretation shrouded in quantification. Given this standard, no matter the evidence, a juror might truly believe, beyond a "moral certainty" that the defendant is guilty, and another juror might believe, in spite of overwhelming evidence to the contrary, that the defendant is innocent. Statistics are about sampling and sample sizes and does not apply directly to burden of proof albeit often implied or implicitly believed in some unknown way by court or jury. Even if a court declared that *beyond a reasonable doubt* required 95 percent certainty, the meaning of 95 percent might be far different for two if not all jurors (and judges).

For Atkins claims the question is not how to interpret the *beyond a reasonable doubt* standard but why this standard is inappropriate when a defendant must prove intellectual disability. If a defendant must prove *beyond a reasonable doubt* that he is intellectually disabled, there is a greater likelihood that he will be executed than if the *preponderance of the evidence* standard were used. Consider the problem faced by courts when interpreting IQ. Applying a decision-making error analysis to IQ, to be even more certain that an IQ score is truly indicative of intellectual disability, one could select a cutoff of 60 (and then apply the margin of error). Even in this case absolutely nothing is certain, as shown by Daryl Atkins IQ of 59, and a determination that he was not mentally retarded. No matter the various justifications of the *beyond a reasonable doubt*, a heightened burden of proof in Atkins claims required to prove intellectual disability is incompatible with the rationale given by the Supreme Court for an IQ cutoff of 75; that is, the Atkins mandate is not to execute the intellectually disabled, increasing the likelihood of executing a defendant who is actually intellectually disabled, is contrary to the underlying principle in Atkins.

For Warren Lee Hill, the United State Court of Appeals for the Eleventh Circuit recognized that "Two kinds of fact determination risks are possible when an offender alleges that he is mentally retarded. The first is that the trier of fact will conclude that the offender is mentally retarded when, in fact, he is not." As previously discussed, this is a Type I error when the correct presumption (or null hypothesis) is rejected and the defendant is incorrectly identified as mentally retarded (i.e., a false positive). The reason why a defendant must prove intellectual disability is because the assumption is that a defendant is not intellectually disabled just as an assumption is made that a defendant is innocent.

The court then explained that the second type of error occurs when "the trier of fact will conclude that the offender is not mentally retarded when, in fact, he is"[197] This is a Type II error. The court correctly recognized the problem of types of error but not the ultimate question. The court reasoned that even a less strict standard, such as preponderance of evidence, will not erase all risk that a mentally retarded person will be wrongly executed. Following this reasoning, because a less strict standard can result in a violation of *Atkins*, every standard of proof is suspect. The logic of here is that the creation of a standard even "beyond" a *beyond a reasonable doubt* would be permissible even though this standard would ensure that most Atkins claims would fail.

The primary concern is which error is to be avoided in Atkins claims: the execution of an offender who is truly (or at least as determined following accepted practice) deserves lesser culpability because of an intellectual disability, or giving life to an offender who is incorrectly identified as intellectually disabled. The preponderance of the evidence standard gives preference to

---

[197]Hill v. Humphrey, 662 F.3d 1335 (2011)

avoiding wrongful execution of someone who is intellectually disabled, while the *beyond a reasonable* and *clear and convincing* standards lean more to the permissibility of execution of someone who is really intellectually disabled.

Georgia met the constitutional obligation banning the execution of the mentally retarded—Georgia abolished the death penalty for the mentally retarded well before *Atkins* in 1988—by providing an Atkins claimant with a variety of safeguards, including "a full and fair plenary trial on his mental retardation claim, as part of the guilt phase of his capital trial," the ability to present evidence, employ experts, to cross-examine State experts, and "to appeal any adverse mental retardation determination." Assuming that there is an actual distinction between the *preponderance of the evidence* and *beyond a reasonable doubt* standard among the various States (considering the possibility that a judge or jury will do whatever it intends to do no matter the standard), an intellectually impaired defendant is more likely to be executed in Georgia than in other States—no matter the list of safeguards or when the safeguards were implemented.

Most troubling about the Warren Hill decision, aside from his execution, is the frequent doing and the undoing of mental retardation/intellectual disability. Warren Hill's mental retardation was acknowledged but denied, then reconsidered but ultimately denied by a habeas court, affirmed by a District Court, then reinstated by a three-judge appellate panel, only to have his mental retardation undone by a decision by the entire appellate court. Not only was the ultimate fact of Hill's mental retardation determined by several courts, these same courts created a clear record of mental retardation. The Americans with Disabilities Act makes no distinction between intellectual disability by a *preponderance of the evidence* and intellectual disability *beyond a reasonable doubt*. There is only a disability that meets the three prongs of the widely accepted professional definitions of intellectual disability and, for purposes of the ADA, someone who has a record of intellectual disability.

One last note about types of error as this relates to the determination intellectual disability for children. For children the type of error analysis is not necessarily the same as for adults. In that the consequence of a finding of intellectual disability for a child can be devastating most would consider the first type of error more serious; that is the goal should be to not misclassify a child as intellectually disabled. As shown below for children a Type I error should be of primary concern: incorrectly determining a child is intellectually disabled. Of course, there are probably those who would contend that finding a child intellectually disabled would provide needed benefits no matter the correctness of the decision. And there are also those who believe that black children are intellectually inferior so that finding a disproportionate number of black children intellectually disabled comports with this racist view.

The "truth"	Childhood Intellectual Disability	
	Not Determined	Determined
No Intellectual Disability	Correct Decision	Type I Error
Intellectual Disability	Type II Error	Correct Decision

For children the task should be to avoid mislabeling a child as intellectually disabled (Type I error), something that has been repeatedly emphasized in the special education law; for adults seeking Atkins relief the task should be to avoid not determining intellectual disability when, in fact, that is the case. For both children and Atkins claimants the essential question is not the type of error but the consequences of the error.

Byron Keith Cooper

Most States use the *preponderance of the evidence* standard for defendants to prove intellectual disability. Several States (viz., Arizona, Colorado, Florida, and Indiana) use the *clear and convincing evidence* standard, and Kansas and Kentucky have no standard. Kansas statute provides limits when sentencing following a determination of intellectual disability. In Kansas (KSA-6622) following a decision that there is sufficient evidence for a hearing to determine intellectual disability, if the court "determines that the defendant is a person with intellectual disability, the court shall sentence the defendant as otherwise provided by law, and no sentence of death, life without the possibility of parole, or mandatory term of imprisonment shall be imposed hereunder."

The *preponderance of the evidence* standard is consistent with the Supreme Court's view that when a defendant "has at stake and interest of transcending value" the "margin of error" is reduced by the heightened *beyond a reasonable doubt* standard.[198] For capital murder the State should use the *beyond a reasonable doubt standard* to ensure that a defendant is not judged "guilty of a criminal offense without convincing a proper factfinder of his guilt with utmost certainty." As explained by the Supreme Court in *Winship* "It is critical that the moral force of the criminal law not be diluted by a standard of proof that leaves people in doubt whether innocent men are being condemned. It is also important in our free society that every individual going about his ordinary affairs have confidence that his government cannot adjudge him guilty of a criminal offense without convincing a proper factfinder of his guilt with utmost certainty."[199]

For an Atkins claim the standard of proof should leave little doubt that someone with an intellectual disability is not executed. If there is error, the error should be on the side of incorrectly finding a claimant to be intellectually disabled rather than incorrectly executing an offender who is intellectually disabled. States have decided that the burden is for the defendant to prove intellectual disability, but States cannot undo the fact that the consequences of failing to prove intellectual disability are far more absolute (viz., death) than when a defendant is found sufficiently intellectual whole to be executed. As Justice Harlan noted in his concurring opinion in *Winship* this is achieved by a *preponderance of the evidence* standard where error is on the side of life rather than execution because "the requirement of proof beyond a reasonable doubt in a criminal case as bottomed on a fundamental value determination of our society that it is far worse to convict an innocent man than to let a guilty man go free."[200] For an Atkins

---

[198]*Ibid.*
[199]In re Winship, 397 U.S. 358 (1970)
[200]In re Winship 397 U.S. 358 (1970)

claimant the "transcending value" at stake is not simply liberty but life itself so that the task should be to minimize error; that is, reduce the error associated with incorrectly accepting the presumption that a defendant is not intellectually disabled.

The Supreme Court did consider the magnitude of doubt for Byron Keith Cooper who was sentenced to death for the 1989 stabbing/murder of 89 year-old Harold Sheppard in Oklahoma City. At the time of his apprehension "he was carrying a portion of a car antenna commonly used as a pipe to smoke crack cocaine." Prior to trial Cooper would not assist counsel and believed that one of his attorneys was the devil.

In 1990 the first of several competency hearings found that Cooper was competent to stand trial (viz., he could assist counsel and understood why he was being tried). In 1995 the Court of Criminal Appeals of Oklahoma explained that "A truly incompetent criminal defendant, through his attorneys and experts, can prove incompetency with relative ease. Therefore, we find forcing a criminal defendant to prove by clear and convincing evidence he is incompetent is not subject to proscription under the Due Process Clause."[201] The higher *clear and convincing evidence* standard, which was required by Cooper's counsel to prove his incompetence to stand trial, was not without merit, especially when considering the possibility of malingering on the part of Cooper (which the Oklahoma court did consider). Oklahoma decided that although the *beyond a reasonable doubt standard* was inappropriate, *clear and convincing evidence* was a reasonable compromise between the rights of the State and the defendant.

The Supreme Court countered in 1996 that "because Oklahoma's procedural rule allows the State to put to trial a defendant who is more likely than not incompetent, the rule is incompatible with the dictates of due process."[202] The reasoning for this is best explained by the Court's reference to the fact that civil commitment requires the *clear and convincing evidence* standard

---

[201]Cooper v. Oklahoma, Court of Criminal Appeals of Oklahoma, No. F-92-533,
1995
[202]Cooper v. Oklahoma, 517 U.S. 348 (1996)

that "protects the individual's fundamental interest in liberty" and "safeguards the fundamental right not to stand trial while incompetent." However, "the prohibition against requiring the criminal defendant to demonstrate incompetence by clear and convincing evidence safeguards the fundamental right not to stand trial while incompetent. Because Oklahoma's procedural rule allows the State to put to trial a defendant who is more likely than not incompetent, the rule is incompatible with the dictates of due process." Cooper has been serving his life without parole sentence in 1997 at Cimarron Correctional Facility near Cushing, Oklahoma.

In Atkins claims a higher burden of proof to protect the States interests should be secondary to protecting "the individual's fundamental interest in liberty." The Court decided that "Oklahoma's practice of requiring the defendant to prove incompetence by *clear and convincing evidence* imposes a significant risk of an erroneous determination that the defendant is competent." The *beyond a reasonable doubt* standard in Georgia imposes an even greater "risk of erroneous determination" that an Atkins claimant is not intellectually disabled. The Court explained in Cooper that the end result of the heightened standard is especially important "for the defendant, the consequences of an erroneous determination of competence are dire."

Morris Leland

States limit an insanity defense (for example Montana, Kansas, Utah and Idaho), but for most States insanity as a defense is a disability unto itself. The disability, when applied to an insanity defense, centers about the crime and whether the defendant knew the wrongfulness of what was done. In addition to the crime itself, insanity can prevent trial (e.g., inability to assist counsel, comprehending the reason for trial, etc.) or execution (viz., the offender does not understand the reason for execution). The criteria for insanity have no professional foundation but is based on the M'Naghten rule where the defendant does "not to know the nature and quality of the act he was doing; or, if he did know it, that he did not know he was doing what was wrong." The Court held that an insanity test that entailed knowing right from wrong did not violate due process.[203]

There is no Diagnostic and Statistical Manual label that would automatically result in a determination that a defendant could not stand trial, could not be sentenced to death, or could not be executed because of a specific mental illness such as schizophrenia, dissociative identity disorder, etc. A specific DSM classification might provide evidence for determining legal insanity, as would be opined by the throng of professionals who descend on courts when sanity is at issue, but the ultimate task is determining whether the defendant understood the wrongfulness of the crime, ability to assist counsel, or understanding the reason for execution.

Georgia has decided that the highest standard (*beyond a reasonable doubt*) is appropriate for Atkins claims. The reasoning is that if the presumption a defendant is innocent until proven guilty, which must be proven *beyond a reasonable doubt*, the presumption that a defendant is not intellectually disabled, should also require the highest standard. The flimsy constitutional basis for this standard dates back to 1952 and a case involving sanity and burden of proof in Leland v. Oregon.[204] All of this was well before *Atkins* in 2002 and *Hall* in 2014 and the Supreme Court's sanction that the Eighth Amendment "places a substantive restriction" on taking the life of an intellectually disabled offender.

Before the reinstitution of the death penalty in 1976, Morris Leland was executed (gas chamber) for the kidnapping and murder of fifteen-year-old Thelma Taylor in 1949 in Portland, Oregon. He was arrested a week or so after the murder and ultimately confessed to the crime. He was tried in October in 1950, sentenced to death in 1951, and executed in 1953. In terms of swiftness, due process was different than today.

Leland raised an insanity defense where the burden of proof was *beyond a reasonable doubt*. Part of his insanity claim was that the

---

[203]Clark v. Arizona, 548 U.S. 735 (2006)
[204]Leland v. Oregon, 343 U.S. 790 (1952)

murder resulted from an "irresistible impulse" but was rejected because the definition of insanity in 1951 in *Oregon* stipulated "insanity as a defense to crime is a disease of the mind which renders the person incapable of understanding the nature, quality and consequences of his act, or of distinguishing between right and wrong in relation to such act."[205] In other words, whether or not the defendant has an "irresistible impulse" is irrelevant. The Supreme Court of Oregon concluded "that insanity as a defense to crime is a disease of the mind which renders the person incapable of understanding the nature, quality and consequences of his act, or of distinguishing between right and wrong in relation to such act."

The Supreme Court agreed with the Oregon court by explaining "We are therefore reluctant to interfere with Oregon's determination of its policy with respect to the burden of proof on the issue of sanity since we cannot say that policy violates generally accepted concepts of basic standards of justice."[206] At the time Oregon was the only State to require the *beyond a reasonable doubt* standard but this was discounted by the Court because "the fact that a practice is followed by a large number of states is not conclusive in a decision as to whether that practice accords with due process." The Court's deference to consensus certainly changed with *Atkins* in 2002.

Because the Supreme Court did not reject the *beyond a reasonable doubt* standard in *Leland* there was no reason to reject this standard in Atkins claims in Georgia. The application of *Leland* to *Atkins* is suspect. *Leland* was based on due process and the Fourteenth Amendment and whether or not the defendant knew what he was doing at the time of the crime and whether what he was doing was wrong. This, as mentioned previously, is the essence of the M'Naghten rule which is void of a specific mental illness designation. As stated by the Supreme Court in Clark v. Arizona in 2006 "Evidence of mental disease, then, can easily mislead; it is very easy to slide from evidence that an individual

---

[205]State of Oregon v. Leland, Supreme Court of Oregon, 190 Or. 598 (1951)
[206]Leland v. Oregon, 343 U.S. 790 (1952)

with a professionally recognized mental disease is very different, into doubting that he has the capacity to form *mens rea*, whereas that doubt may not be justified."[207]

Unlike Leland v. Oregon and Clark v. Arizona, *Atkins* focused on the Eighth Amendment and the belief that the mentally retarded/intellectually disabled deserved lesser culpability. In *Leland* the beyond a reasonable doubt standard was used to prove *mens rea*, intent, or a culpable state of mine. In *Atkins* the task is to determine intellectual disability, using professionally determined criteria, where the disability itself becomes foremost because "some characteristics of mental retardation undermine the strength of the procedural protections that our capital jurisprudence steadfastly guards."[208]

Atkins does not provide a gradient of intellectual disability such as intellectual disability by a *preponderance of the evidence*, by *clear and convincing evidence* or *beyond a reasonable doubt*, but only that professional definitions as adopted by States should be used to determine intellectual disability. Nor does *Atkins* address the various levels of intellectual disability and how each might result in different degree of culpability. For example, *beyond a reasonable doubt* standard suggests a higher level of intellectual disability (e.g., moderate), while a *preponderance* standard suggests a lesser degree of intellectual disability (e.g., mild). Considering IQ alone, an IQ of 75 is certainly not evidence *beyond a reasonable doubt* that a defendant met this criterion of the definition.

There are less persuasive justifications used by Georgia to rationalize the *beyond a reasonable standard*. These include: 1) the Court left the process for determining mental retardation to the States (the rationale used by Florida before Hall in 2014); 2) the Court "praised Georgia as being the first state in the nation to have banned the execution of mentally retarded persons (as mentioned in *Atkins*);" 3) the Court had "no negative comment" regarding Georgia's heightened burden of proof; and 4) other

---

[207]Clark v. Arizona, 548 U.S. 735 (2006)
[208]Atkins v. Virginia, 536 U.S. 304 (2002)

States use a heightened standard (*clear and convincing*) so there is no rationale for not having an even higher standard.

Georgia has an unusual take on *Atkins* where the prohibition on executing the intellectually disabled, and those who are "almost certainly mentally retarded," is more recommendation than prohibition. Judge Leah Ward Sears, Chief Justice of the Georgia Supreme Court at the time, explained that "Despite the federal ban on executing the mentally retarded, Georgia's statute, and the majority decision upholding it, do not prohibit the state from executing mentally retarded people. To the contrary, the State may still execute people who are in all probability mentally retarded. The State may execute people who are more than likely mentally retarded. The State may even execute people who are almost certainly mentally retarded. Only if a mentally retarded person succeeds in proving their retardation *beyond a reasonable doubt* will his or her execution be halted."[209] Georgia's distinction between "people who are almost certainly mentally retarded" and those who are mentally retarded *beyond a reasonable doubt* is a definitional addition not considered by the Supreme Court.

Given the importance of stringent standards required in insanity claims as per Ford v. Wainwright, the goal when considering claims, as explained by Justice Marshall indicates, is "to guard against error" and not enhance the possibility of execution.

> **Although the condemned prisoner does not enjoy the same presumptions accorded a defendant who has yet to be convicted or sentenced, he has not lost the protection of the Constitution altogether; if the Constitution renders the fact or timing of his execution contingent upon establishment of a further fact, then that fact must be determined with the high regard for truth that befits a decision affecting the life or death of a human being. Thus, the ascertainment of a prisoner's sanity**

---

[209]Hill v. Head, Supreme Court of Georgia, Nos. S03A0559, S03X0560, October 6, 2003

> as a predicate to lawful execution calls for no
> less stringent standards than those demanded
> in any other aspect of a capital proceeding.
> Indeed, a particularly acute need for guarding
> against error inheres in a determination that
> "in the present state of the mental sciences is at
> best a hazardous guess however
> conscientious." ... That need is greater still
> because the ultimate decision will turn on the
> finding of a single fact, not on a range of
> equitable considerations ... In light of these
> concerns, the procedures employed in
> petitioner's case do not fare well. [210]

Requiring a State to adhere to stringent procedures when considering insanity claims is incompatible with the employment of a stringent standard for accepting claims. Requiring procedures to guard against "error" then increasing the possibility that someone insane will be executed, is an illogical approach for "the high regard for truth that befits a decision affecting the life or death of a human being."

For Atkins claims Georgia has enhanced the definition of intellectual disability cited in the Georgia code[211] to mean not only "having significantly subaverage general intellectual functioning resulting in or associated with impairments in adaptive behavior which manifested during the developmental period" but to also include "if the jury, or court acting as trier of facts, finds beyond a reasonable doubt that the defendant is guilty of the crime charged and is mentally retarded."

Tommy Cage

In 1986 Tommy Cage, age 19, shot Arthur Johnson in the back and head during the course of a robbery over a medallion Johnson was wearing at a New Orleans bus stop. Cage's conviction and

---

[210]Ford v. Wainwright, 477 U.S. 399 (1986)
[211]Georgia Code, Section 17-7-131(a)(3) and Section 17-7-131[c][3])

sentence were reversed and remanded because of error in the *beyond reasonable doubt* jury instruction. The trial court explained that the doubt of guilt "would give rise to a grave uncertainty" and a doubt that "a reasonable man can seriously entertain. What is required is not an absolute or mathematical certainty, but a moral certainty." In Winship (1970) the Supreme Court emphasized that "Lest there remain any doubt about the constitutional stature of the reasonable doubt standard, we explicitly hold that the Due Process Clause protects the accused against conviction except upon proof beyond a reasonable doubt of every fact necessary to constitute the crime with which he is charged."

The trial court focused on a "moral certainty" of doubt while the Court in Winship explained that a jury must not find a defendant "guilty of a criminal offense without convincing a proper factfinder of his guilt with utmost certainty."[212] In other words "doubt" does not require "moral certainty" (or "grave" or "substantial") but the "utmost certainty." This certainly can be confusing.

The Supreme Court decided that the jury instruction explaining reasonable doubt contained the words "actual substantial doubt," "grave uncertainty," and "moral certainty" so "rather than evidentiary, certainty, a reasonable juror, taking the charge as a whole, could have interpreted the instruction to allow a finding of guilt based on a degree of proof below that required by the Due Process Clause."[213] That is, "moral certainty" is more likely to result in conviction *than beyond a reasonable doubt*.

In 1991 the Supreme Court of Louisiana affirmed Cage's conviction because the court believed that the "erroneous reasonable doubt instruction was subject to harmless error analysis and that this error did not contribute to Cage's sentence.[214] In 1996 the Supreme Court of Louisiana vacated the decision and capital sentence, based on a similar case, because the jury might have misunderstood the jury instructions.

---

[212]In re Winship 397 U.S. 358 (1970)
[213]Cage v. Louisiana, 498 U.S. 39 (1990)
[214]583 So. 2d 1125 (1991)

The guideline seems to be that *beyond a reasonable doubt* requires some degree of "certainty" but a "certainty" that is less than "grave" or "moral." The exception to this uncertain continuum of certainty, as seen in Victor v. Nebraska, is when instructions are "taken as a whole" and "the instructions in question correctly conveyed the concept of reasonable doubt."[215] "Moral certainty" was mentioned by the court in *Victor* but the Supreme Court explained in this case there was sufficient context to correctly interpret the meaning of reasonable doubt. The Supreme Court offered in *Victor* that "a reasonable doubt alternatively as a doubt that would cause a reasonable person to hesitate to act, a formulation which this Court has repeatedly approved and which gives a commonsense benchmark for just how substantial a reasonable doubt must be."

Clarence Victor

If a standard for determining Atkins claims other than *preponderance of the evidence is appropriate,* there is probably no justification for limiting how high the standard might be. In Arizona the court uses the *clear and convincing* standard at a hearing prior to trial,[216] and Florida uses the *clear and convincing* standard in a hearing by the court prior to sentencing.[217] North Carolina has decided that the *clear and convincing* standard is required when the court determines that the defendant has an intellectual disability and the case is declared noncapital. However, if the defendant pursues a claim of intellectual disability, the jury makes the determination using the *preponderance of the evidence* standard.[218]

---

[215]Victor v. Nebraska, 511 U.S. 1 (1994)
[216]Arizona 76 70 65 Ariz. Rev. Stat. Ann. § 13-753
[217]Florida Statute 921.137, Imposition of the death sentence upon a defendant with mental
retardation prohibited
[218]2013 North Carolina General Statutes, Chapter 15A - Criminal Procedure Act. Article 100 - Capital Punishment. Section 15A-2005 - Mentally retarded defendants; death sentence prohibited

As shown by Victor v. Nebraska how a jury conceptualizes standard of proof is anybody's guess. In Nebraska the probability of execution is slim yet the State has not been without influence in death penalty jurisprudence. Only three individuals have been executed in Nebraska since 1976, all by electrocution. Of these three, two were black (the black population in Nebraska was approximately 5 percent in 2015). The last execution in Nebraska was in 1997 when Robert Williams was electrocuted for three murders committed in 1977. Nebraska repealed the death penalty in 2015 but this was overturned in a referendum in November of 2016 by a vote of 60.6 percent.

Clarence Victor was sentenced to death for the 1987 murder of 82 year-old Alice Singleton in 1988. He had previously served time in prison for two previous and separate murders. In 1994 the Supreme Court considered his claim that the jury instructions overstated the degree of doubt needed for conviction:

> **'Reasonable doubt' is such a doubt as would cause a reasonable and prudent person, in one of the graver and more important transactions of life, to pause and hesitate before taking the represented facts as true and relying and acting thereon. It is such a doubt as will not permit you, after full, fair, and impartial consideration of all the evidence, to have an abiding conviction, to a moral certainty, of the guilt of the accused. At the same time, absolute or mathematical certainty is not required. You may be convinced of the truth of a fact beyond a reasonable doubt and yet be fully aware that possibly you may be mistaken. You may find an accused guilty upon the strong probabilities of the case, provided such probabilities are strong enough to exclude any doubt of his guilt that is reasonable. A reasonable doubt is an actual and substantial doubt reasonably arising from the evidence, from the facts or circumstances shown by the evidence, or from the lack of evidence on the part of the State, as**

distinguished from a doubt arising from mere possibility, from bare imagination, or from fanciful conjecture.[219]

The defense argued that the word "substantial" overstated the level of doubt needed to be found not guilty. The Supreme Court rejected Victor's argument because "the context makes clear that 'substantial' is used in the sense of existence rather than magnitude of the doubt, so the same concern is not present." The definition of *reasonable doubt* was "a doubt that would cause a reasonable person to hesitate to act." If the trial court had given an exact percentage, such as 95 percent confidence, the defense might very well asserted that this value overstated (or maybe understated) the degree of confidence necessary to convict using the *beyond a reasonable doubt standard*. The standard could be 95 percent, and at some subliminal level this is what was used, but *beyond a reasonable doubt* can be described but not defined statistically which the Supreme Court referred to as "quantitatively imprecise."[220]

Intelligence scores, no matter how low, are easily discounted or dismissed entirely. The Nebraska legislature prohibited the execution of the mentally retarded in 1998, four years before *Atkins*, and emphasized the importance of a "reliably administered" IQ test so that "An intelligence quotient of seventy or below on a reliably administered intelligence quotient test shall be presumptive evidence of mental retardation."[221] Victor, who had a reported IQ of 65, was presumed to be mentally retarded because of a "reliably administered" test and the State was not able to rebut this presumption by offering other test results or showing there were no deficits in adaptive behavior.

Victor was re-sentenced to life in prison, a decision that was affirmed by the Supreme Court of Nebraska in 2000. Victor did not prevail in convincing the Supreme Court that the jury

---

[219]Victor v. Nebraska, 511 U.S. 1 (1994)
[220]In re Winship 397 U.S. 358 (1970)
[221]Nebraska Rev. Stat. § 28-105.01. An intelligence quotient of seventy or below on a reliably administered intelligence quotient test shall be presumptive evidence of intellectual disability.

instruction for *beyond a reasonable doubt* was unconstitutional, but he was able to show by a *preponderance* of the evidence that he was mentally retarded. The different levels of burden of proof were consistent with avoiding the most dire consequence: convicting an innocent defendant (rejecting the null hypothesis when this hypothesis is correct); and incorrectly deciding a defendant is not intellectually disabled (accepting the null hypothesis when incorrect). Victor died in prison from natural causes at age 82 in 2015.

Alphonso Stripling

In Georgia, for Alphonso Stripling, the *preponderance of the evidence* standard for his Atkins claim was rejected, the *beyond a reasonable doubt* was the acknowledged standard, but in the end no standard was necessary. Stripling was sentenced to death for the shooting of four individuals, two of whom died, at a Kentucky Fried Chicken in Douglasville, Georgia in 1988. The defense claimed that Stripling had met the criteria for mental retardation in Georgia with D's and F's in school, difficulty reading, and an IQ of 68 at age 17 as well as other IQ scores of 64 and 67 (and an improbable score of 111 on a Cultural Fair test).[222]

A determination of Stripling's mental retardation was complicated when the prosecution failed to disclose statements by prison officials attesting to his mental retardation. The reason given why the State did not disclose relevant records was the disingenuous explanation that this information was "confidential." The Georgia Supreme Court believed that a Brady violation was committed, evidence was withheld, and that "Evidence generated by State officials characterizing Stripling as mentally retarded and questioning the only test result relied upon by the State at trial, compiled years before the KFC murders, would have refuted many of the State's arguments and in reasonable probability would have affected the outcome of Stripling's trial."[223]

---

[222]Stripling v. the State, Supreme Court of Georgia, June 13, 2011
[223]Head v. Stripling, Supreme Court of Georgia, No. S03A0525, October 14, 2003

In 2011 the Supreme Court of Georgia agreed that the burden was on the defendant to prove mental retardation, but the trial court had erred by using the *preponderance of the evidence* standard rather than *beyond a reasonable doubt* which resulted in the finding by the trial court that Stripling was mentally retarded.[224] The Supreme Court of Georgia suggested that his Atkins claim could be resolved "through a plea of guilty but mentally retarded if both parties are willing to do so and if the trial court finds a factual basis to enter judgment on such a plea." In 2013 a plea agreement was reached thereby avoiding another evidentiary hearing and possible resentencing. The conclusion that can be drawn is that although the *beyond a reasonable doubt* is a high standard, withholding evidence lessens that height.

Charles Laverne Singleton

The fundamental difference between intellectual disability and insanity is that insanity can be undone to allow for trial or execution. A finding of intellectual disability by the State, regardless of when done, should not be undone, but this is not the case for insanity. For Charles Laverne Singleton sanity as a bar to execution was taken to the extreme. Singleton was convicted for the stabbing and murder of Mary Lou York in Hamburg, Arkansas in June of 1979. While on death row, his mental health deteriorated. He had begun to believe in demons and that his victim was not dead. If he truly believed his victim was alive, he could no longer appreciate the wrongfulness of his crime for he believed there was no crime of murder. One remedy was for the State to administer drugs—by someone not bothered by Hippocratic Oath-type restrictions—to sufficiently restore his sanity whereupon he could be executed.

The Eighth Circuit Court of Appeals decided in 2002 that "the Eighth Amendment did not prohibit executing a prisoner who had become incompetent while on death row but who regained competency through appropriate medical care."[225] Singleton was

---

[224]Stripling v. the State, Supreme Court of Georgia, June 13, 2011

executed in January of 2004. Maybe those who administered antipsychotic drugs believed that the purpose was to improve Singleton's mental health and, after that bit of benevolence was achieved, whatever happened would happen. In the end, for Singleton, benevolent medical intervention was not so benevolent.

Legal insanity has varied meanings depending on what is being considered (viz. the ability to stand trial, a determination of sanity at trial, or sufficient sanity to be executed) and this is often made clear, or at least explained, by statute. For Atkins claims most States consider the totality of the evidence for determining intellectual disability although that determination can be made before trial, during sentencing or while on death row. This is not to say that a State will not treat intellectual disability as an insanity issue as when the *beyond a reasonable doubt* is used, or when intellectual disability has been undone by the curative effects of death row.

The task for an Atkins claim finder of fact is to consider all evidence as a child and as an adult, to evaluate all test scores and reports, all evidence of adaptive behavior, and any and all prior determinations and records of intellectual disability. A determination of intellectual disability as a child, or what should have been determined, is of fundamental importance for the obvious reason that if a State (and the school board or district acting on part of the State) has decided that a child meets the professional criteria for intellectual disability after following extensive regulations for the identification, evaluation and placement of children who need specially designed instruction, a record of intellectual disability has been established. The intent of this action by the State might have been to provide and appropriate education, albeit in a segregated placement apart from the general curriculum. The idea that this prior determination of intellectual disability as a child by the State is irrelevant or should be dismissed is simplistic nonsense.

Much of the problem can be traced to semantics. The Supreme Court said in Atkins the problem is "determining which offenders

---

[225]Singleton v. Norris, 319 F.3d 1018 (2003)

are in fact retarded." Does "are" mean at the time of the crime, at trial, on death row? Or does "are" encompass a broad conceptualization of intellectual disability so that a determination of disability by the State, no matter when, is tantamount to intellectual disability sufficient to allow for lesser culpability?

If a State has correctly identified a child as intellectually disabled and acts accordingly, there is no undoing of this "correct" determination, even if not correct, as when a State rejects the intellectual disability of an Atkins claimant as a child because of the benevolent motives (sometimes) of school officials. If a State has incorrectly identified a child as having an intellectual disability, the resulting stigmatization, segregation and other State actions under the guise of an "appropriate education" would contribute to the reasons for lesser culpability cited by the Supreme Court. Misclassification as having a mild intellectual disability as a child, in explaining the disproportionality of black children in EMR classes in Larry P. v. Riles in 1979, can result "in special classes that doom them to stigma, inadequate education, and failure to develop the skills necessary to productive success in our society."[226]

Because the obligation should be to reduce executing a defendant who is intellectually disabled, there will always be those who are not intellectually disabled who will incorrectly benefit from an Atkins claim. Increasing the probability that someone who is intellectually disabled is found not to be (such as by using the *beyond a reasonable doubt* standard in Georgia or the *clear and convincing standard*), increases the risk for incorrectly executing the intellectually disabled. This is no different than acknowledging that a higher burden of proof in criminal cases will result in some guilty defendants who "are probably guilty" escaping punishment. The Supreme Court is clear that the goal should be a more expansive interpretation of intellectual disability and not an interpretation that increases the likelihood that someone who warrants lesser culpability will be executed. In *Hall* the Court observed that "The death penalty is the gravest sentence our society may impose. Persons facing that most severe sanction

---

[226]Larry P. v. Riles, 495 F. Supp. 926 (1979)

must have a fair opportunity to show that the Constitution prohibits their execution."

5. EMR

"...an unlawful segregative intent..."[227]

Freddie Lee Hall – Circa 1950s

For Freddie Lee Hall the interrelationship between environment, education and racism is essential for understanding why his Atkins claim failed prior to a determination that he did have an intellectual disability in 2016. The Supreme Court of Florida withdrew a previous decision[228] that a "statutorily prescribed" IQ cutoff of 70 was not arbitrary for determining mental retardation and "Hall has demonstrated that he meets the clinical, statutory, and constitutional requirements to establish that his intellectual disability serves as a bar to execution."[229]

The term Educable Mental Retardation (or EMR) is essential for understanding why children were (and are) identified as having intellectual deficiencies sufficient to require special education, individualized programming and educational placements...sometimes in a least restrictive environment and sometimes not. According to the Office of Civil Rights survey data in 1980, approximately 646,000 were identified as having mental retardation, and approximately 85 percent of those identified fell into the EMR category.[230] Black children accounted for 38.7 percent of all children classified as EMR where the black school enrollment was 16.4 percent. However, black children comprised only 27.6 percent of children in the more severe TMR (trainable mental retardation) category, and 15.1 percent of children in the

---

[227]*Ibid.*

[228]Hall v. Florida, Supreme Court of Florida, SC10-1335, December 20, 2012

[229]Hall v. Florida, Supreme Court of Florida, SC10-1335, September 8, 2016: on remand from the Supreme Court as per Hall v. Florida, 572 U.S. ____ (2014), 134 S. Ct. 1986

[230]1980 Elementary and Secondary Schools Civil Rights Survey, National Summaries, Office of Civil Rights (OCR), Washington, D.C., March, 1982 (ED 219 477)

"speech impaired" category which is the least restrictive of all categories.

Many children are identified as having intellectual disability (and other disabilities such as emotional disturbance, specific learning disabilities, and other health impairments) because of poor performance in school, a low score on an IQ test (and this could be a score in excess of 80) and race. For Atkins claims the issue is not the broad category of "intellectual disabilities" to prohibit execution, but that difficult to define category of *mild intellectual disabilities*.

In this work the terms mental retardation and intellectual disabilities refer to **mild intellectual disability** and are used interchangeably depending on the time and source. For example, the 2002 *Atkins* decision used the term *mental retardation* and that is the term which will be used when referencing this decision. In 2010, Public Law 111-256 (Rosa's Law) was enacted to change mental retardation to intellectual disabilities, and the reference of children "having mental retardation" to "having "anachronistic, needlessly insensitive and stigmatizing, and clinically outdated." Regardless of Congressional intent, changing mental retardation to intellectual disability does not alter the disproportionate number of black children who stigmatized and offered inferior and/or limited education which, no matter the name, can result in "classes denies that opportunity through relegation to a markedly inferior, essentially dead-end, track."[231]

From a political standpoint, there is some wisdom for changing the name of mental retardation to show intolerance for "colloquial slurs and pejorative phrases used to demean and insult both persons with and without disabilities."[232] The name change costs nothing and Congress is able to reap the rewards as a defender-of-human-rights. Of course, the term "intellectual disability" does not change what is actually done for or to children. For black children this means that instead of being disproportionally and wrongly categorized as mentally retarded, they will be disproportionally

---

[231]Larry P. v. Riles, 495 F. Supp. 926 (1979)
[232]Senate Report 111-244 for Public Law 111-256 (Rosa's Law)

categorized as children "having intellectual disabilities," and many will nonetheless be deprived of educational opportunity, segregated to varying degrees and otherwise stigmatized (but in a new and more benevolent way by having a new and more benevolent sounding label).

For children the EMR category could, at times, provide necessary educational services; and, conversely, the EMR category could also be used to stigmatize children, especially black children. Conversely, for capital punishment, a previous determination of mental retardation/intellectual disability as a child can be ignored or denied to permit execution. For children and adults, when the result of mental retardation/intellectual disability is necessary services or life (for those condemned to death), race is often a limiting factor; when the result of mental retardation/intellectual disability is stigmatization or execution, race becomes a motivating factor.

For Freddie Lee Hall a reasonable assumption would be that his early education was in segregated schools prior to dropping out in the eleventh grade. The Supreme Court of Florida, in 2016, believed that "based on Hall's academic record, it is reasonable to believe that some testing must have occurred because Hall was referred for placement in Special Education classes and referred to as intellectually disabled in the school record."[233] There were report cards, school grades, samples of school, and possibly standardized achievement test data, but considering the time frame of his early education, there is no reason to believe that a Florida school district would provide an individualized assessment to determine learning needs and an appropriate school placement. Records indicate that teachers thought he needed special education services but Florida, in the 1950s, was hardly of a mind to meet the needs of poor black children or any black children for that matter.

For many black children the Educable Mental Retardation (EMR) category gained increasing popularity in the 1960s in the north (viz., California, New York, Ohio and Pennsylvania) and, in the

---

[233]Freddie Lee Hall v. State of Florida, SC10-1335, September 8, 2016

1970s, in the south. For children, like Freddie Lee Hall in the 1950s, race was one factor that would have prevented an individualized IQ assessment. There was no need to classify black children as intellectual inferior because that was the prevailing belief for all black children. In that the needs of black children in public schools were not of primary importance, there was certainly no incentive to meet the special learning needs of these children.

Following the aggressive efforts by courts to desegregate, testing was often used to identify the needs of children caused by segregation. The circular solution for remedying the effects of an inferior education caused by segregation was more segregation. Intelligence testing provided a ready explanation for poor school performance, rather than prior segregation, and allowed schools to remediate the effects of segregation by segregation in the form of special classes.

As was the case in many States Florida had few provisions for special education in the 1950s. Not until the late 1960s did Florida define the term *exceptional children* to mean a child "who is unsuited for enrollment in a regular class of the public schools or is unable to be adequately educated in the public schools without the provision of special classes, instruction, facilities or related services, or a combination thereof."[234] Before serious desegregation in the South special education was not a mainstay of white schools much less underfunded and unsupported black schools. [235]

In Florida, in 1980, according to the Office of Civil Rights 1980 report, of the approximately 18,500 children identified as EMR, approximately 11,900 (64.3 percent) were black.[236] In perspective, of the approximately 48,700 children in Florida identified as having specific learning disabilities—a less

---

[234]228.041 Statutory Changes-1968 Extraordinary Session
[235]Mackie, Romaine P. Special Education in the United States: Statistics 1948-1966. Teachers College Press: New York, New York, 1969.
[236]1980 Elementary and Secondary Schools Civil Rights Survey State Summaries,, Office of Civil Rights (OCR), Washington, D.C., March, 1982 (ED 219 478)

segregative disability than EMR—only 29.5 percent were black. Even more noteworthy, although one would predict a high level of trainable mental retardation (TMR) among black children, assuming that a greater level of intellectual disability among black children overall—a belief popularized by academics—there were actually more white children (2,646) identified as TMR than black children (1,647). One explanation is that while the EMR category provided exoneration for schools for responsibility for poor black educational performance, the TMR category included children with real cognitive deficits, required greater funding and actually met individual learning needs such as developing independent living skills and meeting basic communication and academic needs.

In all likelihood Freddie Lee Hall should have been classified as educable mentally retarded as a child but, because of limited special education resources and race, was not. One educational report for Hall in the 1950s included comments that he was "mentally retarded," and needed a "special teacher." Long before the Supreme Court's decision in *Hall* in 2014, and after almost 40 years on death row, he was simply "Freddie" who "is slow in all phases of work."[237] The likelihood that someone with Hall's academic record would be classified as educable mentally retarded would have increased as a function of desegregation, especially when EMR could be used to segregate or re-segregate. However, in the 1950s there was no need to classify Hall as EMR in that school segregation provided all that schools thought should be provided black children.

The term Educable Mental Retardation/EMR has been largely abandoned for a variety of reasons. First, the term has assumed very negative connotations. In part this has been the result of the reference to "retardation" which suggests a lesser person, someone deserving lesser respect and a lesser education. Second, racial disproportionality in the EMR category—and, as mentioned, less so in moderate and severe categories— suggests that racial bias rather than need is at play. As the criteria for intellectual

---

[237]Hall v. Florida, On Writ of Certiorari to the Supreme Court of Florida, No. 12-10882

disability become more obvious as the degree of disability increases (e.g., self-care needs, limited language skills, limited independent living skills) race becomes less of a factor. Also, because moderate and severe intellectual disability categories require far more financial resources, there is less incentive to classify black children as having more serious intellectual disabilities.

Finally, eliminating the EMR term allowed States to comingle mild, moderate and severe disabilities into one overall classification. There are serious questions concerning the validity of determining mild intellectual disabilities, but an overall classification includes children with definite cognitive needs which is useful for justifying the overall category—and therefore mild intellectual disabilities which is a part of this overall category. The elimination of EMR as a distinct category, and the aggregation of mild, moderate and profound mental retardation into a single overall category, forgoes the EMR label that has represented stigmatization, racial disproportionality and programs that often precluded educational opportunity. The overall category **intellectual disability** is useful for hiding the unsightly characteristics and racial disproportionality associated with the EMR/mild mental retardation category. By aggregating children with mild intellectual disabilities, where racial disproportionality is at its highest, with moderate and severe intellectual disabilities, the degree of disproportionality is reduced.

The EMR category is very relevant for Atkins claims because this or a similar classification was the prevailing category during the childhood of many claimants. As the EMR label became notorious for not meeting individual learning needs, educational placements became less restrictive and could entail the regular classroom, a resource room, or a special education classroom. Likewise determining exactly how a child was categorized might entail some sleuthing. A school might not use an EMR-type classroom label and opt for a less ominous label such as a 12-1 classroom to indicate a self-contained classroom with 12 students and one teacher. To complicate matters, generic special education placements might include children with varying disabilities so that a child with a learning disability and a child with a mild intellectual disability might be provided the same curriculum.

For defendant's seeking Atkins relief, mild intellectual disabilities as a child should be the foremost factor for substantiating a claim. This includes not only defendants who were formally determined to have a mild intellectual disability, but also defendants who were regarded as having an intellectual disability, defendants who should have been determined to have an intellectual disability, defendants who met all the criteria for an intellectual disability but were either not classified or were classified as having another disability, and for defendants who currently meet the criteria for *Atkins* as manifested by deficits processing information, communication, learning from experience, controlling impulses, the possibility of a false confession, being a poor witness, assisting counsel, etc.

In addition to the various reasons why someone was or was not classified as having an intellectual disability as a child, there is the question of criteria at the time of placement. A retrospective analysis using criteria at the time of *Atkins* might completely overlook the criteria for classification at the time of categorization. An Atkins claimant might have had IQ tests administered as a child when the cutoff was 85, or when the cutoff was whatever the school thought appropriate although "appropriate" for black and white children was not necessarily the same.

Using the same definition of intellectual disability to disproportionately identify black children as having an intellectual disability and denying Atkins relief as an adult is not a paradox but consistent with the general goal, whether intentional or not, to deny black children and adults due process and benefits. When the result is assignment to a restrictive educational placement, intellectual disability is freely bestowed; when intellectual disability means life rather than death, States are frugal to a fault when determining intellectual disability, willingly acknowledge the error of not taking into account environment and cultural factors when a defendant was a child, and are undeterred by evidence showing a previous determination of intellectual disability as a child.

Anderson Hawthorne Jr.

For no other reason than the bizarre status of IQ testing, no Atkins claim can ever be resolved in California. The contentious state of capital punishment in California will likely result in no one on death row among the inordinately large number of death row offenders—from approximately 650 at the time of California's last execution of Clarence Ray Allen in 2006 to 742 as of November, 2018—ever being executed. In California death row is the final punishment unless death by natural causes (79 since 1978), suicide (25), re-sentencing etc. intervenes. The inability of California to resolve *Atkins* claims as per the guidelines expressed in Atkins in 2002 and *Hall* in 2014, especially in regard to IQ, should be a further bar to the imposition of capital punishment. A black child cannot be given an IQ test in California but IQ is an integral part of determining intellectual disability as explained by professionals and the Supreme Court.

California has offered a partial solution to the unique state of IQ testing by de-emphasizing IQ in Atkins claims. Anderson Hawthorne was sentenced to death at age 22 in 1986 for the 1982 murder of two rival gang members. He had reported IQ scores as a child of 86 and 74 (probably in the 1960s or at least before the IQ ban for black children) and an IQ of 71 as an adult. The California Supreme Court explained that "a fixed cutoff is inconsistent with established clinical definitions… and fails to recognize that significantly subaverage intellectual functioning may be established by means other than IQ testing." The court also noted that an IQ below 70 "may be anomalous" and not the result of intellectual disability.[238] California has determined that IQ testing is inappropriate for black children but must contend with the Supreme Court's deference to professional definitions of which IQ is central. The State has decided that IQ lacks precision

---

[238]In re Anderson Hawthorne, Jr., on Habeas Corpus 35 Cal. 4th 40, Supreme Court of California, February 10, 2005, S116670

and there are other means for determining intellectual than IQ testing. The California Supreme Court reasoned that:

> **With respect to the intellectual prong of section 1376, respondent Attorney General urges the court to adopt an IQ of 70 as the upper limit for making a prima facie showing. We decline to do so for several reasons: First, unlike some states, the California Legislature has chosen not to include a numerical IQ score as part of the definition of "mentally retarded." Second, a fixed cutoff is inconsistent with established clinical definitions and fails to recognize that significantly subaverage intellectual functioning may be established by means other than IQ testing. Experts also agree that an IQ score below 70 may be anomalous as to an individual's intellectual functioning and not indicative of mental impairment. Finally, IQ test scores are insufficiently precise to utilize a fixed cutoff in this context.**[239]

The California Supreme Court does not think much of a cutoff of 70, or a cutoff of 75 for that matter, and does not think much of IQ scores in general. Thus far Hawthorne's Atkins claim has not been successful and as of 2019 he remains on California's death row (for 33 years beginning in 1986).

The Supreme Court believes that the SEM solves the question concerning the use of IQ scores, but the application of *Atkins* in California adds a Kafkaesque element to IQ decision making. California has one of the most thorough programs for meeting American with Disabilities Act claims among all the States for prisoners, but exactly how California prisons deal with a determination of intellectual disability after having been sentenced to death is less apparent. Because every inmate in California is evaluated, prison officials could decide that an inmate

---

[239]In re Anderson Hawthorne, Jr., on Habeas Corpus 35 Cal. 4th 40, Supreme Court of California, February 10, 2005, S116670

facing execution (or after an extended period of time on death row) has an intellectual disability, either following an unsuccessful Atkins claim or as part of the normal ADA processing for every prisoner. However, California has de-emphasized the importance of IQ testing for children and adults, yet California prison officials are able to make determinations to meet important developmental needs. At the very least, every offender on death row in California who has developmental needs, as determined by prison officials, should be offered relief via *Atkins*. For that matter every black offender on death row who claims intellectual disability should be removed from death row in that the IQ testing prong cannot be used to determine intellectual ability before age of onset.

DeShawn Lee Campbell

DeShawn Lee Campbell was tried, with special circumstances, for the murder of police officer Jeffrey Fontana on October 28, 2001 whom Campbell had lured to an isolated cul-de-sac and then shot the officer in the head. Following the Atkins decision, California instituted Penal Code § 1376 which allows a defendant to raise an Atkins claim by the court before trial or by a jury following conviction of a capital offense. The code provides that defense and prosecution present evidence for and against an intellectual disability which the defense must prove by a preponderance of the evidence. If the jury does not reach a unanimous decision, a second jury is impaneled to consider the issue of intellectual disability.

In 2007 the trial court decided that Campbell was not mentally retarded. For Campbell IQ was not only important but also an odd metric. In 1997 Campbell received an IQ on the WAIS-R of 65. The record revealed that "In this case, the trial court found that there was no dispute that defendant has IQ scores below 70, consistent with a finding that he is mildly mentally retarded, and that these scores manifested before the age of 18."[240] This results

---

[240]Campbell v. Superior Court of Santa Clara County, Court of Appeal,

in the use of IQ as an adult to determine whether Campbell might have had a similar score on an IQ test that was banned when a child. The retrospective meaningfulness of an IQ test for an adult, when the test was determined to be racial and culturally discriminatory for children, is problematic. Using IQ in Atkins claims, especially when testing an adult, is difficult enough from the standpoint of motivation to perform and possible malingering on tests—and who knows how other life factors would affect an adult accused of a capital crime—but to then use an IQ score for an adult to determine whether intellectual disability was manifested before age 18, on a test that could not be given to a black child in California, is difficult to conceptualize.

In 2008 the appellate court for the sixth district in California vacated the original mental retardation decision because one witness attesting to DeShawn's adaptive behavior had the wrong DeShawn. In addition, the measure of adaptive behavior was "insufficient and unreliable."[241] This resulted in a second Atkins hearing in which the expert evaluated eight informants using various instruments to determine whether or not Campbell had deficits in adaptive behavior. The court believed that Campbell had met the criteria for mental retardation and in December of 2009 he was sentenced to consecutive terms of life without parole and various other sentences in unrelated cases. In 2012 a California appellate court considered a variety of appeals and issued a 74 page decision to include 483 days of presentence custody as credit toward time served.

Ernest Dewayne Jones

The quixotic use of IQ scores in California is part of the overall death penalty jurisprudence where the ultimate penalty is not execution but death row. In 1995 Ernest Dewayne Jones was sentenced to death for the rape and murder of his girlfriend's 50 year-old mother, Julia Miller, in 1992. He was previously convicted of the rape of another girlfriend's mother in 1985. The

---

Sixth District, California, No. H032068, January 30, 2008
[241]*Ibid.*

District Court's interpretation of the 20 year delay was "the dysfunctional administration of California's death penalty system" which resulted "

> **in an inordinate and unpredictable period of delay preceding their actual execution. Indeed, for most, systemic delay has made their - execution so unlikely that the death sentence carefully and deliberately imposed by the jury has been quietly transformed into one no rational jury or legislature could ever impose: *life in prison, with the remote possibility of death*. As for the random few for whom execution does become a reality, they will have languished for so long on Death Row that their execution will serve no retributive or deterrent purpose and will be arbitrary.**[242]

As explained in Jones v. Chappell in 2014, the delay between sentencing and execution begins with the automatic appeal following a death sentence where a condemned prisoner often must wait between 3 to 5 years before qualified counsel is appointed, and the overall review process can be up to 25 years or more. [243] For Alejandro Ruiz, who was sentenced to death in 1980, his appeal was still pending when he died of natural causes in 2007.

Capital punishment has met several stumbling blocks in California. In June of 2014 a District Court judge decided that the death penalty served no penological purpose, other than providing a cruel and unusual punishment, and was unconstitutional.[244] The ruling was based on belief that "when an individual is condemned to death in California, the sentence carries with it an implicit promise from the State that it will actually be carried out." The court then explained that this promise is made to the citizens of

---

[242]Jones v. Chappell, United States District Court for the Central District of California Case No.: CV 09-02158-CJC, Order Declaring California's Death Penalty System Unconstitutional, 2014
[243]*Ibid.*
[244]*Ibid.*

California who underwrite the costly capital proceedings and to those who believe the death penalty is a just punishment and to "to the victims and their loved ones, for whom just punishment might provide some semblance of moral and emotional closure from an otherwise unimaginable loss." Finally, the promise is made to death row prisoners "as a statement their crimes are so heinous they have forfeited their right to life." Because the death penalty is rarely imposed, and when it is imposed (although not carried out) has nothing to do with the crime but cost and budgets, the death penalty in California has no penological purpose and is unrelated to retribution and deterrence. In 2015 a three judge panel for the Ninth Circuit reversed the judge's decision because "federal courts may not consider novel constitutional theories on habeas review, without considering the parties' arguments concerning exhaustion."[245]

In November of 2016 Proposition 62 to eliminate the death penalty was defeated by a 53 percent margin, while proposition 66 to speed up the death penalty process was passed by a 51 percent vote. On March 13, 2019 Governor Gavin Newsom signed executive order N-09-19 which called the death penalty "unfair, unjust, wasteful, protracted and does not make our state safer." He ordered a moratorium on the death penalty, the repeal of the lethal injection procedure, and the closing of the death chamber at San Quentin.[246] This order changed neither conviction nor sentence of prisoners. In April of 2019, contrary to Newsom's executive order, the Supreme Court of California upheld the death sentence for Juan Sanchez for the murder of Ermanda Reyes and Lorena Martinez. This court explained that "Defendant reiterates numerous challenges to California's death penalty law that we have repeatedly rejected. We adhere to our previous decisions."[247]

---

[245]Jones v. Davis (warden), United States Court of Appeals for the Ninth Circuit, No. 14-56373, D.C. No. 2:09-CV-02158-CJC, November 12, 2015
[246]https://www.gov.ca.gov/2019/03/13/governor-gavin-newsom-orders-a-halt-to-the-death-penalty-in-california/
[247]People v. Juan Sanchez, Supreme Court of California, Tulare County Superior Court 40863, April 29, 2019

The odd status of IQ in California is unfair to white offenders who might have any number of IQ scores as children which could show intellectual disability before age of onset. In that IQ really cannot be used in any meaningful way in California to adjudge Atkins claims, and the likelihood no one on California's death row will ever be executed, the logical solution would be to eliminate the death penalty in California. The California citizenry might want capital punishment, but there really isn't a need for the death penalty...unless the ultimate punishment is death row and not execution.

Mendez v. Westminster

The various strategies used to re-interpret and often subvert the definition of intellectual disabilities are similar in purpose to those used to stigmatize and segregate black children as having intellectual disabilities. In many States, following the more aggressive approach in the 1960s used by courts to desegregate after Brown v. Board of Education in 1954, a more paternalistic and benevolent approach to segregation appeared in the form of Educable Mental Retardation (EMR). The great increase in EMR began in California, not with black children, but with the segregation of children of "Mexican and Latin decent." In Mendez v. Westminster School District the District Court found that children of Mexican ancestry ("determined largely by the Latinized or Mexican name of the child") were placed in separate schools until the sixth grade with the ostensible benevolent purpose of improving language skills. The court found in 1946 that this was discriminatory and contrary to the Constitution. The court reasoned that "It is also established by the record that the methods of segregation prevalent in the defendant school districts foster antagonisms in the children and suggest inferiority among them where none exists."

Shortly after *Westminster* was decided California initiated programs for EMR children, as determined by a psychological examination, to provide special education services. The enrollment of EMR classes climbed from approximately 10,000 in

1950 to 57,000 in 1968. In 1972 a District Court decided that IQ tests were the primary mechanism for disproportionately placing black students in EMR classes. As a result the burden shifted to the State to show that IQ "tests were rationally related to the purpose of segregating students according to their ability to learn in regular classes, at least as those tests were applied to black students." California argued that poverty, poor nutrition, problems during pregnancy, black schools, "more white parents than black parents placing their mentally retarded children in private schools" etc. were factors causing disproportionality. Because there was little evidence to support these possibilities, "the court granted the preliminary injunction and restrained the school district from placing black students in classes for the educable mentally retarded on the basis of criteria which placed primary reliance on the results of I.Q. tests."[248]

In response to the problems with IQ testing in California the State Department of Education required testing in a child's primary language (incredibly Spanish-speaking children were sometimes tested in English), the retesting of all children in EMR classes, parent consent for testing and EMR placement, and a reduced IQ cutoff for EMR of 70.[249] The fact that a guideline had to be included in the special education regulations which required that assessments are "not to be discriminatory on a racial or cultural basis" and "provided and administered in the child's native language" indicates the absurd level racism can reach. Specifically, school officials had to be told that giving a Spanish-speaking child or a child who had limited English proficiency, a test in English might somehow impact IQ test performance.

The steps taken by the California State Education Department in 1970, nudged along by the judicial oversight of Larry P. v. Riles, helped reduce the number of children classified as EMR. As a result of court and State legislative findings that EMR classes were

---

[248]Larry P. et al., Plaintiffs, v. Wilson Riles et al., Defendants, United States District Court for the Northern District of California, 343 F. Supp. 1306 (1972)
[249] Hanson, F.M., and Shryock, C. Programs for the educable mentally retarded in public schools. California State Department of Education, Sacramento, California, (Eric #ED 116405), 1974

discriminatory, denied educational opportunity and were segregative, EMR enrollments in California declined to less than 20,000 by 1975,[250] and by 1980 EMR enrollment decreased to 14,448.[251] By the 1970s the Hispanic EMR enrollment decreased but black disproportionality continued where the overall black enrollment was approximately 10 percent but the black EMR enrollment 25 percent.[252] The disproportionality in California was recognized by State officials as a problem, and a solution was sought, but other States latched on to EMR classes as one solution to an entirely different problem: using segregation as a remedial strategy.

As the number of black children identified as EMR decreased in California there was a dramatic increase in EMR enrollments in other States, especially in the South and other havens of segregation (e.g., Chicago). The pretext for this disproportionality was invariably benevolence. In 1972 in Portsmouth, Virginia, an appellate court found that although 75 percent of children assigned to a special school for the mentally retarded were black (the school district had previously operated a dual or segregated system), the "assignments are made to achieve such salutary educational objectives and are in no sense the product of racial discrimination, nothing in Brown, or any subsequent precedents enlarging on Brown, would invalidate such assignments. Brown did not proscribe sound educational practices intended to maximize educational opportunities, when applied in a nondiscriminatory manner."[253] How insightful to use "sound educational practices" to condone segregation.

Did the appellate court really believe the poor educational performance of black children in 1972 in Portsmouth, Virginia was not the result of prior segregation? Or that disproportionately assigning black children to certain schools or classes was not tantamount to segregation but done to "maximize

---

[250]Larry P. v. Riles, 495 F. Supp. 926 (1979)

[251]1980 Elementary and Secondary Schools Civil Rights Survey, State Summaries, Washington, D.C., 1982, ED#219478

[252]See Larry P., 1979, for years 1973-76, EMR SDE enrollments

[253]Copeland v. School Board of the City of Portsmouth, Virginia, 464 F.2d 932 (1972)

educational opportunities"? Then again, there are probably those who believe that lynching was not a product of race, or literacy tests and the various Jim Crow laws were not the result of racial animus. Maybe literacy tests were not the result of invidious intent but to elevate voting standards. This requires disavowing how literacy tests were administered, by whom, and how States used information from these tests to deny voting rights. Even a hint of a racially neutral explanation is difficult other than for the most ardent segregationist for black and white drinking fountains and other popular stains of segregation.

In 1980 in Chicago a District Court judge decided, when considering the disproportionate placement of black children in EMR-type classes that "A motive for unnecessary placement is nonexistent, since the cost to the local system of administering the program far exceeds the state and federal aid received for it."[254] Incredibly, in Chicago with a history of segregation and discrimination, a city which openly practiced *de jure* segregation, financial expenditures was one rationale for segregated EMR classes (EMH classes in Chicago) based on the apparent belief that costly segregation was good segregation.

In Chicago IQ tests were taken at face value. The judge decided that IQ tests in general were not racially biased because there were no specific test questions showing racial bias. The judge responded to the fact the regulations required "procedures to assure that testing and evaluation materials and procedures utilized for the purposes of evaluation and placement of handicapped children will be selected and administered so as not to be racially or culturally discriminatory" by explaining that "the requirement that 'materials and procedures' used for assessment be non-discriminatory, and that no single procedure be the sole criterion for assessment, seems to me to contemplate that the process as a whole be nondiscriminatory." Some discrimination was OK, maybe even a lot of discrimination, but not discrimination "as a whole." In Chicago, if this is to be believed, the intent for

---

[254]Parents in Action on Special Education (PASE) v. Hannon, 506 F. Supp. 831 (1980)

EMR classes, which were disproportionately black, was the result of benevolence and good will

In Georgia a similar convoluted interpretation was used to show there was no invidious intent in the placement of black children in EMR classes.[255] In an excellent example of racial amnesia in Georgia, the District Court decided "the plaintiffs failed to prove that the disparity in the lower achievement groups is the result of the present effects of past discrimination." The explanation for the racial disproportionality is one of benevolence and that "ability grouping as practiced by [the] defendants . . . is designed to remedy the past results of past segregation through better educational opportunity for the present generation of black students." The United States Court of Appeals reasoned that although the classification of EMR is guided by regulations, a child is not necessarily misclassified if the school agency does not comply with regulations and procedural safeguards. Parents are then faced with the impossible task of proving that a child is not EMR, where a determination of EMR is guided by the regulations, by not considering the regulations. A prosecutor can undermine *Atkins* by requiring claimants to prove intellectual disability, as guided by professional definitions, by not considering or re-interpreting the professional regulations to achieve a self-serving State goal (viz., execution).

Florida and other States have not been averse to using a strict IQ cutoff, but for black children in Georgia the appellate court offered the standard error of measurement as an explanation for classifying black children with IQ scores above 70 (or two standard errors of measurement). Even more interesting is how adaptive behavior was assessed. The appellate court explained that in-school adaptive behavior was far more important than out-of-school adaptive behavior. In other words, poor school achievement was used to substantiate mental retardation which was then used to explain poor school achievement. The explanation by the court was that something more than noncompliance with regulations (which the appellate court

---

[255]Georgia State Conference of Branches of NAACP, V. State of Georgia, 775 F.2d 1403 (1985)

remanded for "appropriate relief" as per the Education of All Handicapped Children Act) and procedural safeguards is required for a constitutional violation: "Although noncompliance with procedural safeguards may increase the risk of misclassification, it cannot be said to conclusively establish it. We will not assume, for example, that a child assigned to an EMR program is actually normal simply because his parents did not participate in the evaluation as required by federal regulations."[256] The intent of this is difficult to discern, and maybe the motive was not invidious, but this dubious reasoning provided a justification for the disproportionate placement of black children in EMR classes in Georgia.

The actual intent to disproportionately placing black children in EMR classes, and the very opposite approach used by States to disprove intellectual disability in Atkins claims, might seem at odds but the underlying reasoning for both is completely consistent. For black children, regardless of the professed intent to meet the educational needs of children by disproportionately placing black children in EMR-type classes, the end result was more often than not segregation and an inferior education. For black adults seeking Atkins relief, the ostensible intent might be to somehow pay fidelity to the Eighth Amendment by re-interpreting the definition of intellectual disability and to trivialize relevant evidence, but the end result is death row and, after many years of appeals, sometimes death by natural causes on death row, sometimes suicide, sometimes execution, and possibly resentencing.

The commonality between EMR and capital punishment is not how the definitional criteria for intellectual disability are used but the invidious result for both: segregation and an inferior education for many black children; death row and execution for a disproportionate number of black adults.

Larry P. v. Riles

---

[256]*Ibid.*

Every black inmate on death row could claim intellectual disability as a child, yet California's prohibition against the use of IQ testing for black children would preclude a fair examination of this essential evidence. California recognizes the racial disproportionality caused by IQ testing in children, yet requires this same testing, albeit de-emphasized, for adults seeking Atkins relief.

Not only must the defense for an Atkins claimant consider what time period a claimant was in school, but the criteria used at the time and how the criteria were used (or not). As the resolute California Judge Peckham said in Larry v. Riles in 1979 "It may be that E.M.R. classes and the philosophy underlying them are educational anachronisms. They focus on a label--retardation-- derived for the most part from arbitrary cut-off scores on standardized IQ tests, and that label is used to justify academic isolation in special dead-end classes."[257]

The potential misuse of IQ alone, that a single number could define a child's intellectual ability and terminate educational opportunity, was to be offset by the three prong definition consisting of IQ (the measure of significantly subaverage general intellectual functioning), deficits in adaptive behavior, and age of onset. The three prongs were more theory than fact. As noted in Larry P. v. Riles in 1979, adaptive behavior was not always assessed, and when assessed the data was often not used.[258] For children, then and now, "The record of the I.Q. score was clearly the most scrupulously kept record, and it appears to have been the most important one. The lure of the single, seemingly precise and objective measure is no doubt strong." California schools could use IQ tests to identify mental retardation for black children but there were conditions: the State Board of Education must 1) request that IQ tests be approved, 2) determine that the tests are not racially or culturally discriminatory, 3) ensure that IQ tests have a nondiscriminatory impact, and 4) determine the tests have been validated to place children in EMR classes. Thus far, these requirements have never been met.

---

[257]Larry P. v. Riles, 495 F. Supp. 926 (1979)
[258]Larry P. v. Riles, 495 F. Supp. 926 (1979).

The IQ ban for classifying black children as EMR is often cited as a great civil rights breakthrough for children with disabilities but, in reality, this was nothing more than a quirky California decision that was ignored by every other State. In the 1960s and 1970s the California Legislature and the United States Court for the Northern District of California did more to address racial disproportionality in EMR classes than any State or Court at the time or since.

The use of IQ testing in California is all-important for an adult, yet IQ tests have been banned for use with black children in the State. Black children in California can be placed in an EMR-type classroom (this name has long been abandoned), but IQ is not part of the classification equation. In that professionals and State statutes have defined "significantly subaverage general intellectual functioning" by IQ, an Atkins claimant in California must prove intellectual disability by a preponderance of the evidence using a racially tainted index. This is no small matter for a State with a relatively small black population (6.5 percent), but a death row population having 268 black inmates (36.1 percent) of the 742 prisoners on death row as of November, 2018.

In 1916, the year the Stanford-Binet Intelligence Scale was published, there were 38 lynchings (many lynchings went unreported) in the United States according to the Historical American Lynching (HAL) database.[259] Of these lynchings 37 were black. A primary reason for the disproportionate number of black lynchings (e.g., for disrespect, the pretext of rape) was to maintain white supremacy which was, in a way, no different than white and black drinking fountains and the bevy of other Jim Crow laws. If someone is deemed less than human, what could be wrong with dehumanizing behavior? To this end one can only marvel at our Constitution which reads (Article 1, Section 2) "Representatives and direct Taxes shall be apportioned among the several States which may be included within this Union, according to their respective Numbers, which shall be determined by adding to the whole Number of free Persons, including those bound to Service for a Term of Years, and excluding Indians not taxed, three fifths of all other Persons."

---

[259]http://people.uncw.edu/hinese/HAL/HAL%20Web%20Page.htm

More subtle ways, under the guise of science, were used to show the black inferiority of which and IQ testing plays no small role. For every Atkins in California claim the case of Larry P. v. Riles provides an important historical A framework for the use of IQ. The *Larry P.* case is intriguing because of the fact that the principal defendant, Wilson Riles, the Superintendent of Public Instruction, was African-American. All evidence suggests that the Superintendent and California legislature were aware of black disproportionality in EMR classes and actually did something to rectify the problem. The history of IQ testing in California, coupled with the disproportionate number of blacks on death row, is all the more unusual considering the fact that California is, more or less, the home of IQ testing (viz., the Stanford-Binet tests beginning in 1916).

The tortured history of IQ testing has been sanitized, to a degree, by the Supreme Court by proclaiming an IQ of 75 as a constitutional standard while ignoring the racism long associated with IQ testing and the shaky so-called science of IQ tests. The cutoff of 70 was first proposed by Lewis Madison Terman in 1916.[260] Terman classified children with IQ scores between 70 and 80 as "border-line deficiency, sometimes classifiable as dullness, often as feeble-mindedness." He also asserted that IQ scores of the feeble-minded are "rarely above 75 I.Q" (pp. 79-80). Applying Terman's standard to today's death penalty prohibition, offenders with IQ scores below 70 would "definitely" be ineligible for the death penalty, and those with scores above 75 would "rarely" be eligible. At the time Terman was not encumbered by the added requirement of deficits in adaptive behavior.

Much attention has been given to the margin of error of five points by the Supreme Court to raise the cutoff from 70 to 75 for Atkins claims, but little attention is given the fact the basic cutoff value of 70 is completely arbitrary. The ability to assign great

---

[260]Terman, L. M. The Measurement of Intelligence an Explanation of and a Complete Guide for the Use of the Stanford Revision and Extension of the Binet-Simon Intelligence Scale, Riverside Press: Cambridge, Massachusetts, 1916, p. 91.

constitutional merit to an IQ score of 75, based on an arbitrary base score of 70 and a margin of error of suspicious origin, requires a suspension of belief. The selection of 70 as a basis for determining mental retardation by Terman seems to have been based on data from a study conducted by Fritz Chotzen (a German Psychiatrist in Breslau, Germany) and discussed by William Stern, a German Psychologist, in 1914.[261] Stern provided data showing that when the mental age of a child is six and chronological age eight, the resulting mental quotient of .75 was a useful index for explaining intelligence. His research showed that morons" had "three-fourths" the intellectual ability of a normal child. Interestingly, this esoteric study by a German psychiatrist in 1912, based on a French researcher, re-interpreted by a German psychologist shortly thereafter, and then translated into English in 1914, provides the basic "research" for an IQ score of 70, or about 70 or maybe even 75 or maybe between 70 and 80 or something. This is historical; this is interesting; science it is not.

One of Terman's innovations in 1916 was to multiply the *mental quotient* by 100 to produce the IQ score recognizable today. Rather than a mental quotient of .75, this score is transformed to 75 by

$$IQ = \frac{Mental\ Age}{Chronological\ Age} \times 100$$

When David Wechsler started developing his tests in the 1930's, he decided to avoid the mental age divided by chronological age concept— there were statistical problems inherent in the MA/CA quotient—and calculated IQ scores based on the mean and standard deviation of the test. The Wechsler tests were not made out of whole cloth but were based on tests developed by the United States Army during World War I (the *alpha* and *beta* tests). Today, for individualized tests of intelligence, IQ is no longer a quotient but represents the number of standard deviations a score is above or below the mean. This transformed value, or **z score**,

---

[261]Stern, William, The Psychological Methods of Testing Intelligence (Translated by Guy Montrose Whipple), Warwick and York, Baltimore, 1914.

has a mean of 0 and a standard deviation of 1. Thus, a **z score** of 1 indicates a score one standard deviation above the mean, and a *z score* of -2, a score that is two standard deviations below the mean. This deviation IQ is achieved by first subtracting a person's score on a test from the mean or average test score and then dividing the result by the test's standard deviation or

$$Deviation\ Score\ (z\ score)\ = \frac{(Score - Mean\ Score)}{Standard\ Deviation}$$

To give the appearance of a traditional IQ score, the deviation score is then multiplied by 15 and then 100 is added which is a simple linear transformation and does not change the underlying normal curve meaning.

$Deviation\ IQ\ = z\ score\ X\ 15 + 100$

If the score on a test is 40 and the test's mean is 50 and the standard deviation is 5, the deviation score is (40-50)/5 or -2 which indicates that the score is two standard deviations below the mean. This deviation score or *z score* is then multiplied by 15 and 100 is added or -2 (15) + 100=70. An IQ of 70 means a test is two standard deviations below the mean given a mean of 100 and standard deviation of 15. Scores of 30 and 70 are identical given a mean and standard deviation of 50 and 10 for the former and 100 and 70 for the latter. That is, given these means and standard deviations, scores of 30 and 70 are both two standard deviations below the mean. An IQ of today is many things but a "quotient" it is not.

An IQ point is actually a reference to the normal curve and has no inherent value concerning intelligence. A comparison between IQ based on (MA / CA) X 100 and an IQ based on a deviation score is meaningless. The IQ cutoff of 70 suggested by Terman in 1916 has little or nothing to do with the IQ cutoff (plus the error of measurement) used today. For Wechsler the importance of 70 was that it represented a point at which approximately 2.2 percent have scores below 70 (generally speaking). In 1958

Wechsler cited 69 and below as the cutoff for "defective" based on the premise that this cutoff "seemed reasonable" for defining "the mentally defective group." For the earlier Wechsler-Bellevue Scale in 1939, the cutoff for "defective" was 65 and lower.[262] The *scientific* basis for the IQ cutoff of 70 used today, based on the work of Terman and then Wechsler, is nonexistent.

In 1916 Terman used an IQ cutoff of 70, apparently, because it provided definitive evidence of what he referred to as "feeble-mindedness." The idea of a strict cutoff of 70 or 75 was never proposed by Terman in 1916 but rather "the boundary lines between such groups are absolutely arbitrary." He recognized that "some individuals with IQ somewhat below 75 can hardly be classed as feeble-minded in the ordinary sense of the term, while others with I Q a little above 75 could hardly be classified in any other group" (p. 80).

Wechsler set the mean of IQ tests to 100 and the standard deviation to 15 because it seemed to be in concert with the "historical definition" of IQ and "in line with the order of numerical values of IQ's now in general use."[263] More importantly, who would buy an IQ test—and the bottom line is that IQ testing is a business— where the mean was 0 or something other than 100 or thereabouts? The point is that a score of 70 is not based on science and adding five points does not make the resulting score of 75 more magic or more meaningful.

Given the shaky statistical underpinnings of the IQ concept, where a bright line was disavowed from the beginning of IQ test development, there is considerable wiggle room to use IQ to misclassify children and likewise deny Atkins claims for adults. Racial differences found by intelligence testing was less a discovery than a reinforcement of prevailing attitudes...many of which exist to this day. Terman observed that children who "test at high-grade moronity or at border-line" are very common among "Spanish-Indian and Mexican families of the Southwest and also

---

[262]Wechsler, David. The Measurement and Appraisal of Adult Intelligence (4th Ed.) The Williams and Wilkins Co, Baltimore, 1958, pp. 38-44.
[263]Wechsler, David, The Measurement of Adult Intelligence (3rd Edition), the Williams and Williams Co., Baltimore, 1944.

among negroes. Their dullness seems to be racial, or at least inherent in the family stocks from which they come."

Intelligence tests measure, then and now, a variety of idiosyncratic intellectual tasks (e.g., vocabulary, analogies, mazes, block design, etc.), but IQ tests also measure lack of educational opportunity, poor educational opportunity, poverty, environment, socio-economic factors, unrelenting forms of discrimination, lack of jobs, lack of money, lack of health care, and a lack of whatever there can be a lack of. Terman should have been somewhat aware that the educational facilities for black and white children, teacher training, teacher salaries, transportation and overall educational opportunities might have had some influence on test performance. Just maybe, in 1916, a black child might have been at a disadvantage when asked by a white examiner "If I were to but 4 cents worth of candy and should give the storekeeper 10 cents, how much money would I get back?"[264] Given an unequal education, segregation and discrimination, familiarity with such words (age 12) as *pity, charity, revenge*, and most certainly *justice*, vocabulary of black children might have been less than that of white children in Palo Alto, California—and even less in Jackson, Mississippi or Tuscaloosa, Alabama in 1916.

The 1983 classification manual for the AAMD suggested that the base IQ score of 70 "has been arrived at by professional consensus, after consideration of the consequences of setting a higher or lower value" (p. 22) and "the cut-off IQ at 70 appears to be the best solution for most of the problems encountered with the diagnosis of mental retardation of people who are in the 'gray area' of retardation-average." The solution was not a fixed margin of error (e.g., 5 points) but to treat "IQ with some flexibility" so that some individuals with IQ scores above 70 could be provided special education if necessary, some individuals with IQ scores below 70 would not be identified as having mental retardation (AAMD, 1983, 23-24). The 1983 manual does reference the SEM of 3 to 4 points (depending on whether the test is the Wechsler of Stanford-Binet) and explains that the 95 percent confidence level would be a margin of error of 6 to 8 points or an IQ band of 64 to

---

[264]an actual 1916 question

76 or 62 to 78 (where the band is 2 X SEM). The 1983 classification manual is consistent with Terman's ambiguity concerning IQ categories and is not a ringing endorsement for a bright-line IQ cutoff score.

The racial disproportionality on death row and in the number executions is attributed, in part, to poverty, environment, a resulting increase in crime, and all manner of prior segregation and discrimination. For many black children these factors are readily ignored so that the mild intellectual disability category is used to not only explain educational deficiencies but to rationalize the need to address these deficiencies by segregation.

For adults seeking Atkins relief States routinely attribute low IQ to lack of motivation, malingering or environment; for children States and professionals have historically, and just as routinely, interpreted the low IQ of black children as a valid indicator of intellectual ability. In California in the 1970s State Department of Education officials "testified that they believed the over enrollment of black and Chicano children in the E.M.R. classes accurately reflected the incidence of mental retardation among those children."[265] Today such officials would be far less forthcoming as to underlying beliefs.

For children there was never a loss for reasons to explain the racial disproportionality of EMR classes which included genetics, Fetal Alcohol Syndrome, and the creative explanation "that since black people tend to be poor, and poor pregnant women tend to suffer from inadequate nutrition, it is possible that the brain development of many black children has been retarded by their mothers' poor diet during pregnancy."[266] This type of racism in California would have been far less nuanced than in enclaves of segregation and discrimination.

For Akins claims, IQ and adaptive behavior are often interpreted and/or re-interpreted quite differently. For Atkins claimants IQ is important when scores are above whatever cutoff is used, but if

---

[265]Larry P. v. Riles, 495 F. Supp. 926 (1979)
[266]Larry P. v. Riles, 343 F. Supp. 1306 (1972)

scores exist below the cutoff, IQ becomes less important or dismissed entirely. Likewise, where adaptive behavior for children is often given lesser weight than IQ, the opposite occurs in Atkins claims because this prong can be interpreted to mean the ability to adapt as a child, to adapt before a capital offense, to adapt at the time of the evidentiary hearing, or to adapt while on death row.

When considering the unusual state of IQ testing in California, Larry P. and the ban for the IQ testing of black children, and the disproportionate number of black children in EMR classes in California, much can be traced back to Jim Crow laws and the constant mutation of segregation and discrimination. Solutions for doing away with the problems associated with EMR classes included: 1) providing no services to students with exceptional needs…especially black students, 2) righteously eliminating the EMR label although changing nothing else, or 3) changing the EMR label to something less offensive, and 4) shuffling the students to other categories where oversight was less rigorous (viz., specific learning disabilities),. After a huge reduction in the number of students in EMR classes, the elimination of EMR classes, and the combination of all intellectual disabilities into one category, by 2011 the percent of black students identified as intellectually disabled was less than eleven percent but this still represented a disproportionate number of blacks students based on the 6 to 21 school population.[267] Discrimination and segregation by categorization does not end with the elimination of using IQ tests or eliminating the EMR category to a more acceptable variant. Discrimination and segregation simply mutates to something new, something less obvious, but something.

Hobson v. Hansen

The use of IQ testing of black children was prohibited in California, but mild mental retardation in the South and other States, which operated dual school systems, became a strategy to explain the

---

[267]The ratio of black students per 100 to white students per 100 identified as intellectually disabled was 2.34.

poor educational performance of black children was the result of intellectual inferiority and not prior *de jure* segregation. Following Brown v. Board of Education in 1954, most schools operated dual (segregated) school systems and the 1955 proviso in Brown II that schools create unitary (nonsegregated) school systems with "all deliberate speed" was interpreted to mean *all deliberate delay*. Not until more than a decade after the 1954 decision did courts begin enforcing the *Brown* mandate. In concert with desegregation the classification of children as EMR, especially black children, gained considerable popularity. In addition to the appearance of educational benevolence, the EMR category achieved many of the educational objectives important prior to *Brown* in the form of segregation and the onus of intellectual inferiority.

For many States following desegregation the educational differences between black and white children became obvious. In Washington, D.C., the solution for dealing with the inequities of segregation was segregation.[268] Following Bolling v. Sharpe[269] (the companion decision to Brown v. Board of Education in 1954[270]) and the desegregation of District schools, achievement testing showed that 25 percent of tenth grade black students were below the sixth grade level in reading, and 44 percent were below the sixth grade level in arithmetic. The low achieving students were "predominantly" from Division II (black) schools. The discovery of the "large number of retarded negro children" resulted in a tracking system which had the good intention of providing every student with "the maximum opportunity for self-development...by adjusting curriculum offerings to different levels of need and ability as the pupil moves through the stages of education and growth in our schools."

As with the EMR category/mild mental retardation, tracking was seen as "a legitimate pedagogical method of providing maximum

---

[268]Hobson v. Hansen, 252 F. Supp. 4 (1966), 269 F. Supp. 401 (1967) and 327 F. Supp. 844 (1971)
[269]The Bolling v. Sharpe, 347 U.S. 497 (1954) decision was required because the 5th rather than the 14th Amendment applies to the District.
[270]Bolling v. Sharpe was based on the Fifth Amendment which applied to the District of Columbia rather than the Fourteenth Amendment

educational opportunity for children of widely ranging ability levels; and that any racial effect is but an innocent and unavoidable coincidence of ability grouping." The fact that the "pedagogical method" was little more than repackaged segregation where black children were again denied educational opportunity, not because of race, but because of "legitimate" educational practices under the guise of tracking.
To compensate for the "problems created by the sudden commingling of numerous educationally retarded Negro students with the better educated white students" a four-track system was adopted comprised of gifted, above-average, average, and a Special Academic track. The purpose of the Special Academic track was to provide a highly simplified curriculum for students with IQ scores 75 or lower "who have been variously described as 'slow learners,' 'retarded,' 'academically retarded,' 'retarded slow learners,' or 'stupid.'" The intent of the Special Academic track to help "retarded negro children" was ostensibly benevolent but the connection between the intended "help" and actual help was tenuous. The Special Academic Track was characterized by untrained teachers, an absence of remedial or compensatory educational programs, a "limited or watered down curriculum" resulting in "both physical segregation and a disparity of educational opportunity."[271]

For black students, struggling academically, unable to comprehend the curriculum, repeatedly failing grades, the educational remedy was to direct these students "into a special curriculum geared to his limited abilities and designed to give him a useful 'basic' education - one which makes no pretense of equaling traditionally taught curricula." The solution for treating "the casualties of *de jure* segregation," caused by segregation and the denial of educational opportunity, was segregation and denial of educational opportunity. The intent in the District might have been a good faith effort to meet the learning needs of black children resulting from prior segregation and discrimination but the result was simply a different flavor of segregation and

---

[271]Hobson v. Hansen, 252 F. Supp. 4 (1966), 269 F. Supp. 401 (1967) and 327 F. Supp. 844 (1971)

discrimination where benevolence was proclaimed but segregation and discrimination prevailed.

Mills v. Board of Education

a lack of special education as a child as evidence that an Atkins claimant is not intellectually disabled is to discount history and prior discrimination. For children the refusal to allow participation in regular educational programs, or any programs for that matter, provided the catalyst for the special education law in 1975. In Mills v. the Board of Education of the District of Columbia seven black children (the case was supposedly not about race) were denied access to a public education. Although all members of this suit were black, they represented all students "who are eligible for a free public education and who have been, or may be, excluded from such education or otherwise deprived by defendants of access to publicly supported education."[272] At the time, the primary educational practice for children with disabilities was neglect and exclusion, and for children identified as mild mentally retarded, the result was also neglect and exclusion but more in the manner of traditional segregation. One interesting strategy to inform parents that their child had been excluded from school was not to send the school bus. No call; no notification; just no bus.[273] Of the estimated 22,000 children with disabilities in the District of Columbia in 1971, over 50% were provided no services and were otherwise denied admission, suspended, or expelled from public schools without a hearing or due process.[274]

Lack of financial resources was one of the primary reasons for not providing an appropriate education, but the District Court of the

---

[272]Mills v. Board of Education of the District of Columbia 348 F. Supp. 866 (1972)

[273]The Pennsylvania Association for Retarded Children et al., Plaintiffs, v. Commonwealth of Pennsylvania et al., Defendants, United States District Court For The Eastern District of Pennsylvania, 343 F. Supp. 279; 1972 U.S. Dist.

[274]Mills v. Board of Education of the District of Columbia, 348 F. Supp. 866; 1972 U.S. Dist

District of Columbia was not impressed with the school district's "insufficient funding or administrative inefficiency" difficulties and ordered that no eligible child be excluded from school by "rule, policy, or practice." The result of these abuses and others provided the rationale for the 1975 special education law or Public Law 94-142.

Georgia State Conference v. Georgia

Georgia requires a higher standard for a successful Atkins claim but the State has historically been far more liberal when categorizing black children as EMR. Georgia illustrates how judicial arrogance, as is the case in many Atkins claims, can coincide with segregation. 1983, in Lee County Georgia, the black school enrollment was 33 percent but 82 percent (67 of 82 students) of the children classified as educable mentally retarded were black.[275] In Miller County, in 1978, the enrollment was 40 percent black and 60 percent white, yet 53 of 58 students classified as educable mentally retarded were black.[276] An Appellate Court found numerous procedural violations relating "to the failure to administer psychological exams, assess adaptive behavior, conduct timely placement reevaluations, consider less restrictive alternatives to EMR placement and ensure adequate parental participation in the placement process," but these errors were the result of "human error and financial and administrative difficulties." In other words, there was no intent to discriminate against black children.

The court explained that "noncompliance with procedural safeguards may increase the risk of misclassification, it cannot be said to conclusively establish it. We will not assume, for example, that a child assigned to an EMR program is actually normal simply because his parents did not participate in the evaluation as required by federal regulations." Procedural guidelines are used

---

[275]Georgia State Conference of Branches of NAACP, v. State of Georgia, 775 F.2d 1403 (1985)
[276]Georgia State Conference of Branches of NAACP v. State of Georgia, 99 F.R.D. 16 (1983)

to determine mental retardation; a State does not follow procedural guidelines; and a child (and parents) must somehow show that a determination of mental retardation, based on a misapplication of procedural guidelines, is incorrect! According to the court the disproportionate number of black children classified as educable mentally retarded was not the issue at all. The real problem was the number of black children misclassified as a result of a misapplication of the procedural regulations. Yet, when the misapplication of procedural guidelines was cited, these were rationalized as the result of "human error" and other difficulties.

For the less stigmatizing and segregated specific learning disabilities category used by the Georgia schools, 22% (9) were black and 78% (32) were white.[277] The determination of a child's disability can be based on many factors, of which racism is one (especially in Georgia and other States). For white defendants seeking Atkins relief, a childhood classification of specific learning disability, which could be used to deny the existence of an intellectual disability before age of onset, might have been racially motivated. Odd as it is, a white defendant who was incorrectly classified as having a specific learning disability as a child because of race could be denied Atkins relief because of this racially motivated classification.

To justify the disproportionate identification of black children in EMR classes, Georgia relied on a re-interpretation of adaptive behavior in a way that is not dissimilar from how States re-interpret adaptive behavior to deny Atkins claims. The State can say that a claimant did not show adaptive behavior before age 18, criminal behavior demonstrated the ability to adapt, etc. For black children in Georgia identified as EMR the court decided that the ability to adapt to school was the critical issue because "The District Court's interpretation of the state adaptive behavior regulation was premised on the factual findings that evaluating a student's out-of-school adaptive behavior is not always possible "from a practical and financial standpoint," and that in-school adaptive behavior "is the more important evaluative tool."

---

[277]*Ibid.*

The reasoning used by the Georgia court is circular: a child is not able to adapt to school as shown by poor school performance as a result of various forms of segregation and discrimination; poor school performance is then used as the basis for showing an impairment in adaptive behavior; this impairment in adaptive behavior is then used to support a determination of EMR; the EMR classification is then used to explain poor school performance. The result of this circular reasoning is that poor school performance is used to explain poor school performance.

PASE v. Hannon

The finder of fact in Atkins claims may have absolutely no idea of the history and psychometrics of intellectual disability in much the same way a court can rationalize the disproportionality of black children in EMR classes. In 1980 a District Court judge decided the Chicago Public School System had not discriminated against black school children after reading the IQ test items. He reasoned that IQ tests would not result in the misclassification of a child as having mental retardation because "there is no evidence in this record that such misassessments as do occur are the result of racial bias in test items or in any other aspect of the assessment process currently in use in the Chicago public school system."[278] The psychometric-challenged judge was quite convinced in the absolute ability of IQ tests to determine the underlying intelligence of children while ignoring the pitfalls of environmental deprivation, *de jure* and the very effective form of *de facto* residential/school segregation popular in Chicago.

About the time IQ tests were being lauded in Chicago in the 1980s, the Chicago Public Schools were operating a dual school system—not dissimilar from Alabama and Georgia—and used a variety of segregative strategies to create or maintain racial and ethnic segregation.[279] This unlawful conduct included the alteration of

---

[278]Parents in Action on Special Education (PASE) v. Hannon, United States District Court, 1980 506 F.Supp. 831 (N.D. Ill.)
[279]See United States of America v. Board of Education of the City of Chicago, Case 1:80-cv-05124, Filed 9/24/2009

school attendance boundaries, adjusting grade structures to create or maintain segregation, inferior schools, teacher assignments, transfer policy, associating segregated schools and housing projects, and temporary facilities,—overcrowded black schools were given the notorious Willis Wagons label (mobile school units aka trailers) named after the Superintendent of schools Benjamin Willis, while under-crowded white schools were left under-crowded).

Intelligence tests, vilified in California, were hunky dory in Chicago. Unlike Californians, Illinois psychologist, according to the judge, were able to understand "the milieu of the child" and "correct for cultural bias by asking the questions in a sensitive and intelligent way."[280] As to cost over segregation, "A motive for unnecessary placement is nonexistent, since the cost to the local system of administering the program far exceeds the state and federal aid received for it. The total cost of the Chicago special education program exceeds by 50 million dollars per year the state and federal funds received to support it."

For black children in Chicago in the 1980s, IQ scores were taken at face value when placing a disproportionate number of black children into EMH (Educable Mentally Handicapped) classes. In 1978, 62 percent of the Chicago Public School enrollment was black. Of the 13,225 children enrolled in EMH classes 82 percent were black and 1.3 percent white. The rate per 100 was 4.4 for black children 1.3 for white children, and the risk ratio 3.38 (4.4/1.3).[281]

According to the court "Intelligent administration of the IQ tests by qualified psychologists, followed by the evaluation procedures defendants, should rarely result in the misassessment of a child of normal intelligence as one who is mentally retarded. There is no

---

[280]Parents in Action on Special Education (PASE) v. Hannon, 506 F. Supp. 831 (1980)

[281]As discussed in PASE v. Hannon in 1978, there were 483,209 children enrolled in the Chicago public school system. Of those, 299,590, or 62 per cent, were black. Of the 13,225 children enrolled in EMH classes, 10,833, or 82 per cent, were black. Of the 106,581 white children enrolled in the system, 1,404 were attending EMH classes (1.3 percent).

evidence in this record that such misassessments as do occur are the result of racial bias in test items or in any other aspect of the assessment process currently in use in the Chicago public school system."

Latasha Pulliam

The Illinois court attempted to justify the racial wholesomeness of IQ tests, yet these same tests were largely ignored when considering Latasha Pulliam's Atkins claim. Illinois was notable before the death penalty was abolished in 2011 for the number of exonerations which, at 20, included 14 black, 4 white and 2 death row inmates. The last person executed in Illinois was Andrew Kokoraleis in 1999 for the murder of 21-year-old Lorraine Borowski in 1982.

As recently as 2017 a former Illinois death row inmate (Gabriel Solace) was exonerated because of evidence revealed that his confession was the result of abuse and coercion. His journey did not end with freedom but detention by U.S. Immigration and Customs Enforcement (ICE). As of 2019 Florida leads all other States in exonerations with 29 (17 or 58.6 percent black death row inmates.[282] In January of 2003 the Governor of Illinois, George Ryan, commuted the death sentences of 167 death row inmates and in March of 2011, the death penalty in Illinois was abolished. One of the reasons for abandoning the death penalty in Illinois was the large number of exonerations.

Latasha Pulliam, then 20, was sentenced to death for the 1991 kidnapping, torture, sexual assault, and strangulation of 6 year-old (131 counts in all) Shenosha Richards in an apartment near Washington Park on Chicago's South Side.[283] Pulliam was classified as "mentally impaired" at age five and placed in special education classes. At age 11 Pulliam received a full scale IQ score of 72 on the WISC, a score of 77 at age 13, and a score of 74 at age

---

[282]https://deathpenaltyinfo.org/innocence-list-those-freed-death-row
[283]Illinois v. Latasha Pulliam, 680 N.E.2d 343 (1997) and 794 N.E.2d 214 (2002)

15, a WAIS score of 69 in 1994, and a guestimated IQ of 74 by the State expert (in 1991). Her scores as a child and as an adult were consistent with mental retardation yet the State expert believed that Pulliam was malingering "because she faked mental illness and mental impairment during his examination of her." As a result of the commutation of all death sentences in Illinois in 2003, no further consideration of her Atkins claim was necessary.

Pulliam's horrific crime illustrates the difficulty a judge or jury has when considering an Atkins claim and the specific details surrounding a crime. Probably few who heard the cold-hearted and callous details of the torture and murder of a six year old would believe that such a crime warranted lesser culpability. The task of separating a fair consideration of intellectual disability and the heinousness of a crime is one of the primary reasons why a systematic approach for determining intellectual disability is absolutely necessary. For Pulliam a clear record of a disability as a child should have established her Atkins relief. However, allowing the explanation that low IQ was the result of malingering, based on little or no evidence, has more to do with retribution than lesser culpability.

6. ADA

"the ADA unambiguously extends to state prison inmates"[284]

Pennsylvania Dept. of Corrections v. Yeskey

The State is entitled to present evidence that an Atkins claimant is not intellectually disabled; the decision-maker, judge or jury, is not entitled to pick and choose laws. Of all the various statutes, laws, and guidelines, none is more relevant than the American with Disabilities Act (ADA) for Atkins claims. The ADA provides a meeting place for racism, disability and capital punishment.

Before the special education law of 1975 was passed Congress realized that misclassification could be both stigmatizing and segregative. In 1975 the Senate Report (94-168) for the Education of All Handicapped Children Act (P.L. 94-142) recognized the problem of misclassification, especially regarding minorities. The Senate committee cited a 1974 report by the Children's Defense Fund entitled Children Out of School in America that "There is widespread belief and fear among many black parents and school children that special education placement is used against minority children as a means of re-segregating them in school districts where courts have ordered desegregation or as a means of punishing them for racial reasons" (p. 101). The Senate committee cited three areas of abuse: "(1) The misuse of appropriate identification and classification data within the educational process itself; (2) discriminatory treatment as the result of the identification of a handicapping condition; and (3) misuse of identification procedures or methods which results in erroneous classification of a child as having a handicapping condition" (p. 27).

For children, States have historically disproportionately classified black children as having mental retardation/intellectual disabilities, but States are far more exacting when considering the intellectual ability of Atkins claimants. States seem to believe that

---

[284]524 U.S. 206, 211 (1998)

misclassifying a black child as having an intellectual disability is relatively unimportant or benevolent, but showing that an Atkins claimant is not intellectually disabled is of great constitutional concern.

The Supreme Court has allowed States to determine how an intellectual disability is determined in Atkins clams, although not a completely unfettered determination. The Court has also acknowledged that the ADA applies to prisons and prisoners so that a person with a disability, as defined by the ADA, is entitled to the provisions of the ADA. A defendant or prisoner who met the definition of a disability could not and should not be subject to discrimination because of that disability. A prisoner or defendant, who was intellectually disabled, as provided by the ADA, would be entitled to the lesser culpability standard as used in *Atkins* (given that life in prison is a benefit).

The Americans with Disabilities Act of 1990 and the ADA amendments of 2008[285] is intended to limit discrimination against persons with disabilities, persons with a record of a disability, and persons who are regarded as having a disability. The essence of the ADA is that "society has tended to isolate and segregate individuals with disabilities, and, despite some improvements, such forms of discrimination against individuals with disabilities continue to be a serious and pervasive social problem." Congress found "that people with disabilities, as a group, occupy an inferior status in our society, and are severely disadvantaged socially, vocationally, economically, and educationally."

A disability is defined by the ADA as

> **(A) a physical or mental impairment that substantially limits one or more major life activities of such individual; (B) a record of such an impairment; or (C) being regarded as having such an impairment.**

---

[285]P.L. 110-325

Congress has defined major life activities to "include, but are not limited to, caring for oneself, performing manual tasks, seeing, hearing, eating, sleeping, walking, standing, lifting, bending, speaking, breathing, learning, reading, concentrating, thinking, communicating, and working." In addition to the three ADA prongs there are other specific protections offered by the ADA such as a prohibition against the use of threshold criteria to screen out qualified applicants. In part, a threshold test was exactly what Florida used prior to *Hall* in 2014; that is, a strict IQ cutoff was used to prevent consideration of adaptive behavior. The protection against threshold tests is consistent with the Supreme Court's emphasis on the need for individualization. The Court (citing The Supreme Court of Georgia) provides that "The essential question is not whether our new death statute permits the use of some discretion, because admittedly it does, but, rather, whether the discretion to be exercised is controlled by clear and objective standards so as to produce non-discriminatory application."[286] Ronald R. Yeskey had a relatively short prison term, far removed from death row, and his goal was to reduce his confinement from 18-36 months to six months by participating in a Motivational Boot Camp.[287] Title II states that "Subject to the provisions of this subchapter, no qualified individual with a disability shall, by reason of such disability, be excluded from participation in or be denied the benefits of the services, programs, or activities of a public entity, or be subjected to discrimination by any such entity."[288]

The ADA for Title II defines a qualified individual as someone "with a disability who, with or without reasonable modifications to rules, policies, or practices, the removal of architectural, communication, or transportation barriers, or the provision of auxiliary aids and services, meets the essential eligibility requirements for the receipt of services or the participation in programs or activities provided by a public entity."[289] The Technical Manual for Title II advises that "The 'essential eligibility

---

[286]Gregg v. Georgia, 428 U.S. 153 (1976); Coley v. The State, Supreme Court of Georgia, 231 Ga. 829 (1974)

[287]Pennsylvania Dept. of Corrections v. Yeskey, 524 U.S. 206 (1998)

[288]ADA, §12132. Discrimination

[289]See Title II regulations, September 155, 2010, § 35.104 Definitions

requirements' for participation in many activities of public entities may be minimal. For example, most public entities provide information about their programs, activities, and services upon request. In such situations, the only 'eligibility requirement' for such information would be the request itself. However, under other circumstances, the 'essential eligibility requirements' imposed by a public entity may be quite stringent."[290]

Because of Yeskey's hypertension, his participation in the program was denied. Pennsylvania believed that prisons do not provide benefits and therefore the ADA did not apply. In 1998, in Pennsylvania Department of Corrections v. Yeskey, the Supreme Court decided that the ADA most definitely does apply to prisons and prisoners.[291] The Court reasoned (Justice Scalia provided the unanimous opinion) that inmates receive benefits, such as "recreational 'activities,' medical 'services,' and educational and vocational "programs.'"[292] Just as Florida used the plain text to create a strict IQ cutoff, the Supreme Court determined "the plain text of Title II of the ADA unambiguously extends to state prison inmates." There are exceptions to ADA protection as when a person with a disability poses a threat to the safety of others but this provision, for those on death row eligible for Atkins relief, concerns solitary confinement and not solitary confinement in preparation for execution.

Title II ADA is relatively forthright. Does the person have a disability as outlined by the ADA? If so, is the individual otherwise qualified for the benefit or program? Yeskey's hypertension was recognized as an ADA disability, without re-interpretation, and to qualify for the boot camp program that "the individual with a disability must meet the essential eligibility requirements for receipt of services or participation in a public entity's programs, activities." For Yeskey the boot camp program required that the offender is sentenced to state confinement between 2 and 5 years, has not reached 35 years, and the reason for confinement did not

---

[290]The Americans with Disabilities Act Title II Technical Assistance Manual Covering State and Local Government Programs and Services
[291]Pennsylvania Dept. of Corrections v. Yeskey 524 U.S. 206, 211 (1998)
[292]*Ibid.*

include specific rimes (e.g., murder, voluntary manslaughter, rape, involuntary deviate sexual intercourse, kidnapping, robbery, etc.).

For every offender, where the State is seeking the death penalty, a record of intellectual disability or a determination of intellectual disability as a child should preclude the imposition of the death penalty. There are two possibilities that can occur when an individual had been classified as having an intellectual disability as a child. First, the determination was correct. If this is the case, re-interpreting or ignoring this determination, and then relying on different criteria as an adult Atkins claimant, ignores the very purpose of the professional definition which the Supreme Court has given considerable credence. That is, the primary purpose of the definition first offered in 1959 was for children, and then to ignore a determination of intellectual disability as a child has no rational basis. Second, if the determination was incorrect because of environmental factors or simple racism, the resulting denial of educational opportunity, stigmatization, and segregation should not be discounted as factors contributing to lesser culpability for capital murder. For a State to suggest that an Atkins claimant was incorrectly identified as a child with an intellectual disability, or that the defendant no longer has an intellectual disability, exonerates the State of the responsibility for the stigmatizing and intellectual/educational harmful actions when the defendant was a child.

One purpose of the ADA is to recognize a record of disability and then require that this record cannot be ignored to deny benefits. The ADA should also send a message to States that a determination of intellectual disability for a child is a fundamentally important finding that has far reaching consequences. If the State chooses to identify a child as having an intellectual disability, the child will suffer the consequences as an adult and so should the State when seeking execution.

Florida v. Arline

The history of childhood intellectual disabilities provides the essential foundation for every Atkins claim. The Supreme Court has previously considered a "record" of a disability in Florida v. Arline in 1978 but does so infrequently.[293] Gene Arline was discharged as a teacher because of a reoccurrence of tuberculosis in 1979 by the School Board of Nassau County. The District Court decided that she was not "handicapped" under Section 504 (which is the forerunner of the ADA) because the court did not believe Congress intended a contagious disease such as TB to be protected by the Statute. The Supreme Court disagreed and explained her repertory ailment was a major life activity which, in turn, created a record of a disability. A "record" of a disability is an essential element of the ADA because "such fearful, reflexive reactions with actions based on reasoned and medically sound judgments as to whether contagious handicapped persons are 'otherwise qualified' to do the job." Gene Arline was dismissed as an elementary school teacher because of reoccurrences of TB, yet the school district claimed that she was not "handicapped" (as did the District Court).

For many Atkins claimants, a clear record of a disability is marginalized, dismissed outright or used as a two-step process when determining intellectual disability; that is, intellectual disability must exist prior to age 18 and as an adult. Ignoring or dismissing the importance of intellectual disability as a child runs counter to what the Supreme Court expressed in *Arline* where the ADA is intended "To combat the effects of erroneous but nevertheless prevalent perceptions about the handicapped, Congress expanded the definition of 'handicapped individual' so as to preclude discrimination against '[a] person who has a record of, or is regarded as having, an impairment [but who] may at present have no actual incapacity at all.'"

For Atkins relief the ADA should preclude discrimination against a claimant who has a record or was regarded as intellectually disabled, and who may not meet current criteria or the re-interpretation of criteria. The ADA factor of "regarded as" does not mean a passing reference by a judge during a court proceeding that the defendant is intellectually disabled. For Freddie Lee Hall teachers, judges and a variety of data all suggest he was regarded that he was intellectually. There are other educational scenarios

---

[293]Florida v. Arline, 480 U.S. 273, 1987

where "regarded" can be buttressed by relevant evidence as when a child is educated in a classroom with students classified as intellectually impaired but the child's classification is something other than intellectual disability. If a child is placed in a classroom for children with intellectual disabilities and provided an education commensurate with that classification and placement, the State (or board of education, school district, or classification committee) regards that child as intellectual disability no matter the classification or even data to the contrary.

Clark v. California

As an adult, other disabilities (viz., brain-injury, Alzheimer's, dementia,[294] vascular dementia,[295] etc.) might indicate special services are needed to meet diminished cognitive skills. California provides a Clark v. California Remedial (CRP) Plan or Developmental Disability Plan (DDP) for qualified offenders discussed.[296] **The California memorandum stipulates that "For example, an inmate with advanced dementia requiring 24-hour nursing care may be excluded from the DDP. On the other hand, an inmate outside the hospital setting with mild dementia, who has low cognitive scores and requires adaptive supports to program, should be included in the DDP."** There can be or should be little doubt someone with "advanced dementia" requiring 24-hour nursing care would qualify for lesser culpability even though the determination of intellectual disability would be pointless.

Defense counsel, State officials and legislators would do well to consider the many criteria cited in the Clark remedial plan as relevant for Atkins claims. The report has many examples of specific adaptive skills that might indicate the need for special supports. The Clark report explains that some developmentally disabled inmates might have difficulty with self-advocacy and understanding relevant issues in a hearing" and have difficulty

---

[294]Also referred to in the DSM-5 as Major Neurocognitive Disorder
[295]See the ICD-10-CM code F01
[296]Clark v. California, Remedial Plan, amended March 1, 2002, State of California, Department of Corrections

with "any task requiring reading or processing written material (thus they may have difficulty with disciplinary, classification, and/or appeal processes that require reading and understanding). " In a work environment "DDP inmates may be unable to complete tasks; follow work schedules, seek assistance, take criticism, or improve performance. For socialization skills the Clark report offers the following guidance:

> **The DDP inmates may show difficulty establishing and maintaining positive relationships. They may seem naive with respect to prison routine or culture. They may give up possessions to other inmates. They may become vulnerable to sexual predators, manipulation by other inmates, and/or be recruited for gang activities. The DDP inmates may engage in a repetitive cycle of disciplinary infractions involving other inmates or correctional officers. This could be suggestive of a lack of judgment and failure to understanding the consequences of their actions.**[297]

The Clark report does recognize "Condemned inmates with developmental disabilities affecting placement must be accommodated in existing units for each gender. Condemned inmates with developmental disabilities must receive access to the same type of programs as condemned inmates who are not disabled."[298]

Derrick Clark and Ambrose Woods sought injunctive relief because they were developmental disabled and had difficulty understanding and complying with prison rules. Clark had a reported IQ less than 60 and was not able to read or write. Clark and Woods were subjected to segregation and disciplinary, abuse from other inmates, denied other programs available to inmates, and denied medical services, because of their disability.

---

[297]*Ibid.,* Clark, p.6
[298]*Ibid.,* Clark, p. 34

California is on the forefront for determining disabilities among prisoners and providing appropriate accommodations. In 2001, California recognized the needs of prisoners with developmental disabilities which were defined to include mental retardation, cerebral palsy, epilepsy, and autism. The California definition of developmental disability is more inclusive than intellectual disability because "It also includes disabling conditions found to be closely related to mental retardation or to require treatment similar to that, required for mentally retarded individuals, but does not include other disabling conditions that are solely physical in nature." California's definition of developmental disability is

> **a disability that originates before an individual attains the age of 18, continues-or can be expected to continue-indefinitely, and constitutes a substantial handicap for that individual. It includes mental retardation, cerebral palsy, epilepsy, and autism. It also includes disabling, conditions found to be closely related to mental retardation or to require treatment similar to that required for mentally retarded individuals, but does not include other disabling conditions that are solely physical in nature.**

This is similar to the definition cited in the Developmental Disability Act of 2000:

> **The term "developmental disability" means a severe, chronic disability of an individual that— (i) is attributable to a mental or physical impairment or combination of mental and physical impairments; (ii) is manifested before the individual attains age 22; (iii) is likely to continue indefinitely; (iv) results in substantial functional limitations in 3 or more of the following areas of major life activity: (I) Self-care. (II) Receptive and expressive language. (III) Learning. (IV) Mobility. (V) Self-direction.**

213

> (VI) Capacity for independent living. (VII)
> Economic self-sufficiency; and (v) reflects the
> individual's need for a combination and
> sequence of special, interdisciplinary, or
> generic services, individualized supports, or
> other forms of assistance that are of lifelong or
> extended duration and are individually
> planned and coordinated.[299]

The importance of the term **developmental disability** is that disabilities other than intellectual disability should be included when considering an Atkins claim because a condition other than intellectual disability could result in the same deficits that provide lesser culpability.

California found "in total the evidence demonstrates that mentally retarded prisoners and those with autism spectrum disorders are verbally, physically, and sexually assaulted, exploited, and discriminated against in California prisons."[300] California found that prisoners with disabilities were unable to read important documents, understand prison rules, participate in prison hearings Like almost all services provided by a prison, "daily living activities such as the use of showers, the exchange of laundry, and the receipt of medication constitute 'services, programs, or activities' under the ADA."[301] To address these issues, California required a plan or Clark Remedial Plan (CRP) for prisoners with developmental disabilities: "All inmates will be screened for developmental disabilities using standard instruments, as described below, to ensure uniform application of departmental policies and procedures for screening, identifying, and verifying developmental disabilities and placing identified inmates in appropriate settings."[302]

---

[299]Public Law 106-402, Developmental Disabilities Assistance and Bill of Rights Act of 2000'
[300]Clark v. California, 739 F. Supp. 2d 1168, 2010
[301]*Ibid.*
[302]Clark v. California, Remedial Plan, amended March 1, 2002, State of California, Department of Corrections

As found in California, there are some very specific adaptive skills that are important for prisoners which, when lacking, can result in discriminatory behavior. California responded to this problem by expanding the definition of intellectual disability to meet prisoner needs and to comply with the ADA. California recognizes that all prisoners, included on death row are required to have a CRP. California might well remove all those on death row who have a CRP because of intellectual needs and the corresponding deficits cited in the 2002 CRP memorandum. [303]

Vernon Madison

Dementia, in itself, is not tantamount to intellectual disability but the advent of dementia might suggest that an offender could meet the criteria for intellectual disability. Vernon Madison was tried on three separate occasions for the murder of Mobile, Alabama police officer Julius Schulte in September of 1985. He was convicted and sentenced to death for each of his trials. His first conviction was overturned because of a Batson claim that the prosecution exercised discriminatory juror strikes. His second 1990 trial resulted in a 10 to 2 vote for execution. The second conviction was overturned because an expert witness had relied, in part, on facts not in evidence.[304] After his third trial the jury voted for life in prison but this was overturned by the judge who sentenced Madison to death. In 2016 Madison claimed "that he has experienced multiple strokes including a recent thalamic stroke in January 2016, major vascular neurological disorders, vascular dementia, and other serious medical conditions including diabetes and hypertension. He further alleges that these medical problems have damaged his brain and left him with declining cognitive function, diminished mental capacity, severe memory deficits, dementia, slurred speech, blindness, incontinence, and an inability to walk."[305]

---

[303]*Ibid.*
[304]Madison v. State, 620 So. 2d 62 (1992)
[305]Madison v. Dunn, United States District Court for the Southern District of Alabama Southern Division, Civil Action No. 16-00191-KD-M, May 10, 2016

Madison sought relief from the death penalty because he did not recollect the crime or the reason for his execution. Madison asserted that Ford v. Wainwright (mental illness) and Atkins v. Virginia both provide a constitutional prohibition against his execution. In August of 2017 the United States Court of Appeals decided that Madison did not understand why he was being executed and was therefore not competent to be executed.[306] On November 6, 2017, the Supreme Court engaged in some verbal parsing by explaining that "Neither *Panetti* nor *Ford* 'clearly established' that a prisoner is incompetent to be executed because of a failure to remember his commission of the crime, as distinct from a failure to rationally comprehend the concepts of crime and punishment as applied in his case."[307] The Court concluded that Madison understood that he was tried and convicted of murder and should be executed for that crime. As a result the Court decided that there was no evidence to show that the denial of his claim was "not so lacking in justification as required by the Antiterrorism and Effective Death Penalty Act of 1996." Although Atkins was cited as part of his claim, the criteria under Atkins were not considered by the Court. That is, IQ, adaptive behavior, were not considered or interpreted for cases involving dementia. Madison, age 67 and born in 1950, has been on death row for 32 years. Following the 2017 Supreme Court decision Alabama wasted no time and set a new execution date for January 25, 2018. This was stayed by the Supreme Court to consider the Eighth Amendment relating to his mental disability and memory of the crime.

In 2019 the Supreme Court explicated the standard for when a defendant does not recall the crime but does understand why he is being executed.[308]

---

[306]Madison v. Alabama Dept of Corrections, United States Court of Appeals, Eleventh Circuit, No. 16-12279, March 15, 2017
[307]Dunn v. Madison, 583 U.S. ___ (2017)
[308]Madison v. Alabama, Supreme Court of the United States, No. 17–7505. Argued October 2, 2018—Decided February 27, 2019

In a 5-3 decision Justice Kagan made and important distinction between a label of mental illness and a "rational understanding" of the reason for execution. In Panetti v. Quarterman the Court clarified that eligibility for execution depended on the defendant's ability "reach a rational understanding of the reason for [his] execution" and that "a strict test for competency that treats delusional beliefs as irrelevant" is in error.[309]
The question is not whether the defendant "has any particular memory or any particular mental illness" but a "rational understanding." In the context of Atkins claims, cause is secondary to the effects no matter what that cause might be.   The Court remanded the case to the Alabama court to determine whether he has a "rational understanding" for his execution and not whether he has dementia rather than diagnosed delusional behavior.

Just as dementia does not run afoul of the constitution— providing the Ford v. Wainwright standard is met—nor does age. Walter Leroy Moody, born in 1935 and age 81, was sentenced to death for the 1989 pipe bomb murders of an appellate court judge (Robert Vance) and a civil rights attorney (Robert Robinson). Moody represented himself at trial, put on a feeble defense sans mitigation, and was sentenced to death following an 11 to 1 jury recommendation vote in 1996. Based on the Alabama Department of Labor mortality rates, the 83-year-old Vance had a life expectancy of 5.5 years.[310] For someone age 90 in Alabama the life expectancy would be 3 years. On April 19 the 83-year-old Moody was executed by lethal injection.

There are situations when the ADA does not apply but this is generally not the case for prisons or prisoners. For example, the ADA would not apply if "the public entity can show that the accommodation would impose an "undue hardship" on the operation of its program. In that a successful Atkins claim would result in a placement other than death row, an increase in the number of successful claims would result in a cost saving. Also, the ADA does not apply when a person poses a threat to the health

---

[309]Panetti v. Quarterman, 551 U.S. 930 (2007)
[310]www.aldoi.gov/PDF/Consumers/MortalityTable2001.pdf

and safety of others. Assuming that a death row prisoner is guilty of the most heinous crime imaginable, *Atkins* requires that a person with mental retardation deserves lesser culpability and not lesser culpability *if they no longer pose a threat to others*. States have managed to deal with successful Atkins claims without a massive outcry that the general safety of others in the general prison population has been jeopardized. Finally, to qualify the receipt services (the "benefit") ensured by the ADA, the essential qualification is a determination of intellectual disability where this determination is guided by how disability is defined in the ADA.

If there is a bright line in Atkins claims, it should the prohibition of capital punishment for all claimants with a record of mental retardation/intellectual disability as a child, including those who have been classified as Educable Mentally Retarded, Mentally Retarded, Educable Mentally Handicapped, intellectually disabled, mild intellectually disabled, Mild Cognitive Impaired and the various acronyms (EMR, MR, EMH, ID, MID, MCI, etc.) The fact that someone has been misclassified as having an intellectual disability, but in reality is not, is beside the point. According to the Office of Civil Rights a record of an impairment means that an individual "has a history of, or has been misclassified as having, a mental or physical impairment that substantially limits one or more major life activities[311] and these disorders include "any mental or psychological disorder such as mental retardation, organic brain syndrome, emotional or mental illness, and specific learning disabilities."[312]

For Atkins claims, if a defendant has been classified as having an intellectual disability as a child, especially when the same professional definition is used to determine the merits of an Atkins claim, the State cannot ignore this "record" of intellectual disability to deny the benefit of life rather than death. If the State has used the professional definition to determine that a defendant was intellectually disabled as a child and then provide an education that was often inferior and segregated, these State

---

[311]Regulations of the Offices of the Department of Education 34 CFR § 105.3 Definitions, (7–1–12 Edition)
[312]28 CFR § 35.160

actions cannot be undone when a defendant seeks lesser culpability as an adult as per Atkins.[313]

Toyota v. Williams

Justice Scalia's opinion in Yeskey is emphatic but the Court's position on the ADA has become less inclusive and in disagreement with actual Congressional intent. In Toyota v. Williams, the Court declared that "It is insufficient for individuals attempting to prove disability status under this test to merely submit evidence of a medical diagnosis of an impairment." [314] The Court came to this conclusion by focusing on the first prong of the definition of an ADA disability which requires that "a physical or mental impairment that substantially limits one or more major life activities of such individual." Furthermore, the impairment must involve "doing activities that are of central importance to most people's daily lives." This test, however, was certainly not used in *Yeskey* where Mr. Yeskey was capable of doing all activities in his daily life, including participation in a motivational boot camp. Congress did not agree with the Supreme Court's concept of what Congress intended and said as much in a sternly worded response to the Court, and subsequent decisions, in the amended ADA in 2008 as discussed below.

In *Yeskey* the Supreme Court interpreted the ADA to broaden the concept of disability and coverage. This changed in Toyota v. Williams which entailed the ADA Title I (Employment) and not Title II (Public Services). *Toyota* illustrates how the definition of a disability can be contorted to justify a certain end. Beginning in 1990 Ella Williams worked in a Toyota manufacturing plant in Georgetown, Kentucky and eventually developed carpal tunnel syndrome and related disorders.[315] Toyota provided accommodations but her work requirements were again changed

---

[313]28 § 35.130 General prohibitions against discrimination
[314]Toyota Motor Manufacturing, Kentucky, Inc., Petitioner v. Ella Williams, 534 US 184 (2002)
[315]*Ibid.*

and she developed a muscle inflammation and nerve compression causing upper extremity pain. The District Court found that she had an impairment involving lifting and working but not one that "substantially limited" these activities. The District Court also found that she did not have a "record" of impairment. To decide whether Williams had a disability under the ADA the Supreme Court interpreted the Congressional intent of the ADA "That these terms need to be interpreted strictly to create a demanding standard for qualifying as disabled is confirmed by the first section of the ADA, which lays out the legislative findings and purposes that motivate the Act"[316]

The Court was not sure about a number of factors such as whether "working" was a major life activity. However, if "working" was a major life activity, it must involve a broad class of jobs and not a specific job. For Ella Williams, the Court found that the Court of Appeals was in error by considering only her specific job and not a broad class of activities. Because her work-specific assembly line job was not sufficient proof that she had an impairment involving a broad class of manual tasks involving such tasks as household chores, bating, brushing one's teeth. etc The fact that she avoided household sweeping, dancing, and sometimes needed help dressing ,were not of "central importance to most people's daily lives" to reach the level of disability.

The importance of Toyota is not merely the interpretation of disability but how this interpretation is in direct contrast to the actual Congressional intent for interpreting the ADA. Congressional intent is known because Congress was not shy about correcting the Supreme Court concerning the ADA. In the 2008 ADA Amendments Congress rejected the strict standard of an ADA disability created by the Supreme Court and chided the Court's narrowing "the broad scope of protection intended to be afforded by the ADA" in *Toyota*. Furthermore, "lower courts have incorrectly found in individual cases that people with a range of substantially limiting impairments are not people with disabilities." The ADA is intended to provide "broad scope of protection" and the strict requirements "enunciated by the

---

[316]*Ibid.*

Supreme Court" are rejected. Congress also declared that the Supreme Court has "created an inappropriately high level of limitation necessary to obtain coverage under the ADA" and "to convey that it is the intent of Congress that the primary object of attention in cases brought under the ADA should be whether entities covered under the ADA have complied with their obligations, and to convey that the question of whether an individual's impairment is a disability under the ADA should not demand extensive analysis."[317] Congress' criticism of the Supreme Court's strict interpretation of the ADA is not dissimilar from the Court's criticism for using a strict IQ standard in *Hall*.

The current ADA Title II Assistance Manual (2.5000) states that

> **The ADA protects not only those individuals with disabilities who actually have a physical or mental impairment that substantially limits a major life activity, but also those with a record of such impairment. "This protected group includes 1) a person who has a history of an impairment that substantially limited a major life activity but who has recovered from the impairment. Examples of individuals who have a history of impairment are persons who have histories of mental or emotional illness, drug addiction, alcoholism, heart disease, or cancer. 2) Persons who have been misclassified as having impairment. Examples include persons who have been erroneously diagnosed as mentally retarded or mentally ill.[318]**

Of special importance for Atkins claims is the inclusion of "persons who have been misclassified as having impairment," including those "who have been erroneously diagnosed as mentally retarded." A State's burden of misclassifying a child as having an

---

[317]ADA Amendments Act of 2008 (P.L. 110-325), 534 U.S. 184, 2002
[318]The Americans with Disabilities Act, Title II Technical Assistance Manual, Covering State and Local Government Programs and Services

intellectual disability is great and cannot be ignored or even undone by a court when the child is an adult seeking Atkins relief.

Although the interpretation of the ADA by the Supreme Court in *Toyota* is contrary to the actual Congressional intent as stated by Congress, decisions by the Court, no matter how questionable, have important consequences. In Korematsu v. United States in 1944 then Court considered "the imprisonment of a citizen in a concentration camp solely because of his ancestry, without evidence or inquiry concerning his loyalty and good disposition towards the United States." The Court agreed that "the properly constituted military authorities feared an invasion of our West Coast and felt constrained to take proper security measures" and "the military urgency of the situation demanded that all citizens of Japanese ancestry be segregated from the West Coast temporarily."[319] When deprived of a fundamental right, whether that is imprisonment as in *Korematsu* or capital punishment, the Court should avoid exactly what was done in *Toyota*, but was avoided in *Hall*, and that is a strict rather than individualized and narrowing jurisprudence.

Littleton v. Wal-Mart Stores

The inappropriateness of re-interpreting an intellectual disability under the ADA is never more evident than the quixotic and surreal decision in Littleton v. Wal-Mart Stores in 2007. Charles Irvin Littleton was 29 years old, received social security benefits, and lived at home with his mother. He was classified as having mental retardation as a child, and "graduated" high school with a certificate in special education, and had been a client of public service agencies and organizations.[320] Littleton applied to Walmart in Leeds, Alabama for a job pushing carts (a cart-push "associate") but, following an interview, was not offered the job because of poor interpersonal skills. Littleton contended that he was not offered the job because he was mentally retarded and

---

[319]Korematsu v. United States, 323 U.S. 214 (1944)
[320]Littleton v. Wal-Mart Stores (2007), United States Court of Appeals for the Eleventh Circuit

wanted to know the nondiscriminatory reasons for Walmart's decision. Littleton believed that he was substantially limited in "learning, thinking, communicating, social interaction and working." Walmart countered that, in spite of a record of mental retardation, Littleton was not covered by the ADA (relying on the Supreme Court's interpretation of an ADA disability in Toyota v. Williams) because "there are no jobs he cannot perform because of any alleged disability." Littleton had a clear record of intellectual disability, he was provided an education commensurate with intellectual disability, and he met all criteria for intellectual disability, Walmart asserted that he did not have a substantial limitation in a major life activity and therefore did not have a disability as per the ADA. In this case, a corporate mentality superseded professional definition and common sense.

The District Court believed that Littleton's disability "Viewing the record in the light most favorable to Littleton, there is simply no substantial evidence to support the critical element of his claim that he be 'disabled' and "the overwhelming evidence is that he is not limited in any major life activity."[321] The appellate court affirmed the District Court's opinion and acknowledged his mental retardation, but concluded that mental retardation alone is not sufficient to be disabled under the ADA because the Supreme Court requires a "strict" interpretation of an ADA disability and "a demanding standard for qualifying as disabled."[322] Littleton had a disability that, by definition, involved significantly subaverage general intellectual functioning and impairments in adaptive behavior, and by definition and State action he met any and all criteria for mental retardation. Yet Littleton's record of mental retardation was dismissed in the same way that many Atkins claims are denied by bureaucratic uninformed nitpicking.

The Supreme Court in Toyota imposed a strict interpretation of major life activity, but as explained by Congress the ADA was never intended to be strictly interpreted as was done in Littleton. This is not to say that the Alabama courts were completely wrong.

---

[321]United States District Court for the Northern District of Alabama Southern Division, Civil Action No. 04-AR-0066-S, April 12, 2005
[322]Toyota Motor Manufacturing, Kentucky, Inc. v. Williams, 534 U.S. 184 (2002)

The question was not whether Littleton had an intellectual disability (he clearly did) but whether he was otherwise qualified. For example, if the job Littleton was seeking required specific interpersonal skills, Wal-Mart could have claimed that he was not qualified to hold such a position. The fact that he was applying to push carts, the interpersonal skill requirement, which was the basis for his not being hired, would have been problematic. The court suggested that Littleton was actually quite able and had no problems with major life activities. This is the same stereotypical interpretation of adaptive skills used to deny Atkins claims.

Eugene Milton Clemons II[323]

When a State decides that someone warrants execution, neither double jeopardy nor intellectual disability will stand in the way. Eugene Milton Clemons II shot and killed a Drug Enforcement Administration officer, Douglas Althouse, during a carjacking on May 28, 1992 in Inverness, Alabama south of Birmingham. In 1993 he was sentenced to life in prison in Federal Court. During sentencing his behavior did not endear himself to the Alabama court—smiling at the victim's family and appearing to "gloat" (according to a press report) during sentencing. For Clemons his Federal conviction would seem to put an end to the matter because, as stated in the Alabama Constitution (Article I, § 9) "That no person shall, for the same offense, be twice put in jeopardy of life or limb). However, "The dual sovereignty doctrine is founded on the common-law conception of crime as an offense against the sovereignty of the government. When a defendant in a single act violates the `peace and dignity' of two sovereigns by breaking the laws of each, he has committed two distinct `offences.'" Because the Federal government and the States have separate "inherent sovereignties" for prosecuting crimes, each can punish when the same crime is committed against both.

He was tried a second time and in September of 1994 the jury recommended death which is the sentence the court imposed. Following *Atkins* he claimed mental retardation based on IQ

---

[323]The courts spell his last name "Clemons" but his death row spelling is "Clemmons."

scores of 51, 58 and 67, as well as scores of 73 and 77 on various versions of the WAIS and Stanford-Binet. The circuit court was less than convinced that he was mentally retarded because "The evidence demonstrates that when Clemons puts forward some effort he consistently scores in the 70-80 range on intelligence tests.[324] Further, the evidence demonstrates that when Clemons malingers he consistently scores in the 50-60 range. Clemons has failed to establish that he meets the criteria to establish 'significantly subaverage general intellectual functioning.'" We are left in the dark as to how the court was able to determine when Clemons was malingering.

Of all the IQ scores the most relevant is the Stanford-Binet IQ of 77 when Clemons was six and a half years old and was placed in an EMR class. Clemons attended school until the 10th grade but did not receive a high school diploma. Although the 77 is above the sanctioned Supreme Court cutoff of 75, his IQ score when he was six and a half in the late 1970s was certainly within the range for determining EMR at the time. In 1980 in Alabama there were over 24,000 children classified as EMR of whom 65.8 percent were black (the black enrollment was 36.5 percent). When Clemons was a child, Alabama had no qualms about classifying children, especially black children, as EMR. Most important, his "record" of mental retardation was not linked to his IQ score but his placement in an EMR class because of the belief that he had significantly subaverage general intellectual functioning and impairments in adaptive behavior.

Clemons was regarded by the Alabama as having EMR as a child and provided services for someone having significantly general subaverage intellectual functioning but not as an adult when seeking Atkins relief. His special education placement might have been a legitimate attempt to provide Clemons with an appropriate education, the placement might have been influenced by environment or the inferior education provided black children, an over-reliance on IQ scores, or to the possibility that his IQ score

---

[324]Eugene Milton Clemons II v. State of Alabama, CR-01-1355, August 29, 2003; Eugene Clemons v. State of Alabama, Court of Criminal Appeals, Appeal from Shelby Circuit Court (CC-93-313.61), June, 2012

did not reflect his real intellectual ability. Although he might have been misclassified as EMR, none of these possibilities, or a combination thereof, really matters because for whatever reason(s) his school district decided that he was EMR and provided an education commensurate with that classification. As an adult seeking Atkins relief, Clemons assessment as a child was ignored in favor of a re-interpretation of his IQ and adaptive behavior to conclude that he was not (or no longer) mentally retarded as an adult.

To say that his behavior following his first trial (viz., gloating at the grieving family) or the fact that the murder of an enforcement officer was cold-blooded did not influence the interpretation of his mental retardation claim is difficult to dismiss. For that matter, if his behavior following his Federal trial had been more circumspect, there might not have been a second trial in State court. For Clemons his behavior following the crime might not only have influenced the reason for having a second trial but also to deny his Atkins claim.

In 2007 the Supreme Court of Alabama considered issues including the failure to consider borderline intellectual ability as a mitigating factor and ineffective assistance of counsel. The court decided not to "consider the issue of whether the trial court erred in failing to consider Clemons' borderline intellectual capacity as a mitigating factor in the sentencing phase of his trial because the issue was not presented to the trial court in Clemons's (sic) Rule 32 petition."[325] In 2010 Clemons again filed a petition regarding the failure to consider his low IQ as a mitigating factor which the Supreme Court had decided in Tennard v. Dretke in 2004. In 2012, the Alabama Court of Criminal Appeals determined that his claim was procedurally barred but also observed that "this Court will not address the merits of the claim. This Court notes, however, that Clemons did not present the jury with evidence of his low IQ as mitigation. Accordingly, it is hard to imagine how the State or the circuit court prevented the jury from considering that evidence."[326]

---

[325]Ex Parte Clemons, 55 So. 3d 348 (Ala. 2007)
[326]Clemons v. Alabama, Alabama Court of Criminal Appeals, CR-10-0772,

In 2016 the District Court decided that several of his IQ scores should be dismissed because of malingering and that an overall estimate of four credible IQ scores was 77.[327] Because of malingering and an average IQ score above 75, the court believed that he did not meet the first prong of the definition. Unlike Florida before *Hall* in 2014, although Clemons did not meet the first prong of the definition, adaptive behavior was considered. The court noted that he was more than able to adapt as evidenced by the ability to receive food stamps, because "he had relationships with women and fathered at least two children," he had good literacy skills, "Mr. Clemons' survival on a violent unit may attest to his true ability to function."[328] The District Court also interpreted his score of 77 as a young child as above the cutoff and more important than a diagnosis of EMR.

Nothing that the court said concerning malingering was unreasonable However, expanding the concept of adaptive behavior to include "survival" in a violent prison unit is not something most professionals considered when developing definitions of intellectual disability. Just as the task for courts and juries to put aside the heinousness of a crime is a difficult task, declaring someone intellectually disabled because of a record of intellectual disability as a child when there is evidence to the contrary is difficult. Nonetheless, when he was classified as EMR at age 6-7 years old Alabama made that determination he was intellectually disabled/mentally retarded using a process far more thorough than most evaluations of intellectual disability as an adult by a court.

Currently, the decision to determine that a child has an intellectual disability is usually made a team which generally includes the classroom teacher, special education teacher, special education supervisor, the parents and "one person qualified to conduct

---

June 29, 2012
[327]Clemons v. Thomas (Commissioner), United States District Court for the Northern District of Alabama, Southern Division, 2:10-cv-02218-LSC, March 28, 2016.
[328]As cited in Eugene Milton Clemons II v. State of Alabama, CR-01-1355, August 29, 2003.

individual diagnostic examinations of children, such as a school psychologist, speech-language pathologist, or remedial reading teacher,"[329] and even the child when appropriate. The prevailing belief in the late 1970s, after Public Law 94-142 was passed in 1975, was more consist with Terman's recommendation (in 1916) that IQ scores between 70 and 80 were considered border-line deficiency, and that some in this category were and others not mentally retarded. The "border-line deficiency" category was not meant to dismiss the possibility of intellectual disability but to emphasize the need to use careful clinical judgment to identify those who are and who are not identified.   All of this must also be seen in the context of racism in Alabama in the 1970s and the use of testing to segregate and stigmatize.

If Clemons was appropriately identified as EMR as a child, this provided a record of intellectual disability. If Clemons was misclassified, the consequences were even more serious because of denial of educational opportunity, stigmatization, a less than appropriate curriculum, and segregation. Likewise there should be consequences for a State at a later time when considering intellectual disability to prohibit the death penalty, and one consequence should be that when a defendant was classified as EMR as a child this should be a bright-line bar to execution, as per the ADA, as an adult. As of January 2020 Clemons remains on Alabama's Holman death row.

Marvin Charles Gabrion

For Clemons his Federal prosecution resulted in a sentence of life, but the State sentence was death. Federal prosecution is not always so benevolent, even in Michigan where the death penalty was abolished in 1847. Marvin Charles Gabrion was sentenced to death in 2002 for the 1997 kidnapping and murder of Rachael Timmerman the victim he was about to stand trial in Michigan for rape. [330] He had kidnapped Ms. Timmerman, weighed her down

---

[329]34 § 300.308 Additional group members (for determining a specific learning disability
[330]United States Court of Appeals, Sixth Circuit. United States v. Marvin

with rocks and threw her overboard in a lake on Federal land. He also is suspected of having murdered Timmerman's 11-month old daughter, and suspected of killing at least three others. Death penalty or not, Gabrion was tried in Michigan in Federal Court (he United States District Court for the Western District of Michigan) and sentenced to death. His sentence was overturned in 2011 by a three-member Federal appellate panel because the trial court did not inform jurors that if tried in State court he would not have faced the death penalty. The full appellate court for the Sixth Circuit disagreed and Gabrion's death sentence was reinstated in 2013. Gabrion is currently on death row in USP Terre Haute, Indiana.

Leon Jermain Winston

A record of intellectual disability, for the purpose of the ADA, is inextricably linked to age of onset and the determination of intellectual disability as a child. As with other States, Virginia differentiates between a record of intellectual disability before age of onset and intellectual disability for adults in Atkins claims by asserting the former is a matter of benevolence while the latter is the result of a more exacting determination. Leon Jermain Winston, black, was sentenced to death in 2004, at the age of 23, for the 2002 murder of Rhonda (who was pregnant) and Anthony Robinson during a home robbery in Lynchburg, Virginia. Winston was identified as having mild mental retardation by the Fairfax County Public Schools at age 16. Born in 1980, Winston was given four IQ tests between 1987 and 1995 which included three WISC-R scores of 77, 76 and 73.[331] The Commonwealth re-characterized this prior determination as a child as "'mildly mentally retarded' for the purposes of special education." This suggests that the determination of mental retardation in Virginia, when Winston was a child was not a real determination of intellectual disability

---

Charles Gabrion, II, Nos. 02–1386, 02–1461, 02–1570. Decided: May 28, 2013

[331]Winston v. Warden of the Sussex I State Prison, Supreme Court of Virginia, March 7, 2007.

but a bureaucratic necessity to provide needed special education services.

Placement in a special education classroom by the Fairfax Public Schools required the identification of one of the listed disabilities in the regulations and a need for special education. These requirements were guided by fairly explicit regulatory guidelines although often not followed. Characterizing Winston's classification as "described as mildly mentally retarded" discounts the fact that a determination of mental retardation required extensive due process rights (e.g., independent evaluations, prior written notice, parental consent, etc.), a full and individual evaluation, a determination by a team of qualified individuals and the parents, an individualized education program, and the placement in the least restrictive environment. This process is in contrast to Atkins claims where the finder of fact, often with little or no experience regarding intellectual disabilities, is provided barebones guidelines for understanding data and criteria for making a valid determination of intellectual disabilities. This lack of knowledge of intellectual disabilities is the reason for the various plain language interpretations of statutes for adults in Atkins claims. With limited knowledge of intellectual disabilities, and little if any understanding of the psychometrics underling IQ, how assessment data should be interpreted and the various regulatory guidelines, one recourse is a rigid and "plain language" adherence to statute. As it is a rigid statutory interpretation of intellectual disability, which is supposedly based on professional definitions, is contrary to the history of intellectual disability professional definitions and guidelines.

The Virginia Supreme Court decided that Winston had not met the first prong of the definition because his IQ scores were above 70, exactly what Florida decided before the 2014 Supreme Court *Hall* decision. Although the same essential elements of the professional definition cited by the Virginia Supreme Court were used to identify Winston as mentally retarded as a child, for purposes of an Atkins claim, and supposedly the Eighth Amendment, the prior determination was incorrect and "petitioner offers no objective data in support of his claim of mental retardation" (aside from IQ scores and the fact that he was determined to be mentally retarded by a group of qualified professionals under the auspices of the State agency as a child). The court offered that Winston's determination of mental retardation as a child, based on what should have been explicit criteria, was irrelevant because he did not provide "documentation that he was diagnosed as being mentally retarded before the age of 18 in accordance with the legal definition of mental retardation established by the legislature." The professional definition used to classify Winston as a child was the very definition used to create the "legal definition" which, in turn, was then used to nullify the definition that was used when he was a child.

No matter the reason, no matter if his IQ scores were above 70 or above 80, no matter the underlying basis for deficits in adaptive behavior, no matter if the identification of mental retardation as a child was legitimate or based on flat-out racism (of which Virginia has some history), if the Commonwealth, as represented by the Fairfax County public schools and the Board of Education, placed Winston in special education because of mild mental retardation, his record of disability is established as mentally retarded/intellectual disabled for purposes of the ADA . Virginia might very well contend that the ADA does not apply, as was the case for Pennsylvania in *Yeskey* (which was undone by the Supreme Court), but the finder of fact must at least consider the ADA and its applicability to Winston.

In 2010 the Court of Appeals for the Fourth Circuit revisited his developmental period and found that "in defense counsel's possession, but not submitted to the jury, were additional records from the Fairfax County Department of Student Services and Special Education. These records showed that Winston was eligible for special education due to mild retardation, he performed at a reduced rate of development and of academic achievement, and that he demonstrated concurrent deficits in adaptive behavior.[332] Showing a marvelous talent for sleuthing, Winston's counsel located the psychologist who had examined Winston in 1997 and, lo and behold, records were found showing

---

[332]Winston v. Kelly, 592 F.3d 535 (4th Cir. 2010)

that his IQ score for that testing was 66. In 1998, 47.6 percent of the children identified as having mental retardation in Virginia were black, in contrast to the 25.7 percent of black children comprising the 6-21 population, so that finding a black child having mental retardation would not have been an uncommon occurrence.

The appellate court did not declare that Winston was mentally retarded but decided his Atkins evaluation was incomplete, vacated the District Court's judgment, and remanded his claim for further consideration. Following remand, the District Court decided "that but for counsel's unprofessional errors" Virginia must determine his mental retardation by trial or resentence with the possibility of the death penalty.[333] In 2012 the Commonwealth again appealed the decision but the appellate court was firm that the Winston's Atkins claim was not adjudicated on its merits. The appellate court attributed Winston's unsuccessful Atkins claim to the "deficient performance" of his counsel for not collecting all the data, especially the IQ of 66, his classification as mentally retarded, "and testimony from school officials and counselors would have significantly strengthened Winston's sentencing case such that we can confidently ascertain a 'reasonable probability that, but for counsel's unprofessional errors,' the court would not have sentenced Winston to death."[334] In February of 2013, after the Supreme Court denied certiorari, the Commonwealth decided not to pursue the death penalty.

As was the case with Daryl Atkins, the result for Winston was life in prison rather than the death penalty because of errors when resolving his Atkins claim— and not because he was determined to be exempt from the death penalty because of mental retardation (although everyone seems to agree, aside from the prosecution, that he was mentally retarded).

Daniel Lee Bedford

---

[333]Winston v. Kelly, 784 F.Supp.2d 623,□634□(W.D. Va. 2011)
[334]Winston v. Pearson, 683 F.3d 489 (2012)

There are many ways to discount a record of intellectual disability as a child, including the assertion that the data represents something other than intellectual disability. While environment is often a primary factor in the determination of intellectual disability for black children—but given little notice because mild intellectual disabilities so conveniently explains educational deficits and provides exoneration for all past discriminatory misdeeds—environment is readily acknowledged as the cause for poor performance on IQ tests for adults seeking Atkins relief and therefore the claimant is not really, and never was intellectually disabled. Racism is used to classify black children, and then to permit the execution of black adults.

To a large extent the role of environment could well be the underlying cause of adult intellectual disability as it is for many children. No one knows what causes a person to score low on an IQ test. Poor test performance could be an actual reflection of poor skills as measured by the test, poor educational skills, inadequate instruction or poor school attendance, environment, prior discrimination, socio-economic factors, fetal alcohol syndrome, specific learning disabilities or another disability,, personality factors, "extreme Stress and depression" (noted by the court in *Bedford*), poor verbal skills, genetics, being tested by a white psychologist, not having enough to eat, malingering, a lack of general motivation, a lack of motivation to do well because maximum performance on an IQ test could result in execution, or even that nebulous subaverage general intellectual functioning. All of these factors should have been considered at the time school officials decided that a classification of intellectual disability was appropriate. However, once the classification has been made, causation is irrelevant, and the eggs not to be unbroken no matter the proffered judicial wisdom.

Intelligence testing is not the end-all of assessment but can, potentially, provide useful information. The regulations for the special education law (P.L. 108-446) state that no single measure (viz., IQ) should be used as the sole criterion for determining a disability and an appropriate education, and that "Assessments and other evaluation materials include those tailored to assess specific areas of educational need and not merely those that are designed to provide a single general intelligence quotient."[335] Courts frequently give undue weight to IQ scores because of the misguided belief that a single score can indicate intellectual potential and all that needs to be known about an individual.

The essential purpose of the ADA is to dispel stereotypes and "to provide clear, strong, consistent, enforceable standards addressing discrimination against individuals with disabilities."[336] Some of the more egregious stereotypes are that individuals who have been identified as intellectually disabled have an absolute limit on what they can or cannot achieve. Common stereotypes include not being able to drive a car, work, have a family, participate in community activities, read, write, have a bank account, function independently, etc. If an Atkins claimant has demonstrated any of these types of skills, the presumption is that this is evidence of someone who is not truly intellectually disabled.

If a State had decided that an intellectual disability classification was appropriate, the State must have also decided that the child had significantly subaverage general intellectual functioning, deficits in adaptive behavior and needed special education. If one of these three conditions was not met, the child was misclassified. If the first possibility is true, that the classification was correct and the individual benefited from the specially designed instruction, the very purpose of special education was achieved and individual performance was enhanced. If the classification is incorrect, the intellectual and educational harm is inestimable. When the determination of intellectual disability is a result of racism, either intentionally or not, a child might well develop independent living skills beyond those of a child who is actually intellectually disabled. Correct or not, a determination of intellectual disability as a child warrants lesser culpability as an adult.

Daniel Lee Bedford was sentenced to death in Ohio for the murder of his ex-girlfriend and her boyfriend in 1984 in Cincinnati. In 2011 the Ohio Court of Appeals decided that he was

---

[335] 34 CFR § 300.304 Evaluation procedures
[336] 42 USC 126.12101(b)(2)

presumptively not mentally retarded because he had IQ scores of 70 (in 1960 at age 13) and 76 in 1984. The IQ of 70 in 1960 when he was 13 is especially important in that the professional cutoff at the time was an IQ score of 85, well within the range of Educable Mental Retardation. Ohio has always had a high rate of children classified as intellectually disabled. In 1998 Ohio accounted for 8.5 percent of all children in the United States identified as having mental retardation. Of the 50,535 children 6 to 21 reported in the mental retardation category in Ohio in 1998 (followed by Florida with 38,086) 29 percent were black and 69 percent white. The racial disproportionality is different than that of Florida in 1998 where 51 percent of the children identified as having mental retardation were black and 37 percent white.

The Ohio appellate court found that Bedford's illiteracy and poor school performance indicated some intellectual limitations, "But this evidence does not conclusively demonstrate significant intellectual limitations when considered with the evidence of his sporadic school attendance and defense counsel's assertion that Bedford had, while awaiting trial, taught himself to read, and when viewed in the context of his dysfunctional home life when these matters manifested themselves."[337] The court concluded that "the record does not demonstrate that his adaptive-behavior limitations, however significant, were the product of limitations in his intellectual functioning. Again, his illiteracy may as well have been attributable to his dysfunctional home life during his formative years.

Both clinical psychologists who examined Bedford attributed his social-skills limitations to a borderline personality disorder resulting from his early childhood development and alcohol abuse. By focusing on the myth of causation for a determination of mild intellectual disability, no one would receive Atkins relief because every adaptive deficit could be attributed to home life, environment, and an endless list of Diagnostic and Statistical Manual codes. For the vast majority of children identified as having a mild intellectual disability, unlike more severe forms

---

[337]Ohio v. Bedford, Court of Appeals, First Appellate District of Ohio, Appeal NO. C-100735, 2011

caused by Down syndrome, Fragile X syndrome, brain injury, etc., the underlying cause is not known. This includes the inclusion of many children in the EMR category because of factors unrelated to intellectual ability. The question is not what causes EMR but rather what are the reasons for classifying a child as EMR. Reasons for classification could have been a problem at birth, genetics, brain injury, fetal alcohol spectrum disorder, etc., and a host of other reasons related to environment, educational opportunity, socio-economic conditions and, of course, racism. There is no such thing as EMR or mild intellectual disability as a concrete entity but rather a combination of mostly unknown, and sometimes known or acknowledged factors. For Daniel Lee Bedford Ohio chose to focus on the impossible task of determining causation which, for Bedford, resulted in his execution at age 63 on May 17, 2011.

Andre R. Williams

The question of causation arose again in Ohio in Williams v. Mitchell. In 1988 Andre R. Williams murdered, George Melnick, age 65, in Warren, Ohio during a robbery. His accomplice, Christopher Daniel, was sentenced to 37 to 100 years for the murder. Following Williams' trial in 1989 he was sentenced to death. Williams initiated his Atkins in 2003. His defense contended that Williams had at age 15 an IQ of 67 and deficits in adaptive behavior, including "'deficiencies in communication, locomotion, occupation and self-direction.'"[338] Testimony revealed in 2006 that in the fourth grade (about 1976-77) Williams was enrolled in a special education program referred to as an Adjusted Curriculum Program/Developmentally Handicapped Program. Inclusion in this program required "a measured intelligence or IQ of 80 or below and have deficiencies in two areas of what is called adaptive behavior."[339] Prior to 1973 the AAMR cutoff was an IQ score of 85 and many States continued to use a cutoff higher than 70 well after the professional guideline

---

[338]Williams v. Mitchell, United States Court for the Northern District of Ohio, Case No. 1:09 CV2246, September 27, 2012
[339]State v. Williams, 2006-Ohio-617

changed to 70. For example, in 1966 the Minnesota Department of Education explained that "Although the majority of children with I.Q.'s between approximately 50 and 80 on individual intelligence tests will require special class assignment, there may be problems encountered in the placement of pupils who score at the upper and lower extremes of this range."[340] The placement of Bedford as a child with an IQ above a score of 75 was consistent with the prevailing concept of EMR at the time.

The State contended that Williams' IQ score of 67 was outweighed by three IQ scores above 70 and "evidence of the underlying crimes and prison records indicated that Williams did not have current limitations in adaptive skills." His petition for a hearing to determine mental retardation was denied. The Ohio appellate court decided that Williams did not meet the IQ and adaptive behavior prongs of the definition of mental retardation but he did meet the third showing mental retardation before age 18. By this conclusion the court acknowledged his *record* of mental retardation but explained that his "present" levels did not indicate mental retardation.[341]

In 2015 the United States Court of Appeals for the Fifth Circuit was intrigued by the fact that the Ohio "court of appeals rejected outright any pre-1989 evidence from its analysis of Williams's intellectual functioning and adaptive skills, despite finding this same evidence showed that Williams was intellectually disabled before he turned eighteen."[342] The Ohio court not only gave less weight to the IQ score of 67 at age 15 but no weight at all. This was based on the belief that this score and other evidence was the result of developmental delay and not really an intellectual disability which is a lifelong disability. If evidence as an adult was insufficient to prove intellectual disability, the diagnosed intellectual disability as a child must have been in error and the

---

[340] A Resource Guide for Teachers ff Educable Mentally Retarded Children in Minnesota Public Schools, Department of Education, 1966.
[341] Williams v. Mitchell, United States District Court for the Northern District of Ohio, Eastern Division, CASE No. 1:09 CV 2246, September 28, 2012
[342] Williams v. Mitchell, United States Court of Appeals for the Fifth Circuit, Nos. 03-3626/12-4269, July 7, 2015

result of developmental delay (or something other than intellectual disability).

The U.S. Appellate Court concluded that "there is no basis for the Ohio Court of Appeals to have assumed, as it apparently did, that most low childhood IQ scores (or, to be precise, age-fifteen IQ scores) are the result of developmental delays. The Ohio Court of Appeals determination that William's age-fifteen IQ score was not competent evidence to show present intellectual limitations was thus an unreasonable application of Lott"[343] .

The Ohio Court of Appeals offered that evidence before 1989 was not "competent evidence" of his 'present functioning' as a matter of law. [344] The court suggested that the cause of low IQ as a child might have been the result of developmental delay, and that the only way to determine whether or not an Atkins claimant is truly intellectually disabled is to consider "current" levels of intellectual performance. As for Daniel Lee Bedford, determining the actual cause for why a child was identified as having an intellectual disability is irrelevant—aside from the fact that he was executed in spite of this irrelevant interpretation of cause. As for Bedford the actual cause could be racism, prior discrimination, developmental delay, lack of educational opportunity environment, lack of motivation, socio-economic factors and just about anything. "Could be" is irrelevant; what is relevant is an actual determination of intellectual disability during childhood or after. Contrary to the ADA's concept of how a disability should be defined and the importance of a record of a disability, the impossible task of determining cause obfuscates the actual record of an intellectual disability and how this record should guide an Atkins claim.

The United States Court of Appeals believed that "pursuant to the clinical definitions in *Atkins*, past evidence of intellectual disability—including evidence of intellectual disability from an individual's childhood—is relevant to an analysis of an individual's present intellectual functioning." The Court of

---

[343]*Ibid.*
[344]*Ibid.*

Appeals criticized the Ohio court of appeals for completely "rejecting past evidence of intellectual deficiencies wholesale" which is "contrary to clearly established Federal law."[345]

The Court of Appeals' emphasis on evidence prior to age of onset is consistent with the essential principle in Ford v. Wainwright in 1986, in Atkins v. Virginia in 2002, and Hall v. Florida in 2014 that (in *Ford*) "in all other proceedings leading to the execution of an accused, we have said that the factfinder must 'have before it all possible relevant information about the individual defendant whose fate it must determine.'"[346] The court also addressed the self-serving weighting of evidence where subjective reports by prison officials was considered far more meaningful than more objective data (e.g., school records, reports) and informed decision-making by the qualified group of professionals for children. Finally, the court confirmed the underlying theme in the ADA that a "record" of a disability should not be dismissed so that "By rejecting past evidence of intellectual deficiencies wholesale, the Ohio Court of Appeals reached a decision opposite to the clearly established Federal law set forth in *Atkins/Lott*."

In a concurring opinion, Judge Gibbons observed that "If Williams was intellectually disabled in 1989, he remains intellectually disabled now. By excluding the pre-1989 evidence, the state court severely limited its own ability to make a reasoned assessment of Williams's condition according to the legal and medical standard that *Atkins* and *Hall* plainly require." This is exactly what the ADA requires. Williams had a record of mental retardation before age 18 and he therefore has a record of mental retardation for all time. After his record of intellectual disability had been established by the State (i.e., those representing the State) as a child, he could have an IQ of 100 as an adult, but for purposes of *Atkins* and the ADA, he has an intellectual disability that should exclude execution. The moral of all of this is that identification of intellectual disability as a child—whether the classification is correct or not—can have consequences for a child in terms of

---

[345]Williams v. Betty Mitchell (Warden), United States Court of Appeals for the Sixth Circuit, Nos. 03-3626/12-4269, July 7, 2015
[346]Ford v. Wainwright, 477 U.S. 399 (1986)

educational opportunity or lack thereof; and when that child is an adult seeking Atkins relief these consequences cannot be undone and cannot be ignored.

The reference "to substantial limitations in present functioning" in the 1992 definition, illustrates the unique ability of States to capitalize on attempts by professionals to better meet individual learning needs of children and then transform these attempts in ways never imagined. Just as Florida used a plain language of the 70 cutoff to deny relevant evidence, Ohio and other States use the "present functioning" reference to deny all evidence of prior determinations of intellectual disability.

The 1992 definition attempted to focus on supports rather than deficiencies. The goal was to do more than provide a statement that a child was mentally retarded and somehow someone somewhere would do something. The 1992 definition was intended to emphasize what could be done for a child, especially supports for regular classroom inclusion. Needless to say, this notion of inclusion is not exactly consistent with the concept of the EMR classroom as a place, especially for black children. Whereas the 1992 definition was a step toward inclusion and what could be done to support "present functioning," States then use this to suggest that this means that evidence before "present" is unimportant and does not warrant consideration. For Williams, "present" does not undo the past and a record of intellectual disability. For Williams, who remains on death row as of February his Atkins petition was reassessed and rejected by a Trumbull County court in April of 2019.

Gary Eldon Alvord

The criteria for insanity (or criterion) is very unlike that of the three-prong definition of intellectual disability. For insanity claims, under Ford v. Wainwright, the definition of disability is a purely legal construct and time specific: 1) too insane to be tried (i.e., unable to understand the wrongfulness of the crime, to assist counsel); 2) insane when the murder occurred (or some variation of the M'Naghten rule to distinguish right from wrong); and 3) the ability to understand the crime and reason for execution. A defendant might have a record of mental illness as a child or before a capital murder, and received services for that disability (viz., emotional disturbance). However, a "record" of mental illness is not how mental illness or insanity is conceptualized by courts at the time of the crime, to stand trial, or to be executed. For insanity claims the test is not a professional or a DSM label (as it is with intellectual disability) but the ability to understand the crime, the reason for trial, to assist counsel, or the reason for execution.

In addition to the distinct time-specific characteristics, insanity presents unique ethical questions. For Gary Eldon Alvord medical personnel were aware that medication for Alvord, voluntary or not, would result in his execution and the furtherance of this outcome poised an ethical dilemma. In 1973 Gary Eldon Alvord strangled three women to death during a robbery in Tampa, Florida and was sentenced to death in 1974.[347] Alvord had been committed to a Michigan mental hospital for the 1967 kidnapping and rape of a 10-year old girl. In 1973 he escaped from the Michigan facility and three murders followed in five months. In 1984 the Supreme Court denied certiorari but not without dissent from Justices Marshall and Brennan who believed that Alvord's counsel should have done more to pursue an insanity defense.[348] In 1984, before his scheduled execution, he was evaluated by a team of psychiatrists who found that he was too incompetent to be executed. Alvord was sent to the Florida State Hospital in Chattahoochee where the ethics of providing treatment to allow for eventual execution came into question. The staff boycotted treatment and competency assessment that would have resulted in execution. He was transferred to another facility but in 1987 refused to participate in a competency assessment.

Alvord's 1998 Supreme Court appeal was denied. However, until his death from cancer in 2013 the governor did not sign a death warrant because, in all likelihood, this would have resulted in

---

[347]Alvord v. State of Florida, 396 So.2d 184 (1981) and 725 F. 2d 1282 (1984)
[348]Alvord v. Wainwright, 469 U.S. 956 (1984)

another competency examination, for which he would likely have refused and the delay would continue. As with Freddie Lee Hall, the result of this was almost 40 years on death row.[349]

Gary Otte

Gary Otte was sentenced to death in Ohio for the two murders committed during the course of separate robberies in 1992 in Parma, Ohio. Otte reportedly had an IQ of 85.[350] When considering the first prong of the definition of intellectual disability, an IQ above 75 and certainly an IQ above 80 would exclude an offender from Atkins relief. According to the defense Otte had a hearing loss, hyperactivity, a speech and language disorder (stuttering), and a learning disability, emotional disturbance (he attempted suicide twice), and "at the age of ten began using drugs and alcohol."[351] At some point as a child special education must have been considered. If Otte were black, and his IQ was in line with the 15 point discrepancy between white and black IQ test takers, he would have very likely been identified as having EMR—especially when considering his various other disabilities which would have been neatly addressed by a simple EMR classification. For Otte race might very well have been instrumental in his execution on September 13, 2017.

---

[349]Florida Administrative Code, 33-601.830 Death Row
[350]State v. Otte, 74 Ohio St.3d 555 (1996)
[351]*Ibid.*

7. Adaptive Behavior

"This Court does not, under normal circumstances, create law."[352]

Jose Garcia Briseno

In Texas normal death penalty jurisprudence is not the norm. Where IQ can always be questioned because of malingering or validity, re-adjusted, re-interpreted, not believed for a variety of reasons, dismissed because of a lack of IQ scores before age 18, or simply ignored, the second prong of the definition requiring deficits in adaptive behavior is easily used to reject most if not all Atkins claims if that is the real intent of a State. On this count, no State has incurred the ire of professional groups and defense attorney's more than Texas and the so-called Briseno factors.

Unlike other States, Texas did not undertake "the task of developing appropriate ways to enforce the constitutional restriction" when sentencing the mentally retarded/intellectually disabled. Rather, in 2004, the Court of Criminal Appeals in Texas decided, out of necessity, to undertake the task to define mental retardation in a way that would assist Texas courts.[353] After considering the unique needs of Texas and Texans, the concept of adaptive behavior was changed to place emphasis on a variety of factors that were subjectively evaluated such as the ability to hide facts, leadership, and respond coherently. This provided a mechanism for not only assisting Texas courts, but to replace the professional criteria for adaptive behavior by focusing on, for the most part, behavior associated with the capital murder.

Texas stands out for evaluating adaptive behavior for several reasons. Texas is the leader in executions in the United States since the Supreme Court reinstated the death penalty in 1976. Of the 1,517 executions in the United States as of March, 2020, 571

---

[352]In the Court Of Criminal Appeals of Texas, *Ex parte* Briseno, 135 S.W.3d 1, 3 (Tex. Crim. App. 2004)
[353]*Ibid.*

executions have been in Texas which accounts for 37.6 percent of all executions since 1976. Of the executions in Texas, 207 or 36.3 percent have been black. In comparison there have been 113 executions in Virginia (52 black) since 1976 which accounts for 7.5 percent of all executions since 1976. Also, of the 129 Latino executions in the United States 85.3 percent (110) have been in Texas. The combined number (317) of black and Latino executions comprise 55.5 percent of all executions in Texas. This is in contrast to the 71.6 percent black/Latino prisoners on death row in Texas. Again, the difference between race, executions and death row has more to do with scrutiny than racial/ethnic benevolence.

The prolific application of the death penalty for minorities was facilitated by the Texas Court of Appeals which provided a means, now prohibited by the Supreme Court, to circumvent the elements of the adaptive behavior prong by focusing on anecdotal, stereotypic, and idiosyncratic behavior (the Briseno factors) to offset a record of intellectual disability and a fair consideration of professional criteria.

Jose Garcia Briseno was sentenced to death in Webb County for the January 1991 murder of Sheriff Ben Murray. The sheriff was robbed, stabbed, and then shot in the head in his home. Briseno was captured but then escaped from jail with two other inmates. He was soon re-captured and subsequently confessed to one of the other escapees how Sheriff Murray was killed. He was convicted of capital murder and sentenced to death. After all appeals were denied, he filed an Atkins claim on the day of his scheduled execution in 2002 which resulted in a stay to determine whether he was mentally retarded. As a result of this appeal, the trial judge conducted a five day evidentiary hearing and decided that Briseno was not mentally retarded.

Because there were no statutory guidelines for Atkins claims in Texas, the trial judge determined the merits of a claim of mental retardation and this decision was then reviewed by the Texas Court of Appeals. The resulting 2004 Texas appellate court decision was the source of the great uproar among professional groups. The center of controversy was whether Texas can create a standard for mental retardation different from those "who might legitimately qualify for assistance under the social services" but use a different standard when determining culpability for an Atkins claim. One professional organization believed that the task of determining Atkins claims given to the States by the Supreme Court was not unfettered and "this case provides the Court with an appropriate vehicle to remind lower courts that fidelity to the holding of *Atkins* requires even-handed application of the definition *Atkins* embraced, and requires adherence to the scientific and clinical understanding of mental retardation that are its foundation."[354] The Texas court believed otherwise because

> **We, however, must define that level and degree of mental retardation at which a consensus of Texas citizens would agree that a person should be exempted from the death penalty. Most Texas citizens might agree that Steinbeck's Lennie should, by virtue of his lack of reasoning ability and adaptive skills, be exempt. But, does a consensus of Texas citizens agree that all persons who might legitimately qualify for assistance under the social services definition of mental retardation be exempt from an otherwise constitutional penalty?**

The Texas court has been much criticized for the "Lennie" comment but critics seem disinterested in the important distinction that the court was trying to make between mild and moderate/severe levels of intellectual disabilities. To a large degree a death sentence would be less likely as the degree of intellectual disability becomes more pronounced. In that Lennie in Of Mice and Men was greatly dependent on George (and thus had obvious deficits in independent living skills), and had what would seem to be deficits involving language (such that George felt he had to speak on Lennie's behalf), this stereotype of a

---

[354]Briseno v. Quarterman, Brief of the American Association on Intellectual and Developmental Disabilities (AAIDD) and the Arc of the United States as *Amici Curiae* in Support of Petitioner

fictional character would "by virtue of his lack of reasoning ability and adaptive skills, be exempt" from the death penalty.

Because the Texas citizenry, via the legislature, had been unable to decide criteria for intellectual disabilities, the court of criminal appeals of Texas created its own standard which might be called the "Lennie Test" where someone who behaves like Lennie Small exemplifies the type of person who should be exempt from the death penalty. This reasoning suggests that Atkins only applies to individuals with moderate or severe intellectual disabilities and not to the vast majority of persons with IQ scores in the 55 to 75 or mild intellectual disability range. As already discussed, Atkins had a reported IQ of 59 but was said not to be mentally retarded because of his adaptive skills (but was eventually sentenced to life in prison for a reason other than intellectual disability). Unlike the fortunate Daryl Atkins, Marvin Wilson had a reported IQ of 61 in 2006 but was nonetheless executed in Texas in August of 2012. The Texas court decided that the key for determining that Wilson was not mentally retarded was not IQ but adaptive skills including being able to formulate "a plan to kill the victim because he believed that the victim had informed on him to the police."

Most States would agree that moderate and severe levels of intellectual disabilities would exempt an individual from the death penalty. This was essentially the position of Justice O'Connor in 1989 in Penry v. Lynaugh, well before the 2002 Atkins decision. She explained that "The common law prohibition against punishing 'idiots' generally applied, however, to persons of such severe disability that they lacked the reasoning capacity to form criminal intent or to understand the difference between good and evil. In the 19th and early 20th centuries, the term 'idiot' was used to describe the most retarded of persons, corresponding to what is called 'profound' and 'severe' retardation today. Justice O'Connor concluded that "The common law prohibition against punishing 'idiots' for their crimes suggests that it may indeed be 'cruel and unusual' punishment to execute persons who are profoundly or severely retarded and wholly lacking the capacity to appreciate the wrongfulness of their actions. Because of the protections afforded by the insanity defense today, such a person is not likely to be convicted or face the prospect of punishment."[355] This is essentially what the Texas Court of Appeals argues by the reference to Of Mice and Men.

For Jose Briseno, his IQ scores of 72 and 74 were both over the cutoff of 70, but a cutoff of 75 would not have helped much because "the preponderance of the evidence does not show that these test scores over-state the actual intellectual functioning of Applicant; the evidence in fact showed that there are good indications that the test scores understated Applicant's intellectual functioning" and "in sum, we conclude that, while there is expert opinion testimony in this record that would support a finding of mental retardation, there is also ample evidence, including expert and lay opinion testimony, as well as written records, to support the trial court's finding that applicant failed to prove that he is mentally retarded."[356]

One problem with a purely professional guideline for determining intellectual disability when used in Atkins claims is a disavowal of the adversarial process that can be just as self-serving as that used by States. The professional approach seems to be that the definition intellectual disability, having been created by professionals, is above adversarial bickering. In many Atkins claims the prosecution focuses on strengths (especially as an adult), and the defense on a more liberal interpretation of criteria. Considering either only strengths or deficits would hinder the flow of relevant evidence in a manner similar to that in *Ford* or when a strict IQ cutoff of 70 is used in *Hall*. Historically, adaptive behavior (in 1961) was proposed as "a composite of many aspects of behavior and a function of a wide range of specific abilities and disabilities."

Finally, both States and defendants make illogical comparisons when considering strengths and deficits. The cafeteria-style items listed for adaptive behavior in the definitions (viz., communication, self-care, home living, social skills, community use, self-direction, health and safety, functional academics, leisure,

---

[355]Penry v. Lynaugh, 492 US 302, 1989
[356]Criminal Appeals of Texas, *Ex parte* Briseno, 135 S.W.3d 1, 3 (Tex. Crim. App. 2004)

and work suggest that two deficits (e.g., community use, health and safety) could be used to meet the adaptive behavior prong, and would outweigh strengths in academic and communication skills. This would be an unrealistic weighting of the adaptive criteria. For example, a child who had no academic deficits and did not need special education would not meet the standard for having an intellectual disability as per the special education law.[357] To receive special education, a child must have one of the specified disabilities and *need* special education. For the almost 7,000,000 receiving special education under IDEA, approximately 6.3 percent have been identified as having intellectual disabilities. Theoretically, all of these children have educational needs which require special education and an individualized educational program. For IDEA and the 436,000 identified as having intellectual disabilities the ability to adapt to school is the foremost need.[358]

There should be consideration of evidence that would contradict low IQ or deficits in adaptive behavior but using a completely subjective criterion (e.g., "Does his conduct show leadership or does it show that he is led around by others?") to counter an assessment as a child or adult does not enhance the fact-finding process. The problem is not necessarily subjective criteria but when these criteria become the key element, and possibly the only element in the fact-finding process. Thus ability to plan a crime or to conceal participation in a crime is used to contravene a lack of successful school performance, independent living skills, and deficits in language.

Absolute bright lines for IQ or adaptive behavior can easily preclude the consideration of relevant evidence. A defendant might have an IQ below 70, but other IQ scores above 75, and the

---

[357]IDEA or the Individuals with Disabilities Education Act, Public Law 108-446 (2004)

[358]National Center for Education Statistics, Table 204.30. Children 3 to 21 years old served under Individuals with Disabilities Education Act (IDEA), Part B, by type of disability: Selected years, 1976-77 through 2017-18, https://nces.ed.gov/programs/digest/d18/tables/dt18_204.30.asp

meaning of this type of discrepancy would need to be considered by the finder of fact. Likewise, the finder of fact must be allowed to consider all data relating to adaptive behavior, especially data linked to the professional definition and a prior determination of intellectual disability.

Whether or not a defendant graduated from high school will often provide insight as to the type of educational placement. For many children identified as intellectually disabled who are placed in special education, when special education services are terminated, an IEP certificate will be given rather than a high school diploma. However, with extensive supports the ability of a student correctly identified as having an intellectual disability to graduate with a high school diploma is more than a possibility. According to the 30th annual report on the implementation of the IDEA amendments, between 1996 and 2005 the average percentage of students between the ages of 14 and 21 identified as having an intellectual disability and graduating with a high school diploma was 35.8 percent in comparison to an overall average of 49.7 percent of all students with a disability receiving a regular high school diploma.[359] In comparison 32.9 percent of students with emotional disturbance received a regular high school diploma and 55.2 percent of students with specific learning disabilities. A high school diploma or GED does not nullify intellectual disability but provides evidence of the effectiveness of individualized programming and supplementary aids and services. In Florida William Donald Dufour's adaptive skills included receiving a GED, having mechanical skills and "street smarts."[360] These skills were used to show his adaptive strengths and thereby support his death penalty sentence.

State prosecutors certainly can and should weigh strengths and weaknesses, but both strengths and weaknesses cannot be evaluated in isolation. A high school, diploma is often a reflection of successful special education services and supplementary aids and services—and not that reasoning skills, the possibility of a

---

[359] 30th Annual Report to Congress on the Implementation of the *Individuals with Disabilities Education Act*, 2008, p. 65.
[360] Dufour v. Florida, February 3, 2011

false confession, the ability to assist counsel, etc. are no longer suspect and that lesser culpability for capital murder is not appropriate.

Standardized assessments of adaptive behavior can be useful, especially when obtained for children. These assessments are based on interviews with respondents and may or may not be appropriate in an Atkins claim. A self-care item such as "Uses public restroom alone" or "Carries scissors safely" can be very useful for identifying needs for a child or someone with extensive cognitive deficits but this type of data is less useful for Atkins claimants. Defense counsel might consider designing a relatively simple Atkins rating scale with items that address the various behaviors and traits suggested by the Supreme Court (and in *Briseno*) including ability to assist counsel, advocating needs, showing mitigation and lack of remorse, serving as an effective witness, processing the concept of a death penalty as a deterrent, processing information, communicating, independent living skills, learning from experience, engaging in logical reasoning, understanding the reactions of others, acting on impulse, planning, being a leader, etc. Defense should consider multidimensional data that would indicate a finding of intellectual disability and lesser culpability.

When using standardized assessments in Atkins claims, multiple respondents should be used. Unlike the collection of objective data, the type of possible respondents suggested for collecting data should be many and varied ("family members, professional caregivers, supervisors, or the individual"[361]). Responses should be solicited from not only those in the penal system such as prison personnel but others who knew the defendant as a child, teachers, work situations, family members, etc. All data should be considered.

The Briseno factors allowed Texas courts to transcend the professional definition of intellectual disability and focus on traits and behavior at the time of the crime. If a defendant can plan a

---

[361]From the Adaptive Behavior Assessment System–II, Psychological Corporation, 2003.

murder, lie about his/her involvement, the defendant cannot be intellectually disabled. The factors cited in 2004 by the Texas Court of Appeals included the following questions to help the finder of fact in the determination of mental retardation:

1. **Did those who knew the person best during the developmental stage-his family, friends, teachers, employers, authorities-think he was mentally retarded at that time, and, if so, act in accordance with that determination?**
2. **Has the person formulated plans and carried them through or is his conduct impulsive?**
3. **Does his conduct show leadership or does it show that he is led around by others?**
4. **Is his conduct in response to external stimuli rational and appropriate, regardless of whether it is socially acceptable?**
5. **Does he respond coherently, rationally, and on point to oral or written questions or do his responses wander from subject to subject?**
6. **Can the person hide facts or lie effectively in his own or others' interests?**
7. **Putting aside any heinousness or gruesomeness surrounding the capital offense, did the commission of that offense require forethought, planning, and complex execution of purpose?[362]**

Professional groups have disavowed the Briseno factors because "States that adopt non-clinical, non-scientific, and idiosyncratic definitions of mental retardation are abusing the responsibility entrusted to them in *Atkins*, and are defying the clear constitutional mandate from this Court" and contrary to the "accepted and established scientific understanding of mental retardation" and the "scientific mooring" of mental retardation.[363]

---

[362]In the Court Of Criminal Appeals of Texas, *Ex parte* Briseno, 135 S.W.3d 1, 3 (Tex. Crim. App. 2004)

The notion that the definition is remotely related to *science* is a stretch but the factors do represent a combination of reasonable concerns as well as assorted stereotypes. The fact that the Supreme Court was slow[364] in admonishing Texas, as it did for Florida in *Hall* in 2014 regarding the strict IQ cutoff of 70, is not surprising. In Ford v. Wainwright in 1986 the basic problem was a process that restricted the admission of evidence such as not being able to cross-examine witnesses in an insanity hearing. The Briseno factors did raise legitimate concerns that arise in every Atkins claim. The problem was that these factors became the *de facto* definition of intellectual disability which was then used to ignore other commonly accepted elements of adaptive behavior.

The Briseno factors allow a subjective evaluation of "forethought, planning, and complex execution of purpose" to become more relevant than childhood data, assessment reports, a variety of assessments and samples of work, teacher-made tests, State assessments, statistical data concerning overall school grades, rating scales, curriculum-based assessments, reports from parents and teachers, reports from other school personnel such as reading and speech teachers, behavior reports, data pertaining to adaptive behavior, and an individualized education program.

The Supreme Court explained that the rationale for the Eighth Amendment prohibition for capital punishment for the intellectually disabled is based on difficulty involving logical reasoning, understanding information, learning from experience, assisting counsel, etc. These abilities flow from the concept of intellectual disability as defined by professionals, and were not intended to be a list of traits to re-define intellectual disability. One might conclude that someone identified as intellectually disabled would have difficulty processing information, but this does not mean that an opinion by a judge or prison official that

---

[363]Briseno v. Quarterman (Director, Texas Department of Criminal Justice, On Petition for a Writ of Certiorari To the United States Court of Appeals for the Fifth Circuit, Brief of the American Association on Intellectual and Developmental Disabilities (AAIDD) And the Arc of the United States as *Amici Curiae in* Support of Petitioner
[364]Which the Supreme Court did in March of 2017 in Moore v. Texas. See Moore v. Texas, Supreme Court of the United States, March 28, 2017

someone who *seems* able to process information is not intellectually disabled. The Supreme Court gave deference to the professional definition for identifying intellectual disability, but never suggested a subjective evaluation of intellectual disability, based most often on stereotype, should replace the professional definition.

The importance of IQ tests, even after considering the many problems associated with IQ testing, are to show, as best as possible, whether someone has diminished capacity to understand verbal concepts and to engage in logical reasoning. In this respect, these assessments and others, especially before age of onset, provide some measure of a standardized interpretation of intellectual functioning. The Texas court did not simply identify factors that "might" help "weighing evidence" but made these factors the overwhelming evidence of all data considered. With the exception of someone with extensive disabilities, virtually everyone can show "complex execution of purpose" or the ability to "formulate plans." The Briseno factors are not simply factors that "might" help "weighing evidence" but become the overwhelming evidence of all the evidence considered. With the exception of someone with extensive disabilities, virtually everyone can show "complex execution of purpose" or the ability to "formulate plans."

In addition to the faulty logic underlying the Briseno factors, there is also the matter of stereotype which was certainly emphasized in the Lennie analogy in *Briseno Ex Parte*. The ability to "hide facts or lie effectively in his own or others' interests" is based more on an apparent stereotype t someone who is intellectually disabled is not be able to lie "effectively."

The professional definition of intellectual disability is not without fault. Intelligence testing is clouded by environmental and racial concerns and the adaptive behavior prong has been misused or ignored in the misclassification of children and adults. To this end professionals have been less than helpful concerning the importance of IQ and adaptive behavior during the developmental period, the ADA implications for Atkins claimants, and the inclusion of criteria that would assist in the definition of disabilities in Atkins claims. Professionals could formulate a definition that considered the many factors pertinent to *Atkins* and adults and even consider some adaptation or inclusion of the Briseno factors but within the context of the professional definition of intellectual disability.

Even considering the many shortcomings of the professional definition of intellectual disability for adults, the Briseno factors are far more devious in that they can be used to minimize standardized assessments, a record of intellectual disability, developmental history, and the somewhat agreed upon assessment of adaptive behavior. In Texas the finder of fact may know little or nothing about testing or adaptive behavior and thus stereotypic criteria for determining intellectual disability provides a simple solution to a very complex problem—not a good solution but simple nonetheless.

For all the consternation caused by the Briseno factors, where the factors were used to show that Jose Briseno was not mentally retarded and therefore could be executed, he was not executed. In 2010, the Texas Criminal Court of Appeals decided that the jury instruction given during Briseno's sentencing did not adequately explain that sub-average intellectual functioning (low IQ) could be a mitigating factor that would disallow the death penalty. After 20 years of litigation, Jose Briseno's death sentence was commuted to life. He will be eligible for parole in 2028 at the age of 70.

As explained by the Court of Criminal Appeals of Texas (and the Supreme Court in Penry v. Johnson in 2001[365]), the instruction did "'not adequately inform the jury that it may assess a punishment less than death on account of [the mitigating evidence] irrespective of what the evidence shows as to [the defendant's] deliberateness and future dangerousness.'" If jury was able to interpret the above instruction, which is more riddle than instruction, it failed to reveal that a sentence less than death could be imposed no matter the extent (or vote) of deliberateness and future-dangerousness.

---

[365]Penry v. Johnson, 532 US 782, 2001

Bobby James Moore

The Briseno factors were eventually undone, not by Texas, but by Bobby James Moore and the Supreme Court. In 1980 Moore murdered James McCarble, a 73-year old grocery clerk in Houston, Texas during an attempted robbery at the Birdsall Super Market. Following a second punishment hearing in 2001 he was again sentenced to death. In 2014 a habeas court found that Moore met the criteria for intellectual disability and was not eligible for the death penalty. In 2015 the Court of Criminal Appeals of Texas found that the habeas judge erred "by disregarding case law requiring relatedness between any adaptive behavior deficits and sub-average general intellectual functioning."[366]

A variety of test scores were reported for Moore including an IQ score of 77 when he was 12, a full scale IQ of 78 on the WISC when he was 13, and various scores on different versions of the WAIS following his death sentence (71, 57, 74, 59 and 85). A psychologist recommended that Moore, as a child, "stay in regular classes, but suggested that the school modify his program by using certain specific teaching techniques to strengthen his areas of academic weakness." Exactly what disability was identified for Moore as a child (e.g., mental retardation, specific learning disability, etc.) and by whom, was not discussed. The habeas court adjusted IQ scores for the so-called Flynn effect and decided that he met the first prong. The Texas Court of Appeals ignored various IQ scores because of the type of test used (e.g., a group test) and considered only IQ scores of 74 at age 13 and 78 at age 30. The court interpreted the different tests scores as caused by something other than intellectual disability (e.g., reduced effort) and therefore did not support the first prong (low IQ) of the definition of intellectual disability.

Although acknowledging some deficits in adaptive behavior such as academic deficits, the court believed these were caused by factors other than intellectual disability and was more impressed

---

[366]Ex Parte Bobby James Moore, Court of Criminal Appeals of Texas, 470 S.W.3d 481, 2015

with adaptive strengths cited by the State expert which included the adaptive tidbit "that applicant had lived in the back of a pool hall, as well as evidence that he had played pool and mowed lawns for money." After considering testimony from various experts, the Court of Appeals decided the State's expert was "more credible and reliable" and therefore Moore did not meet the second prong of the definition. The conclusion that Moore did not have deficits in adaptive behavior was supported by his "significant advances" while on death row and an evaluation of the Briseno factors. To show his ability to plan the Court of Appeals noted that Moore "doggedly pursued his desire to obtain new appellate counsel after his 1980 trial by writing to various courts, attorneys, and organizations, filing pleadings and motions, and marshaling exhibits." In other words, seeking to prove he was mentally retarded proved that he was not.

The ultimate argument offered by the Texas appellate court for rejecting Moore's claim of intellectual disability was that in Ex Parte Briseno the Texas court used the 1992 AAMR definition. This definition required that a defendant's "significantly subaverage general intellectual functioning is accompanied by related and significant limitations in adaptive functioning." The habeas court used the 2010 AAIDD definition which defined intellectual disability "as a condition 'characterized by significant limitations both in intellectual functioning and in adaptive behavior as expressed in conceptual, social, and practical adaptive skills'" rather than the 1992 AAMR definition. By using the most recent definition, according to the Texas Court of Appeals, the habeas court did not follow the 1992 "requirement that an individual's adaptive behavior deficits, if any, must be 'related to' significantly subaverage general intellectual functioning."

According to the appellate court, an Atkins claimant must not only establish by a preponderance of the evidence deficits in significantly subaverage general intellectual functioning and adaptive behavior but that the former must be related to the latter. The fallacy of this argument is that "related" is used as a synonym for "caused." For example, the inability to adapt to school as evidenced by poor achievement scores must be related or "caused" by low intelligence and not "caused" by motivation, environment, emotional disturbance or specific learning disabilities (among many other factors). There has never been a hint of **causation** between IQ and adaptive behavior until the DSM-5 stipulated that "to meet diagnostic criteria for intellectual disability, the deficits in adaptive functioning must be directly related to the intellectual impairments described in Criterion A." Citing the first Briseno factor (did those who knew him as a child think he was mentally retarded), the court observed that as a child a physician thought that emotional problems were the cause of poor school performance, he was never diagnosed as mentally retarded, and never placed in a special education class. As a result, whatever his IQ, a significantly subaverage general intellectual functioning was not related to adaptive behavior.

In an article by Tasse, Luckasson, and Schalock in 2016 the notion of causation between significantly subaverage general intellectual functioning and adaptive behavior was emphatically denounced.[367] These authors state that "the DSM-5 inadvertently created a fourth diagnostic criterion, one that is virtually impossible for clinicians to implement and is unsupported by science." For Atkins claims courts and experts have not been adverse to demand a need for a show of causation.

There is no way to determine the exact cause of mild intellectual disability or to partition a certain percentage of cause to the various possible underlying factors. The term *cultural-familial* intellectual disability represents the majority (75 to 85 percent) of persons with intellectual disabilities. This is in contrast to intellectual disabilities where there is a known etiology such as Down syndrome, PKU, Fragile X syndrome, fetal alcohol syndrome, etc. The Texas appellate court required evidence of the cause of intellectual disability, a cause which is mired in the interaction of environment, genetics, and organic causes.

---

[367]Marc J. Tasse, Ruth Luckasson, and Robert L. Schalock, The Relation Intellectual and Developmental Disabilities Between Intellectual Functioning and Adaptive Behavior in the Diagnosis of Intellectual Disability, Intellectual and Developmental Disabilities, 2016, Vol. 54, No. 6, 381–390.

For someone identified as having an intellectual disability as a child, the adaptive deficits might have been the result of learning disabilities, environment, or socio-economic factors, genetics, brain-injury, prenatal factors, etc., and, of course, significantly subaverage general intellectual functioning. The definition does not eliminate misclassification, as evidenced by the disproportionate number of black children identified as having intellectual disabilities, but what the definition does is to provide a framework for identifying a very complex disability that, in most cases, cause is not readily identifiable. When a child is classified as having a mild intellectual disability, in most cases, causation is simply not known. By considering the professional definition of intellectual disability, using relatively accepted criteria, some semblance of definitional standardization is achieved. For whatever reason, once the State has pronounced a person intellectually disabled, or regarded a person as intellectually disabled, as a child or as an adult, that identification should mandate lesser culpability for an adult seeking Atkins relief.

The Texas appellate court decided "the record overwhelmingly supports the conclusion that applicant's academic difficulties were caused by a variety of factors, including trauma from the emotionally and physically abusive atmosphere in which he was raised, undiagnosed learning disorders, changing elementary schools three times in three years, racially motivated harassment and violence at school, a history of academic failure, drug abuse, and absenteeism. The same is true of any social difficulty that applicant experienced during the developmental period." Of course, all of this could be true for the majority of children identified as intellectually disabled as a child or adult.

In 2017 the Supreme Court reviewed the Texas Court of Appeals decision and concluded that in several ways the Texas Court of Appeals decision was inconsistent with *Atkins*, *Hall* and the Eighth Amendment.[368] In a 5 to 3 vote the Court not only rejected the Briseno factors but provided some guidance concerning how intellectual disability should be interpreted by courts.

---

[368]Moore v. Texas, Supreme Court of the United States, March 28, 2017

First, the Court offered an indirect comment on how to deal with multiple scores. In the hodgepodge of IQ scores offered on behalf of Moore, the Court cited the score of 74 as meeting the significantly subaverage intellectual functioning prong of the definition. The Court suggested a single credible IQ score is sufficient to move on to the next prong (adaptive behavior). More importantly, the Court focused on the IQ score of 74 at age 30 (of the two IQ scores worthy of consideration).

Aside from this is the fact that the score of 78 at age 13 (Moore was born in 1959) is even more relevant than a score of 74 as an adult. Not only was there less likelihood of malingering as a child, but a score of 78 in the 1960s would have been well below the IQ cutoff of 85 as per the 1959 and 1961 AAMR guidelines. In the 1960s, even having met the criteria for mental retardation, Moore would not necessarily have been classified. The probability of classification would have increased as schools became desegregated.

Second, the Supreme Court attempted to clarify that stereotype should not guide the determination of adaptive behavior. The Court explained that "The CCA overemphasized Moore's perceived adaptive strengths—living on the streets, mowing lawns, and playing pool for money—when the medical community focuses the adaptive-functioning inquiry on adaptive *deficits*." The problem is not simply that strengths were emphasized but that all meaningful and thoughtful behavior above drooling was used to show that Moore was not intellectually disabled. The idea that a defendant with mild intellectual disability would be able to read— based on an observation by a jail guard that the "applicant had been in jail awaiting the retrial, he had seen applicant reading a newspaper"—was deemed revealing and demonstrated that an inmate was not intellectually disabled.

Third, the Briseno factors were rejected entirely as a means for denying a determination of intellectual disability. The Court explained that the Briseno factors were "Not aligned with the medical community's information, and drawing no strength from our precedent, the *Briseno* factors created an unacceptable risk that persons with intellectual disability will be executed." By considering the Briseno factors the Court explained that this "pervasively infected the CCA's analysis, the decision of that court cannot stand. Skeptical of what it viewed as "exceedingly subjective" medical and clinical standards, the CCA in *Briseno* advanced lay perceptions of intellectual disability."

Fourth, the "relatedness" criterion created by the Texas Court of Appeals was rejected. The court offered multiple causes for Moore's deficits including adaptive deficits involving "an abuse-filled childhood, undiagnosed learning disorders, multiple elementary-school transfers, racially motivated assessment, violence at school, and a history of academic failure, drug abuse, and absenteeism." What should be obvious in determining mild intellectual disabilities is that all of these could be contributing factors in addition to many other possible "causes." The idea that a defendant must "show that his adaptive deficits were not related to 'a personality disorder' is not only an impossible task but a ridiculous one to boot.

The Court of Criminal Appeals of Texas again, upon remand, tackled the issue of whether Moore was intellectually disabled and again found that he was not.[369] The CCA, relying on a self-serving interpretation of the DSM-5, concluded that Moore did not have sufficient deficits in adaptive behavior to make a determination of intellectual disability. Evidence discounting his intellectual disability included "Applicant's ability to copy such documents by hand would indicate an understanding and ability to write that would be within the realm of only a few intellectually disabled people." The CCA also found that his prison adaptive skills were not within the realm of intellectual disability. For example, "one of applicant's sisters testified that Applicant's reading and writing ability had greatly improved since his imprisonment. She further acknowledged that, in prison, his ability to count had greatly improved." The court then assumed a mantel of expertise in not only intellectual disability but "learning" as when 'the amount and pace of Applicant's improvement in reading and writing is simply

---

[369]*Ex parte Moore II*, 548 S. W. 3d, at 555, Court of Criminal Appeals of Texas
June 6, 201

inconsistent with the habeas court's description of Applicant as a 'slow learner.'"

As with the first review by the CCA the court fell back on the need for causation as when the "evidence fails to suggest that the cause of Applicant's deficient social behavior was related to any deficits in general mental abilities, suggesting instead that the cause was "most likely emotional problems." Although the court supposedly abandoned the Briseno factors there was a Briseno-type quality to what the CCA seemed important: "His testimony was coherent and sometimes lengthy. Dr. Compton said that Applicant's responses to questions during his trial showed that he could 'conceptualize what was being asked and form exculpatory statements or responses' and indicated 'an ability to engage in abstract reasoning to some degree."

The Supreme Court again rejected the decision by the Court of Criminal Appeals because of three factors: 1) an over-emphasis on current adaptive skills (especially in prison) while ignoring Moore's history of poor adaptive functioning, 2) suggesting that the cause of his deficits must be intellectual disability, and 3) while having said the Briseno factors were abandoned the CCA (and the court's most "credible" expert) as exemplified by Moore's ability to conceptualize and engage in abstract reasoning as noted above.[370] The Court reversed the CCA decision and stated that "Moore has shown he is a person with intellectual disability." The task left to States in *Atkins* to determine intellectual disability has been modified: if a State is unable to make a proper determination of intellectual disability, the Supreme Court will. Moore is no longer on death row (the Polunsky Unit) and is currently serving a life sentence at the Ramsey Unit near Rosharon, Texas. His co-defendant, Willie Albert Koonce, who is reported to have actually committed the murder, received a life sentence and was paroled in 2012.

Kenneth D. Williams

---

[370]Moore v. Texas, 586 U. S. ___ (2019)

The Supreme Court's 2017 Moore v. Texas decision provides very important guidelines for Atkins claims (maybe not so important when considered by the CCA in 2018) but the decision is bothered by the question of retroactivity. In 1999 Kenny Williams escaped from Cummins Unit prison in Arkansas where he had been serving a life sentence for the murder of cheerleader Dominique Hurd. Following his escape, he stole the truck of Cecil Boren who he then murdered. Williams fled to Missouri, crashed Boren's truck killing the driver of a water delivery truck. In 2000 he was sentenced to death. His appeals were denied and shortly before his execution he sought relief under Moore v. Texas.[371]

Williams had been given a variety of IQ tests, some above 75 and some below. His appeal placed considerable emphasis on the Flynn effect whereby IQ scores should be adjusted downward depending on when a test was standardized and then administered. In addition, his appeal cited various adaptive deficits that should be considered. Probably more emphasis should have been placed on whether or not Arkansas considered him mentally retarded or intellectually disabled before age of onset and whether he was in special education as a child. In the end the United States Court of Appeals for the Eighth Circuit decided on April 27 that Moore discussed "purely procedural issues"[372] and thus did not apply retroactively. On April 27, 2017 one day after his final appeal citing *Moore*, Kenneth Williams age 38, was executed by lethal injection in the Cummins Unit, the same prison he had escaped from in 1999.

Williams' argument was that *Moore* was a new substantive rule and that he was intellectually disabled based on the guidance provided in *Moore*. There was a leap of logic in his appeal to the United States Court of Appeals for the Eighth Circuit. He asserted

---

[371]Kenneth Dewayne Williams, applicant-petitioner v. Wendy Kelley, Director, Arkansas Department of Correction, respondent , Protective application to file a second or successive petition pursuant to 28 U.S.C. § 2244, The United States Court of Appeals for the Eighth Circuit, filed April 26, 2017.

[372]Kenneth Dewayne Williams Petitioner v. Wendy Kelley, Director, Arkansas Department of Correction Respondent, No. 17-1892, No. 17-1893, No. 17-1896

that "Moore was made retroactive to cases by the Supreme Court that was previously unavailable." This was based on a claim that *Moore* was a new substantive rule of law." The difficulty with this argument is the presumption that *Moore* is, indeed, a new rule of law. The United States Court of Appeals disagreed, decided that Moore was not "a new rule of constitutional procedure," but then acknowledged that the Supreme Court's decision "may presage an eventual ruling by the Court that Moore will be given a Montgomery-like effect" as per the 2012 the Supreme Court's decision in Miller v. Alabama that life without parole for defendants under 18 was mandated.[373]

Miller v. Alabama involved a life without parole sentence for a 14-year-old offender. Evan Miller and a friend had beat a neighbor (52-year-old Cole Cannon) and set fire to his trailer. Cannon died and Miller was sentenced to life without parole. The Court decided that "the Eighth Amendment forbids a sentencing scheme that mandates life in prison without possibility of parole for juvenile offenders." The reasoning for this decision by Justice Kagan was that "By requiring that all children convicted of homicide receive life time incarceration without possibility of parole, regardless of their age and age-related characteristics and the nature of their crimes, the mandatory sentencing schemes before us violate this principle of proportionality."[374]

In Montgomery v. Louisiana, in 2016, the Supreme Court explained that "Substantive rules, then, set forth categorical constitutional guarantees that place certain criminal laws and punishments altogether beyond the State's power to impose."[375] In 1963 Henry Montgomery murdered a deputy sheriff (Charles Hurt) in East Baton Rouge, Louisiana. He was convicted and sentenced to life without parole as a 17-year-old. The Court announced that *Miller* was a "substantive rule of constitutional law." The Court did not mandate parole for juvenile offenders sentenced to life without parole but suggested that States can remedy the unconstitutional sentencing of juvenile offenders by

---

[373]Miller v. Alabama, 567 U. S. ___ (2012)
[374]Miller v. Alabama, 567 U. S. ___ (2012)
[375]Montgomery v. Louisiana, 577 U.S. __ (2016)

allowing the consideration of parole rather than re-sentencing. *Consideration* does not mean *leniency*. In Pennsylvania George Gregory Elliot was sentenced to life without parole for a murder committed at age 17. He was then resentenced to 50 years with the possibility of parole and will be eligible for parole at age 70. The result of Montgomery the Montgomery v. Louisiana had a similar result. In April, 2019 the 72-year-old Montgomery was denied parole while having served 55 years at the Louisiana State Penitentiary at Angola. The parole board denied his request because one board member believed he needed additional guidance and coursework.

Danny Hill

In September of 1985 Danny Hill tortured and murdered Raymond Fife, age 12 in Warren, Ohio. Hill was sentenced to death in 1986. After initiating an Atkins claim in 2002, which was denied, in 2018 the United States Court of Appeals for the Sixth Circuit faulted the trial court's interpretation of the criteria for *Atkins* because "the state trial court focused extensively on Hill's interview with a reporter, his demeanor in interacting with law enforcement and the legal system, and the circumstances surrounding the Fife murder.[376] Those supposed adaptive strengths convinced the state trial court that Hill could not be intellectually disabled because he had "remarkable" communication and vocabulary skills and was self-directed." As was decided improper in Moore, the appellate court believed that the State placed too much emphasis on not only adaptive strengths but the ability to adapt in prison.

The court of appeals relied heavily on *Moore* but the Supreme Court decided that the interpretation of Atkins was contrary to clearly established law. The appellate court did not need *Moore* to establish intellectual disability because all evidence suggested that Danny Hill had a clear history of intellectual disability including an

---

[376]Hill v. Anderson, 881 F.3d 483, February 2, 2018

IQ score below 70, great difficulty in school, and many other acknowledged adaptive deficits such as poor communication skills. Most important, he was in special education and, in Ohio at the time this, would have meant inclusion in an EMR designated classroom. Ohio had already decided that Hill was mentally retarded as a child, provided an education commensurate with this decision, and then decided to recant this decision for the purpose of execution.

Because the court of appeals emphasis on *Moore* (in 2017) which came many years after the determination that he was not intellectually disabled, the Supreme Court vacated the decision.[377] In Shoop v. Hill, decided on January 7, 2019, (Tim Shoop was the warden) the Court cited the Antiterrorism and Effective Death Penalty Act of 1996 (AEDPA) and how this "imposes important limitations on the power of federal courts to overturn the judgments of state courts in criminal cases." The Court then decided to "consider what was clearly established regarding the execution of the intellectually disabled in 2008, when the Ohio Court of Appeals rejected Hill's *Atkins* claim." In other words, *Moore* is not retroactive and using *Moore* as a guideline in this fashion is an inappropriate application of the law.

There seems little doubt that the court of appeals need only consider the criteria for Atkins in 2002 to come to the conclusion that Hill is intellectually disabled. Hill's appeal was first based on "an unreasonable determination of the facts" and not the retroactive application of *Moore* (which the Supreme Court found unreasonable). This is another example where a murder was so horrific, so beyond the pale of human behavior that if there is to be a death penalty, the torture and murder of a 12-year-old might well be most deserving of capital punishment. In all likelihood this could be one of the factors that resulted in a determination that he was not intellectually disabled. The ultimate task for resolving every Atkins claim is objectivity, and a fair interpretation of the criteria and evidence for intellectuality—a task made difficulty by the circumstances of the crime and the victim. Hill remains on death row as of 2020.

---

[377]Shoop v. Hill, 586 U.S. __ (2019)

Robert James Tennard

The Supreme Court has tried to narrow its death penalty jurisprudence for the most heinous crimes and most deserving defendants as shown by *Atkins* and *Hall*. However, the line between mild intellectual disability and not is often slim and the line between life and death as per *Atkins* is even more so. If there is insufficient evidence for a determination of an intellectual disability, the next obvious question is whether low intelligence is a mitigating factor and how much weight should be given to this factor.

Robert James Tennard and accomplices killed (by stabbing and hatchet) two neighbors as part of a robbery in 1985 in Harris County, Texas. At trial his parole officer testified that Tennard had an IQ of 67 which was administered as part of a prior felony-rape trial and conviction. Texas decided that low intellectual ability was not a sufficient mitigating factor and he was sentenced to death.

Upon appeal the Fifth Circuit Court of Appeals also did not believe the murder was caused (the "nexus" test) by his IQ, but the Supreme Court explained that "impaired intellectual functioning is inherently mitigating" and that the appellate court's "nexus" test was rejected.[378] The Court explained that in Atkins "Nothing in our opinion suggested that a mentally retarded individual must establish a nexus between her mental capacity and her crime before the Eighth Amendment prohibition on executing her is triggered."[379] The "nexus" claim is similar to a causation requirement whereby a defendant must not only prove intellectual disability, but prove the impossible task that intellectual disability was the cause of the murder. The Supreme Court remanded the case and the circuit court, in 2006, found "that the state court failed to ensure that the jury was able to give sufficient mitigating effect to Tennard's evidence of diminished

---

[378]Tennard v. Dretke, 542 U.S. 274 (2004)
[379]Sandra Day O'Connor gave the opinion for the majority 6-3 decision

cognitive capacity, in violation of the Eighth and Fourteenth Amendments."[380] Before a re-trial to consider his IQ score of 67 as a mitigating factor, Tennard negotiated a sentence for two life terms for the 1985 murder and an assault on a prison guard in 2005, and agreed to not ask for parole.

Holly Wood

Other States distort and re-interpret the adaptive behavior prong of the definition of intellectual disability but are far more subtle than Texas. Alabama does not use the Briseno factors *per se* but it was able to invent the concept of "regrettable adaptability"—regrettably. For Holly Wood a record of mental retardation did not prevent his execution at the Holman Correctional Facility in September of 2010 by lethal injection. He was executed not because of an IQ cutoff and not because of a clinical definition, or in spite of the clinical definition, but because Alabama did not consider all the evidence that showed that he was mentally retarded.

For the much arrested Wood (18 prior arrests in all), the death penalty was given for the murder of his girlfriend, Ruby Lois Gosh ("I shot that bitch in the head"). He had abused Gosh prior to the murder, attacked her with a knife, and eventually shot her in the face with a 12-gauge shotgun in her home. In 1994 he was sentenced to death but claimed he had ineffective counsel and was mentally retarded. To counter Wood's claim of ineffective counsel for not presenting evidence of mental retardation, the State contended that this was a decision by counsel. In 2006 the District Court found "a finding by the state courts that a strategic decision was made not to investigate or introduce to the sentencing jury evidence of mental retardation is an unreasonable determination of the facts in light of the clear and convincing evidence presented in the record." This might have been due, in part, to the inexperience of his counsel, or the inability to gather relevant information for whatever reasons. His counsel never discussed

---

[380]Tennard v. Dretke, United States Court of Appeals for the Fifth Circuit, No. 00-20915,March 1, 2006

Wood's education. For some unknown reason, although school records were subpoenaed, no records were forthcoming. Considering that the vote for the death penalty was 10 to 2, the minimum required, additional mitigating evidence could have been relevant to the outcome of vote.

Following *Atkins* in 2002 Wood claimed mental retardation. During his evidentiary hearing, State experts found that in spite of an IQ of 64, he was able to adapt and was not mentally retarded. Wood's defense contended that he had adaptive deficits in functional academics, communication, social skills, and self-direction. As done in other States (viz., Texas), Alabama focused on strengths rather than deficits.[381] The case for mental retardation was hampered, for a time, when the circuit court refused to hear the expert testimony of an out-of-state psychologist unless proof to practice psychology in Alabama could be shown. As a further incentive not to testify, her testimony was said to have entailed practicing without a license in Alabama. The Alabama Court of Criminal Appeals, in 2004, decided otherwise because "if we were to adopt [the circuit court's position], we would in effect preclude expert testimony from, for example, Archimedes himself, the Greek mathematician, physicist, and inventor credited with the discovery of the principle of the lever."[382]

In spite of testimony to the contrary, the State argued that Wood was not mentally retarded because he was able to maintain employment, drive a car ("...and paid cash for most of them"), "was an automobile enthusiast who subscribed to Hot Rod magazine" and was able to communicate, solve problems, maintain relationships and was able to devise a plan to shoot a former girlfriend which the court referred to as "regrettable adaptability."

A special education teacher testified that Wood was in her class for two years and that placements were based on IQ scores.[383] In addition, there is a statement that "Wood was probably classified

---

[381]Wood v. Allen, 465 F. Supp. 2d 1211 (M.D. Ala. 2006)
[382]Wood v. State, 891 So. 2d 398 (Ala. Crim. App. 2004)
[383]Wood v. Allen, 465 F.Supp.2d 1211 (2006)

as educable mentally retarded, which meant he was more productive than the students classified as trainable mentally retarded." The State circumvented his prior mental retardation by the implausible argument that he was actually average because he "was in the middle range of the educable mentally retarded group of students, had an IQ in the low to mid 60s, and got C-range grades. Wood never failed and attended class on a regular basis, although he was quiet and did not always put forth maximum effort." One witness "confirmed Wood was very clean and had a very neat appearance." His special education teacher testified that he was just an "average" student (in an EMR class), passed all his classes and was not truant. Alabama decided that he was mentally retarded as a child as evidenced by his classification and school placement, but State experts determined that he was no longer mentally retarded as per *Atkins*...regrettably.

The "court rejected the expert testimony that Wood was mentally retarded as being incredible because it was based on information which was inconsistent with his actual functioning in the community. "[384] Not only are there strengths and deficits, but if the court agrees with testimony attesting to strengths ("to drive a forklift, to manage money, to maintain a relationship with his girlfriend, and other similar evidence)," opinions to the contrary must be based on evidence that is not reliable. In other words, if there is evidence contrary to the Alabama's interpretation of the evidence, that evidence is unreliable (or "incredible").

Howard Dean Goodin

The dilemma for Howard Dean Goodin was a Catch-22.[385] An Atkins claim would prevent his execution if he were intellectually disabled, but asserting his constitutional claim of intellectual disability would show that he was not intellectually disabled. This is a State's ultimate trump card in Atkins claims: asserting a claim

---

[384]Wood v. Allen, 465 F. Supp. 2d 1211 (M.D. Ala. 2006)
[385]The famous Catch-22 book/movie phrase where a claim of "crazy" by a flyer to avoid dangerous missions during the war indicated that the flyer was not really crazy and so had to fly more dangerous missions.

is a strength that shows the claim should be denied. In the end his claim of intellectual disability prevailed but not before much bureaucratic nitpicking by Mississippi.

In support of an IQ cutoff of 75 in oral arguments on behalf of Freddie Lee Hall in 2014, Mississippi (along with Oklahoma) was offered as examples of States that met the constitutional requirement in *Atkins*. In Mississippi, in 1999, Howard Dean Goodin (born in 1954) was sentenced to death by lethal injection for the 1998 robbery, kidnapping and murder of store owner Willis Rigdon. Rigdon was taken from his store, shot in the head and neck, and then dumped in a ditch along a dirt road. As a teenager, in 1971, as part of a vocational rehabilitation evaluation, Goodin's full scale WAIS IQ was 62 (with a performance score of 49). In 1973 his full scale WAIS score was 63, and in 1999 his WAIS-Revised full scale IQ score was 60. In 2004, his WAIS-III full scale IQ was reported to be 52 which would, if accurate, indicate extensive cognitive impairment.

In 2003 the State argued that his test performance was the result of malingering and a trial report "which found that Goodin was attentive, cooperative and polite. The State argued that Goodin's behavior during and after the shooting/robbery showed a level of intelligence, reasoning and planning that was inconsistent with a finding of mental retardation." This is a variation of the Briseno factors where test evidence is dismissed and "intelligence" is determined by a subjective evaluation of behavior pursuant to the offense.[386]

To receive an Atkins hearing in Mississippi, as outlined in Chase v. Mississippi in 2004, the defendant must have a timely motion that includes an affidavit that contains the opinion by at least one expert that "(1) the defendant has a combined Intelligence Quotient ("IQ") of 75 or below, and; (2) in the opinion of the expert, there is a reasonable basis to believe that, upon further testing, the defendant will be found to be mentally retarded." In a footnote (#20) to the 2004 Supreme Court of Mississippi decision,

---

[386]Goodin V. Mississippi, Supreme Court of Mississippi, No. 2002-DR-00686-SCT, August 7, 2003

the court explained that "the cutoff score for the intellectual functioning prong of the test is 75" and "defendants with an IQ of 76 or above do not qualify for Eighth Amendment protection."[387]

A four person evaluation team decided that Goodin was not mentally retarded because he could consult with his attorneys, was able to understand the various legal proceedings and was able to "assert his constitutional rights."[388] For Goodin, if he did not assist counsel, his Atkins would be difficult to substantiate; if he did assist counsel, this would show that he was not mentally retarded. Courts and experts decided that he was not "genuinely mentally retarded" because, among other factors, he had "the present capacity to understand and knowingly, intelligently, and voluntarily to waive or assert his constitutional rights." More importantly, "he had exaggerated his limitations in past testing and that his use of language and his ability to learn and apply basic legal concepts was incompatible with someone who was genuinely mentally retarded." This is another revision of the definition of intellectual disability: criteria for intellectual disability are secondary to a determination of *genuine intellectual disability/mental retardation* which is somehow divined by judge, jury and/or prosecutor.

In 2010, Goodin's full scale IQ had rebounded to 64 with no evidence of malingering. For all on death row the possibility of malingering when taking an IQ test, or anything that would delay execution, is not an inconsequential consideration. Justice Scalia, in his dissent in *Atkins*, offered that

> **One need only read the definitions of mental retardation adopted by the American Association on Mental Retardation and the American Psychiatric Association (set forth in the Court's opinion, *ante*, at 308, n. 3) to realize that the symptoms of this condition can readily be feigned. And whereas the capital defendant**

[387]Chase v. Mississippi, Supreme Court of Mississippi, 873 So.2d 1013 (2004)
[388]Goodin v. Mississippi, Supreme Court of Mississippi, No. 2010-CA-01762-SCT, December 13, 2012

who feigns insanity risks commitment to a mental institution until he can be cured (and then tried and executed), *Jones* v. *United States,* 463 U. S. 354, 370, and n. 20 (1983), the capital defendant who feigns mental retardation risks nothing at all.

For Goodin there were a variety of attempts to determine malingering. A forensic psychiatrist commented on reasons why she thought Goodin was not malingering: "(1) his symptoms had been consistent since 1971; (2) he had nothing to gain by malingering in 1971, and he had never used his mental symptoms as an excuse for prior offenses; (3) he had harmed his credibility when he testified at his trial; and (4) he had continued to report auditory hallucinations when examined at Whitfield in 2004." [389] Of particular importance is that he had nothing to gain by malingering in 1971, at age 12, or when he had a reported IQ of 62 and an IQ of 63 two years later. Courts are not hesitant to devalue the importance of IQ tests given prior to age 18 when malingering is less likely but place great value on IQ assessments after age of onset when the possibility of malingering is far more likely.

The court decided that his IQ scores were low, maybe believable and maybe not, and that "Despite scoring poorly on tests measuring intellectual functioning, Goodin's cognitive abilities are beyond that of a person who is genuinely mentally retarded." [390] The circuit court found in 2012 that "Any deficits in adaptive functioning were certainly affected by the fact that Goodin has been incarcerated for most of his adult life. Therefore, Goodin has not proven by a preponderance of evidence that he is mentally retarded." For Goodin IQ scores were not credible and deficits in adaptive behavior were probably the result of incarceration.

The Mississippi Supreme Court regarded allegations of malingering as unsubstantiated and discounted the subjective determination that Goodin was "too adept at using language." The Mississippi Supreme Court decided that "the evidence that Goodin

---

[389] *Ibid.*
[390] *Ibid.*

has met this Court's standard for mental retardation is overwhelming and may not be discounted by the assertion that he is too adept at using language or by other unsupported allegations of malingering."[391]

Joseph Daniel Miller

In 1993, Joseph Daniel Miller was sentenced to death for kidnapping and the first degree murder of Selina Franklin and Stephanie McDuffey in Pennsylvania. Shortly after *Atkins* in 2002 Virginia Miller claimed that he was mentally retarded. The court reviewed evidence relating to psychological reports, school reports and expert testimony showing Miller had IQ scores of 66, 67, 55 and 59 between the ages of 6 and 12, and was placed in special education classes for the educable mentally retarded.[392] In 2008 the Supreme Court of Pennsylvania considered Miller's claim and focused, not on IQ scores, but adaptive behavior. The defense cited adaptive behavior deficits consistent with the professional definitions while the State offered testimony by an expert who believed Miller was mentally retarded before his death sentence, but not mentally retarded as a result of his time on death row where he was able to adapt. In Mississippi death row explained an ability to adapt; in Pennsylvania death row improved adaptive behavior to a level above that of mental retardation. As is in other States, the theory is that "adapt" is not interpreted with anything remotely related to the professional definition but some range of behaviors unique to death row where a prisoner apparently adapts to strip searches, 22-23 hours of solitary confinement, minimal contact with other prisoners, and two hour caged recreation and/or library time. Pennsylvania in a very Florida and Texas-like way, "expressed the opinion that the relevant community for consideration of adaptive defects was the prison, death-row community." This approach offers a unique interpretation of professional definitions of intellectual disability,

---

[391]*Ibid.*

[392]Pennsylvania v Miller, Supreme Court of Pennsylvania, 888 A.2d 624 (2005)

sans an adherence to professional guidance, that was rejected by the Supreme Court Moore v. Texas in 2017.[393]

In the end, following claims by the Commonwealth of judicial impartiality, the Supreme Court of Pennsylvania[394] sided with the Post Conviction Relief Act court because the evidence showed that Miller was placed in special education classes beginning in first grade for the 'educable' mentally retarded; during his early years, his IQ was repeatedly tested and he tested in the 50's and 60's; in his early teens." The court also noted that "all five mental health experts who testified during the penalty phase and at the first PCRA hearing, including the Commonwealth's expert at the PCRA hearing, agreed that Appellee was borderline retarded or mentally retarded. Accordingly, the court concluded that Appellee proved by a preponderance of the evidence that he is mentally retarded."[395]

---

[393]Moore v. Texas, Supreme Court of the United States, March 28, 2017
[394]Commonwealth of Pennsylvania v. Miller, 951 A.2d 322 (2008)
[395]Pennsylvania v Miller, Supreme Court of Pennsylvania, 888 A.2d 624 (2005)

8. Age of Onset

**"It is implicit in that definition that the IQ and
deficits in adaptive behavior exist not only prior to the
age of 18 but also both at the time of the crime and currently."**[396]

Eddie Duval Powell

The third criterion, which is more guideline than criterion, for defining intellectual disability is interpreted, contrary to the intent in 1959, to establish an a completely unjustifiable and egregiously strict criterion for Atkins claims. For Eddie Duval Powell this enhancement of the definition of mental retardation was too difficult to overcome and he was executed on June 16, 2011, by lethal injection. Age of onset played a key role in his execution.

In various forms, States can ensure the likelihood an Atkins claim will fail by a "plain language" requirement that a claimant must meet the definitional criteria for intellectual disability before age 18, after age 18, at the time of the crime, and/or on death row. This use of the third element of the definition for intellectual disabilities, *age of onset*, is nothing less than definitional sleight of hand to deny Atkins claims. To counter deficits in adaptive behavior, the defense is faulted for not showing deficits as a child, or emphasizing strengths at the time of the crime, or the ability to adapt to prison life. If childhood intellectual ability is considered, these data are given lesser importance because they were to provide social services and not really to identify intellectual disability. Even more disingenuous, claiming that classification as a child as intellectually disabled must have been incorrect because of the new found re-interpretation of the definition of intellectual disability as an adult, by paying homage to the Eight Amendment, or by a "plain language" adherence to regulations.

The use of age of onset to deny Atkins claims is the ultimate in hypocrisy. Black children are denied an appropriate education by

---

[396]Powell v. Allen, United States Court of Appeals for the Eleventh Circuit, 602 F.3d 1263 (2010)

using intellectual disabilities to explain the substantial effects of environment, segregation and discrimination on school performance; Atkins claims for adults are denied by disingenuously adhering to a strict interpretation of the definition intellectual disability, and then a feigned allegiance to culture and environment as factors which might have impacted IQ and adaptive performance as a child. Race is blithely ignored when evaluating the intellectual disability of a child but then given great importance for an Atkins claimant to show that IQ and other deficits are the result of environment or something other than true ("genuine") intellectual disability.

In Powell v. Allen, in 2010, the United States Court of Appeals for the Eleventh Circuit Court acknowledged the standard definition of mental retardation "but also clarified that it is implicit in that definition that the IQ and deficits in adaptive behavior exist not only prior to the age of eighteen but also both at the time of the crime and currently."[397] In 1998 a jury recommended the death penalty by a 10-1 vote for Eddie Duval Powell for the 1995 murder of 70 year old Mattie Lee Wesson in Holt, Alabama. The court followed the jury's recommendation and imposed the death penalty. In the fifth grade Powell, who was born in 1969, was determined to have mild mental retardation in Lake County, Illinois. Nonetheless, the court decided that because Powell did not provide evidence that he had an IQ of 70 or below, he was not mentally retarded. This revisionist approach for interpreting IQ is contrary to how IQ was used to determine mental retardation when Powell was a child and the concept of *age of onset*. Putting aside the factor of race in the determination of mental retardation in Illinois and Alabama, a child might have had an IQ above 70 (or even 80) and been determined to have EMR or placed in an EMR classroom when Powell was a child. No matter the criteria for determining EMR, the State cannot undo a prior determination of intellectual disability.

No matter whether Powell's IQ was 71, or 76, or 81 as a child, if he was classified as mentally retarded as a child and placed him accordingly, there is no more relevant evidence for meeting the

---

[397] *Ibid.*

standard necessary for *Atkins*. This is because his classification was not based on a strict interpretation of IQ but rather relied on IQ, adaptive behavior, and all other data prior which was then used to determine (by a qualified group of professionals and the parents in theory) an appropriate category and placement. This determination was dismissed in Alabama because of a practice that is not based on federal law federal or State regulatory guidelines, but is only consistent with a court's limited understanding of intellectual disabilities and a disregard for the ADA, federal (i.e., Individuals with Disabilities Education Act) guidelines, and State regulations and for determining intellectual disabilities.

In Illinois, when Powell was 11, the black EMR enrollment in 1980 was approximately 49 percent and the overall black enrollment 21 percent. In Alabama of the over 30,000 children classified as EMR in 1980, 61.6 percent were black in comparison to a black enrollment of 33.1 percent. For Powell a standard created by an Alabama court was used to dismiss his prior determination of mental retardation because a current and more exacting definition was deemed more appropriate. The concept of an "exacting" or "plain language" interpretation of intellectual disability is a misnomer. A "plain language" interpretation does not represent a more exacting or scientific interpretation of data but, just the opposite, is used to over-simplify the definition, to create a bright-line, and ignore the history, best practice and professional guidelines for determining intellectual disability.

When Powell was a child, his IQ, adaptive deficits, and other data were deemed sufficient to warrant an interpretation of significantly subaverage intellectual functioning. True, race was likely a part of the decision making but that does not matter. If the State made a decision, no matter the process used, that Powell was intellectually disabled as a child, he is intellectually disabled as an adult for the purpose of an Atkins claim. By Alabama's reckoning, as an adult, he was no longer mentally retarded because he is able to maintain a neat death row cell and his "current" adaptive behavior was not indicative of someone who was truly mentally retarded.

In *Hall* the Supreme Court commented that "This last factor, referred to as 'age of onset'" is not at issue" and "The first and second criteria—deficits in intellectual functioning and deficits in adaptive functioning—are central here." Contrary to this compartmentalized interpretation, age of onset is of primary importance because of the emphasis given to the early manifestation of intellectual disability and developmental skills when the definition of mental retardation was first proposed in 1959. Age of onset was never a bright line for intellectual disability but was added to the definition to emphasize the importance of developmental information as a child, and to differentiate childhood intellectual disability from low IQ and deficits in adaptive behavior as an adult that could be explained by other disabilities (e.g., traumatic brain-injury, dementia, etc). There is no logical basis to deny lesser culpability because there was no evidence of disability before age 18, or that a defendant did not have an IQ score as a child, or was not considered intellectually disabled as a child. The age of onset prong was not intended to deny the existence of intellectual disability as an adult but to emphasize the importance of childhood data before age of onset. Age of onset is often used to deny Atkins claims in a way that is contrary to the original intent of the 1959 definition. [398]

There is a conflict between the acknowledged vagaries for criteria for determining intellectual disability and the judicial inclination for simplification and bright line. In Roper v. Simmons the Court cited the Eighth Amendment as the reason for rejecting the death penalty for juvenile offenders where *juvenile* is defined as an age less than 18 at the time of the crime.[399] The Court explained that because "society draws the line for many purposes between childhood and adulthood" and this is "the age at which the line for death eligibility ought to rest." A juvenile who commits a murder one day before reaching the age of 18 is ineligible for the death penalty, but a State can "extinguish his life and his potential to attain a mature understanding of his own humanity" for a crime committed one day later or one second after age of onset. The

[398]Heber, Rick, A Manual on Terminology and Classification in Mental Retardation, Monograph Supplement, American Journal of Mental Deficiency (2nd ed.), 1959 and 1961
[399]543 U.S. 551 (2005)

Court acknowledged that "drawing the line at 18 is subject to the objections always raised against categorical rules," but something had to be done and for *Roper* and *Hall* a bright-line of 18 and an IQ of 75 in *Hall* was that something. For *Roper* a cutoff of 18, just as an IQ of 75 in *Hall*, is more a nod to cruel and unusual punishment and evolving standards of decency than some hard and fast science that 18 should define a juvenile or that an IQ above 75 should deny a claim of intellectual disability.

Ricky R. Chase

In Mississippi, Ricky Chase was sentenced to death in 1990 for the murder of Elmer Hart. Chase was tested in 2010 and found to have an IQ score of 72. After a scoring error reduced the score to 71, and then the Flynn effect was taken into account, his score was further reduced to 70 which placed him in the mental retardation range. The State characterized Chase's evidence showing intellectual disability as "based largely on personal opinions and moral judgment, not science." For both prosecution and defense, contradictory evidence is regarded as "not science" or the even more belittling "junk science." Aside from the scientific name calling, IQ testing has little to do with science, and bickering about an IQ point or two as being determinative of intellectual disability is anything but science.

In 2004 the State believed that "numerous portions of Chase's testimony are cited to demonstrate that Chase speaks and reasons too well to be mentally retarded,"[400] but that a deficit in adaptive behavior such as failing a civics class was "based on personal beliefs, not science." Part of the problem might have been the trivialization of deficits in adaptive behavior offered by the defense. For example, adaptive deficits were said to be exemplified by washing "salt off prepackaged noodles" and "a significant deficit in social responsibility by unknowingly fathering a child out of wedlock."[401]

---

[400]Chase v. State of Mississippi, 873 So.2d 1013 (2004)
[401]Chase v. State of Mississippi, Brief of Appellee, Office of the Attorney General, 2014

An evidentiary hearing for Chase was held in August of 2010 and the circuit court decided that he was not mentally retarded. In April of 2013 the Supreme Court of Mississippi faulted the circuit court for relying too heavily by facts and conclusions provided by the State, and remanded the case back to the court to draw its own facts and conclusions. In other words, the circuit court was instructed to conduct an actual evidentiary hearing.[402] In May of 2013 the circuit court again found that Chase was not mentally retarded which was affirmed by the Supreme Court of Mississippi in April of 2015. This decision was appealed by Chase but Mississippi believed that his claim should be denied because it had already been "presented in a prior application" and he had not presented a *prima facie* case showing an intellectual disability. In October of 2015 the United States Court of Appeals for the Fifth District did not rule on Chase's intellectual disability but that "The question whether Chase is intellectually disabled and ineligible for execution under *Atkins* was neither presented to nor decided by the District Court when it ruled on Chase's first federal habeas petition," and that he had made a *prima facie* showing of intellectual disability. Because a claim under *Atkins* was never decided, the appellate court authorized a successive claim to determine intellectually disability.[403]

The difference between a label of mental retardation and the reasons for lesser culpability as per *Atkins* was explained by Justice David Chandler's dissent in Chase v. Mississippi in 2015. He noted that the age of onset criterion is "wholly insignificant" when considering the Eighth Amendment. He then gave an example of an individual who, if brain injured after age 18 which resulted in low IQ and deficits in adaptive behavior, would be eligible for the death penalty "simply because his mental disability did not manifest prior to age eighteen" and "While manifestation prior to age eighteen may be significant in acquiring the mental health label of intellectual disability, it is wholly insignificant with respect to the Eighth Amendment concerns voiced by the Atkins

---

[402]Chase v. State, 112 So.3d 421, 422 (Miss.2013)
[403]United States Court of Appeals for the Fifth Circuit, In Re: Ricky R. Chase, No. 15-60452, October, 26, 2015

Court."[404] Justice Chandler believed that Ricky Chase had met the professional criteria for proving intellectual disability. His concern stemmed from the Supreme Court's rationale for assigning lesser culpability to mentally retarded offenders which included the risk of false confessions, the lesser ability to show remorse, being a poor witness, demeanor, and assisting counsel. As of February 2020 Chase, remains on Mississippi's death row (with a "Tentative Release" date of Death.

Harry Franklin Phillips

In 2008 the Supreme Court of Florida decided that the age of onset criterion was not simply less important but that a diagnosis is "insufficient to satisfy the second retrospective prong of the mental retardation definition." In 1984 Harry Franklin Phillips was sentence to death for the 1982 revenge murder of his parole officer in Miami, Florida. As a child "Phillips's school history also revealed that he attended school when the system was segregated and special education was not available to him."

The Supreme Court of Florida found in 2008 "that both the statute and the rule require significantly subaverage general intellectual functioning to exist *concurrently with* deficits in adaptive behavior."[405] The word *concurrent* is equated with *present* so regardless of a previous determination of intellectual disability or an overwhelming record of intellectual disability as a child prior to age 18, a failure to show *present* deficits in adaptive behavior would invalidate an Atkins claim. Having decided that *current* adaptive behavior was central, the court then explained the claimant's adaptive strengths showed that he had a "position as a short-order cook was an 'unusually high level' job for someone who has mental retardation." The emphasis on adult skills suggested that an effective special education program as a child eradicated intellectual disability as an adult. An effective special education program as a child is not used to show that the child's

---

[404]Ricky Chase v. State of Mississippi, Supreme Court of Mississippi, No. 2013–CA–01089–SCT. Decided: April 23, 2015
[405]Phillips v. State, 984 So. 2d 503 (Fla. 2008)

cognitive and adaptive skills have been maximized within the scope of intellectual disability but that cognition and the ability to adapt are no longer consistent with the criteria for intellectual disability.

In 2014 the Supreme Court of Florida explained that the trial court believed that the appropriate measure for concurrent deficits in adaptive behavior for Freddie Lee Hall "'would have been to interview correction officers or classification officers, or perhaps, to review records documenting the Defendant's existence and interactions while in the custody of such evidence, he could not meet the adaptive behavior prong.'" This not only diminishes or eliminates the basic definition of intellectual disabilities and the role of professionals, but creates an entirely new standard whereby the subjective and anecdotal impressions of prison officials would be the primary source of data for determining intellectual disability.

When the primary elements of the definition of mental retardation were first proposed in 1959 the difficulty specifying the developmental cutoff was acknowledged because "for practical purposes," the age limit was designated as 16 (later changed to 18).[406] Age of onset was more a dimension to understand and define a specific category of disability rather than a requirement to nullify similar disability characteristics that occur after age of onset. For Freddie Lee Hall the trial court created a new criterion for intellectual disability. If an Atkins claimant's IQ was not tested before age 18, age of onset could not be determined, and the age of onset prong could not be satisfied. For Freddie Lee Hall, he did not "'satisfy the third prong—manifestation prior to age 18—because his IQ was not tested before age 18.'"[407] Of course, this reasoning ignores the racism and school segregation when Hall was a child and the fact in the early 1950s in Florida, and in many other States both South and North, an inferior segregation education would have been all that a school would have provided

---

[406]Heber, Rick, A Manual on Terminology and Classification in Mental Retardation, Monograph Supplement, American Journal of Mental Deficiency (2nd ed.), 1959 and 1961
[407]Hall v. Florida, Supreme Court of Florida, Case No. SC10-1335, Circuit Case No. 1978-CF-0052, 201

to meet any and all learning needs of a black child. Racism was used to deny special education, and than the lack of special education was used to deny Atkins relief.

Florida had no problems arresting four teenagers at a King Street Woolworth in St. Augustine in 1963 for having the audacity to sit and order at a whites-only lunch counter. This example of the prevailing discrimination provides some insight into the likelihood that a black child in Florida would be tested to determine special learning needs, as for Freddie Lee Hall, is small. For Hall the ongoing racism that would have prevented IQ testing as a child is then used to not-so-cleverly show that Hall was never tested and therefore did not have an intellectual disability before age of onset.

The age of onset prong was never intended to suggest that there was an Eighth Amendment difference between individuals with low IQ and deficits in adaptive behavior before and after age of onset. Because of the ability to minimize IQ and creatively use adaptive behavior to deny many Atkins claims, the importance of age of onset in the determination of intellectual disability is marginalized or dismissed entirely. What is especially egregious by a State's self-serving use of the age of onset criterion is to bypass the ADA and a record of intellectual disability as a child, or what should have been a determination of a disability were it not for prevailing racism. If a defendant was identified as having an intellectual disability as a child because of race, an Atkins claim as an adult is denied because the determination as a child might have been the result of race; if a child was classified as EMR as a child, the State then asserts that the childhood classification was in error, or irrelevant because of current guidelines.

Virginia is one of the few States that addresses the issue of "developmental period" (in some ways) in the determination of intellectual disability for adults by identifying a variety of sources which should be the basis of every Atkins claim:

> **Assessment of developmental origin shall be**
> **based on multiple sources of information**
> **generally accepted by the field of psychological**

> testing and appropriate for the particular
> defendant being assessed, including, whenever
> available, educational, social service, medical
> records, prior disability assessments, parental
> or caregiver reports, and other collateral data,
> recognizing that valid clinical assessment
> conducted during the defendant's childhood
> may not have conformed to current practice
> standards.[408]

The seemingly high-minded nod to professional scrutiny that an assessment "may not have conformed to current practice standards" suggests that if the cutoff for placing a child was an IQ of 85, the more guideline (an IQ of 70 or 75) for an Atkins claim could be used to refute the earlier determination because it did not conform to "current practice standards."[409]

Age of onset is not only important because of the relevance of the data for a child but also because how data is interpreted for children and for Atkins claimants. In Atkins claims a judge or jury is expected to interpret technical data and the nuances of disabilities in addition to contending with an adversarial process. The views of expert witnesses often provide anything but an unbiased evaluation of the data or how data should be interpreted. The defendant must prove intellectual disability to a finder of fact who may be knowledgeable about intellectual disabilities, or who is completely ill-equipped to make such a determination and has no idea of the meaning of IQ, validity, reliability, the normal curve, the history of the definitions of intellectual disability, or the Supreme Court's reasoning for lesser culpability. For many the standard error of measurement could very well be a crater on the moon rather a porous statistical index based on a group reliability statistic.

For an adult, the finder of fact must consider multiple IQ scores, malingering, and conflicting expert testimony concerning Atkins

---

[408]Code of Virginia, § 19.2-264.3:1.1. Capital cases; determination of mental retardation.
[409]*Ibid.*

claims which can complicate rather than clarify a determination of intellectual disability. In Mississippi, the Minnesota Multiphasic Personality Inventory is used to assess malingering, but interpreting the results for someone who might actually have an intellectual disability on a test which includes over 560 true/false items (depending on the version) that are read by the examinee would be difficult for an expert much less a judge or jury. The Supreme Court of Mississippi has said that "the Minnesota Multiphasic Personality Inventory-II (MMPI-II) should be administered, because 'its associated validity scales make the test best suited to detect malingering'" which would mean that no matter the reading ability of a defendant, or that the defendant might be functionally illiterate, suspect data from the MMPI would be used to determine malingering.

In addition to the self-anointed test expertise of courts, one might assume that actual experts involved in the administration and interpretation of tests would help clarify a determination of intellectual disability. In spite of self-proclaimed professionalism, finders of fact are guided by expert witnesses who almost always reach diametrically opposed determinations depending on whether the expert represents the State or defense.

Contrary to the flimsy guidelines used by the finder of fact in Atkins claims (disregarding the now unconstitutional guidelines offered by Texas courts in the form of the Briseno factors), the special education law has been revised to meet the needs of children and overcome obstacles relating to assessment and placement. Even with these many changes from 1975 to the present, problems remain especially involving the disproportionate classification of many black children as intellectually disabled. Unlike the finder of fact in Atkins claims the determination of a disability for children is made by a group of qualified professionals and the parents. In Atkins claims the finder of fact must rely on consistently divergent expert testimony; for the determination of a disability for a child there are a variety of regulatory requirements and safeguards. When assessing a disability for a child the determination must be made using "a variety of assessment tools and strategies to gather relevant functional, developmental, and academic information about the child," "not use any single measure or assessment as the sole criterion for determining whether a child is a child with a disability," and "use technically sound instruments that may assess the relative contribution of cognitive and behavioral factors, in addition to physical or developmental factors."[410]

Cecil Clayton

Cecil Clayton, age 74, was executed in Missouri in March of 2015 for the murder of sheriff's deputy Chris Castetter in 1996. Following a sawmill accident in 1972 part of his frontal lobe was removed. Clayton's claim of incompetence as a result of brain injury was rejected because he understood the reason for his execution and that he was to be executed.

Missouri uses the essential professional definition to determine intellectual disability which refers "to a condition involving substantial limitations in general functioning characterized by significantly subaverage intellectual functioning with continual extensive related deficits and limitations in two or more adaptive behaviors such as communication, self-care, home living, social skills, community use, self-direction, health and safety, functional academics, leisure and work, which conditions are manifested and documented before eighteen years of age."[411] Clayton's Atkins claim failed "because 'he has not presented evidence that any of his symptoms manifested before the age of eighteen – a necessary requirement under the [Missouri] statutory definition.'"[412] He apparently was a "good student" in elementary grades but dropped out of school in the 10th grade and had not received a GED. Having made this determination, his claim was considered more of a Ford claim (insanity) than an Atkins claim. That is, as per *Ford*, he could understand the legal process, was able to communicate with his counsel, and understood the basis for his death sentence.

---

[410]Regulations for Public Law 108-446, § 300.304 Evaluation procedures
[411]§ 565.030 RSMo Supp. 2013
[412]Clayton v. Griffiths, Supreme Court of Missouri, No. SC94841, March 14, 2015

In her 2015 dissent, Judge Laura Denvir Stith argued that a recent testing revealed an IQ score of 71 in contrast to an earlier full scale IQ score of 86. The Judge then exclaimed in bold text that "This is **exactly what the Supreme Court in *Hall* disallowed**."[413] Clayton's Atkins claim was rejected because of the age of onset criterion. Judge Stith argued that "the presumptive purpose of requiring a disability to manifest itself by age 18 is to preclude later faking of intellectual disability."[414] This is one reason for age of onset in Atkins claim although the original purpose was to focus attention on cognitive deficits occurring prior to age of onset and to distinguish intellectual disability manifested as a child from other adult disabilities such as dementia and, for Cecil Clayton, brain injury.

Judge Stith believed there was no faking his disability that occurred after age 18. If a specific hearing was held for Clayton's Atkins claim, as suggested by Judge Stith, Clayton probably would have shown deficits in adaptive behavior to warrant a determination of mental retardation. She argued that an intellectual disability certainly can occur after age 18 that would meet the Supreme Court's rationale for lesser culpability. If an Atkins claimant was determined to be intellectually disabled, it would be illogical to negate this finding because a similar determination was not made prior to age 18. Furthermore, whatever the statute, it is axiomatic that the Eighth Amendment applies to all persons so that someone who becomes intellectually disabled after age 18 should also be able to seek relief from execution as per *Atkins*.

The interpretation of the age of onset criterion is often contradictory: evidence of intellectual disability at the time of the crime is given priority over evidence of intellectual disability before age of onset. Unless, however, there is a lack of evidence of intellectual disability prior to age 18 because a defendant was not tested as a child, was not in special education, was said to have a

---

[413]Clayton v. Luebbers, United States District Court for the Western District of Missouri, Case No. 02-8001-CV-W-NKL, April 27, 2006
[414]Clayton v. Griffiths, Supreme Court of Missouri, No. SC94841, March 14, 2015

disability other than mental retardation, etc. In which case all evidence after age 18 is devalued and the lack of evidence prior to age 18 is given new found importance. These definitional contortions are glued together by a passing reference to the Eighth Amendment and the prohibition against cruel and unusual punishment.

The primary vehicle for misclassification for children has always been an over-reliance on IQ. For adults IQ testing becomes even more problematic because of the more complex nature of adult behavior and accumulated experiences, the unique circumstances when assessing Atkins claimants, and the possibility of malingering. For children by considering developmental data, the ability to adapt in school and in other environments, and a less-than rigid interpretation of IQ to account for cultural factors, as much as possible, misclassification is reduced. Nonetheless, the age of onset criterion is not a bright line but a guide to consider the importance of developmental factors for children and not to discount evidence of intellectual disability for adults.

Age of onset emphasizes the importance of the various classification criteria, and provides a mechanism for triangulating data to reach a relatively accurate classification. For adults common sense should indicate that other conditions can also result in lesser culpability. The purpose of *Atkins*, and the holding that the intellectually disabled require lesser culpability, was not in response to an iconic label of mental retardation or intellectual disability, but because of specific behaviors the Supreme Court believed to be associated with intellectual disability including "diminished capacities to understand and process information, to communicate, to abstract from mistakes and learn from experience, to engage in logical reasoning, to control impulses, and to understand others' reactions," an inability to understand "execution as a penalty," the likelihood of false confessions, the inability to assist counsel, and because "they are typically poor witnesses and that their demeanor may create an unwarranted impression of lack of remorse for their crimes."[415]

---

[415]Atkins v. Virginia, 536 U. S. 304 (2002)

Age of onset is important for focusing attention on childhood behavior, but age of onset cannot preclude Atkins protection for a defendant who meets all the criteria for lesser culpability. An Atkins claimant who had no record of intellectual disability as a child, had a disability other than intellectual disability as a child, or whose intellectual disability occurred after age of onset (e.g., brain injury, dementia, Alzheimer's) would require Atkins protection and lesser culpability if all the criteria for a determination of intellectual disability have been met.

Victor Tony Jones

Age of onset is a bright-line obstacle for successful Atkins claims. If there is no record of an intellectual disability, or the defendant had a disability other than intellectual, the claim can be denied because the definitions cited in Atkins clearly state that "Mental retardation manifests before age 18" (AAMR) and the more emphatic DSM-4 definition that "The onset must occur before age 18 years." Florida, not satisfied with a single age of onset bright-line, made the task for a successful Atkins claim more difficult by creating a twofold standard: a showing of mental retardation before and after age of onset.

In 1993, Victor Tony Jones, born in 1961, was sentenced to death for the 1990 murders of Matilda and Jacob Nestor in Dade County, Florida. Before he died, Jacob Nestor shot Jones in the head. Records indicated that Jones had a horrific childhood (alcoholic mother, school dropout, drug abuse) and, between 1991 and 2005 as an adult, Jones received IQ scores of 72, 70, 67, 72, and 75. As a child testimony indicated that Jones might have been average or somewhat above average in both school and intelligence. Because Florida used the strict IQ cutoff of 70 (rejected by the Supreme Court in Hall in 2014), the court decided that Jones did not have significantly subaverage general intellectual functioning.

The Supreme Court of Florida reasoned that a "diagnosis of mental retardation in an adult must be based on present or current intellectual functioning and adaptive skills and information that the condition also existed in childhood." According to the Florida court in 2007 "the question is whether a defendant 'is' mentally retarded, not whether he was."[416] A neuropsychologist who testified on Jones' behalf believed that the definition requires a consideration of adaptive behavior before age of onset and attempted to show that Jones had deficits in at least two areas as a child.

The Florida court accepted the plain language of the statute, as it did for IQ, and rejected all data prior to age onset because the statute is interpreted to mean "is" mentally retarded rather than "was." The reasoning was that mental retardation is required before age of onset, but the relevant evidence considered for an Atkins claim is current evidence of intellectual disability. Jones' expert believed all that mattered was a retrospective analysis of mental retardation before age 18 which, to the expert, showed deficits in communication, academic function, self-direction, and social interpersonal skills. The State believed that current ability to adapt was all important as evidenced by anecdotal data showing that Jones adapted well to prison life, was able to communicate, could understand his medical needs, and had other "strong" intellectual skills.

The State expert believed that "true mental retardation is lifelong and "a child deemed mentally retarded actually may be experiencing a developmental delay." With appropriate training and skill development, that individual may, as an adult, no longer have the level of impairment required for the diagnosis."[417] This re-interpretation of the definition of mental retardation as a child is the same tactic used in Ohio for Andre R. Williams where the State believed that evidence of intellectual disability as a child was not "competent evidence" of "present" intellectual disability as an adult.

For Jones the expert concluded that "a diagnosis of an adult, based solely on the person's adaptive functioning as a child, is invalid." There is no professional guideline that has ever stated that a determination of mental retardation cannot be "based solely" on

---

[416]Jones v. State of Florida, 966 So.2d 319, 330 (Fla. 2007)
[417]*Ibid.*

childhood data. much less that a "record" of intellectual is irrelevant. The expert recognized that the purpose of the age of onset criterion was to rule out other causes; what the expert did not consider was a record of disability, the ADA, and the reason for the lesser culpability underpinning *Atkins*. The Supreme Court of Florida used a definition designed for children to interpret adult adaptive behavior. The court then decided that a "diagnosis of mental retardation in an adult must be based on present or current intellectual functioning and adaptive skills and information that the condition also existed in childhood."

If a State has decided that a child has an intellectual disability, and then provides an environment and curriculum that supposedly addresses that disability, it is disingenuous to suggest that, for the purposes of Atkins and the Eighth Amendment, this disability determination was in error, or no longer exists, or that factors never considered by professionals should guide the determination of intellectual disability. For Victor Jones his ability to keep a clean cell, seem polite, request medical help and the ability to stowaway o n a plane at age 11 (which showed "a tremendous amount of sophistication" but apparently not enough to be successful) were used to demonstrate his ability to adapt. There is no way to refute information that suggests "sophisticated" intellectual functioning when there is no foundation that these behaviors are actually beyond the ability of someone with mild intellectual disability. Jones did have one IQ score below 70 but his scores were "consistently above 70," and he appeared to be able to adapt to a life on death row. Although the standard for the defense in an Atkins claim in Florida is *clear and convincing evidence*, the Supreme Court of Florida gratuitously explained that Jones did not even meet the lesser *preponderance of the evidence* standard...just in case.

The finder of fact in death penalty cases does not have an envious task, especially when the capital murder is unimaginably heinous. However difficult that task might be, for an Atkins claim the goal should be to consider, as was done in *Ford,* all relevant evidence to determine if a defendant's intellectual ability warrants lesser culpability. If an error is to be made, given the Supreme Court's belief in the "evolving standards of decency" and "narrowing jurisprudence" for those deserving the death penalty, the error should be on the side of life and not execution. The Court did not say that a subjective analysis of criminal behavior at the time of the crime was the central issue, or that stereotypic behavior of intellectual disability was primary (e.g., being able to read, drive a car, being polite, keeping a clean cell, and being able to stowaway on a plane), but that professional definitions should provide substantial guidance in the determination of intellectual disability.

Beyond Age of Onset

The twofold purpose of the death penalty, "the retribution and deterrence of capital crimes," might be an important consideration in some States but not so in California where death row, itself, is the ultimate punishment. California's death row includes 163 inmates aged 60-69, 53 inmates aged 70-79, and 5 inmates aged 80-89. The over-80 inmates include serial killers Joseph Naso, now 86, sentenced to death in 2013 in Marin County for the murder of six women, and 89 year old David Carpenter (the "trailside killer") sentenced to death in 1984 for multiple murders. [418] Considering the advancing age of California death row prisoners, these prisoners could make a Ford claim (inability to assist in defense, to understand the crime, or the death penalty) or an Atkins claim (low IQ and deficits in adaptive behavior) because of dementia or Alzheimer's. The probability that California will ever conduct another execution is small, and the probability that Carpenter will be executed is almost nonexistent. The Sacramento Bee reported (April 21, 2017) that California's death row has become a home for seniors and "the number of seniors on death row has grown by nearly 500 percent since early 2006, when the state housed 16 seniors."[419] According to the California Department of Corrections on August 21, 2018 there were 201 offenders 60 or older on death row.

---

[418]As of June 2019, California Department of Corrections and Rehabilitation, Division Of Adult Operations, condemned Inmate Summary List
[419]https://www.sacbee.com/news/local/article145889979.html

Other States such as Florida might very well follow California where death row, and not execution, is the ultimate punishment. As of February 2020, there are 340 offenders on death row in Florida of whom 126 or 37.1 percent were black. There are more than 25 inmates on Florida's death row 70 years or older, and more than 75 who are 60 years or older. The average amount of time on death row for those 60 years or older has been approximately 30 years. According to the Supreme Court of Florida in 2002 "an extended stay on death row does not constitute cruel and unusual punishment."[420] The oldest prisoner on death row in Florida is Nelson Ivan Serrano (born in 1938) for the 1997 murder of four business associates in Bartow, Florida. He was sentenced to death following a 9 to 3 jury recommendation on all four counts in 2006. Because the jury did not unanimously recommend death as per *Hurst*, the Florida Supreme Court set aside his conviction in May of 2017 because this "error" was not harmless and remanded for new sentencing. As of 2020 Serrano remains on death row.

The various constitutional violations which have involved Florida (especially *Hall* and 2014 and *Hurst* in 2016) may or may not result Florida achieving California death row proportions. Taken together, California and Florida account for approximately 40 percent of all death row inmates in the United States. Florida, unlike California, has not been totally stymied by the various constitutional issues as shown by the execution of Patrick Charles Hannon on November 8, 0217 for the 1991 murder of two men in Tampa in 1991. One co-offender (James Acker) received a life sentence while a second a five-year sentence for testimony against Hannon and Acker. More recently, Eric Scott Branch (white) was executed in Florida on February 22, 2018 for the 1993 rape and murder of 21 year-old college student Susan Morris. Morris was sentenced to death by a 10 to 2 jury recommendation in 1994 which the Florida Supreme Court found unconstitutional but not for those sentenced before 2002 (Ring. v. Arizona) which required that a jury not a judge decide the ultimate punishment.[421] Gary R.

---

[420]Foster v. Florida, Supreme Court of Florida, SC01-767, February 14, 2002

[421]Ring v. Arizona, 536 U.S. 584 (2002)

Bowles, white, was the most recent execution in Florida for the murder of six men in the vicinity of Interstate 95 in 1994. He was subsequently resentenced to death in 1999 and executed on August 22, 2019.

Viva Leroy Nash

Viva Leroy Nash, white, was a notable death row inmate for having survived on death row for 27 years until his death of natural causes at the age of 94 (he was born in September of 1915 and died in February of 2010). He was sentenced to death for the murder of Gregory D. West, owner of the Moon Valley Coin Shop in Phoenix, Arizona in 1982. Nash was 67 when sentenced in 1983. He had previously been sentenced to life for the murder of postal worker David J. Woodhurst in 1977. Nash escaped from prison and murdered West in 1982. He was sentenced to death the following year. At age 90 the District Court denied all of Nash's claims for relief as well as an evidentiary hearing. Much of this decision centered about his crime and his sanity at the time (he was found "legally sane under the *M'Naghten* standard") but little consideration was given to the mental status of a 90 year-old man who had been on death row for 27 years.[422] The court found three aggravating but no mitigating factors (including his "old age" at age 67 at the time of the murder).

In Arizona the death row environment requires that

> **All inmates are in single cells which are equipped with a toilet, sink, bed and mattress. Each Death Row inmate has no contact with any other inmate. Out-of-cell time is limited to outdoor exercise in a secured area, two hours a day, three times a week, and a shower, three times a week. All meals are delivered by correction officers at the cell front. Limited non-contact visitation is available. Death Row**

---

[422]Nash v. Schriro, United States District Court of Arizona, Case 2:97-cv-01104-MHM, July 7, 2006.

> inmates may place two ten minute telephone
> calls per week. Personal property is limited to
> hygiene items, two appliances, two books and
> writing materials, which can be purchased
> from the inmate commissary. Health care is
> provided at the Health Unit; medication is
> passed out at the cell front. Clergy contacts are
> provided at the cell.[423]

Considering Nash's age, his time on death row, and a variety of expected medical problems as well as being described as a "wacky" and a "doddering old man," the logical solution was to wait for Nash to die of natural causes which is exactly what Arizona did.

Capital punishment sentencing is not always about execution when death row itself can be even more cruel, unusual and prolonged form of punishment. As with Nash waiting for death by natural causes is the preferred strategy for inmates in their 80's, much less 90's might be a less than a viable public relations strategy. Unfortunately there is not an abundance of research on age, dementia and death row confinement, much less the prolonged cognitive consequences of solitary confinement. The use of IQ tests and other measures becomes very problematic with older death row inmates. The WAIS-IV was standardized on ages between 16 and 90. When considering age, motivation, dementia, environment, the very idea of a 94 year old on death row does seem unusual if not a cruel punishment. Maybe an even more cruel and unusual punishment would be giving an IQ test to someone 90 plus.

There is an obvious relationship between the criteria cited in *Atkins* warranting lesser culpability for capital murder and the various categories of adult cognitive disturbances (including Alzheimer's, traumatic brain injury, Chronic Traumatic Encephalopathy, mixed dementia, Vascular Cognitive Impairment

---

[423]From the Arizona Department of Corrections website at https://corrections.az.gov/public-resources/death-row/death-row-information-and-frequently-asked-questions

or VCI, Mild Cognitive Impairment or MCI, and other disorders). Unlike a relatively consistent level of low cognitive performance for someone who was diagnosed as having an intellectual disability as a child, the development of cognitive impairment likely increases with increasing age.

The Alzheimer's Association[424] list various symptoms for Alzheimer's and dementia including difficulty remembering newly learned information, disorientation, behavior changes, confusion, difficulty speaking, understanding speech, poor judgment, social withdrawal. For a death row inmate with one of the various forms of dementia how the reason for execution is conceptualized is anybody's guess. In that the ability to assess intelligence past age 90 is highly problematic, the Supreme Court might well reserve execution for those between 18 and 79. n that the average time from sentencing to execution has steadily increased from 6 years in 1984 to almost 16 years in 2012 according to U.S. Department of Justice data, the probability of ever executing an offender sentenced after age 70 decreases. This would not result in a huge reduction of those on death row, but it would provide some recognition that age is a variable that simply can go unnoticed by States. Race also becomes a factor for determining a bright line for age in that the life expectancy of white males (76.3 years) is 4.4 years higher than that of black males.[425] The life expectancy for Hispanic males (79.3 years) is three years higher than white males.

Regardless of race, age at some point becomes a salient variable when evaluating mental ability and competence. In Alabama, of the 175 inmates on death row as of February 2020, 87 or 49.7 percent are black, while the percentage of black inmates executed is 42.4 (28 of 66 executions) following the execution of Christopher Price in May of 2019. Alabama has executed offenders in their seventies including 75 year-old Thomas Douglas Arthur, white, on May 26, 2017.[426] Arthur was convicted by three

---

[424]https://www.alz.org/what-is-dementia.asp
[425]https://www.cdc.gov/nchs/data/hus/hus16.pdf#015
[426]Supreme Court of Alabama, Ex parte Thomas Douglas Arthur, 1951985, Decided: April 04, 2017

juries (the first two convictions were overturned) for the 1982 contract murder of Troy Wicker. Following years of appeals, the Supreme Court of Alabama set the date for execution. At the time Arthur was 75 and in Ex Parte Thomas Douglas Arthur (April 4, 2017) the following footnote was added:

> **The mortality tables set out by the Alabama Department of Insurance show that someone who is 75 years of age, as is Arthur, should have, on average, 9.4 more years left on this Earth. At this point, I posit, only partially facetiously, that perhaps the fairest, least cruel, and most humane eighth execution date for Arthur and perhaps for the forgotten victim's friends and family (at least those still living) might be a date sometime in 2026, so Arthur has the statistical maximum time left on his mortality table in which to continue his challenges.**

In any case, the execution of Arthur (as well as 74-year-old James Barney Hubbard in 2004) did skew the execution of the average age for white offenders

The overall declining cognitive performance for prisoners with dementia (or neurocognitive disorder) is accompanied by declining language and independent living skills. Cognition, language, and independent living skills are essential components of the definition of intellectual disability so that decreased test performance in these areas, especially low IQ and adaptive behavior, might well meet the first two criteria for intellectual disability. For older death row prisoners, the cause of this cognitive impairment would have occurred well after age of onset. A paper by Maschi, et al. suggested that the percent of inmates 65 an older with some degree of dementia was 13 percent.[427] Even this rather high estimate would underestimate the degree of

---

[427]Forget Me Not: Dementia in Prison, Tina Maschi, Jung Kwak, Eunjeong Ko, Mary B. Morrissey, *The Gerontologist*, Volume 52, Issue 4, 1 August 2012, Pages 441–451, https://doi.org/10.1093/geront/gnr131

dementia on death row when considering the effects of prior environment and life choices, time on death row, solitary confinement, race, and the various effects of prior discrimination and deprivation.

Considering the disproportionate number of black inmates, and the aging death row population, Alzheimer's and dementia take on added weight for those seeking Atkins relief. According to a 1999 study by Gurland and others[428] the prevalence of dementia for the 65-74 age group was 9.1 percent for African-Americans, 7.5 percent for Hispanics and 2.9 percent for whites   For ages 75 to 84, cognitive impairment increased to 19.9 percent for African-Americans, 27.9 percent for Hispanics, and 10.9 percent for whites. For ages 85 and older the percent increased to 58.6 percent for African-Americans, 62.9 percent for Hispanics, and 30.2 percent for whites.[429]

In a study by Goodman and others in 2017[430], of the over 21,000,000 Medicare data files examined, services needed for dementia (including Alzheimer's, vascular, alcohol induced dementia, etc.) were found in 14.4 percent of over 3,000,000 claims. For ages 68-69 Medicare dementia claims were 2.7 percent, 10.1 percent for ages 70-74, 15.5 percent for ages 75-79, 21.7 percent for ages 80-84, and 50 percent for ages 85+.

The Goodman study also found that dementia was somewhat higher in 9.2 percent of black claims which accounted for 7.2 percent of all claims examined in the study population. The lower number of black claims in comparison to the number of claims in

---

[428]Barry J. Gurland, David E. Wilder, Rafael Lantigua, Yaakov Stern, Jiming Chen, Eloise H. P. Killeffer,
Richard Mayeux, Rates of dementia in three ethnoracial groups, International Journal of Geriatric Psychiatry, 14, 481-493, 1999.
[429]Health and RetirementStudy, unpublished data from the 2006 survey provided under contract to the Alzheimer's Association by K. Langa, M. Kabeto, and D. Weir, Jan. 8, 2010.
[430]Richard A. Goodman, Kimberly A. Lochner, Madhav Thambisetty, Thomas S. Wingo, Samuel F. Posner, Shari M. Ling, Prevalence of dementia subtypes in United States Medicare fee-for-service beneficiaries, 2011–2013, Alzheimer's & Dementia, 13 (2017), 28-37.

the population (13.3 percent) is probably attributed to life expectancy and the fact that when services and benefits are provided, black Americans receive fewer (including the "benefit" of lesser culpability as per *Atkins*). There was also a finding that Alzheimer's disease was highest among Hispanics which is important in California where Hispanics on death row (183 of the 735 on death row as of June 2019[431]) account for 52.1 percent of all "Latino/Latina" (351[432]) on death row in the United States.

For black Americans race is a confounding factor. Race is related to environment, opportunity in every phase of daily living, arrests for capital murder, convictions, death penalty sentences, and executions. All of this forms a toxic soup when added to the length of time between sentence and execution, the longevity of black Americans, age becomes an extremely important variable which serves to further deny black prisoners on death row, when appropriate, lesser culpability. The admonition in *Furman* by the Supreme Court that "the application of the penalty was discretionary, haphazard, and discriminatory in that it was inflicted in a small number of the total possible cases and primarily against certain minority groups" has not changed in over four decades. As of the Fall of 2019 the percent of white (46.9) and black (46.4) of the 2,369 total inmates on death row is in far contrast to the percent of black (13.4) and white (76.5) Americans in the general populations., Justice Stewart, in his concurring opinion in *Furman*, suggested that if there was any basis for rejecting the death penalty, "it is the constitutionally impermissible basis of race."

For whatever reasons, race is inextricably associate with age. Young black Americans are disproportionally identified as having intellectual disability or treated as if they were intellectually disabled but via a different disability category. Older black

---

[431]https://www.cdcr.ca.gov/Capital_Punishment/docs/CondemnedInma teSummary.pdf?pdf=Condemned-Inmates

[432]Source: DEATH ROW U.S.A., A quarterly report by the Criminal Justice Project of the NAACP Legal Defense and Educational Fund, Inc., Deborah Fins, Esq. Consultant to the Criminal Justice Project NAACP Legal Defense and Educational Fund, Inc. at https://www.naacpldf.org/wp-content/uploads/DRUSAFALL2019_.pdf

Americans are disproportionally sentenced to death but are then held to a strict standard, unlike that for black children, when the death penalty is considered.

For *Atkins* the question is not intent or that when the death penalty is considered that race is intentionally used to deny black defendants lesser culpability, but that race, from birth to death row, contaminates fair decision making. This is not dissimilar to the finding in 1971 in Griggs v. the Duke Power Company that "unnecessary barriers to employment that operate invidiously to discriminate on the basis of race" must be eliminated "if, as here, an employment practice that operates to exclude Negroes cannot be shown to be related to job performance, it is prohibited, notwithstanding the employer's lack of discriminatory intent."

9. Narrowing Jurisprudence

"to ensure that only the most deserving of execution are put to death, an exclusion for the mentally retarded is appropriate"[433]

What is the underlying intent when black children are disproportionately identified as having intellectual disabilities but Atkins claimants are subjected to careful scrutiny to show that they are not and therefore eligible for execution? When the special education law (Education for All Handicapped Children Act or P.L. 94-142 in 1975) was first proposed in the early 1970s Congress expressed concern for "the misuse of appropriate identification and classification data within the educational process itself; (2) discriminatory treatment as the result of the identification of a handicapping condition; and (3) misuse of identification procedures or methods which results in erroneous classification of a child as having a handicapping condition."[434] The law mandated full educational opportunity, a free appropriate public education (FAPE), and that all children who need special education are identified, located, and evaluated. Before this law services for many children with disabilities were often few or nonexistent. Congress realized that to ensure that children with disabilities are not deprived of necessary services regulations were needed to ensure compliance which was sometimes achieved and sometimes not. The goal in *Atkins* is of a similar vein: offenders who are intellectually disabled should not be executed and guidelines are needed to ensure States comply with this mandate. For Atkins claims the guidelines are flimsy at best, sometimes followed, often times not.

Justice Frankfurter explained in a concurring opinion in Sweezy v. New Hampshire in 1957 that "For a citizen to be made to forego even a part of so basic a liberty as his political autonomy, the subordinating interest of the State must be compelling. Inquiry pursued in safeguarding a State's security against threatened force

---

[433]Atkins v. Virginia, 536 U.S. 304 (2002)
[434]Senate Report 94-168, Education for All Handicapped Children Act, 1975, pp. 26-27

and violence cannot be shut off by mere disclaimer, though of course a relevant claim may be made to the privilege against self-incrimination."[435] For children there is a compelling interest to provide an appropriate education, and for some offenders found guilty of capital murder the compelling interest is the twofold purpose of retribution and deterrence.

The Senate Report for Public Law 94-142 recognized that disability classifications could result in an inappropriate education. The Senate Report cautioned that "the Committee believes that the greatest possible care must be taken to assure that the identification and classification process is utilized solely for designing an individually tailored educational program for each handicapped child. The Committee directs the Commissioner and each State educational agency to assure that information required for planning and provision of special education and related services, and the administration of such services, does not get carried over into the educational process in a way which results in distinguishing handicapped children as having lesser rights."[436]

Congress has long been aware of racial disproportionality in mental retardation/intellectual disability and has assiduously attempted to narrowly define the law to meet the State's compelling interest to provide an appropriate education. The misclassification of children as intellectually disabled, or when an appropriate classification results in an inappropriate education, is often a function of race, environment and poverty.

The process for balancing a compelling State interest to execute with the essential constitutional right of life and liberty must be, as explained by the Court in *Enmund*, "tailored to… personal responsibility and moral guilt."[437] Justice Douglas, in his concurring opinion in *Furman,* acknowledged the "prejudice against discrete and insular minorities"[438] that the "proscription

---

[435]354 U.S. 234 (1957)
[436]Senate Report 94-168
[437]Enmund v. Florida, 458 U. S. 782 (1982)
[438]The now famous footnote 4 in United States v. Carolene Products Co.,

against selective and irregular use of penalties, suggest it is "cruel and unusual" to apply the death penalty -- or any other penalty -- selectively to minorities whose numbers are few, who are outcasts of society, and who are unpopular, but whom society is willing to see suffer though it would not countenance general application of the same penalty across the board."[439] The concept of "severity and irrevocability" can also be applied to a determination by the State that a child is mentally retarded, intellectually disabled, cognitively impaired, etc. The labels are many; the consequences are severe and not undone by a judge or jury who decide that an offender is eligible for execution because the impairment of intellectual disability (and the educational consequences of this determination) as a child has been undone by a whimsical application of the professional definitions.

The task to eliminate racial disproportionality in the intellectual disability category has been glacially slow. The process has been further hindered by label shuffling where a less noisome label results in the same inappropriate education. If States were aware that the consequences of labeling a child intellectually disabled had irrevocable results, including shelter from the death penalty for a capital offender as an adult, States would be less cavalier with educational labels, stigmatization, and segregative placements.

The justification for classifying children as having a disability is the need for a free appropriate public education. Congress has repeatedly used criteria that would pass the test of strict scrutiny: a **narrowly tailored** program and **least restrictive means** are needed to achieve the compelling interest of a free appropriate public education; that is, narrowly tailored and least restrictive criteria are needed to provide an appropriate education but to prevent misclassification. The requirement that an individualized education program and placement must be narrowly tailored to meet a child's needs acknowledges the importance of strict scrutiny when determining a disability and providing and an educational placement.

---

304 U.S. 144 (1938)
[439]Furman v. Georgia, 408 U.S. 238 (1972)

Congress provided a framework for scrutinizing the determination of disabilities but the Supreme Court has a different view of the relationship between strict scrutiny and intellectual disability. The Court decided in Cleburne v. Cleburne Living Center that mental retardation was not a quasi-suspect classification and therefore did not require heightened scrutiny.[440] The reasoning for this decision was threefold: First, there is great variability among those classified as intellectually disabled who "range from those whose disability is not immediately evident to those who must be constantly cared for." The Court cautioned that "How this large and diversified group is to be treated under the law is a difficult and often a technical matter, very much a task for legislators guided by qualified professionals, and not by the perhaps ill-informed opinions of the judiciary." Second, this diversified group is not powerless as evidenced by the various laws and statutes such as the Rehabilitation Act of 1973 and the Education of the Handicapped Act (the Education for All Handicapped Children Act or P.L. 94-142) of 1975. Third, requiring heightened scrutiny for this "amorphous class" would be a difficult task because of "a variety of other groups who have perhaps immutable disabilities."

The explanation by the Court as to why the general category mental retardation is not a suspect or quasi-suspect classification also provides a rationale why those sentenced to death seeking Atkins relief should be a suspect classification and require heightened scrutiny. Those on death row do not represent an "amorphous class" but are distinguished by race, gender and "mild intellectual disability." Unlike the overall class of those having mental retardation described in *Cleburne*, the intellectual and adaptive variability of those on death row is far more restricted. There is no one (hopefully) on death row who is dependent on others for self-care, daily living, who cannot communicate and who would otherwise be identified as having a more severe intellectual or developmental disorder. Unlike the statutes cited in *Cleburne*, the statutory protections offered those seeking Atkins relief lack specificity and often rely on idiosyncratic and

---

[440]Cleburne v. Cleburne Living Ctr., 473 U.S. 432 (1985)

stereotypic interpretations of professional guidelines for determining intellectual disability. The class of Atkins offenders seeking Atkins relief is not a wide ranging class of those having intellectual disabilities, is comprised of a large subclass requiring heightened scrutiny, and does not have the type of legislation showing that "negates any claim that the mentally retarded are politically powerless in the sense that they have no ability to attract the attention of the lawmakers."[441]

Although the Supreme Court believed that the wide-ranging class of those having mental retardation did not require heightened scrutiny, the Court decided in favor of Cleburne Living Center (after having concluded that mental retardation was not a quasi-classification) because the denial of a permit was not rationally related to a compelling State interest. For capital punishment the Supreme Court has recognized, at least for the time being, the compelling interest of a State to execute, providing that the laws permitting execution is narrowly tailored. This tailoring of the law was achieved by Georgia in 1976[442] to the extent "that the infliction of death as a punishment for murder is not without justification, and thus is not unconstitutionally severe." Whatever the level of scrutiny deemed appropriate by the Court, *Atkins, Hall* and *Moore* show that if States will not narrowly tailor death penalty statues, especially those regarding the determination of intellectual disability, the Court will.

For Atkins claimants the only rational method for not executing those who warrant lesser culpability is to provide the same type of guidance that assists in the identification of children. For Atkins claimants the primary obstacle is a porous and re-interpreted definition of intellectual disability used to achieve the supposedly compelling, albeit irrevocable State interest of execution. The substance of virtually every statute or judicial guidance concerning Atkins centers about professional definitions. The task to enforce Atkins, as expressed by the Supreme Court," did not give the States unfettered discretion to define the full scope of the constitutional protection." [443] Gregg provided some guidelines for

---

[441]Cleburne v. Cleburne Living Ctr., 473 U.S. 432 (1985)
[442]Gregg v. Georgia, 428 U.S. 153 (1976)

the death penalty that would elevate execution above the level of haphazard and discriminatory but not by much. For Atkins claims many of the problems could be alleviated by following the Supreme Court's guidance in Dunn v. Blumstein in 1972 where "a heavy burden of justification is on the State, and that the statute will be closely scrutinized in light of its asserted purposes.[444]

The following are points that should be considered when evaluating an Atkins claim and thereby provide a degree of scrutiny or, at least, a rational basis for determining intellectual disability for those belonging to this narrow and small category of offenders:

- The importance of childhood data, especially IQ scores
- the likelihood that IQ scores before age of onset will be less influenced by malingering than those obtained in pursuit of an Atkins claim
- recognition of the ADA and a record of a disability as substantiating the existence of an intellectual disability
- acknowledging that no record of intellectual disability does not demonstrate that a person did not meet the criteria for lesser culpability
- a determination that a child has a disability other than intellectual disability does not demonstrate that the criteria for intellectual disability could not have been met
- the complex racial implications of IQ testing for children and adults and the anomalous use of IQ in States (e.g., California and the banning of IQ testing for black children and the "any" IQ score above 75 in Oklahoma)
- the statistical portrait of racism—including school demographics for disability categories, the prosecution of black defendants, victim race, jury selection, etc.— should be carefully examined
- the consideration of the criteria for mental retardation/intellectual disability at or about the time

---

[443]Hall v. Florida, 572 U.S. ___ (2014)
[444]Dunn v. Blumstein, 405 U.S. 330 (1972)

of assessment. If an IQ of 80 resulted in a determination by a State that a child was intellectually impaired, this same score should not be used to show no intellectual disability

- abandoning stereotypic interpretations of adaptive behavior such as being able to read, drive a car, or assist counsel
- the need to assess adaptive behavior using criteria appropriate for prisons (e.g., assessment criteria for Clark remedial plans) but as one element of an individual's ability to adapt as per the criteria for intellectual disability
- the preponderance of the evidence standard as standard of proof when considering Atkins claims
- Abandoning strict guidelines when interpreting criteria for intellectual disability

The racial characteristics of every State are unique. The complex racial landscape for determining intellectual disability for Atkins claimants is inextricably related to how intellectual disability was determined and used for claimants as children. California has by far the largest death row (735 as of June, 2019) population of whom 36.2 percent are black (266), 33.5 percent white (246) and 25 percent Hispanic (177).[445] More than half of those on death row (233) are from Los Angeles County. In spite of the large percent of black inmates on death row in relation to the general population (where the Black/African American population is approximately 6.5 percent) every Atkins claim for this large subgroup is confounded by the fact that black children cannot be given IQ tests in California to determine intellectual disability. Intelligence quotients, so central to the 2014 *Hall* decision, is lacking for California capital offenders who were educated within the State.

Georgia has a long history of racism and disproportionately classifying black children as having -intellectual disability yet disingenuously uses the highest burden of proof for deciding the

---

[445]https://www.cdcr.ca.gov/Capital_Punishment/docs/CondemnedInma teSummary.pdf?pdf=Condemned-Inmates

merits of Atkins claims. Louisiana has only executed 28 offenders since 1976 (of whom 13 or 46.4 percent were black). Louisiana has not imposed the death penalty since the 2010 the execution of Gerald Bordelon (white) for the 2002 murder of his 12-year-old stepdaughter. The last execution before Bordelon's was that of Leslie Martin in 2002. Although infrequently used in Louisiana the racial complexity in the State suggests that no one, white or black, should ever be executed which, indeed, might very well be the case. Just as in Brown v. Board of Education where the Supreme Court found that segregation deprives "children of the minority group of equal educational opportunities" regardless of the pretense of "separate but equal," discrimination and for the most part *de facto* segregation is part of the fabric of Louisiana (and every other State for that matter).

Not only is Louisiana's death row comprised, to a large extent, of a suspect class (47 of the 71 or 66.2 percent are black[446]), there is a large contingent seeking Atkins relief. In a brief on behalf of Kevan Brumfield, 19 Atkins claims in Louisiana were discussed (of 87 on death row in Louisiana at the time of *Atkins* in 2002).[447] The percent of black inmates on death row is similar to the percent of black children in the mental retardation category in 1980 where 72.4 percent of the almost 13,000 children classified as EMR in Louisiana were black, 68.5 percent in 1998, and 64.3 percent in 2011. As is often the case, fewer black children were identified as having the more serious Trainable Mental Retardation (59.7 percent) in 1980. In contrast to the EMR category in Louisiana in 1980, only 33.1 percent of the almost 20,000 classified as having specific learning disabilities were black. The percent of black children in the specific learning disability in Louisiana in 2011

---

[446]Source: DEATH ROW U.S.A., A quarterly report by the Criminal Justice Project of the NAACP Legal Defense and Educational Fund, Inc., Deborah Fins, Esq. Consultant to the Criminal Justice Project NAACP Legal Defense and Educational Fund, Inc. at https://www.naacpldf.org/wp-content/uploads/DRUSAWinter2018_.pdf

[447]Kevan Brumfield v. Burl Cain, Warden, Louisiana State Penitentiary, On Writ of Certiorari to the United States Court of Appeals, No. 13-1433, Brief Amici Curiae of Chief Justice Pascal F. Calogero, Jr., The Louisiana Association of Criminal Defense Lawyers (LACDL), & The Promise Of Justice Initiative (PJI) In Support Of Petitioner

increased to 56.3 percent in contrast to the black 6 to 21 population of 38.1 (the black student enrollment was approximately 45 percent). The increase of black children in the specific learning disability category says nothing of the restrictiveness of the specific learning disability environment or the type/quality of services received. The interpretation of all of these data is complicated by the racial makeup of schools, the influx of school options (charter schools, virtual charter schools, private schools, home schooling, etc.), and socio-economic factors . In 2014 approximately 49 percent of black children in Louisiana were living in poverty as compared to 14 percent of white students.[448]

A report from the General Accountability Office in 2016 indicated that between 2000 and 20014 the percentage of schools with poor Black and Hispanic enrollments grew from 9 to 16 percent and "these schools offered disproportionately fewer math, science, and college preparatory courses and had disproportionately higher rates of students who were held back in 9th grade, suspended, or expelled."[449] Attempts to remedy the deleterious effects of the substandard education provided black children further confound the problem. For example, creating charter schools can actually enhance racial disproportionality. The essential point is that segregation is infectious and difficult to remedy. More importantly, there is no way of knowing the extent that racism has contributed to the number for black offenders on death row and executed, or to what extent racism prevented successful Atkins claims or exonerations.

Kevan Brumfield

In 1993 Kevan Brumfield murdered off-duty Baton Rouge police officer Betty Smothers in an ambush shooting outside of a bank.

---

[448]According to the Kids Count data center at http://datacenter.kidscount.org
[449]file:///C:/Users/ed/Documents/race-education-gao-2016.pdf, Better Use of Information Could Help Agencies Identify Disparities and Address Racial Discrimination, GAO, April 16.

Officer Smothers was providing security for store-manager Kimen Lee who was making a deposit. Brumfield was sentenced to death in 1995. The trial court considered the possibility of mental retardation and agreed with one expert's assessment that "he did have an anti-social personality or sociopath, and explained it as someone with no conscience, and the defendant hadn't carried his burden placing the claim of mental retardation at issue." The anti-personality designation provided an explanation for his various scores and deficits and also suggested that someone with this disorder could not be mentally retarded. The determination that Brumfield was not intellectually disabled could only be appealed to the District Court if the decision was contrary to a reasonable standard or application of the law.[450]

The District Court decided that the trial court's failure to hold an evidentiary hearing to consider his Atkins claim was an unreasonable application of the law. As a result, the District Court conducted its own evidentiary hearing and decided that Brumfield was mentally retarded and therefore ineligible for the death penalty. The United State Court of Appeals for the Fifth Circuit reversed this decision, not because of evidence of intellectual disability, but because the court believed that the trial court did not make an unreasonable decision by not granting Brumfield an Atkins evidentiary hearing. In 2015 the Supreme Court believed that Brumfield had provided sufficient data (an IQ of 75 and deficits in adaptive behavior), not to prove intellectual disability, but to provide a reasonable ground for an evidentiary hearing. A side note to the Supreme Court's decision was a lengthy dissent by Judge Thomas who did bring up a vexing problem related to the standard error of measurement. Contrary to the Court's bright-line of an IQ score of 75 or less indicating intellectual disability (this centered about Brumfield's IQ score of 75), Thomas pointed out that the actual standard error of measurement resulted in a band of confidence of 66 to 74 so that a score of 75 was not in the intellectually disabled range. In any case, consistent with the Court's majority opinion, in 2016 the Fifth Circuit decided that

---

[450]according to the Antiterrorism and Effective Death Penalty Act of 1996 or AEDPA (28 U.S.C. § 2254[d]).

Brumfield was intellectually disabled and not eligible for execution.

One criticism of AEDPA is that, although the intent is to limit frivolous appeals, the law could also maintain a wrongful conviction. The decision that Brumfield was intellectually disabled by the District Court was not considered by the Fifth Circuit which "rejected the District Court's conclusion that the state court had unreasonably applied clearly established federal law."[451] On remand from the Supreme Court the Fifth Circuit then reasoned that "Because the District Court's determination that Brumfield is intellectually disabled is plausible in light of the record as a whole, its determination is not clearly erroneous. Accordingly, we AFFIRM the ruling of the District Court."[452]
In 2016 Brumfield was re-sentenced to life in prison. Brumfield's journey is unusual because of his curious path toward a successful Atkins claim: His claim was first dismissed, then he was intellectually disabled, then not intellectually disabled, then at least entitled to show that he was intellectually disabled, and then again determined to be intellectually disabled.

Kevan Brumfield is typical of a large class of those on death row, a class far more distinct than the "amorphous class" of mental retardation described in *Cleburne*. As opposed to a wide range of individuals having an intellectual disability, many Atkins claimants are black and Atkins legislation or the interpretation of legislation, weighs heavily on black defendants by ignoring childhood data, a previous determination of intellectual disability, a misinterpretation of the age of onset prong of the professional definition, and an often stereotypic interpretation of adaptive behavior. Unlike children who are "not politically powerless" as evidenced by State and federal legislation cited in *Cleburne*, many Atkins claimants have been subjected to discrimination by the very legislation designed to provide relief. The interpretation of Atkins legislation is used to vanquish all responsibility by the State

---

[451]See the Supreme Court's June 18 decision Brumfield v. Cain, 76 U.S. ___ (2015)
[452]Brumfield v. Cain, United States Court of Appeals for the Fifth Circuit, No. 12-30256, Revised February 10, 2016

for a prior determination of intellectual disability by claiming a not "unreasonable" interpretation of the law.

For Atkins claimants the law for determining intellectual disability is vaguely explained, variously defined and used with limited guidance—albeit acknowledging the stereotypic guidance as provided in Texas in *Briseno*. Unlike death penalty statutes the special education law has been assiduously modified to better identify children with disabilities. The 1975 special education law was, as best as possible, narrowly defined to meet the compelling interest of the State to provide an appropriate education by requiring a written individualized education program and placement in the least restrictive environment. In spite of these efforts, black children have always been disproportionately identified as having mental retardation or mild intellectual disabilities. For some States the intent of these placements might be benevolent and based on the belief that the ill effects of prior segregation and discrimination are best remedied by a special form of segregation under the guise of special education.

Judges, juries, and prosecutors often accept IQ as an absolute standard and, when IQ is of questionable validity, the cause of low IQ is the child or claimant and not those who use, administer or interpret scores. For children the P.L. 94-142 1975 law required "positive action be taken against erroneous classification of poor, minority and bilingual children and against the invalid use of testing."[453] Of particular importance for Atkins claims is not only the "the invalid use of testing" but the peculiar interpretation of the professional definition of intellectual disability which is just as onerous as the misclassification of children. For children the burden is an inferior education; for Atkins claimants the burden can be death row (California), the possibility of death (other States) and a very good probability of death (Texas).

Data for children is essential for understanding the role of race for Atkins claimants seeking relief. The table below[454] shows the

---

[453]Senate Report 94-168, p. 28

[454]22nd Annual Report to Congress, Appendix A, 1998 school year, see https://www2.ed.gov/about/reports/annual/osep/2000/appendix-a.pdf

number of black and white children identified as having mental retardation for selected States when racial data was first reported in 1998 for the Individuals with Disabilities Education Act.[455] Data for racial disproportionality is, by and large, unique to each State in that each State seems to have a unique flavor of racism. Washington D.C. in 1998 had 1,157 children classified as mentally retarded but no white children. The District of Columbia Public School (DCPS) has long been characterized by segregated and then re-segregated public schools.

In Georgia the number of black children identified as having mental retardation in 1998 was 18,257 in comparison to 10,479 white children. The black 6 to 21 population in 1998 was 614,238, the white 6-21 population 1,836,494, and the ratio per 100 for black children identified as mentally retarded was 2.97.[456] The rate per 100 for white children was .98. A comparison of these two rates (2.09/.98) yields a risk ratio of 3.03 which indicates approximately three times as many black children were identified as having mental retardation as white children in Georgia in 1998.

1998 Mental Retardation Data Black and White children (6-21) [457]					
State	**Black MR**	**White MR**	**Black Rate**	**White Rate**	**Risk**
Alabama	14,516	7,599	4.46	1.19	3.77
California	4,004	11,487	0.69	0.43	1.89
DC	1,157	0	1.97	---	---
Florida	19,080	13,833	2.88	0.75	3.83

---

[455]The disability data for 1998 is important for two reasons: First, this is when race and ethnicity data were first reported. Second, these data provide a better description of race and disability for Atkins claimants in relation to when they were in school than more recent data. Also, beginning in 1998, the data were based on actual child counts rather than survey data (as was the 1980 Office of Civil Rights survey data.
[456]Or 2.97 = 18,257/614,238 X 100
[457]*Ibid.*

Georgia	18,257	10,479	2.97	0.98	3.03
Mississippi	5,226	1,441	1.67	0.39	4.26
New Jersey	1,665	1,787	0.59	0.17	3.59
New York	5,144	7,555	0.75	0.32	2.33
Ohio	14,741	34,778	4.12	1.63	2.53
South Carolina	12,580	4,916	3.86	0.93	4.17
Texas	7,433	8,412	1.14	0.36	3.18
Virginia	6,952	6,746	1.98	0.66	2.98

In 1998 Florida was the leader for the identification of mental retardation (19,080) and the risk factor between the black and white rates was 3.83. What is amazing is that with so many children identified as having mental retardation in Florida as children, there have been so few successful *Atkins* claims. The risk ratio for black/white mental retardation was 3.03 in Illinois in 1998. In Illinois the psychometrically challenged United States District Court judge believed he had great insight into the usefulness of EMR classes where "The curriculum thus involves much repetition and concrete teaching. Subjects are taught for short periods of time, in recognition of the children's short attention spans. The subject matter of the EMH courses is oriented toward socialization, language skills and vocational training. Academic subjects are taught, but on an elementary level and with the objective of helping the child become economically independent."[458] All that can be said of this fictional account of EMR classes is that it offers an expeditious way to ignore racial disproportionality, the preclusion of educational opportunity, and segregation (more about Chicago and this regrettable decision shortly). Considering that the overall number of exonerations in Illinois (214 according to the National Registry of Exonerations) consists primarily of black defendants wrongfully convicted (an astonishing 68 percent or 137), Illinois has a history of mingling race and disability identification to ostensible "help" black children and then to wrongfully convict black adults. Not only did

---

[458]Parents in Action on Special Education (PASE) v. Hannon, 506 F. Supp. 831 (1980)

Chicago stigmatize and segregate children via mental retardation, for adults, false confessions seem to have been a popular method for solving crimes as demonstrated by a false confession rate three times that of the national average.

Alabama, in 1998, had a relatively large rate of black children classified as mentally retarded (4.46 per 100), and the ratio of black to white mental retardation was approximately 3.8. The black to white ratios in Mississippi (4.26) and South Carolina (4.17) indicated that more than four times as many black children were classified as mentally retarded than white children. New Jersey (which, by the way, abolished the death penalty in 2007) illustrates the difficulty interpreting disproportionality statistics. New Jersey has one of the smallest black rates of mental retardation per 100 children (.57), similar to that of California, but the white ratio was significantly smaller (.17). In 1998 the risk ratio for mental retardation in New Jersey was a very high 3.59 (and an even higher risk of 3.92 in 2011).

The Alabama black mental retardation rate (4.46) is very high in comparison to Mississippi (1.67) suggests that there would be fewer Atkins claims in Alabama than Mississippi. These data actually obfuscate how intellectual disability is used in relation to *de jure* and *de facto* segregation and available State educational resources. In Atkins claims the use of mental retardation and other disabilities should be carefully examined to understand the extent of racial bias, the use of other disabilities to categorize children, and the process used to determine disability categorization. For example, the low rate of black mental retardation in Mississippi in 1998 was likely attributed to race just as race was the underlying cause of over-identification of black children in Alabama. There is no incentive to disproportionally identify black children as intellectually disabled when resources are lacking and when and traditional segregation/grouping is more than sufficient to meet the racial needs of a State.

In 1998, of all the children identified as having mental retardation in Alabama, 65.2 percent were black. In 2011 this was reduced to 50.4 percent. Also, in 1998 in Alabama, 32.6 percent of the children identified as having specific learning disabilities were black (which increased to 46 percent in 2011) and 35 percent of the 15,977 children identified as having speech and language disabilities were black in 1998. Alabama has significantly reduced the disproportionality in intellectual disability, and increased the identification of black children as having specific learning disabilities.

Participation in the least restrictive category (speech or language impairments) decreased from 35 percent in 1998 to 30 percent in 2011. The fact that so many black children had intellectual disabilities but had far fewer speech and language disorders is telling. Then, and now, IQ tests measure, to a great extent, verbal ability, but the reason for so fewer black children in the speech and language disability category is the result of the multiple character of might be explained by the varied character of racism. Mental retardation provides one of the most restrictive environments and speech or language impairments the least restrictive educational environment of all disability categories. In addition, if black children did have greater language needs, these needs were simply ignored. One disability provided a segregated environment (which was readily given), another needed disability provided necessary services (which were readily ignored). Maybe the intent was to place black children in segregative environments to remedy the effects of segregation as was the apparent intent in Washington, D.C. in Hobson v. Hansen in 1971. However, fewer black children in the speech and language impairments (and specific learning disabilities) category suggest segregation rather than need was the primary concern.

The lesson to be learned from childhood disability data, especially when applied to an Atkins claim, is that the intent for identifying a child as having a disability and why/how children are placed in educational environments is not always apparent. There is a clear history of using the EMR category to segregate black children, regardless of benevolent intent, but the category itself is less significant than the result of the categorization. If an EMR-type placement results in segregation from the regular school population and denial of educational opportunity, rebranding this placement by another name does not change the dire educational consequences, especially when race is a factor.

There is no question that many black children were disproportionally identified as having mental retardation/intellectual disability. Likewise, there are many black adults who attended segregated schools, *de facto* or otherwise, who could or should have been identified as needing special education, and who were either denied services or provided with less than appropriate services. On the other side of the coin there are probably white children who were not identified as having an intellectual disability because of race. For both black and white children, who should merit lesser culpability as an adult, there are innumerable reasons why a child was not classified or classified as having a disability with a less onerous label than EMR.

Intellectual disability was and is not the only category subject to misclassification. New York's risk factor for mental retardation in 1998 was 2.33 but New York has a reputation for using the emotional disturbance category to segregate. In New York, in 1998, there were 26,751 black and Hispanic children identified as having emotional disturbance (58 percent). The problem of disproportionality in this disability category was highlighted 20 years earlier in a 1978 case involving the misplacement of black and Hispanic children. At the time the racial composition of special day schools was 68 percent black and 27 percent Hispanic.[459] New York has a penchant for using the emotional disturbance category to provide a segregated environment.

What was the intent of assigning disproportionate number of black and Hispanic children to special day schools?   The plaintiffs contended that the disproportionality was the result of intentional segregation without due process. The defendants were aghast that such a service—placement in special day schools—to needy children and the community would be eliminated. In the end, the Court found that "good intentions" do not compensate for inadequacies in evaluation, due process, and appropriate educational programming...a finding that could easily apply to Atkins claims. One key issue was the fact that while minority

---

[459]Lora v. The Board of Education of the City of New York, 456 F. Supp. 1211 (1978)

students were placed in special day schools, white students were often placed in private schools where treatment was better and more costly.

Part of the problem, a problem currently exhibited in very wealthy States like New Jersey and Massachusetts, is the ability of more affluent parents to better manipulate the system. In Lora v. Board of Education, in 1978, the Court found that the minority children assigned to special day schools were drawn from "largely underprivileged, often broken homes, and with parents who are, more likely than not, poorly educated, harried, beset by their own personal problems and intimidated by authority and a plethora of forms." These factors could easily be applied to black defendants in all phases of the death penalty jurisprudence, especially Atkins claims.

Washington v. Davis

A narrowing jurisprudence of the death penalty and the fact that the death penalty weighs more heavily on black than white defendants is not without boundaries. In Washington v. Davis the issue was the disproportionate number of black police applicants who failed a written test and whether the test was related to job performance.[460] The District Court decided that the test and the actions of the District of Columbia Metropolitan Police Department were not discriminatory. As stated by the court, "It would be a setback for blacks and whites alike to lower standards of recruitment." The court of appeals found that, regardless of intent, test performance disproportionality, standing alone and based on the Title VII standard, was a constitutional violation. In *Davis,* the Supreme Court explained that the appellate court was in error for not considering discriminatory intent and shifting the burden to offer a race neutral explanation for the poor black test performance. As stated by the Court

---

[460]Washington v. Davis, 426 U.S. 229 (1976)

nevertheless a law, neutral on its face and serving ends otherwise within the power of government to pursue, is not invalid under the equal protection clause of the Fourteenth Amendment simply because it may affect a greater proportion of one race than of another; while disproportionate impact is not irrelevant, it is not the sole touchstone of an invidious racial discrimination forbidden by the Federal Constitution, and standing alone, disproportionate impact does not trigger the rule that racial classifications are to be subjected to the strictest scrutiny and are justifiable only by the weightiest of considerations.

For Atkins claims the areas relating to disproportionality are pervasive and include racial disproportionality in school districts when classifying children, disproportionality in the type of restrictive services provided children, the lack of disproportionality in certain disabilities (e.g., speech or language disorders), the history of disproportionality from lynchings to State sanctioned executions, disproportionality in sentencing, disproportionality on death row, disproportionality in exonerations (where the high percentage of black exonerations speaks of the fairness of prior judicial proceedings), and the disproportionality of judges, prosecutors, and jurors. In every phase of an Atkins claim, the dimensions of history and disproportionality triangulate to invidious intent. Nonetheless, the Court did conclude that "Though the Due Process Clause of the Fifth Amendment contains an equal protection component prohibiting the Government from invidious discrimination, it does not follow that a law or other official act is unconstitutional solely because it has a racially disproportionate impact regardless of whether it reflects a racially discriminatory purpose."

Bobby Tarver

When considering an Atkins claim, the circumstances that surround the claim, often strange, demand careful attention. The murder of cab driver Percy Gibson in Mobile, Alabama near a Seven Eleven by Bobby Tarver, age 21 and black, in 1981 highlights the complexity of intellectual disability, race and odd jurisprudence. Tarver had originally intended to rob the convenience store but, because the store was crowded, robbed taxi driver Percy Gibson outside of the store for all of 40 cents. Tarver had ordered Gibson out of the cab and, according to Tarver, accidentally dropped the shotgun resulting in Gibson's death. However, the evidence demonstrated that Gibson died of a contact wound. Tarver eventually called the police and reported that he witnessed a murder. Shortly thereafter Gibson was arrested, convicted of capital murder and sentenced to death. Because the district attorney "exceeded the bounds of prosecutorial ethics and propriety" by serving as a prosecutor and witness (he took the stand) the case was remanded for a new trial.[461] Tarver was again convicted of murder but the jury recommended life without parole. This "recommendation" was ignored by the court, via jury override, and he was again sentenced to death.

The murder of the cab driver, the 40 cents stolen, the calling of police and the pathetic explanation for the murder might suggest someone who was not engaging in a great deal of planning or forethought. Some years later Tarver sought relief from his death sentence under *Atkins* but his claim was denied. Tarver had a WISC IQ of 61 at age 14 and was placed in a class for the mentally retarded. At age 16 he had an IQ of 72 on the WAIS, and in 1995 an IQ of 76 on the WAIS-R and then a score of 74 by the State's psychologist on the same test. In 2005 a State expert found that Tarver had IQ scores of 59 and 61 on the WAIS-III and decided that he was mentally retarded. The court reasoned that Tarver must have been malingering to receive such low IQ scores.[462] Considering all the data, his IQ scores before 18, and the fact that

---

[461]Court of Criminal Appeals of Alabama, 492 So. 2d 328 (1986)
[462]United States District Court for the Southern District of Alabama Southern Division, Civil Action No. 07-00294-CG-B, Bobby Tarver v. Kim T. Thomas, Commissioner, Alabama Department of Corrections, Respondent. 09-24-2012

Alabama had decided that he was mentally retarded as a child, racial intent might well have been part of the decision-making process to deny his Atkins claim.

Every State has a unique character when addressing the mental retardation/EMR/intellectual disability category for children and adults. In spite of the complexity of data, how intellectual disability is interrelated with race, and how specific school districts deal with race and disability all provide a backdrop for understanding Atkins claims. The United States District Court decided that "the evidence of Tarver's mental retardation is overwhelming." The idiosyncratic and subjective interpretation of the definition of mental retardation by the court was summarily rebuked by the District Court. Not only was important evidence concerning IQ selectively ignored, the court ignored evidence that Tarver was functionally illiterate, never functioned independently and had a record of mental retardation. The District Court decided that there was clear evidence that Tarver was mentally retarded and his death sentence was vacated.

Another Tarver, Robert Lee, was also sentenced to death as a result of jury override. The vote by the jury was 7 to 5 for life in prison without parole. His death sentence was given for the murder of store owner Hugh Sims Kite in Cottonton, Alabama in 1984. In 2000 the Supreme Court decided not to review Tarver's appeal which claimed that the electric chair was cruel and unusual punishment. This Tarver was less fortunate and was executed by electrocution in 2000.

In addition to complex racial data involving disability categories, black children and adults must deal with a double standard whenever testing is involved. To understand the less than beneficial role of testing for both children and Atkins claimants, tests should be considered for what they measure and not an iconic concept such as an *intelligence quotient* (which IQ is not as discussed previously). If low IQ or adaptive deficits suggest intellectual disability, race is ignored for children but for adults these data are rationalized as being attributed to race and environment and not a real disability.

Courts have, at times, been mindful of racial bias and the interpretation of test scores. In 1986 Alice Richardson, who had failed the Alabama Initial Teacher Certification Test on several occasions, was not rehired as a teacher following a school consolidation.[463] Richardson claimed that the test had an adverse impact resulting from race. If this were the case, Alabama would then need to show that the use of the test was justified for employment purposes. Of the 4,144 white test takers, 93.8 percent passed the test between 1981 and 1985, and 49.6 percent of the 496 black test takers passed.

Much of the problem faced by the court in this case, as was the problem faced by the Supreme Court in *Hall*, centered about the use of cutoff scores. For the Alabama court, the essential problem was not reliability or estimating true scores, but about test validity—a concept that the Supreme Court has been loath to consider (although not so in Griggs v. Duke Power Company in 1971[464]). The Alabama court explained that "cut scores cannot be determined with mathematical certainty, and political considerations may properly enter into cut-score decisions" but decided that for the "Alabama Initial Teacher Certification test, and in particular with the early childhood education and elementary education examinations" the "evidence reflects that the test falls so far below acceptable and reasonable minimum standards that the test could not be reasonably understood to do what it purports to do." The result of all of this was the re-employment of Richardson, backpay, and attorney fees. The same standard expressed by this court could be used in Atkins claims where consideration of the total evidence, from birth to murder, "falls so far below acceptable and reasonable minimum standards" that the criteria for determining intellectual disability "could not be reasonably understood to do what it purports to do."

Ehrlich Anthony Coker

---

[463]Richardson v. Lamar County Board of Education, 729 F.Supp. 806 (1989)
[464]Griggs v. Duke Power Co., 401 U.S. 424 (1971)

There is one area of racial disproportionality that is especially telling when attempting to understand intent: rape. For black defendants rape has always been a pretext for both lynching and legalized forms of execution. According to national data retrieved from the Espy file which lists executions between 1608 and 2002,[465] between 1930 when Georgia executed Frank Jackson by electrocution for murder (Georgia changed from hanging to electrocution in 1924) to 1967 with the execution of Luis Monge in Colorado, there were 3,891 executions in the United States and of these 2,034 were for black offenders (52.3 percent black).

Of the 423 executions for rape between 1930 and 1967, 370 (87.5 percent) of those executed were black.[466] The use execution for rape is better understood when considering the fact that rape is not a black crime. The arrest rate for murder and nonnegligent homicide for white suspects is 45.9 percent and 51.1 percent for black suspects according to 2015 FBI statistics. On the other hand, the arrest rate for rape is 68 percent for white suspects and 28.2 percent for black suspects.[467] Prosecution for rape and execution are inextricably tied to other dimensions of racism (e.g., juror selection). For example, Robert Swain was sentenced to death for rape when an Alabama court reasoned that challenging all potential black jurors was constitutional as long as they were allowed to be called for jury service.

The disproportionate use of the death penalty for black defendants involving rape came to an end with Ehrlich Anthony Coker who was, not surprisingly, white. In September of 1974, Coker escaped from a Georgia prison, entered a home, subdued the occupants, then raped and kidnapped the wife of Allen Carver.

---

[465]Espy, M. Watt, and John Ortiz Smykla. Executions in the United States, 1608-2002: The ESPY File. ICPSR08451-v5. Ann Arbor, MI: Inter-university Consortium for Political and Social Research

[466]The ESPY file was "compiled by M. Watt Espy and John Ortiz Smykla, and was made available through the Inter-University Consortium for Political and Social Research" and accessed through the Death Penalty Information Center at http://www.deathpenaltyinfo.org/executions-us-1608-2002-espy-file

[467]2015 FBI report Crime in the United States: https://ucr.fbi.gov/crime-in-the-u.s/2015/crime-in-the-u.s.-2015/tables/table-43

On December 4, 1974, Coker was sentenced to death for the rape with aggravating circumstances. In 1977, in Coker v. Georgia, the Supreme Court decided in a 7-2 decision that "although rape deserves serious punishment, the death penalty, which is unique in its severity and irrevocability, is an excessive penalty for the rapist who, as such and as opposed to the murderer, does not unjustifiably take human life."[468] Coker was resentenced to life in prison.

Historically, whether the data involve lynchings, jury selection, executions, or Atkins claims, race is always lurking in the background. Nonetheless, there are many confounding variables that are not only difficult to explain but suggest invidious intent when considered in isolation. According to an ACLU report black inmates comprise 38.3 percent of those serving life prison terms but 56.4 percent of those serving sentences of life without parole (LWOP). At first blush this disproportionality seems obvious but the possible causes are many. One possibility is that the excessive percent of black defendants receiving LWOP terms is an artifact of prior segregation and discrimination which then resulted in fewer educational opportunities, socio-economic mobility which then resulted in fewer resources to negotiate more equitable representation, trials and/or sentencing.[469]

Prosecutorial discretion is another factor that must be considered. In Georgia 98.4 percent of prisoners serving life sentences, where prosecutors have discretion following a second drug offense, are black. In United States v. Booker in 2005 the Supreme Court decided that "the Sixth Amendment requires juries, not judges, to find facts relevant to sentencing" and that mandatory federal sentencing guidelines are unconstitutional and must be advisory.[470]

As stated by the 2014 ACLU report "These racial disparities result from disparate treatment of black defendants at every stage of the

---

[468]Coker v. Georgia, 433 U.S. 584 (1977)
[469]Written Submission of the American Civil Liberties Union on Racial Disparities in Sentencing Hearing on Reports of Racism in the Justice System of the United States Submitted to the Inter-American Commission on Human Rights 153rd Session, October 27, 2014
[470]United States v. Booker, 543 U.S. 220 (2005)

criminal justice system, including stops and searches, arrests, prosecutions and plea negotiations, trials, and sentencing." What must be added to this list of racial disparities is the historical basis of racism, including lynching, which provide evidence that the essential problem is not only sentencing guidelines but a manifestation of how black Americans have always been treated.

Executions 1608 – 2020			
Year	Total	Black	Percent
1608-1880	4,831	2,212	45.8
1880-1929	5,767	2,838	49.2
1930-1967	3,891	2,034	52.3
1976-2020	1,517	517	34.1

One area of consistency in death penalty data is the disproportionate number of black inmates on death row and those executed. From data gathered from the ESPY file,[471] the percent of black inmates executed between 1608 and 1880 was 45.8 percent. Between 1880 and 1929 the percent of black executions was 49.2, and between 1930 and 1967 the percent was 52.3. Of the 1,517 executions (as of March, 2020) in the United States occurring after the death penalty was reinstated in 1976 (with the Utah firing squad execution of Gary Gilmore, white, in January of 1977), 34 percent (517) of those executed have been black.[472] The fact that there has been a reduction in black executions since the death penalty was reinstated likely the result of racial bias in the initial application of the death penalty; that is, on appeal the appropriateness of the death penalty has received a degree of closer scrutiny.

---

[471]The ESPY file was downloaded from the DPIC and was compiled by Espy, M. Watt, and John Ortiz Smykla. Executions in the United States, 1608-2002: The ESPY File ICPSR08451-v5. Ann Arbor, MI: Inter-university Consortium for Political and Social Research [distributor], 2016-07-20. http://doi.org/10.3886/ICPSR08451.v5
[472]All data is from the Death Penalty Information Center

The number of black executions before and after 1976 suggests that as courts became more conscious of racial overtones (but not for all), the result was a decrease in the number of black inmates executed from 52.3 percent between 1930 and 1967 to 34 percent after 1976. Similar to the percent of black executions, in 1998-99 the percent (33.5) of children ages 6-21 identified as having mental retardation were black. The gradual decrease of black executions after 1976 has been small. Between 1976 and 1999 there were 598 executions of which 211 or 35.3 percent were black. From January of 2000 to March 2020 there were 919 executions of which 306 or 33.3 percent were black. In 2000 the U.S. population census estimate was 12.9 percent Black or African American alone, and this increased to 13.4 in 2018.

Executions: 1976-2020			
Year	Total	Black	Percent
1976-1999	598	211	35.3
2000-2020	919	306	33.3
Total	1,517	517	34.1

The percent of black inmates executed since 1976 is similar to the percent of black children identified as having mental retardation/intellectual disabilities. From a 38.7 percent black EMR enrollment in 1980 to approximately 34 percent of black children identified as having mental retardation in 1998, black children have routinely been disproportionately identified and misclassified. The reduction of intellectual disabilities for black children does not take into account the use of other disabilities to provide a segregated environment, and, more likely than not, an inferior education. For example, rather than an EMR classroom the less stigmatizing special education classroom, self-contained classroom, specific learning disabilities classroom, or 12-1-1 classroom (12 students of varying disabilities in one classroom with one teacher and one aide) are among the many possibilities for repackaging EMR into the same educational diet but with a much more appealing menu.

A comparison between the percent of black inmates on death row and black executions provides yet another index, albeit indirect, of racial intent underlying death penalty jurisprudence. have been black. In contrast to the percent (34) of executions, 41.7 percent of death row inmates are black.[473] There are many reasons for this discrepancy including the unlikely possibility that States are particularly benevolent when addressing the needs of black prisoners on death row—all history to the contrary. A more likely possibility is that when death penalty cases are given a higher degree of scrutiny during the appellate process, the lack of fairness and racism become more obvious.

The death row population is disproportionally black (1,100 of 2,639 death row prisoners reported in 2019) but the extent of the disproportionally depends on the State.[474] Louisiana has one of the largest percentages (66.7%) of black inmates on death row (46 of 69 death row inmates are black). In contrast, California has by far the largest number death row inmates overall (over 727) of whom 36 (262) percent are black[475] (compared to a relatively small black population in California of 6.5 percent).[476] California alone accounts for 27.5 percent of all those on death row in the United States.[477]

States with the highest Black Death Row/census ratios are Ohio (4.4), Pennsylvania (4.5), and Oklahoma (5.7). The ratio is slightly smaller for California than Oklahoma, but the number of black prisoners on death row is far greater in California (262 to 21). Unlike the large number of executions in Texas, the ratio of death

---

[473]See NAACP, Legal Defense Fund, https://www.naacpldf.org/our-thinking/death-row-usa/ Fall, 2019

[474]See NAACP, Legal Defense Fund, https://www.naacpldf.org/wp-content/uploads/DRUSAWinter2020.pdf

[475]California Department of Corrections and Rehabilitation 04/11/2018, Division of Adult Operations Printed Date: Death Row Tracking System Condemned Inmate Summary List, https://www.cdcr.ca.gov/Capital_Punishment/docs/CondemnedInmate Summary.pdf?pdf=Condemned-Inmates

[476]Source: DEATH ROW U.S.A., A quarterly report by the Criminal Justice Project of the NAACP Legal Defense and Educational Fund, Inc., Deborah Fins, Esq. Consultant to the Criminal Justice Project NAACP Legal Defense and Educational Fund, Inc. at https://www.naacpldf.org/wp-content/uploads/DRUSAWinter2020.pdf

[477]*Ibid.*

row prisoners (44.3 percent black) is 3.5. The table shown below lists the number of prisoners on death row, the number of black prisoners, the percent of black prisoners, census data for "Black or African American alone," and the ratio of the percent of black prisoners to census data for selected States. Although most States with a large percentage of black inmates (in excess of 50 percent) are in the South, California, Pennsylvania and Ohio have the largest disparity between census data and percent of black inmates on death row (and Mississippi the lowest disparity).

Black Offenders on Death Row for Selected States (from Death Row U.S.A. 2019)					
State	All	Black	Percent	Census	Ratio
California	727	262	36.0	6.5	5.5
Florida	348	132	37.9	16.8	2.3
Texas	219	97	44.3	12.7	3.5
Alabama	177	91	51.4	26.8	1.9
Pennsylvania	152	81	53.3	11.8	4.5
North Carolina	144	77	53.5	22.2	2.4
Ohio	140	79	56.4	12.8	4.4
Arizona	120	18	15.0	5	3.0
Nevada	74	28	37.8	9.8	3.9
Louisiana	69	46	66.7	32.6	2.0
Federal	61	25	41.0	13.4	3.1
Tennessee	54	26	48.1	17.1	2.8
Georgia	49	25	51.0	32.2	1.6
Oklahoma	47	21	44.7	7.8	5.7
Mississippi	43	24	55.8	37.7	1.5
South Carolina	40	22	55.0	27.5	2.0
Kentucky	30	4	13.3	8.4	1.6
Oregon	31	2	6.5	2.2	2.9
Arkansas	32	17	53.1	15.7	3.4
Missouri	24	7	29.2	11.8	2.5
Total	2,581	1,084	42.0	17.2	2.4
Total (all States)	2,620	1,089	41.7	13.3	3.0

Since the execution of Jimmy Gray for rape and murder in 1983 following the reinstatement of the death penalty in 1976, there have been 27 executions in Mississippi of which 9 were black offenders.

States with the highest Black Death Row/census ratios are Ohio (4.4), Pennsylvania (4.5), and Oklahoma (5.7). The ratio is slightly smaller for California than Oklahoma, but the number of black prisoners on death row is far greater in California (262 to 21). Unlike the large number of executions in Texas, the ratio of death row prisoners (44.3 percent black) is 3.5. The table shown below lists the number of prisoners on death row, the number of black prisoners, the percent of black prisoners, census data for "Black or African American alone," and the ratio of the percent of black prisoners to census data for selected States. Although most States with a large percentage of black inmates (in excess of 50 percent) are in the South, California, Pennsylvania and Ohio have the largest disparity between census data and percent of black inmates on death row (and Mississippi the lowest disparity). Since the execution of Jimmy Gray for rape and murder in 1983 following the reinstatement of the death penalty in 1976, there have been 27 executions in Mississippi of which 9 were black offenders.

The data show that States are not easily categorized when trying to conceptualize an overall theory of death row and the racial composition for various States. In Virginia, 46 percent (52) of the 113 executions have been for black offenders since the execution of Frank Coppola in 1982. The most recent execution occurred July 6, 2017 when William Morva, white, was executed by lethal injection at the Greensville Correctional Center for the murders of security guard Derrick McFarland and County deputy Eric Sutphin. Notwithstanding the execution of Morva, the death row population in Virginia has been greatly reduced (two black and one white) as of fall 2017.[478]

---

[478]*Ibid.*

One of obstacle to the death penalty in Virginia is death row itself. To be executed in Virginia there must be at least one aggravating factor of which future dangerousness to society is one. However, if a determination is made that a prisoner is not a future danger to society in prison or on death row, does this impact this aggravating factor. On November 27, 2018 the United States Court of Appeals for the Fourth Circuit decided that lower courts were incorrect when considering mitigating evidence for Mark Eric Lawlor for the rape and murder of Genevieve Orange in 2008. Lawlor was sentenced to death in 2011 because of the vileness of the murder and that he was a future danger to society. The Virginia courts believed that a defense expert should opine on future dangerousness to society as a whole and not only in prison. The appellate court reversed by deciding that the special circumstance of future dangerousness cannot be restricted to society as a whole but must include potential prison conduct as a mitigating factor. This was explained by the Supreme Court in 1978 that "The Eighth and Fourteenth Amendments require that the sentencer, in all but the rarest kind of capital case, not be precluded from considering as a mitigating factor, any aspect of a defendant's character or record and any of the circumstances of the offense that the defendant proffers as a basis for a sentence less than death."[479]

Benjamin Rauf

The interpretation of execution and death row data must take into consideration the skewed nature of data, especially when considering the disproportionality of data by specific States. As shown in the table below the States having the largest number of executions since 1976 are Texas (557), Virginia (113), Oklahoma (112), Florida (96), Missouri (88), Georgia (72), Alabama (63), Ohio (55), North Carolina (43) and South Carolina (43). These States account for 94.6 percent of the 1,491 executions since 1976 and 96.9 percent (493) of all black executions (509).[480]

---

[479]Lockett v. Ohio, 438 U.S. 586 (1978)
[480]As of December 6, 2018

The Supreme Court of Delaware (in Rauf v. Delaware) declared the death penalty unconstitutional on August 2, 2016. The decision was based on Hurst v. Florida band the importance of the jury rather than judge in death penalty decisions. The Delaware court went further by stating that "Because the respective roles of the judge and jury are so complicated under § 4209, we are unable to discern a method by which to parse the statute so as to preserve it. Because we see no way to sever § 4209, the decision whether to reinstate the death penalty—if our ruling ultimately becomes final—and under what procedures, should be left to the General Assembly.

Benjamin Rauf was convicted of murdering Shazim Uppal, a fellow law student and former law school classmate at Temple University in 2015. This case (similar to that of *Hurst* in Florida) ruled the death penalty unconstitutional because the jury must unanimously find the aggravating factors necessary for the death penalty and not the sentencing court.[481] Rauf may or may not end the death penalty in Delaware. House Bill 125 was introduced in 2017 to amend the death penalty so that it was in compliance with *Hurst* and *Rauf.* This bill would allow the imposition of the death penalty if a jury determined unanimously and beyond a reasonable doubt that at least one aggravating existed and aggravating factor(s) outweighed all fact outweighed all mitigating factors.[482] As it is, in 2015 Rauf was re-sentenced to 15 years in prison for manslaughter.

As shown in the following table the States with the highest percent of black executions are Louisiana (46.4), Virginia (46.0), Alabama (42.4), Missouri (38.6), South Carolina (37.2), Texas (36.3) and Ohio (33.9). Of the 16 executions in Delaware prior to being abolished in 2016, 7 were black (43.8 percent).

Percentages can be deceptive. Texas does have a relatively large number of black executions (207 of the overall 571 executions in Texas) in comparison to the July, 2017 "Black or African American

---

[481]Benjamin Rauf v. State of Delaware, Supreme Court of the State of Delaware, § No. 39, 2016, § No. 39, 2016, Decided: August 2, 2016
[482]https://legis.delaware.gov/BillDetail?LegislationId=2559

alone" census of 12.7 percent). On the other hand, Texas accounts for 37.8 percent of all executions in the United States since 1976 and 40.1 percent of all black executions (207 of the 516 black executions). The death penalty in Texas is freakish for the sheer number of Texans executed. Harris County (Houston), Texas, alone is responsible for 129 executions, followed by Dallas County (Dallas/Fort Worth) with 62 executions. Harris County has more executions than either Virginia or Oklahoma (the two States with the next most executions following Texas). Of those executed from Harris county 69 (53.5 percent) have been black. The Black or African alone population in Harris County is 19.9 percent.[483]

In contrast to Texas, there are currently 116 inmates on Arizona's death row of whom 18 (15.5 percent) are black. The Black or African alone population in Arizona is approximately 5.6 percent. Of the 37 executions in Arizona since 1976 only one African America has been executed. In 2011 Eric John King, black, was executed by lethal injection for the 1989 murder of two convenience store employees during a robbery which netted $73. On the other hand, there have been 5 "Latino" executions (13.5 percent) Mexican Americans. According to Death Row USA of the 120 prisoners on Arizona's death row 18 are black and 24 Latino (of the 120 on death row). The black census population in Arizona is 5.1 percent and the Hispanic or Latino 31.6 percent.

---

[483] From Death Penalty Information Center county database at https://deathpenaltyinfo.org/executions/executions-overview/executions-by-county

Most Executions by State as of April, 2020			
State	Total	Black	Percent
Texas	571	207	36.3
Virginia	113	52	46.0
Oklahoma	113	35	31.0
Florida	99	28	28.3
Missouri	88	34	38.6
Georgia	76	28	36.8
Alabama	66	28	42.4
Ohio	56	19	33.9
North Carolina	43	13	30.2
South Carolina	43	16	37.2
Arizona	37	1	2.7
Arkansas	31	10	32.3
Louisiana	28	13	46.4
Mississippi	21	6	28.6
Indiana	20	3	15.0
Delaware	16	7	43.8
California	13	2	15.4
Summary of Above	1,434	502	35.0
Total All Executions	1,517	517	34.8

Mississippi has a legacy of segregation and discrimination including a sordid history of lynchings, the murder of Emmett Till and Medgar Evers, the Ole Miss riot of 1962 in Oxford, the murder of three civil rights works in 1964, segregation laws following *Brown* in 1954, etc. Although Mississippi has a very large "Black or African American alone" population (37.8 percent), of the 21 executions in Mississippi 6 were black offenders (28.6 percent). Of the 43 prisoners on Mississippi's death row, 55.8 percent are black. In contrast, 40 percent of Mississippi death row are white but of the 21 executions 15 (71.4 percent) have been white. The statistics comparing Mississippi's death row and execution rates for black and white prisoners indicates a readiness to sentence blacks to death but a much greater reluctance to actually carry out that sentence. Again, this is more the result of appellate scrutiny than benevolence as shown by the many trials of Curtis Flowers.[484]

Mississippi	Death Row	Executions
White	17 (41%)	15 (71%)
Black	24 (59%)	6 (29%)

Curtis Flowers

In spite of *Foster* and the racial bias in jury selection States cling to this strategy in violation of *Batson*. In 2019 the Supreme Court found Mississippi was motivated by discriminatory intent to strike a black prospective juror at Flowers' sixth trial.[485] The history of his various trials does provide several interesting statistics. Curtis Flowers had been tried six times for four murders committed in Winona, Mississippi in 1996 at the Tardy Furniture Store. The Court believed that the history of peremptory challenges for Flowers "first four trials strongly supports the conclusion that the State's use of peremptory strikes in Flowers' sixth trial was motivated in substantial part by discriminatory intent." For Flowers first four trials the State struck all 36 black prospective jurors. No racial data was available for his fifth trial and during his sixth trial 5 prospective jurors were struck and one black juror seated. One reason why Carolyn Wright was struck was because she knew defense witnesses, "but three white prospective jurors also knew many individuals involved in the case, and the State asked them no individual questions about their connections to

---

[484]For those interested the Chi Square for these data is significant at lean than the .05 level.
[485]Flowers v. Mississippi, Supreme Court of the United States, decided June 21, 2019.

witnesses." The Court referred to the striking of black prospective jurors as a "relentless and determined effort."

For Curtis Flowers the history of striking black prospective jurors was a critical factor for the Supreme Court to conclude that the underlying cause was discriminatory intent. Likewise, every Atkins claim should take into account the history of EMR, the overall intellectual disability category, and other disability categories. For the much beleaguered Florida, and other States, Atkins claims have resulted in an inexplicable anomaly. In spite of considerable efforts to ensure that Atkins claimants are truly intellectually disabled, States have been less strict when identifying children. A 1996 report of Florida schools showed that 54.8 percent of the 26,143 children identified as EMH were black, 34.4 percent white and 10 percent Hispanic. [486]

As is usually found, the disproportionality decreases as the severity of the intellectual disability increases. Of the 7,699 children identified as Trainable Mentally Handicapped (TMH) in this Florida report 37 percent were black and 45.9 percent white. The only explanation for the racial difference with respect to the degree of intellectual disability is that the more severe disability (TMH) is less susceptible to misidentification because cognitive needs become much more pronounced. A related explanation is that for the more severe disabilities services are more costly and, as is often the case, denied to many black children. In 1998 the two largest categories of disabilities, Speech/Language Handicapped and Specific Learning Disabilities, were 60.6 percent and 59.5 percent white.

The intent that underlies these data is difficult to establish. Maybe black children were not incorrectly identified as EMH because of race; and maybe white children have some unique nature/nurture mechanism that results in a high percentage of speech or language impairments and specific learning disabilities which black children have apparently been spared (IQ data which relies

---

[486]Profiles of Florida School Districts, Florida Department of Education, Education Information & Accountability Services, Statistical Report, Student Characteristics, 1996-1997, January 1998.

heavily on verbal behavior to the contrary). All this could be, but all is unlikely.

In 2006-2007 the EMH enrollment in Florida decreased to 24,026 of whom 49.4 percent were black, 32.4 percent white, and 15.5 percent Hispanic.[487] For the TMH category 39.3 percent were white and 35.1 percent black. As was done in many States, Florida abandoned the EMH category for a single intellectual disability category which combines all severity intellectual disability categories into one overall category. This relabeling does not necessarily change how children are educated but the change does decrease the percent of black disproportionality (by about five percent) because of the greater racial parity in the more severe categories. More recently, in 2016 in Florida, the percent of black children in the intellectual disabilities was reduced to 36.5. In spite of explicit regulatory goals to reduce disproportionality, black children are still overrepresented.[488]

Florida is not unique in the disproportionate identification of black children as having intellectual disabilities. In 1998, in comparison to 50.1 percent of black children identified as having mental retardations, the percent of black children in the mental retardation category was 59.1 percent in North Carolina, 60 percent in Georgia, 65.2 percent in Alabama, 68.5 percent in Louisiana, 71.4 percent in South Carolina 71.4 percent in Mississippi, and 78.1 percent in Louisiana. In 1998, overall, 34.3 percent of the children identified as having mental retardation were black (given a black 6 to 21 population of 14.8 percent).[489] These percentages were for all levels of mental retardation so that the percentage of children in the EMR category would have been larger. There is an interesting similarity in the percent of black children identified as having mental retardation in 1998 (34.3 percent) and the percent of black inmates executed between 1976 and 2020 also 34.2 percent).

---

[487]Profiles of Florida School Districts 2006-2007, Student and Staff Data, Florida Department of Education, May, 2008.
[488]Data source:
http://www.fldoe.org/core/fileparse.php/7584/urlt/MPES.xls
[489]Twenty-Second Annual Report to Congress on the Implementation of the Individuals with Disabilities Education Act, Appendix A

In the United States, in 1991, the death row population was 2,507.[490] Of these, 1,306 were white (51.3 percent), 986 black (38.7 percent), and 181 Hispanic (7.1 percent). In the Fall of 2019, the death row population was 2,639.[491] Of these 1,112 were white (42.1 percent), 1,100 black (41.7 percent) and 351 Latino/Latina (13.3 percent). The change from 1991 to 2019 has been a decrease of white offenders on death row, an increase, of black offenders, and a significant increase in the percent of Latino/Latina prisoners on death row.[492]

As with executions (and Texas) death row data is skewed. California alone accounts for 27 percent of all those on death row. The five States with the largest death row populations account for 61 percent of all death row prisoners. Death row data is quixotic. In California, in spite of the large number on death row, the likelihood that no one will ever be executed is small. As of 2019 there were 727 offenders on death (36 percent black) in comparison to 586 in 2000.[493] Execution is not the vehicle for exiting death row in California but death by natural causes (79 since 1978), suicide (26) and assorted other deaths (11) have supplanted execution. There have been 120 non-execution deaths on death row in California since 1978 in comparison to 13 executions (Clarence Allen being the last in 2006).

---

[490]https://www.naacpldf.org/wp-content/uploads/DRUSA_1991_Winter.pdf
[491]https://www.naacpldf.org/wp-content/uploads/DRUSAFall2019.pdf
[492]Source: DEATH ROW U.S.A., A quarterly report by the Criminal Justice Project of the NAACP Legal Defense and Educational Fund, Inc., Deborah Fins, Esq. Consultant to the Criminal Justice Project NAACP Legal Defense and Educational Fund, Inc. at https://www.naacpldf.org/wp-content/uploads/DRUSAWinter2020.pdf
[493]December 2001, NCJ 190598

10. Selection, Exoneration, Execution

"Colored Men and Hombres Aqui"[494]

Pete Hernandez

Jury selection has provided compelling data showing invidious intent and some of the more incredulous explanations for what is said to be racially neutral juror selection. For statistical chutzpah in juror selection, a case in 1950 Texas illustrates not only a clear pattern of invidious intent but how data, no matter how compelling, is easily dismissed. Pete Hernandez, age 26, was insulted by Joe Espinosa in a Café in Edna, Texas, retrieved a rifle, returned 20 minutes later and shot Espinosa in the heart. There was little doubt about his guilt. He was tried and convicted in 1951 by an all-white jury and sentenced to life in prison for murdering Espinosa. One of the focal points of Hernandez's appeal was that there were no Hispanics on his jury. His appeal was rejected based on the theory that the equal protection clause of the Fourteenth Amendment "recognized only two classes as coming within that guarantee: the white race, comprising one class, and the Negro race, comprising the other class."

Hernandez's all-white jury, according to the court, did not violate the Constitution because Mexican people are "white people of Spanish descent" and "to say that members of the various nationalities and groups composing the white race must be represented on grand and petit juries would destroy our jury system, for it would be impossible to meet such requirement."[495] The fact that there were no white persons of Mexican descent on juries for over 25 years, according to Texas' courts, was the result of chance rather than invidious intent. The Supreme Court ruled that the jury selection system in Texas was fair on its face and the law was not the problem; the problem was the administration of the law to exclude "otherwise eligible persons from jury service

---

[494]See an excellent article entitled The Message of Gustavo Garcia by Steve A. Peirce in the San Antonio Lawyer, May-June, 2014.
[495]Texas Court of Criminal Appeals, 1952, 251 S.W.2d 531

solely because of their ancestry or national origin is discrimination prohibited by the Fourteenth Amendment."[496]

The Supreme Court acknowledged the possibility that chance could play a role in jury selection "but it taxes our credulity to say that mere chance resulted in their being no members of this class among the over six thousand jurors called in the past 25 years." The idea that race/ethnicity was not a factor in jury selection might also have been contraindicated by the two separate restrooms in the Jackson County courthouse where the case was being tried. One sign cautioned that one of the restrooms was for "Colored Men" followed by "Hombres Aqui." How difficult it is, when discriminating, to take care of every loose end, much less a restroom sign revealing segregative intent. Pete Hernandez was eventually retried with a jury that included two Mexican Americans and convicted.

James Kirkland Batson

There is no way to eradicate what a judge or jury might think; or whether the underlying intent of an action was the result of racial bias. In particular, every Atkins claim is tainted by a history of racial bias that a black claimant experiences in the educational process and, following a long journey of *de jure* and *de facto* segregation, strategies to dismiss the need to award lesser culpability. Peremptory challenges is often revealing of invidious intent and racial bias...sometimes. If jury selection is suspect, so to must the racial intent of jurists when considering intellectual disability and lesser culpability.

The Supreme Court made this clear when deciding that James Kirkland Batson was not given a fair trial because the prosecution used peremptory challenges to strike all four black members from the venire (the panel selected from the State's master list of eligible jurors) for his 1983 trial.[497] Prior to Batson v. Kentucky, in 1986, instances of individual discrimination in the selection of

---

[496] Hernandez v. Texas, 347 U.S. 475 (1954)
[497] Batson v. Kentucky, 476 U.S. 79 (1986)

jurors was insufficient to prove purposeful discrimination but rather the requirement was the "system as a whole was being perverted" as decided by the Supreme Court in Swain v. Alabama in 1965. [498] In Alabama, at the time, black citizens were included in the venire but were "always" (at least since 1950 or so) excluded from petit jury selection.[499]

Before *Batson* Robert Swain, who was black, was sentenced to death for the 1962 rape of a seventeen-year-old white girl in Talladega County. He appealed his death penalty decision because of the exclusion of six black members from the venire to serve as jury members. The Supreme Court of Alabama touted the fairness of the venire selection but believed that peremptory challenges were a sacred right and to challenge this would undermine the jury selection process. Even if there was purposeful discrimination under the Fourteenth Amendment, according to the Alabama court, there was insufficient evidence to show a systematic striking of black jurors in the county.

The Supreme Court agreed with Alabama, in *Swain* in 1963, and offered the high-minded explanation that "In the light of the purpose of the peremptory system and the function it serves in a pluralistic society in connection with the institution of jury trial, we cannot hold that the Constitution requires an examination of the prosecutor's reasons for the exercise of his challenges in any given case."[500] The Court decided that the prohibition against racial bias involved the selection of the venire and not the selection of the actual jury from the pool. By this reasoning systematic racial bias in the selection of the venire was prohibited but not peremptory challenges.

The Supreme Court's footwork for circumventing the obvious fact that the system as a whole was "perverted" is artful. The Court acknowledged that jurors were rarely (just short of never) selected as jurors "But the responsibility of the prosecutor is not illuminated in this record. There is no allegation or explanation,

---

[498]Swain v. Alabama, 380 U.S. 202 (1965)
[499]Swain v. State, Supreme Court of Alabama, 156 So. 2d 368 (1963)
[500]*Ibid.*

and hence no opportunity for the State to rebut, as to when, why and under what circumstances in cases previous to this one the prosecutor used his strikes to remove Negroes. In short, petitioner has not laid the proper predicate for attacking the peremptory strikes as they were used in this case. Petitioner has the burden of proof and he has failed to carry it." Swain's sentence was vacated in 1972[501] by the Supreme Court following Furman v. Georgia on the same date (June 29, 1972) as a result of deficiencies in the death penalty jurisprudence as a whole and not his jury selection. In 1973 he was resentenced by the Supreme Court of Alabama to a life.[502]

The partial undoing of *Swain* was the result of James Batson's trial for burglary and receiving stolen property in Jefferson County, Kentucky. For Batson, who was black, this was not so much a question of evidence, there seemed little doubt that Batson was guilty, but about the Sixth (jury selection) and Fourteenth (equal rights) Amendments. The Supreme Court reversed *Swain* and the evidentiary burden placed on the defendant to the extent that peremptory challenges can be used "for any reason" providing that the reason "is related to his [the prosecutor] view concerning the outcome of the case to be tried." A defendant is not entitled to a jury of only members of his or her race, but "the Equal Protection Clause forbids the prosecutor to challenge potential jurors solely on account of their race or on the assumption that black jurors as a group will be unable impartially to consider the State's case against a black defendant."[503] Later, in Foster v. Chatman in 2016, the "reason" for a challenge had to be applied to all races on equal terms.[504]

What is known as a Batson challenge entails first making a prima facie case showing purposeful discrimination, and then shifting the burden to the proponent of the strike to provide a neutral explanation. The trial judge's experience can be used to determine whether peremptory challenges give rise to a *prima facie* case of purposeful racial discrimination. A *prima facie* case showing

---

[501]Swain v. Alabama, 408 U.S. 936, June. 29, 1972.
[502]Swain v. State, Supreme Court of Alabama, 274 So. 2d 305 (1973)
[503]Batson v. Kentucky, 476 U.S. 79 (1986)
[504]Foster v. Chatman, Warden, May 23, 2016

discriminatory purpose can be the result of disproportionate impact, non neutral selection procedures, and "facts and any other relevant circumstances raise an inference that the prosecutor used peremptory challenges to exclude the veniremen from the petit jury on account of their race."[505] Following a *prima facie* case the second step shifts the burden of proof "to the state to rebut the presumption of unconstitutional action by showing that permissible racially neutral selection criteria and procedures have produced the monochromatic result."[506]

In *Batson* the Court ordered that if a neutral explanation is provided but is not credible showing purposeful discrimination, the conviction must be reversed. Credibility is a leaky boat but the Court did say that "The prosecutor may not rebut a prima facie showing by stating that he challenged the jurors on the assumption that they would be partial to the defendant because of their shared race or by affirming his good faith in individual selections."[507]

The third step in a Batson challenge requires the court to determine whether or not purposeful discrimination occurred. In Title VII (the Civil Rights Act of 1964) employment claims this step allows the employee to rebut the neutral claim by showing that it was a pretext for invidious discrimination. [508] The Court did not decide that the peremptory challenges used by the prosecution were at fault but that the trial court was in error by not requiring a racial neutral explanation for the challenges. Following the 1986 decision the case was remanded. Batson, who was serving a 20-year prison term for the burglary, pleaded guilty and was resentenced to a five-year term.

Thomas Joe Miller-El

---

[505]Batson v. Kentucky, 476 U.S. 79 (1986)
[506]Washington v. Davis, 426 U.S. 229 (1976)
[507]*Ibid.*
[508]McDonnell v. Green, 411 U.S. 792 (1973)

Thomas Joe Miller-El was sentenced to death for a Holiday Inn robbery and murder of 25 year-old Douglas Walker in Irving, Texas in 1985. During jury selection peremptory strikes were used to reject 10 black venirepersons. In all, 19 of the 20 black venire members were rejected from the 108 member venire panel. Miller-El's defense believed that the use of peremptory strikes was the result of purposeful discrimination.

The history of executions in the United States, along with all other data relating to race, does suggest "a clear pattern, unexplainable on grounds other than race, emerges from the effect of the state action even when the governing legislation appears neutral on its face." [509] Factors that can be used to determine credibility include "the prosecutor's demeanor; by how reasonable, or how improbable, the explanations are; and by whether the proffered rationale has some basis in accepted trial strategy." [510]

Miller-El's appeal rested on the third Batson test of credibility. He contended that there was a history of discrimination in the prosecutor's office. The defense believed that excluding black citizens from jury selection was the "unofficial policy," [511] and there were similarities between non-black venire members selected and black members who were struck from jury selection. Miller-El's appeal also observed that the process of jury selection was unique to Texas. Harkening back to the unrelenting strategies to thwart desegregation following Brown in 1954, States and prosecutors have been no less creative when selecting jurors or, more precisely, to avoid selecting black jurors. One technique, that few would even imagine, is known as "jury shuffling" or, more poignantly, the "Texas shuffle" which, as explained by the Supreme Court, entails

> **the prosecution's use of a Texas criminal procedure practice known as jury shuffling. This practice permits parties to rearrange the order in which members of the venire are**

[509] Arlington Heights v. Metropolitan Housing Corp., 429 U.S. 252 (1977)
[510] Miller-El v. Cockrell, 537 U.S. 322 (2003)
[511] Miller-El v. Dretke, United States Court of Appeals for the Fifth Circuit, NO. 00-10784, 2004.

examined so as to increase the likelihood that visually preferable venire members will be moved forward and empanelled. With no information about the prospective jurors other than their appearance, the party requesting the procedure literally shuffles the juror cards, and the venire members are then reseated in the new order.[512]

Because jurors who are "shuffled" to the back, the likelihood they will be questioned to serve is decreased. Miller-El was tried and sentenced to death. Prior to trial in 1986, 10 of 11 eligible African-Americans were excluded from serving via peremptory challenges (and 9 were excused for cause). The trial court, using the standard before the *Batson* decision, found no discrimination in the selection of jurors. Following the 1986 Batson decision and guidelines for evaluating claims (a *prima facie* case, race neutral explanations and proof by the defendant of purposeful discrimination) the Texas appellate court, in 1988, remanded the case to the trial court.[513] In 1989 the trail court found that Miller-El had not even met the first prong of the three-part test for establishing a *prima facie* case. In 1993 the Texas appellate court agreed with this decision.

In 2003 the Supreme Court reversed and remanded the decision because the reasons for excluding black members also pertained to white members, and the process of jury shuffling was suspect.[514] The Court found the finding by trial court "that there was not even the inference of discrimination to support a prima facie case" was less than credible and a "clear error." Such is the nature of discrimination: The trial court was not credible when determining credibility.

---

[512]Miller-El v. Cockrell (01-7662) 537 U.S. 322 (2003)
[513]Miller-El v. State, 748 S.W.2d 459, 461 (Tex. Crim. App. 1988)
[514]Miller-El v. Cockrell (01-7662) 537 U.S. 322 (2003)

The Fifth Circuit Court of Appeals found, in 2004, no discrimination by interpreting the Antiterrorism and Effective Death Penalty Act of 1996 to show that this conclusion was not "an unreasonable determination of the facts in light of the evidence presented in the State court proceeding." Miller-El failed to show purposeful discrimination by clear and convincing evidence. The Supreme Court again disagreed and decided, in 2005, that the Fifth Circuit's conclusion regarding purposeful discrimination "unsupportable as the 'dismissive and strained interpretation' of his evidence that we disapproved when we decided Miller-El was entitled to a certificate of appealability." The Court further concluded that "The prosecutors' chosen race-neutral reasons for the strikes do not hold up and are so far at odds with the evidence that pretext is the fair conclusion, indicating the very discrimination the explanations were meant to deny." In 2008 Miller-El was resentenced to life in prison.

Allen Snyder

Allen Snyder was tried by an all-white jury in 1996 for the stabbing and murder of Howard Wilson who was on a first date with Snyder's estranged wife in 1995 in a New Orleans suburb. He was tried in 1996 and sentenced to death. During the initial juror selection 36 prospective jurors were considered. Of the five black potential jury members available, all were rejected. The Supreme Court of Louisiana denied his Batson claim of racial bias in jury selection in 2005. The Court believed that the explanation for the strike of one black juror was implausible, and the trial court failed to consider the reasoning for the challenge. In 2012 Snyder was convicted of second-degree murder and sentenced "to life imprisonment at hard labor, without benefit of parole, probation, or suspension of sentence." If he couldn't be executed, Louisiana had a plan B. He is currently serving his sentence in the "Angola" Louisiana Penitentiary.

The task for determining invidious intent is difficult and often impossible. The United States is good at racism and neither children nor adults can match the guile, legal maneuverings, and ability to stigmatize, segregate and discriminate— and for Atkins claims, to feign honor to the Eighth Amendment. There are, many decades after *Brown*, schools operating under court jurisdiction because they have not achieved unitary status. There are many schools that are completely segregated as a result of prior segregation and discrimination but this segregation cannot be traced to a current and identifiable invidious intent. The suggestion is that *de facto* segregation is more a mysterious apparition that is void of history. This is not dissimilar from the idea that and Atkins claim can be evaluated sans racial bias by adhering to an easily misinterpreted definition. Invidious intent is a slippery fish.

Marcus Erik Robinson

The 2009 Racial Justice Act (Senate Bill 461) in North Carolina was, for four years while it lasted, one of the few attempts to eliminate racial bias in jury selection.[515] The Act provided that racial intent could be established if "race was a significant factor in decisions to seek or impose the sentence of death in the county, the prosecutorial district, the judicial division, or the State at the time the death sentence was sought or imposed." Evidence of racial intent could include testimony that "death sentences were sought or imposed significantly more frequently upon persons of one race," and "race was a significant factor in decisions to exercise peremptory challenges during jury selection."

Marcus Erik Robinson was sentenced to death in 1994 in North Carolina for the murder of 17 year old Erik Tornblom by a shotgun blast to the head during a robbery.[516] The selection of jurors was Robinson's basis for racial bias. Nine peremptory challenges were made when selecting jurors, four involving 28 potential white jury members and five of 10 potential black jury members. As a result 50 percent of the black and 14 percent of the white venire members were peremptorily excused. One black was excused

---

[515]General Assembly of North Carolina, Senate Bill 461, 2009, § 15A-2011, Proof of racial discrimination
[516]State of North Carolina v. Marcus Reymond Robinson, Superior Court, Cumberland County, April 20, 2012

because of "public drunkenness while two white venire members with driving intoxication convictions were not." In the end, the court found that race was a significant factor in the peremptory striking of black venire members. Having established a statistical basis for the disproportionate striking of black venire members, the burden shifted to the State to rebut this evidence which the prosecution was not able to do. The court observed that "Prosecutors intentionally used the race of venire members as a significant factor in decisions to exercise peremptory strikes in capital cases." One statistical tidbit added a new dimension to probability and statistics. While most researchers are satisfied with the five percent or one percent level (.05 or .01 levels) the court cited statistics which showed that prosecutors struck 56 percent of black venire members but 24.8 percent of all others eligible for jury selection which was significant at the <.001. The court then observed that the probability of this occurring by chance was "less than one in 10,000,000,000,000,000,000,000,000,000,000,000." The court vacated his death sentence and re-sentenced Robison to life without the possibility of parole.[517]

In addition to Robinson, other cases in North Carolina resulted in vacated death sentences because race was a factor when selecting jurors.[518] In 1998 Tilmon Golphin was convicted for the 1997 murders of Edward Lowery and David Hathcock. During jury selection 5 of 7 black jurors were excused in comparison to 24 of 67 white jurors. In 2000, Christina Walters was convicted in 1998 for the murder of Susan Moore and Tracey Lambert. During her jury selection 10 of 19 black jurors were excused but only 4 of 27 white jurors. Quintel Augustine was convicted for the 2001 murder of Roy Gene Turner and sentenced to death in 2002. During his jury selection all five black venire members were excused. The North Carolina Superior Court vacated the death sentences of all three defendants because prosecutors relied on race, supported by "facially unbelievable" evidence, pretextual explanations, and "incredible" reasons, to rationalize the

---

[517]*Ibid.*
[518]State of North Carolina v. Tilmon Golphin, Christina Walters, and Quintel Augustine, 2012

disproportionate peremptory strikes of black venire members in death penalty cases.

In 2013, the Racial Justice Act was repealed because of the apparent belief that the statute was tantamount to eliminating the death penalty as a form of punishment. As of April, 2019, there are 141 offenders on North Carolina's death row of whom 78 (55.3 percent) are black.[519] According to the U.S. Census in 2017 the Black or African American population in North Carolina was 22.2 percent. Of the 43 executions since 1984, 13 (30.2 percent) have been for black offenders suggesting a greater degree of racial consciousness for executions but less so for seeking the death penalty for black defendants or at least the percent of black offenders on death row. Of the 269 prisoners removed from death row in North Carolina since 1977, beginning with the suicide of Daniel Webster in 1977, approximately 50 percent were black. Most were removed because of resentencing to life (primarily because of court ordered resentencing, vacated sentences, Atkins claims, and the Racial Justice Act). Of those removed because of resentencing, approximately 50 percent (69) have been black inmates.[520] With legal challenges pending there has not been an execution in North Carolina since that of Samuel R. Flippen in 2006. There are currently (June 2019) 142 offenders on death row the majority of whom (54.9 percent) are black.[521] Of the 43 executions in North Carolina, 13 or 30.2 percent have been black offenders.

Willie Horne and others

Considering the various dimensions of invidious intent, such as juror selection, can obscure the overwhelming and collective nature of racism and death penalty jurisprudence. For defendants

---

[519]https://www.ncdps.gov/adult-corrections/prisons/death-penalty/death-row-roster
[520]https://www.ncdps.gov/our-organization/adult-correction/prisons/death-penalty/list-removed-death-row
[521]https://www.ncdps.gov/adult-corrections/prisons/death-penalty/death-row-roster

such as Freddie Lee Hall "all of the circumstances that bear upon the issue of racial animosity" also include racial issues when Hall was a child, his education or lack thereof, the reasons for seeking the death penalty by the prosecution, the crime itself, the victim, juror selection, jury sentencing recommendation, jury vote, the climate of racial bias at trial, racial bias in the imposition of the death penalty, and racial bias when interpreting intellectual disability as a child and as an adult.

Because of race and the fact that providing special services for black children was hardly a priority in Florida—in 1963 four black teenagers were jailed and sent to reform school for ordering a hamburger and coke at a Woolworth on King Street in St. Augustine, Florida—black children were segregated for the simple reason that they were deemed inferior (and not worthy of being allowed to order a hamburger at a public lunch counter). Florida was not always kind to black teenagers;
and even less so for black adults.

Between 1950 and the execution of Henry Tillman, white, and the execution by electrocution of Blake Emmet (white) in 1964 there were 61 executions in Florida of whom 39 were black (63.9 percent). During that time frame there were 12 executions for rape. Except for one all were black.[522] In 1959 alone three black men were executed for rape (Willie Horne, Sam Odom and John Paul). The governor at the time was Leroy Collins who was considered a moderate and was in favor of desegregation. Collins was opposed to the death penalty and did commute a number of death sentences while in office but not for Willie Horne whose victim was white. The legislature in Florida was not inclined to end the death penalty for fear that this would renew lynchings.

More Florida racial history: in 1949 four black men were accused of raping a white woman in Groveland, Lake County, Florida just west of Orlando. Following the reported rape of Norma Padgett black homes were burned and property stolen. Shortly thereafter

---

[522]Espy, M. Watt, and John Ortiz Smykla. Executions in the United States, 1608-2002: The ESPY File. ICPSR08451-v5. Ann Arbor, MI: Inter-university Consortium for Political and Social Research

Ernest Thomas was lynched (shot by a deputized "posse" which is a euphemism for "deputized mob"). According to the Orlando Sentinel (April 17, 2017) Thomas "fled to the Panhandle, where he was hunted down by a posse of 1,000 men and fatally shot more than 400 times."

In 1951 one of the Groveland Four, Samuel Shepherd, was executed by Sheriff Willis McCall while handcuffed to Walter Irvin who was also shot but survived. Supposedly, both attempted to escape while being transported by the Sheriff in 1951. Irvin's troubles were not over. He would again stand trial but refused to say he raped Norma Padgett. No one other than Thurgood Marshall had said that, for a plea of guilty, and a sentence of life in prison would be given. This was rejected by Irvin and he was convicted and sentenced to death as expected. Governor Collins commuted his sentence in 1955. Norma Padgett later recanted that the rape never happened. Irvin was paroled in 1968 and died of a heart attack shortly thereafter. Charles Greenlee, who was 16 when the supposed rape occurred, was sentenced to life and paroled after 12 years in prison.

For black offenders there have always been special circumstances for the death penalty as when the victim or reported victim is white. Likewise, there are special rules for identifying black children with intellectual disabilities. Freddie Lee Hall should have been identified as having a disability as a child but there was no need for segregating young Hall in that prevailing school segregation was working nicely. After school desegregation and the rise of EMR as a strategy to segregate, Hall most certainly would have been identified as EMH but for almost forty years while Hall was on death row, before his death sentence was vacated, a blind eye was given the history of segregation and education, how children were first not identified then disproportionally identified as having intellectual disabilities, and professing a plain interpretation of the law demanded adherence to a
fixed IQ cutoff score of 70, a score tainted by racial shortcomings.

Mitchell Adams

The elements required for invidious intent cited in *Arlington Heights* by the Supreme Court are often difficult to establish, especially for Atkins claims, because departures from normal procedures, contemporary statements, and historical background (cited in *Arlington*) are given little consideration or dismissed entirely. For Atkins claims departures from normal procedures and accompanying statements are the norm. Professional guidelines should suggest a normal procedure but developmental data is deemed important when not showing intellectual disability, or ignored when showing intellectual disability. Great importance is given IQ when not showing intellectual disability but these data are dismissed because of malingering, lack of motivation, lack of education, etc. when indicating subaverage intellectual ability. The various guidelines for identifying intellectual disability are ignored in favor of stereotypic impressions of what someone with an intellectual disability can and cannot do. Common sense would indicate that teachers and other professionals should provide insights into the intellectual ability of an Atkins claimant but somehow prison officials or behavior on death row provide the most salient data.

The execution of blacks, legal or otherwise, follows a course similar to that of slavery to Jim Crow laws, and to *de jure* and *de facto* segregation. The disproportionate percent of black offenders on death row and black executions is high but not at the level of lynchings identified in the Historic American Lynching database (or Project HAL) between 1882 and 1930.[523] Of the 2,806 victims, 2,462 were black (87.7 percent). For victims where rape was cited as at least part of the offense—which included rape, attempted rape, rape & murder, assaulted girl (rape), attacked woman (rape), Criminal assault (rape), etc.—750 or 95.3 percent were black. Of the 223 victims lynched for "attempted rape," the euphemism for any real or perceived slight, 218 were black (97.7percent).

The only explanation for the collective thought process for rationalizing a lynching is that this barbarism is somehow

---

[523]http://people.uncw.edu/hinese/HAL/HAL%20Web%20Page.htm

righteous and good. In December of 1904 eight black prisoners were taken from the Barnwell, South Carolina jail by a white mob and lynched ("riddled with bullets" according to one report). The crime was, for the most part, for being black. Two of the victims were thought to have participated in the murder of a white man while the other six were in the wrong place at the wrong time and black. Included among the eight victims was Mitchell Adams, 65, who was found with "nine balls in his body." Sometimes intent is difficult to establish but for the Barnwell eight and Mitchell Adams there is little doubt of the racial intent.

Jerome Bowden

Before Georgia's 1988 statute that prohibited the execution of the mentally retarded (well before *Atkins* in 2002), a black defendant faced multiple racial obstacles during trial and sentencing including a history of racism in virtually all areas of life, a showing of mental retardation that might enhance the likelihood of execution (as suggested in *Atkins*), the ineffectiveness of counsel to offer appropriate mitigation, and the enhanced probability that the State would seek the death penalty when the victim was white and the defendant black. In Georgia no white offender has ever been executed for the murder of a black victim. Of the 76 (of whom 28 were black) executions in Georgia 9 have been when the victim and offender were black, 19 executions when the offender was black and the victim white; and 48 when both offender and victim were white. As of 2020 there were 41 inmates on death row in Georgia of whom 20 or 48.8 percent were black. In contrast, since the electrocution of John Smith in 1983 and the lethal injection of Donnie Lance, white, on January 29, 2020, 28 or 36.8 percent have been black.[524] As previously discussed the difference between the percent of black inmates on death row and the percent of black prisoners executed can be attributed, in part, to the increased scrutiny of convictions for capital murder upon appeal.

---

[524]Georgia Department of Corrections at http://www.dcor.state.ga.us/sites/all/themes/gdc/pdf/Profile_death_row_2020_01.pdf

In 1976 Jerome Bowden and an accomplice burglarized the home of 55-year-old Kathryn Stryker of Columbus, Georgia. Bowden attacked and murdered Ms. Bowden and then assaulted Stryker's seventy-six year old mother. During jury selection all black potential jurors were rejected by peremptory challenges. This issue was dismissed on appeal because "at trial, petitioner did not object to the manner in which the prosecutor exercised the State's peremptory challenges." Bowden also claimed ineffective counsel because readily available evidence of mental retardation was not presented during trial. Records indicated that Bowden had an IQ of 59, a report by a school psychologist indicated he was in the low mild mental retardation range, he was employed for a period of time in a sheltered workshop, and he was in special education.[525] While on death row he was given another IQ test which resulted in a score of 65.

The United States Court of Appeals for the 11th District decided that "the jury had ample opportunity to observe Bowden and no doubt drew the same conclusion about his mental state as it would have drawn had it been given the additional evidence now before us. In sum, there is no reason to believe that the jury on the basis of this additional evidence of Bowden's low intelligence would have recommended a different sentence. We conclude, as the Georgia courts have, that 'Bowden's trial counsel easily met the test of reasonably effective counsel.'"[526] Notwithstanding the failure of counsel to present all relevant evidence and the utmost certainty that he did meet the criteria for intellectual disability, Bowden was executed in 1986 by lethal injection.[527] For Bowden, before the 1988 Georgia statute prohibiting the execution of the mentally retarded, the overriding concern was not necessarily presenting all the relevant evidence but that he was black and murdered a white woman, and he had the misfortune to commit this horrendous act in Georgia.

---

[525]Bowden v. Kemp, 793 F.2d 273 (11th Cir. 1986)
[526]Bowden v. Francis, 733 F.2d 740, 1984
[527]*Ibid.*

Timothy Tyrone Foster

A claim of intellectual disability cannot be viewed by focusing on the trees (the criteria for intellectual disability) but ignoring the forest ("circumstantial and direct evidence of intent"). For those seeking Atkins relief an essential question is whether an unfavorable Atkins decision for a defendant can be tainted by an explicit showing of invidious intent.

Timothy Tyrone Foster was sentenced to death in 1987 by an all-white jury in Georgia for the 1986 sexual assault and strangulation of 79-year-old Queen Madge White in Rome, Georgia. His claim of mental retardation was rejected but his Batson challenge, the use of peremptory challenges, persisted for almost 30 years. The State had used peremptory challenges to strike four prospective black jurors.[528] The Supreme Court of Georgia concluded that Foster's Batson challenge was without merit. Although Foster had made a prima facie case, the State successfully rebutted this case because the explanations for the peremptory strikes were "neutral" and "reasonable specific."

Eventually the jury venire list used by the prosecution was obtained by the Georgia Open Records Act which contradicted the racial neutral explanations offered by the prosecution and the finding of non-purposeful discrimination by the trial court. The prosecutor's notes showed that all black jurors were identified by race and had been listed as "N" (for "No" or something more descriptive) before the challenges were made. The Supreme Court found that the racial neutral explanations were less than truthful. For example, the prosecution asserted that a black juror was excused because of membership in the Church of Christ and then argued that three white members were excused for the same reason when, in fact, this was not the case.

The less than believable reason given by the prosecution for focusing on black jurors was "an effort to develop and maintain a detailed account should the prosecution need a defense against any suggestion that its reasons were pretextual." The Supreme

---

[528]Foster v. Chatman, Warden, May 23, 2016

Court commented that this "argument, having never before been raised in the 30 years since Foster's trial, 'reeks of afterthought.' And the focus on race in the prosecution's file plainly demonstrates a concerted effort to keep black prospective jurors off the jury." The Supreme Court rejected Georgia's race neutral explanations and, more importantly, added an element of internal consistency to Batson claims. Prosecutors may be able to provide "any reason" for a peremptory challenge but the reason must be consistent for all jurors. If age is the reason for rejecting a black juror, it must be used for all jurors. If the reason for striking a black juror is divorce, this reasoning must be used for all possible jurors otherwise the inconsistency "undermines the justifications proffered by the State to the trial court for the strike." One additional point made by the Court is that the Constitution is not simply intolerant of a pattern of racial bias but for any and all racial bias peremptory challenges so that "Two peremptory strikes on the basis of race are two more than the Constitution allows."

In Foster v. Chatman in 2016, the Supreme Court did exactly what was suggested in Arlington Heights in 1977 by "Determining whether invidious discriminatory purpose was a motivating factor" which "demands a sensitive inquiry into such circumstantial and direct evidence of intent as may be available." Although the State provided racially neutral explanations for striking black jurors in *Foster*, the inquiry was less than sensitive. The Court explained that "the focus on race in the prosecution's file plainly demonstrates a concerted effort to keep black prospective jurors off the jury." Without the newly discovered notes showing racial bias, the nonracial explanation for juror selection offered by the prosecution would have been accepted as it was by the trial court and the Supreme Court of Georgia. The Supreme Court considered all the evidence, including handwritten notes, and decided that "Our independent examination of the record, however, reveals that much of the reasoning provided by" the district attorney "has no grounding in fact." The Court then referred to the nonracial explanations offered as "elaborate" but "misrepresentations" nonetheless.

The Supreme Court's vote in *Foster* of 7 to 1 is a clear message that the Court believed the intent of the prosecution was racially motivated. Nonetheless, Justice Thomas' dissent illustrates how, no matter the data, invidious intent is easily disbelieved...and disbelieved with conviction. Thomas stated that "The notion that this 'newly discovered evidence' could warrant relitigation of a *Batson* claim is flabbergasting" and that "The most obvious ground for deciding that Foster's claim lacked 'arguable merit' is that the Supreme Court of Georgia already considered that claim and rejected it decades ago." Apparently the other Justices were not flabbergasted by the "newly discovered evidence" and that "a sensitive inquiry" of available evidence was appropriate for determining invidious intent. The fact that Georgia had litigated this issue "decades ago" probably needs to be considered in light of the racial judicial climate in Georgia decades ago and the whole point for relitigation in 2016. All of this would come under the category of "history" as discussed in *Arlington Heights*.

In *Foster* the prosecution (the district attorney at the time is now deceased) was caught with its hand in the cookie jar of notes as it were because the evidence showed inconsistencies, misrepresentations and improbable explanations. *Foster* provides an inkling of the reasoning that underlies purposeful discrimination, but for many black claimants seeking relief under *Atkins,* the reasoning used to deny claims is just as discriminatory.

Unfortunately, for Atkins claims, the discovery of incriminating notes showing racial bias is extremely unlikely. Yet, for Foster, if racial bias occurred in jury selection, there is reason to assume that such bias would have tainted his Atkins claim. To this end the Supreme Court of Georgia decided that his subsequent IQ scores were the result of "depression and malingering" and that "his letter writing, newspaper reading, and sports activities all indicated that Foster did not meet the statutory definition of mental retardation."[529] Only this court knows how newspaper reading and sports activities became part of a statutory definition.

---

[529]Supreme Court of Georgia, Foster v. The State, No. S99P1800, Decided: January 18, 2000

For Foster there were three possible outcomes which included a new trial, vacating the death sentence for life in prison, or, as suggested by Justice Alito in his concurring opinion, "On remand, the Georgia Supreme Court is bound to accept that evaluation of the federal question, but whether that conclusion justifies relief under state *res judicata* law is a matter for that court to decide." In other words, the Georgia court could decide whether, on remand from the Supreme Court, Foster deserves relief for a decision that has already been decided. In 2017 he was removed from Georgia's death row (Georgia Diagnostic and Classification Prison), arrested thereafter, and sent to the Floyd County jail in Rome, Georgia where he is being held without bond awaiting retrial in Floyd County Superior Court (amidst a barrage of motions tentatively set for January of 2021). Although his Atkins claim was denied, the defense seeks to re-evaluate this issue because of the contention that this is a new case following the Supreme Court decision.[530]

Georgia does seem to be making headway for addressing racial bias in death penalty jurisprudence, but not so much in reducing racial disproportionality in the determination of intellectual disabilities for children. In 1998 over 18,000 black children were identified as mentally retarded (63.5 percent). During Foster's schooling in the late 1970s and 1980s the percent of black children in the mental retardation category was even greater. This does not mean that Foster would have been identified as EMR. This would depend on services available for black children and whether classification as EMR would achieve some segregation purpose. More recently, in 2016 intellectual disabilities was the most disproportionate special education category (55 percent were comprised of black children) according to the Georgia Department of Education data. These data are further complicated by a high public-school black enrollment of 44 percent in 2016 but very high (75 percent) white private school enrollment.

Blume and others found that in 2014, only one of nine Atkins claims in Georgia have been successful.[531] Georgia is one of the

---

[530]See the Rome News-Tribune, December 2, 2019

leaders in the identification of black children as having intellectual disabilities, but has mysteriously and conveniently solved the problem of intellectual disabilities for black Atkins claimants by suggesting that, for adults, the rules for determining intellectual disabilities no longer apply. There is also the implication that environment could be an important factor when deciding Atkins claims; that is, environment is unimportant for the identification of children but very important for Atkins claimants.

Elzie Ball

The American with Disabilities Act has important implications for Atkins claims in that the ADA definition of disability includes "a record of such an impairment" or "being regarded as having such an impairment." The Supreme Court has said that the ADA unambiguously applies to prisons and, therefore, one must assume that this application includes death row. Prison officials should extend considerable effort to ensure that the disability needs of prisoners are met on death row. California has by far the most considered policy concerning the ADA and prisoners but how ADA needs are met on death row is less apparent.

For Elzie Ball and several others on death row the ADA was not at the forefront of their treatment on death but their various needs were part of a claim of cruel and unusual punishment. For the disproportionate number of black offenders on death row, death row is often the ultimate and truly cruel and unusual punishment. This is then magnified by time on death row and various disabilities. Ball has been on death row at the Louisiana State Penitentiary (Angola or "the farm") following his conviction for killing a Budweiser delivery man during a robbery in 1997; Nathaniel Code was on death row after killing at least eight people; and James Magee was on death row following the killing of his estranged wife and 5-year old child. The plaintiffs claimed that prison officials violated "their rights under the Eighth

---

[531]From the Southern Education Foundation at http://www.southerneducation.org/Publications/Race-Ethnicity-State-Profiles/GA-State-Profile.aspx and file:///C:/Users/ed/Documents/private%20schools%20race.pdf

Amendment, ADA, ADAAA, and Rehabilitation Act by subjecting them to excessive heat, acting with deliberate indifference to their health and safety, and discriminating against them on the basis of their disabilities."[532]

Death row inmates at the Louisiana State Penitentiary in West Feliciana Parish were confined to cells 23 hours a day with "sink, mirror, toilet, bed, desk, and chair," but no windows or air conditioning. The ventilation system did not reduce the temperature, humidity or the heat index, and the 100 degree plus water temperature for daily showering provided no relief from the heat. In the hotter months, the cooler floor and fire ants were often preferred for sleeping than sweltering beds. The Middle District Court of Louisiana ruled that "Defendants disregarded the substantial risk of serious harm to Plaintiffs' health and safety. Accordingly, the Court concludes that Plaintiffs have met their burden of proving that Defendants acted with deliberate indifference. Thus, the Court concludes that the conditions of confinement at Angola's death row do not meet constitutional standards, and Defendants have violated the Eighth Amendment." The court also ruled that although the plaintiffs had a variety of medical conditions (e.g., high blood pressure, hypertension, obesity, hepatitis, depression, high cholesterol), they did not provide evidence that these conditions limited a major life activity such as "caring for oneself, performing manual tasks, seeing, hearing, eating, sleeping, walking, standing, sitting, reaching, lifting, bending, speaking, breathing, learning, reading, concentrating, thinking, communicating, interacting with others, and working." Yet, Ronald Yeskey was denied benefits when seeking a participation in a prison program but for the plaintiffs on death row sleeping and existing in abominable conditions were not considered "major life" activities. All this begs the question if a death row inmate had a record of intellectual disability, or a disability that was consistent with the Supreme Court's reasons for lesser culpability, would the District Court have prohibited the imposition of the death penalty under the ADA?

---

[532]See Ball v. LeBlanc, United States District Court, Middle District of Louisiana, Ruling and Order, 12/19/13.

Ralph Daniel Wright

As of 2020 there have been 167 exonerations from death row.[533]
Florida is the leader in the number of exonerations with 29,
followed by Illinois (20) which, as was discussed, has since
abandoned the death penalty,[534] Texas (13), Louisiana (11),
Oklahoma (10), North Carolina (10), Arizona (9), Ohio (9),
Pennsylvania (7), Alabama (6), Georgia (6), and California (5).[535]
Illinois no longer has the death penalty and for good reason
considering that there were 20 exonerations in comparison to 12
executions. Pennsylvania also exonerated 6 inmates in
comparison to 3 executions while Louisiana has had 11
exonerations and 28 executions.

For the extremely large number of inmates on death row in
California, few have been exonerated. The five exonerations in
California have been for three black, one American Indian or
Alaska Native, and one Latino inmates. One possibility for the
small number of exonerations, especially when compared to the
exceedingly large number of prisoners on death row, might be the
same glacial approach for enacting the death penalty. In Texas
there have been 13 exonerations (three black) in comparisons to
561 executions. Of the 167 exonerations listed in the Innocence
Project database, the reasons for exoneration included charges
dismissed, acquitted, pardoned, official misconduct, mistaken
witness identification, perjury or false accusation, etc.[536] Of the
167 exonerations cited, 87 (52.1 percent) were black.

---

[533]Death Penalty Information Center at
https://deathpenaltyinfo.org/policy-issues/innocence-database
[534]In 2017 the charges for Gabriel Solache, who had been on death row,
were dismissed
[535]From Innocence database at
https://deathpenaltyinfo.org/innocence?inno_name=&exonerated=&stat
e_innocence=8&race=All&dna=All&page=1

When race is a factor, often from the initial investigation of the crime to death sentence, the standard of proof is not necessarily a standard at all and the road to exoneration is not that complicated. In 2007 Paula O'Conner, white, and her 15-month-old baby were strangled to death. The State argued that Ralph Daniel Wright, black, had committed the murders to avoid child support and to continue his "bachelor lifestyle." The jury recommended death by a vote of 7 to 5. On May 11, 2017 the Supreme Court of Florida explained that "In this case, none of the evidence presented at trial directly tied Wright to the murders. Most of the State's evidence was intended to how that Wright had a motive to commit the murders and that other potential suspects did not."[537] In July of 2017 Wright was released from prison.

Wright was acquitted of murder because there was not a "moral certainty" (for guilt and not doubt) that Wright had committed the murders. Whether race was a factor during the investigation, or for not investigating other suspects, or in seeking the penalty, or the jury recommendation, or the sentence of death by the judge is not certain. What the Supreme Court of Florida did say was that suspicion alone would not sustain a guilty verdict. The court also stated that "no rational trier of fact could have found the existence of all the elements necessary to prove Wright guilty of the murders—specifically, the identity element—beyond a reasonable doubt." For Wright his guilt may have been influenced by the heinousness of the crime with an undercurrent of racial motive.

Of the 99 executed in Florida, from John Spenkelink's execution in 1979 to 2020, 28.3 percent have been black (28) compared to 36.9 percent black offenders (125 of 339[538]) on death row in Florida as 0f March, 2020. However, of the death row exonerations in Florida, 17 of the 29 have been black defendants (58.6 percent). Although black defendants have more exonerations than white defendants, the length of time from conviction to exoneration is

---

[536]https://deathpenaltyinfo.org/number-executions-state-and-region-1976
[537]Wright v. Florida, Supreme Court of Florida, SC14-2410, May 11, 2017
[538]March 15, 2020
http://www.dc.state.fl.us/OffenderSearch/deathrowroster.aspx

13.6 years for black exonerees in comparison to 9.2 years for white exonerees. Not only is racism a likely factor in wrongful conviction, but also in the length of time for determining that a conviction has been wrongful. [539]

As shown below the relationship in the United States between exonerations, death row and executions suggests greater judicial scrutiny regarding the many racial factors preceding a death sentence for capital murder: 52.1 percent of exonerations have been for black prisoners, death row is comprised of 42.1 percent black offenders[540], and 34.1 percent of those executed have been black.[541]

Exonerations, Death Row and Executions in the United States			
Race	Exonerations[542]	Death Row	Executions
Black	52,1% (87)	42.1% (1,103)	34.1% (517)
White	37.1% (62)	41.6% (1,089	57.8% (846)
Latino/Latina	9.0% (15)	13.5% (353)	8.5% (129)
Number	167	2,620[543]	1,517

---

[539]From Innocence database at https://deathpenaltyinfo.org/innocence?inno_name=&exonerated=&state_innocence=8&race=All&dna=All&page=1
[540]Source: DEATH ROW U.S.A., A quarterly report by the Criminal Justice Project of the NAACP Legal Defense and Educational Fund, Inc., Deborah Fins, Esq. Consultant to the Criminal Justice Project NAACP Legal Defense and Educational Fund, Inc. at https://www.naacpldf.org/wp-content/uploads/DRUSAWinter2020.pdf
[541]Death Penalty Information Center at https://deathpenaltyinfo.org/race-death-row-inmates-executed-1976
[542]From Innocence database
[543]This number includes States such as California where there has been a moratorium on executions

Of course, there are many possible reasons for the large number of black exonerations, the percentage of black inmates on death row, and the number of black executions. One explanation for these data might be attributed to invidious intent where more blacks are prosecuted for capital murder and convicted because, to some extent, of race. As already mentioned, race taints the prosecution of blacks from the race of judges, prosecutors, juries, juror selection, consideration of mitigating factors, constitutional issues such as those involving Atkins claims, and financial resources. Admittedly, the degree that the extent race is the cause is difficult to determine, especially when considering the ever confounding variables of prior segregation and discrimination.   However, there is an element of linearity from executions, to death row, to exonerations that is difficult to explain other than by race.

Henry Lee "Buddy" McCollum

One would think that following an exoneration life would be good and all problems solved, especially when the State provides financial compensation. Not necessarily. Henry McCollum was sentenced to death in 1984 for the rape and murder of Sabrina Buie, an 11-year old girl, in Red Springs, County, North Carolina. Following court errors he was tried again in 1991 and again sentenced to death following a jury recommendation. In a dissenting Supreme Court decision in 1994 Justice Blackmun opined that Henry "Buddy McCollum is mentally retarded. He has an IQ between 60 and 69 and the mental age of a 9-year old. He reads on a second grade level. This factor alone persuades me that the death penalty in his case is unconstitutional."[544] McCollum actually had a reported IQ of 51 and his half-brother an IQ of 49. In 2014 McCollum and his half-brother were exonerated based on DNA evidence[545] and each awarded $750,000. Alas, following "legal fees" and financial guidance of sorts, District Court judge Terrence Boyle, on October 23 of 2017, appointed a guardian *ad litem* to oversee his McCollum's financial situation. Consistent

---

[544] McCollum v. North Carolina, 512 U.S. 1254 (1994)
[545]North Carolina v. Henry Lee McCollum, Superior Court, September, 2, 2014.

with his intellectual level, McCollum was apparently satisfied with his various legal financial obligations. McCollum was also receiving SSI benefits and the court observed "That McCollum would qualify for SSI today raises a serious concern regarding his ability to manage his financial and personal affairs, despite the fact that McCollum has stated that he understands how to set aside money for rent and bills each month."[546]

Kenneth Earl Fults

From the beginning of the process from arrest to execution, including police, prosecutors, judges, juror selection and decision-making by all parties, race is a factor. Blacks account for approximately 7 to 9 percent of judges, less than 5 percent of elected prosecutors [547](as reported in a study by the Women Donors Network). Considering the racial history of many States, racial bias in jury selection, no matter how egregious, is not surprising.

In Georgia, for Kenneth Earl Fults, neither an Atkins claim nor juror comments prevented his execution. Georgia rejected Fults' claim of intellectual disability but had the foresight to consider evidence (as opposed to "disregard" as Florida did before *Hall* in 2014). The appellate court reasoned "the state habeas court found Mr. Fults' evidence to be not credible is not an indication, on this record, that it failed to follow the dictates of *Atkins*. As we read its order, the state habeas court characterized Mr. Fults' evidence as not credible with respect to the ultimate issue of mental retardation, and not as shorthand for utter disregard or disbelief." To support a claim of mental retardation, his defense showed IQ scores of 68 (when he was 20), 74, and 72. His reading level was reported to be at the fifth grade level and he had third-grade math skills. The State rejected this evidence because it "was

---

[546]Raymond Tarlton, as guardian ad litem for Henry Lee McCollum and J. Duane Gilliam, as guardian of the estate of LEON BROWN v. Town of Red Springs, United States District Court for the Eastern District of North Carolina Western Division, No; 5:15-CV-451-BO.
[547]See https://mic.com/articles/121919/79-percent-of-criminal-prosecutors-are-white-and-male#.T2do7Yajn

not credible or persuasive." The court noted that two of his scores were above 70 which suggested some indifference to the margin of error of five demanded by the Supreme Court. The prosecution believed that his IQ was actually higher, he was "street smart," and he could "make decisions and choices, and did not have to rely on someone to support him."[548] Thus a new definition of intelligence has emerged comprised, in part, of street smartness which was determined by an expert who was apparently *smart* in *street smartness*. Although street smartness was explained as being "able to survive on the street" an explanation of this explanation was not provided.

The problem found by the Supreme Court with Florida's interpretation of the definition of intellectual disability in 2014 was not so much rejecting his IQ scores, or his claim of intellectual disability, but not "considering" other relevant evidence of intellectual disability. A State can regard scores of less than 75 as not indicative of intellectual disability providing that the scores are not used to preclude the "consideration" of other relevant evidence such as adaptive behavior. This is done by many States because of the belief, or expressed belief, that low IQ scores are the result of malingering, lack of motivation, or simply not credible. The flaw in the Supreme Court's dictum is that the error of measurement requirement is easily bypassed by first considering scores and then finding the now-considered-scores not credible or persuasive.

Fults pleaded guilty to malice murder and felony murder of next-door neighbor Cathy Bounds in 1996. In 1997 the jury found that two aggravating circumstances (murder that was "outrageously and wantonly vile, horrible, or inhuman" committed during a kidnapping with bodily injury) and recommended a death sentence. In 2014 the United States Court of Appeals for the Eleventh District considered juror racism and his mental retardation claim. This court believed that Fults was not able to rebut the State court's contention that he was not mentally retarded by clear and convincing evidence.

---

[548]Fults v. Warden, United States Court of Appeals for the Eleventh District, Case: 12-13563 Date Filed: 08/26/2014

Fults' claim of racial bias by a juror was no more successful than his claim of mental retardation. In 2005 a sworn affidavit was produced with juror statements that included "I don't know if he ever killed anybody, but that nigger got just what should have happened" and "Once he pleaded guilty, I knew I would vote for the death penalty because that's what that nigger deserved." The appellate court denied his claim because "Mr. Fults, in sum, has failed to provide any specifics to the state or federal courts as to why the claim of racial prejudice relating to Mr. Buffington was not raised until 2005." The court also noted that the death penalty was not a "fundamental miscarriage of justice" because the assertion for racial bias was procedurally barred and no showing was made that the racial bias in question was responsible for the death sentence.[549] Fults was executed by lethal injection in Jackson, Georgia on April 11, 2016. Aside from the niceties of procedurally barred factors, the language used by jurors suggests some degree of racial bias, or maybe even a whole bunch of racial bias.

Contemporary statements supporting an invidious racial motive are rare but not uncommon, and even more rarely will public officials reveal the true basis for an action that is discriminatory. When contemporary statements do suggest invidious intent, as evidenced by the execution of Kenneth Faults, "contemporary statements by members of the decision making body" are easily dismissed.[550] Academics have been on the forefront for using non-experimental, correlational nonsense purporting to show, often very vocally and spouting all sorts of statistical significance gibberish, the intellectual inferiority of blacks via a mish-mash of IQ tests. Public officials are cautious or quickly learn to be cautious. In Larry P. v. Riles (1979), in California, State Education department officials testified that the disproportionate placement of "black and Chicano children in the E.M.R. classes accurately reflected the incidence of mental retardation among those

---

[549]Fults v. Warden, United States Court of Appeals for the Eleventh District, Case: 12-13563 Date Filed: 08/26/2014
[550]Arlington Heights v. Metropolitan Housing Dev. Corp., 429 U.S. 252 (1977)

children." The lesson learned by State officials everywhere from Larry P. was not that the disproportionate placement was improper but to be more circumspect when discussing the reasons for racial disproportionality.

When dealing with Atkins claims success is relative and, as with Brown v. Board of Education, not particularly speedy. Freddie Lee Hall had been on death row since 1978 and was unsuccessful to have mental retardation as a reason to reverse his death sentence. Following Atkins in 2002 and an evidentiary hearing in 2010, his Atkins claim was unsuccessful because of the strict cutoff IQ score of 70 used in Florida. In 2012 his appeal to the Supreme Court of Florida was unsuccessful because "we have concluded that because a defendant must establish all three elements of such a claim, the failure to establish any one element will end the inquiry." In 2014 the Supreme Court decided that the strict IQ cutoff was unconstitutional but did not conclude that Hall's death sentence was in error. After 38 years on death row Hall was finally successful when the Supreme Court of Florida decided that he was intellectually disabled, referencing three definitions no less, and could not be executed.[551] Success for an Atkins claim can be slow going. As of 2019 Hall resides at the Lake Correctional Institution where he is serving his sentence of life.

Data for Atkins claims are obviously not something that States openly present for all to inspect. What data that has been compiled is disturbing although consistent with the overwhelming "clear pattern" of invidious intent. According to a report by Blume and others, African Americans comprised 57 percent of Atkins claims of 232 adjudicated on merit.[552] Blume offers possible explanations for this finding, including cultural stereotypes, racial disadvantages, and the possibility that there might actually be more persons with intellectual disabilities on death row. What we do know is that a disproportionate number of black children are

---

[551]Hall v. State of Florida, SC10-1335, September 8, 2016
[552]Blume, John H.; Johnson, Sheri Lynn; and Seeds, Christopher, "An Empirical Look at Atkins v. Virginia and its Application in Capital Cases," 2009, *Cornell Law Faculty Publications.* Paper 7
http://scholarship.law.cornell.edu/facpub/7

identified as having intellectual disabilities, and there are many offenders on death row, especially African American defendants, who have a record of intellectual disability. Considering the extent of racial disproportionality in intellectual disabilities in childhood, and the high percent of blacks on death row in comparison to the percent of blacks in the general population, the fact that 57 percent of Atkins claims involved African Americans as found by Blume, and 57 percent of successful Atkins claims were for African Americans, is not all that surprising. In view of the racial disproportionality of childhood intellectual disabilities, and the racial inequities in the legal process resulting in a sentence of death, the number of Atkins claims and successful Atkins claims by black offenders would be expected.

The complexity of the death penalty and race is unique to each State but one conclusion that can be drawn is that many are sentenced to death and executed because of race. In Louisiana 47 of the 71 inmates (66.2 percent) on death row are black.[553] Yet, of those executed in Louisiana (28) 46.4 percent have been black (13). The number of black offenders on death row is not dissimilar from the disproportionate number of children (64.3 percent) classified as intellectually disabled in Louisiana in 2011.

According to Blume, 91 percent (11) of Atkins claims in Louisiana were for African Americans. The large number of black Atkins claims found by Blume in Louisiana is consistent with the large number of children identified as having mental retardation, and with data for death penalty reversals and exonerations. In an article examining death sentences and their reversals, Frank R. Baumgartner and Tim Lyman examined 241 death sentences in Louisiana since 1976[554]. Of these there were 127 reversals 79 were for black defendants (62.2 percent) and 9 exonerations (6 for black defendants). The Black or African American alone

---

[553]Source: DEATH ROW U.S.A., A quarterly report by the Criminal Justice Project of the NAACP Legal Defense and Educational Fund, Inc., Deborah Fins, Esq. Consultant to the Criminal Justice Project NAACP Legal Defense and Educational Fund, Inc. at https://www.naacpldf.org/wp-content/uploads/DRUSAWinter2020.pdf
[554]Louisiana Death-Sentenced Cases and Their Reversals, 1976-2015, The Journal of Race, Gender, and Poverty, Volume VII, p. 58-75

population in Louisiana in 2018 was 32.7 percent. For black children intellectual disability provides a handy explanation for prior segregation, discrimination and socio-economic disparities; for black adults the milieu giving rise to increased crime and capital murder, caused in no small part by segregation, discrimination and socio-economic disparities, are disingenuously when sentencing.

Race is an important factor when identifying children as having mental retardation, death penalty sentencing, Atkins claims, reversals and exonerations. Added to this is the importance of the victim's race. Of the 20,942 homicides committed in Louisiana since 1976, 72 percent have been for blacks, yet 79 percent of those executed have been when the victim is white.[555] In Louisiana the greatest probability that someone will be executed is when the victim is a white female, and the lowest probability is when the victim is a black male. In Louisiana and other States the importance of life depends, to a large extent, on race.

Given childhood data regarding intellectual disability, the large number of unsuccessful Atkins claims is difficult to explain for reasons other than racial. In 2014 Blume and colleagues examined 304 claims decided on merit and 38 percent were successful.[556] Justice Scalia in *Atkins* suggested that the process of claiming mental retardation would become a "game" because "the capital defendant who feigns mental retardation risks nothing at all." Justice Scalia did not address the disproportionate number of black children identified as having an intellectual disability or why this fact would not result in correspondingly disproportionate number of black Atkins claims.

---

[555]Frank R. Baumgartner & Tim Lyman, Race-of-Victim Discrepancies in Homicides and Executions, Louisiana 1976-2015, Loyola Journal of Public Interest Law, Vol. 17, 2015, pp. 130-144.
[556]John H. Blume, Sheri Lynn Johnson, Paul Marcus and Emily Paavola, A Tale of Two (and Possibly Three) *Atkins*:
Intellectual Disability and Capital Punishment Creation of a Categorical Bar, William & Mary Law School Research Paper No. 09-294 23 Wm. & Mary Bill Rts. J. 393 (2014)

Blume found that approximately 7 percent of death row inmates filed claims pursuant to *Atkins* but data for individual States are varied. According to this report, there were 34 claims in North Carolina and 28 were successful or 82.3 percent. This was before North Carolina repealed the Racial Justice Act in 2013. In Texas Blume found that 8 of 45 claims were successful before the Supreme Court decided that the Briseno factors "do not comport with the Eighth Amendment" [557] so that Atkins claims in Texas are no longer burdened by a judicial definition of intellectual disability. In any case this is the theory. If not theory, hope. In Alabama of the 34 Atkins claims decided on merit, 5 or 14.7 percent were successful. There were 24 claims in Florida and all were unsuccessful until *Hall*. Blume noted that "the Supreme Court reversed Hall's conviction in its case, *Hall v. Florida*, 134 S. Ct. 1986 (2014), improving Florida's success rate to 1 in 24."

In 2014 the Supreme Court did not declare Hall was intellectually disabled but only that IQ scores of 75 or less must be considered. The Florida Supreme Court eventually did intercede on Hall's behalf in 2016 by acknowledging the importance of evidence of intellectual disabilities before age of onset and the importance of evidence other than IQ. As a result, the Florida Atkins success rate has improved when the court decided that Hall met the criteria for intellectual disability, vacated his death sentence and instructed the trial court to sentence Hall to life.[558]

The resolution of the effects of intellectual disability are not always forthright or clearly determined by an Atkins claims and a determination of intellectual disability by judge or jury. Charles Michael Kight (white) was sentenced to death for the murder of black cabdriver Herman McGoogin in 1982. He had a reported IQ of 69, was in special education, had limited literacy skills, and was considered mentally retarded. However, before Atkins, his mental retardation was not considered a sufficient mitigating factor to prevent a sentence of death. The fact that Kight was white and in Florida in 1980 over 64 percent of children in EMR classes were

---

[557]Moore v. Texas, Supreme Court of the United States, March 28, 2017.
[558]Freddie Lee Hall v. State of Florida, SC10-, September 8, 2016

black, there is every reason to believe that Florida regarded Kight as mentally retarded. Eventually he was re-sentenced to life.

The Florida Supreme Court's 2016 decision has provided excellent guidance for future Atkins claims but considering the fact that Florida has one of the highest rates of childhood intellectual disabilities, the rarity of successful Atkins claims, is perplexing.

William L. Maxwell

The relevant question is whether, in the complex decision making of judge or jury, the application of the death penalty and executions weighs more heavily on blacks than whites. Homicide is, for the most part, not interracial. According to the 2017 FBI Crime in the United States statistical report, of the 3,203 homicides committed by black offenders 82 percent occurred when both offender and victim were black, and 18 percent when the victim was white; on the other hand, of the 3,125 homicides committed by white offenders 91.6 percent occurred when the victim was white, and 8.4 percent when the was victim black.

The following is the 2017 offender/victim homicide breakdown by race as per FBI statistics.[559] These data include only include black/white racial categories.

FBI Homicides 2017 (N=6,537)			
		Victim	
	Race	Black (n=3,203)	White (n=3,125)
Offender	Black	82.0	18.0
	White	8.4	91.6

The 2020 Death Penalty U.S.A. database shows that for 491 black executions by race and 826 white executions only 21 white offenders have been executed when the victim was black,[560]

---

[559]https://ucr.fbi.gov/crime-in-the-u.s/2017/crime-in-the-u.s.-2017/topic-pages/tables/expanded-homicide-data-table-6.xls

2892when the offender was black and the victim white, and 176 (58.7 percent) when both offender and victim were black. Black defendants tend to murder (82 percent or thereabouts) black victims but the death penalty is imposed far more frequently when the victim is white rather than black. Whereas the homicide rate for blacks killing whites is 18 percent, the execution rate when the offender is black and the victim white is 57.9 percent.

United States Executions[561]			
		Victim	
	Race	**Black**	**White**
Offender	**Black** **(n=504)**	34.9	57.9
	White **(n=826)**	2.5	94.6

The Death Penalty Information Center database yields similar data although not exactly the same as for Death Row U.S.A. data. Discrepancies can be attributed to race/ethnicity categories, census categories, an "other race' category, and multiple victims comprised of different racial categories.   For example, Sahib Al-Mosawi, who was executed on December 6, 2001 in Oklahoma for the stabbing death of his wife and uncle, the victims are listed as "other race" in the DPIC database but white in Death Penalty U.S.A.

---

[560]Source: DEATH ROW U.S.A., A quarterly report by the Criminal Justice Project of the NAACP Legal Defense and Educational Fund, Inc., Deborah Fins, Esq. Consultant to the Criminal Justice Project NAACP Legal Dense and Educational Fund, Inc. at https://www.naacpldf.org/wp-content/uploads/DRUSAWinter2020.pdf
[561]Ibid.

National: Offender/Victim Executions Death Penalty Information Center Database[562]		
	Victim	
Race	Black	White
Offender		
Black (n=517)	36.2	60.0
White (n=846)	4.0	94.3

Alas, no matter the pattern or how clear the pattern, statistics are easily dismissed. William L. Maxwell was sentenced to death for a rape committed in Hot Springs, Arkansas in 1961. One reason for Maxwell's appeal was that race played an important role when determining the death penalty. For his 1968 appeal, statistical evidence suggested that a black man has a 50 percent greater chance of receiving a death sentence when the victim is white as opposed to a 14 percent chance when the victim is black.[563] Evidence was presented that from 1913 to 1963-64 there were 21 men executed for rape, 19 of these were black, and 19 of the victims of those executed were white. During this time period there were 176 executions in Arkansas and of these 130 or 73.9 percent were black.

Of the nine blacks considered for Maxwell's jury all were excused for cause (three by the court and six by peremptory challenges). The court concluded that the data and other evidence (e.g., racial name calling) that "These facts do not seem to us to establish a pattern or something specific or useful here, or to provide anything other than a weak basis for suspicion on the part of the defense. Also, other evidence showing racial bias was dismissed

---

[562]https://deathpenaltyinfo.org/executions/execution-database
[563]Maxwell v. Stephens, 348 F.2d 325 (8th Cir. 1965)

as being insignificant such as "The 'nigger' references, while unfortunate, are only two in number and no objection was made to either." The defense also believed that because the jury was elected from a racial poll tax book, the jury was racially biased. The appellate court disagreed and explained that the primary source for jury selection was "independently prepared," the poll tax book was used for verification, and that a handwritten "c" next to eight on the list of 36 possible jurors did not designate the color of jurors. Indeed, the clerk testified he could not recall whether he might have done this, but he just could not remember.

In June of 1970 the Supreme Court remanded the case to the District Court to determine whether potential jurors were excluded because of a general belief against the death penalty (and not because of race).[564] For example, one juror was removed because of the response "No, I don't believe in capital punishment." In Witherspoon v. Illinois the Supreme Court decided that "unless a venireman states unambiguously that he would automatically vote against the imposition of capital punishment no matter what the trial might reveal" an assumption cannot be made that the venireman would not follow the court's instructions and fairly consider all possible sentences (including the death penalty).[565]

The Arkansas court might have been unimpressed with statistics showing racial bias but not so the Governor. On December 29, 1970, Governor Winthrop Rockefeller commuted the death sentences of the 15 condemned prisoners (11 of whom were black) on death row at the Tucker Prison Farm before leaving office. William Maxwell was among this group. Arkansas did not resume executions until 1990 with the execution of John Edward Swindler for the murder of Fort Smith police officer Randy Basnett in 1976. Since that time Arkansas has executed 31 (10 of whom were black). No white offender has ever been executed for the murder of a black victim. Of the 10 blacks executed in Arkansas, three of the victims were black and seven white. Of the 21 white executions, 20 of the victims were white and one Latino.

---

[564]Maxwell v. Bishop, 398 U.S. 262 (1970)
[565]Witherspoon v. Illinois, 391 U.S. 510 (1968)

Phillip Wayne Tomlin

Unlike other States, Alabama had for many years a festering data point in the form of jury override where a judge could sentence a defendant to death no matter the jury vote. In 1997 Phillip Wayne Tomlin was convicted for the fourth time for the murders of 19 year-old Richard Brune and 15 year-old Cheryl Moore in Mobile County, Alabama. Following Tomlin's fourth conviction, the jury recommended life in prison without the possibility of parole by a 12 to 0 vote. The trial judge used the override prerogative and sentenced Tomlin to death because that was the sentence received by the actual killer, John Ronald Daniels (he died in 1995 of a heart attack while on death row). The court reasoned that not to sentence the person who planned the murders would be, paraphrasing the Supreme Court when declaring a moratorium on capital punishment in 1972,[566] "freakish, arbitrary, wanton or capricious."[567] His death sentence was eventually remanded with instructions to resentence Tomlin to life without the possibility of parole.

Mario Dion Woodward

Jury override ended in Alabama in April of 2017 but the practice does illustrate how death penalty jurisprudence can be complicated by judicial interpretation. In 2006 Mario Dion Woodward, black, was sentenced to death for the murder of Keith Houts, a Montgomery police officer, in 2006. The jury voted 8 to 4 for life in prison without the possibility of parole but the trial court sentenced Woodward to death. The jury did find two aggravating factors (a previous violent felony conviction and "capital murder to disrupt or hinder the lawful exercise of a governmental function") but the trial court found otherwise.[568]

---

[566]Furman v. Georgia, 408 U.S. 238, 1972
[567]Ex Partee Tomlin, 909 So. 2d 283 (Ala. 2003)
[568]Woodward v. Alabama, Court of Criminal Appeals of Alabama, CR–08–

The explanation for the override was that "evidence the jury did not hear diminished the mitigating evidence and arguments Woodward offered."[569]

In 2013 the Supreme Court denied certiorari for Mario Woodward but not without a harsh dissent by Justice Sotomayor.[570] She cited two factors that should have resulted in the review of Woodward's trial court override death penalty sentence. Justice Sotomayor voiced a common criticism of jury override that "Alabama judges, who are elected in partisan proceedings, appear to have succumbed to electoral pressures." Second, Ring v. Arizona requires a "jury determination of any fact on which the legislature conditions an increase in their maximum punishment." The jury for Woodward did find two aggravating factors but the jury also believed that, by an 8-4 vote, the mitigating factors outweighed the aggravating factors. Justice Sotomayor believed that the override by the trial judge was "constitutionally suspect." This is slightly different than *Hurst* where no one knew exactly what aggravating factors the jury had actually found. The Alabama trial court decided that the jury did find the necessary aggravating factors although the jury also decided these factors were outweighed by the mitigating factors.

Statistics, no matter how clear the pattern, invidious intent do not make. An underlying cause of the long and seemingly never ending history of segregation and discrimination might suggest a degree of moral responsibility for the increase of criminality among blacks. Although a horrendous environment and egregious family circumstances are often offered as mitigation, this element of "historical background" (as noted in *Arlington Heights*) is often marginalized as are most factors that militate against execution.

As with all other factors relating to the death penalty, jury override and race go hand in hand. As suggested by Justice Sotomayor in her dissenting opinion in Woodward v. Alabama

---

0145, December 16, 2011
[569]Mario Dion Woodward v. State of Alabama, Court of Criminal Appeals of Alabama
CR–08–0145, December 16, 2011
[570]Woodward v. Alabama, 134 S. Ct. 405 (2013)

in 2013 the ability of Alabama judges to override jury verdicts "casts a cloud of illegitimacy over the criminal justice system: Alabama judges, who are elected in partisan proceedings, appear to have succumbed to electoral pressures."[571]

The use of jury override in Alabama has been criticized, not for illicit racial motive, but because of the politicalization of the judicial process. The result of this is a process that weighs more heavily when the offender is black and the victim white, or simply when the offender is black. Unlike the unique case Timothy Tyrone Foster in Georgia where newly discovered notes revealed race was a factor for striking black jurors during jury selection, judges in Alabama have left scant information as to a precise parsing of motive when overriding jury verdicts other than a noble tough-on-crime stance, especially during election years.

Equal Justice Initiative jury override data from life to death in Alabama provide a another perspective of racial motive.[572] Of 101 override cases from life to death, 53 have been for black and 48 for white offenders.[573] Of the 101 overrides, 24.8 percent have been when the victim was black and 75.1 percent when the victim was white. As shown below, there have been 23 jury overrides in Alabama from life to death when both defendant and victim were black (43.4 percent), and 30 when the defendant was black and the victim white (56.6 percent).

---

[571]Woodward v. Alabama, 134 S. Ct. 405 (2013)
[572]Alabama Overrides from Life to Death, from Equal Justice Initiative
[573]Equal Justice Initiative https://eji.org/sites/default/files/list-alabama-override-cases.pdf, downloaded March 7, 2018.

Alabama Jury Override: Life to Death (N=101)			
		Victim	
	Race	Black	White
Defendant	Black (n=53)	43.4	56.6
	White (n=48)	4.2	95.8

There have been 67 executions in Alabama since the reinstatement of the death penalty in 1976 beginning with the execution of John Louis Evans (white) in 1983.

Alabama Executions (N=66)			
		Victim	
	Race	Black	White
Offender	Black (n=28)	39.3	60.7
	White (n=39)	2.6	97.4

Of the 28 blacks (41.8 percent of the 67 total executions) in Alabama since 1976, 11 (39.3 percent) have been when the victims were black and 17(60.7 percent) when at least one of the victims was white.   Of the 28 black executions, 14 involved white females and seven black females. For black offenders these data suggest that the risk of execution is greater when the victim is female and especially when the victim is a white female. This might be attributed, in part, to the lynching effect when rape was the rationale for barbaric execution.

For the 39 whites executed in Alabama all but one the victims were white. In 1997 Henry Francis Hays, a KKK member, was executed by electrocution for the 1981 murder of 19-year old Michael Donald who was black. According to the Associated Press the young man "was abducted at random from a Mobile street by two men, then beaten, cut and strangled. His body was strung up in a tree" (AP, June 6, 1997). Most often jury override has very negative racial consequences and, in an unusual judicial twist, the consequence was execution for Hays. In this case the jury (11 whites and one black) had recommended life in prison without parole but the trial court imposed a sentence of death. Two of Hays' accomplices received lengthy sentences but Frank Cox was released in 2000, and James Knowles (the principal witness against Hays who was 17 at the time of the murder) in 2010.

Of the 67 executions, only one was female. In 2002 Lynda Block, white, was executed for the murder of police officer Roger Motley. George Sibley, her common law husband, was executed in 2005 for his involvement in the murder.

One explanation for the disproportionality when the offender is black and the victim is white is the unlikely possibility that this is a reflection of the disproportionate number of blacks who murder whites. In Alabama in 2016 there were 316 homicides. Of these 194 were by black offenders and 78 by white offenders. For black offenders 163 occurred when the offender and victim were black (84.0 percent, and 31 (16.0 percent) when the offender was black and the victim white. For white offenders 9 when the offender was white and the victim black (11.5 percent), and 85.5 percent then both offender and victim were white.

Alabama Homicides in 2016 (N=272[574])			
		Victim	
	Race	Black	White
Offender	Black (n=194)	84.0	16.0
	White (n=78)	11.5	85.5

The above data must be viewed in the context of history and not as a single point that is without reference. George Wallace, in his 1963 University of Alabama Foster Auditorium speech (the "schoolhouse door" speech) attempted to prevent two black

---

[574]Of the 316 homicides in Alabama 272 involved black/white offender/victim combinations.

students from attending based on the high-minded constitutional belief that the tenth amendment ("The powers not delegated to the United States by the Constitution, nor prohibited by it to the States, are reserved to the States respectively, or to the people"). According to Wallace, the Constitution would be forever compromised and "state sovereignty sacrificed on the altar of political expediency" if Vivian Malone and James Hood were allowed to attend the University of Alabama. More recently, and hard to believe for most observers, Alabama attempted to repeal Section 256 of the Alabama constitution which reads "Separate schools shall be provided for white and colored children, and no child of either race shall be permitted to attend a school of the other race." This section is now meaningless although the attempt to repeal this noisome statute of racist language in 2012 was defeated.[575] On the bright side of the Alabama Constitution, the State did repeal the miscegenation law in 2000.

This racist language in the Alabama's constitution is consistent with the past and current history of racism from lynchings to executions. The Atkins claimant must not only tiptoe through a minefield of racism including apprehension for a murder, interrogation, prosecutors seeking the death penalty, juror selection, the race and sex of the victim, jury override, the imposition of the death penalty and possible execution, but a long history of segregation and discrimination. This tapestry of racism provides a backdrop for understanding, to some degree, the intent of capital punishment decisions. For Alabama and other States, an understanding of racial motive must be evaluated through the lens of history. An Atkins claim is not a separate entity but an integral part of this racial history.

Because *Hurst* focused on the fact that the jury rather than trial court must find the necessary aggravating factors, the Supreme Court probably did not envision the ability of a trial court to diminish the weight of mitigating factors as a rationale for imposing the death sentence. This statutory nitpicking is what Alabama did following Brown v. Board of Education in 1954, and

---

[575]https://law.justia.com/constitution/alabama/CA-245806.html

this is certainly what Alabama does when considering the death penalty.

In February the Alabama Senate voted to remove jury override from the Alabama Code (13A-5-45 to 13A-5-47) by striking references to "advisory verdict" to simply "verdict" ("Where a sentence of death is not returned by the jury, the court shall sentence the defendant to life imprisonment without parole.") by a vote of 30 to 1 and the House of Representatives followed suit by a vote of 78 to 19 in April of 2017. A sentence of death requires a vote by at least 10 jurors. This would have been a straightforward law to enact following Governor Bentley's signature were it not for a sex scandal that forced the governor to resign on April 10, 2017. Kay Ivey was appointed Governor on April 11 and her first official act was to sign the bill abolishing judicial override. End of story: not quite.

There is also the matter of retroactivity which creeps into the picture because those charged with murder does not apply before April 11. The law states that "Sections 13A-5-45 , 13A-5-46 , and 13A-5-47 shall apply to any defendant who is charged with capital murder after April 11, 2017, and shall not apply retroactively to any defendant who has previously been convicted of capital murder and sentenced to death prior to April 11, 2017" (§ 13A-5-47.1). Does this mean that those "charged" with murder before April 11 are eligible for judicial override and execution? Maybe yes, maybe no. Bright lines are not always so simple. Judicial override could have resulted in the death penalty for Richard Burgin who had been charged with the murders of Anthony and Terry Jackson. These murders occurred at West Huntsville United Methodist Church food bank before 2013 but Burgin was convicted after that date. The court eventually did agree with the jury decision to impose a penalty of life in prison without the possibility of parole, but the court (county circuit judge Karen Hall) believed that because Burgin was charged (in 2014) before the 2017, April 11 cutoff, and he was convicted in May of 2017, she could have used judicial override to sentence Burgin to death.

For 69-year-old Vernon Madison in Alabama, already discussed because of his various disabilities (viz., dementia), his sentence by a vote of 8 to 4 t0 life in prison following his third trial was overridden by the court for a sentence of death.[576] Madison dies in February of 2020 while on death row. Gregory Lance Henderson was convicted of the 2009 murder of Deputy James Anderson. The jury voted 9 to 3 for life in prison without the possibility of parole. The Court of Criminal of Appeals of Alabama in January of 2017 concurred with the trial court "that the aggravating circumstances vastly outweighed the mitigating circumstances and sentenced Henderson to death."[577] As of 2020 Henderson and others who were sentenced to death as a result of jury override before the 2017 cutoff date remain on Alabama's death row at the Holman Correctional Facility.

Marvin Rice

And then there is the oblique approach to jury override in Missouri. Marvin Rice, a former deputy sheriff, was sentenced to death for the murder of the mother of his child Annette Durham in December of 2011. In October of 2017 the jury was deadlocked at 11 to 1 in favor of a life sentence. But the court sentenced Rice to death according to Missouri statute. When there is a hung jury (no matter the vote).[578] The death sentence was unconstitutional but the Missouri Supreme Court decided that the circuit court erred by not including proposed jury instructions for one of the victims (the second-degree murder of Steven Strotkamp), and because of inappropriate comments during the prosecutions closing. The

---

[576]Dunn v. Madison, 583 U.S. __ (2017)

[577]Henderson v. Alabama, Court of Criminal Appeals of Alabama, CR-12-0043, Decided: February 10, 2017

[578]Missouri Statute 565.030.4(4) now reads " "If the trier is a jury it shall be instructed before the case is submitted that if it is unable to decide or agree upon the punishment the court shall assess and declare the punishment at life imprisonment without eligibility for probation, parole, or release except by act of the governor or death. The court shall follow the same procedure as set out in this section whenever it is required to determine punishment for murder in the first degree."

prosecutor had referenced Rice's decision not to testify in closing arguments.

11. Invidious Intent

"...an evil eye and an unequal hand..."[579]

Arlington Heights v. Metropolitan Corp

In Arlington Heights v. Metropolitan Housing Corp. (1977) the Supreme Court required that "racially discriminatory intent or purpose" must be "a motivating factor" to rise to a level of a constitutional violation. Invidious purpose does not mean an evil purpose, and the underlying purpose could even be benevolent. Of course, deep down in the heart of hearts, what one truly believes is often a mystery to all concerned. The ostensible reason for President Wilson's endorsement of segregation in 1913 was to prevent discrimination and to help workers...maybe.

In Kalamazoo, Michigan, the appellate court offered that "benevolence of motive does not excuse segregative acts."[580] Discriminatory and benevolent purpose become entangled when government officials truly believe that segregation is good, when a decision, albeit discriminatory, is in the best interest of black children or adults, or when a white prosecutor, judge or jury believes that a black defendant is more likely guilty than a white defendant and more likely to commit a heinous crime where "more likely" is the product of race.

The racial element of Atkins claims, when consideration in isolation, is easily ignored or dismissed as courts have readily shown. However, Atkins claims is simply part of a matrix showing a "clear pattern" invidious intent. There is no way to disentangle Atkins claims from *de jure* and *de facto* segregation, the history of segregation and discrimination, the relationship between intellectual disabilities and race, and all aspects of death penalty jurisprudence. Guidance for understanding Atkins claims comes from Illinois and the Village of Arlington Heights.

---

[579]118 US 356 Yick Wo v. Hopkins 118 U.S. 356 (1886).
[580]Oliver v. Michigan State Board of Education, 508 F.2d 178 (1974)

In *Arlington Heights* the Court found that the Village in Illinois did not discriminate against the Metropolitan Housing Development by denying a rezoning permit to build racially integrated housing. At the time the Village had a population of approximately 64,000 of whom 27 were black. The District Court believed that the vote against the integrated housing was intended to maintain property values and was not racially motivated. The appellate court disagreed and decided the vote not to rezone was discriminatory, was consistent with ongoing residential segregation, and violated the Fourteenth Amendment. The key finding by the Supreme Court was that the purpose of the decision not to rezone was central for a finding of racially discriminatory purpose and not the result (the "ultimate effect"). Disproportionate impact, as viewed by the Court, is not irrelevant but is more a "starting" point" than the determinative factor...usually. The task before a court is to examine the underlying purpose. The Court of Appeals Court was aware that disproportionate impact alone would not necessitate strict scrutiny and a reason to prevent rezoning. However, the court decided that Arlington Heights was not able to show rezoning served a compelling interest. The Supreme Court believed that an initial showing of discriminatory purpose had not been met—which would have shifted the burden to the village to establish "that the same decision would have resulted even had the impermissible purpose not been considered— and the development corporation "simply failed to carry their burden of proving that discriminatory purpose was a motivating factor in the Village's decision."

The impact of official actions concerning intentionally discrimination "may provide an important starting point. Sometimes a clear pattern, unexplainable on grounds other than race, emerges from the effect of the state action even when the governing legislation appears neutral on its face."[581] The Court was aware that, barring a "clear pattern" of disproportionality, "significant" disproportionality could be useful for determining invidious intent but not determinative in and of itself. Examples of a clear pattern given by the Court in Arlington *Heights* included Lane v. Wilson (307 U.S. 268, 1939) and Gomillion v. Lightfoot

---

[581]Arlington Heights v. Metropolitan Housing Corp., 429 U.S. 252 (1977)

(*364 U.S. 339, 1960*). In *Lane* the Court objected to the grandfather clause which exempted those who had voted (whites) in 1914 from a literacy test requirement. In *Gomillion* the City of Tuskegee boundaries were changed from a four sided square to a 28-sided figure which resulted in most blacks within the city being denied the ability to vote (as if no one would notice).[582] In terms of racial bureaucratic nitpicking and farfetched statistics few strategies rival those used by the Virginia officials. During the "massive resistance" saga opposing desegregation following *Brown* in 1954, the Pupil Placement Boards in Virginia screened more than 450,000 students but a black child was never placed in a white school...what are the odds?[583]

In *Arlington Heights* in 1977 Justice Powell explained that "A racially discriminatory intent, as evidenced by such factors as disproportionate impact, the historical background of the challenged decision, the specific antecedent events, departures from normal procedures, and contemporary statements of the decision makers, must be shown." Atkins claims provide considerable insight into the intricacies of racism and invidious intent when the factors outlined by Justice Powell are considered.

For every Atkins claimant the most relevant data is a complete history of mental retardation/intellectual disability, the history of how a claimant received educational services, and the history of segregation and discrimination relating to the claimant. For some Atkins claimants (e.g., Freddie Lee Hall), who were in segregated schools as children, there were likely limited or no services for black children. As school districts desegregated mild intellectual disability (Educable Mental Retardation or EMR during Hall's childhood) became a means to explain prior educational inequities: poor educational performance was not the result of prior segregation or an inferior education but because of intellectual disability. Just as important as educational history, every attempt should be made to explain the sordid history of the death penalty and race—from the terror of lynchings, to prosecution and race, to death row and executions, to the bizarre

---

[582]Gomillion v. Lightfoot, 364 U.S. 339 (1960)
[583]Farley v. Turner, 281 F2d 131 (1960)

statistics concerning executions (e.g., Texas), and to the myriad strategies used to deny Atkins claims. One important theme in the Arlington decision is the context of discrimination. An Atkins claim cannot be viewed in racial isolation but is an element of the history relating to intellectual disability, the Supreme Court's reasoning for lesser culpability and, for many, racial discrimination.

An understanding of the complex maze of racial disproportionality is to consider **all** relevant data. These data include lynchings, the historical pattern of race and executions, executions and geography, a State's history of segregation and discrimination, school segregation, residential segregation, race and targeting, race and job opportunity, law enforcement, pretextual reasons for executions such as rape, race and the judiciary, race and juror selection, race as a factor when seeking the death penalty, race and exonerations, and of course, race and Atkins claims .

After the Supreme Court's Arlington decision the court of appeals considered a possible statutory violation as per the Fair Housing Act (Title VIII of the Civil Rights Act of 1968). The court was aware of the distinction between "intent" and actual racial discrimination because "A strict focus on intent permits racial discrimination to go unpunished in the absence of evidence of overt bigotry. As overtly bigoted behavior has become more unfashionable, evidence of intent has become harder to find. But this does not mean that racial discrimination has disappeared."[584] For Atkins claims there is a historical framework to show the overwhelming effects of racial bias. Nonetheless, invidious intent is buried beneath statute, interpretation, and disingenuous guidelines.
As is often the case when racial intent is difficult to ignore, the solution is often a nod to the possibility of discrimination and nothing more. Following the *Arlington Heights* decision the court approved a settlement and consent decree which provided land for the development of affordable housing. This is not unlike the ultimate outcome for Daryl Renard Atkins who claimed

---

[584]Metropolitan Housing Development Corp. v. Village of Arlington Heights, 558 F.2d 1283, July 7, 1977 and Rehearing August 25, 1977

intellectual disability but who was spared the death penalty for other reasons.

The small percentage of black residents in 1977 in Arlington Heights, coupled with rezoning, might suggest (to some) an underlying discriminatory motive but racial disproportionality does not prove invidious intent. Today, there are schools that are primarily or completely black or white. Bergen County Academies in New Jersey is a competitive public magnet high school with very few black students albeit a very large Asian student population. Camden High School, on the other hand, is 70 percent black and 25 percent Hispanic. East Saint Louis School District 189 is 97.3 percent black and 82.5 percent of these students are from low income families.[585] The cause of this so-called *de facto* segregation might be the result of environment, residential segregation, financial resources, the effects of prior segregation and discrimination, etc. In any case, whatever the complex underlying cause, racial disproportionality is evident but not so intent because discriminatory actions are secreted in history.

The disproportionality of blacks on death row is not dissimilar from that of town, school, workplace, etc. disproportionality. Although death row is over 41 percent black this, by itself, does not mean an invidious motive by prosecutors, juries and/or judges. One might argue that from arrest to execution, laws and regulations are racially neutral and applied evenhandedly. The actual underlying cause of racial death row disproportionality could be the result of prior *de jure* segregation and discrimination, which resulted in disproportionate socio-economic factors, which then resulted in increased criminality. Likewise, the underlying cause of racial disproportionality from childhood intellectual disability to executions might be the result of prior invidious intent— but history is easily dismissed when the intent is to provide a racially neutral application of the law.

In Plain Dealing, Louisiana a court plan was approved whereby students would be assigned to one of two schools based on

---

[585]https://www.illinoisreportcard.com/district.aspx?source=studentcha racteristics&source2=lowincome&Districtid=50082189022

California Achievement Test scores.[586] One obvious result of this seemingly benign educational strategy would be a black school (low scores) and a white school (high scores). Schools officials knew that students in segregated schools were provided an inferior education as reflected by poor test performance. The appellate court would not allow the use of test scores for grouping until a district had achieved unitary status (i.e., they were not segregated). In 1975, several years later, the court explained that "whether in classrooms or in schools, ability grouping may nevertheless be permitted in an otherwise unitary system if the school district can demonstrate that its assignment method is not based on the present results of past segregation or will remedy such results through better educational opportunities" and that "Such a bar period may be lifted when the district can show that steps taken to bring disadvantaged students to peer status have ended the educational disadvantages caused by prior segregation."[587] The length of time required to counter the effects of segregation was said to be the operation of a school as unitary "for several years." The theory was (and is) the effects of slavery, Jim Crow laws, and educational segregation could be undone in a little more than several years! Such grandiose hopes or grandiose naiveté.

To use the distinction made by the Supreme Court in Washington v. Davis in 1976, the disproportionate number of blacks on death row is (or could be) the result of *de facto* segregation rather than *de jure* segregation; there is obviously a disproportionate number of blacks on death row but to rise to the level of a constitutional violation, intentional discrimination must be shown.[588] Evidence garnered as part of the "sensitive inquiry" which considers all relevant data including but not limited to disparate impact, historical background, policies, procedures and practices, departures from normal procedures), specific sequence of events, testimony and administrative background, and comments by decision makers.

---

[586]Lemon v. Bossier, 444 F.2d 1400 (1971)
[587]McNeal v. Tate County School District, 508 F.2d 1017 (1975)
[588]Washington v. Davis, 426 U.S. 229 (1976)

Intent to discriminate is difficult if not impossible to prove. What is the real intent when a prosecutor seeks the death penalty, or selects only white jurors when the defendant is black, when the death penalty is a more likely outcome when the defendant is black, or when a judge could override a jury decision and sentences a black defendant to death? The history of unmitigated discrimination in every aspect of the lives of many on death row, and many who are executed, might suggest that a race neutral explanation is virtually impossible but the standard for reaching the level of constitutional violation is extremely high.

The most elusive strategy to contend with when attempting to understand invidious intent is benevolence which might be real, feigned or somewhere in between. For children, the goal might be to provide an appropriate education and not to place a disproportionate number of black children into dead-end classes; for adults that once benevolence associated with EMR placement is transformed into a self-serving and a strict interpretation of intellectual disability which promotes a dismissal of "the lesser culpability for the mentally retarded offender." [589] One could also suppose that the administration of drugs to render someone on death row eligible for execution is really an act of benevolence (aside from the execution part). An invidious purpose does not mean an evil purpose, and the intended or at least professed purpose, feigned or not, might be benevolent.

In Kalamazoo in the 1970s, one explanation for assigning black teachers to black schools was "to provide Black students with suitable role models and to decrease the tensions between teacher and pupil in the classroom."[590] The effect of the Kalamazoo program was to contain the future growth of the black elementary student population. The Court of Appeals for the Sixth Circuit explained that when there is a failure to act (or not), when the foreseeable result is segregation, "a presumption of segregation arises" which becomes proof "unless defendants affirmatively

---

[589]Atkins v. Virginia, 536 U.S. 304 (2002)
[590]Oliver v. Michigan State Board of Education, 508 F.2d 178 (1974)

establish that their action or inaction was a consistent and resolute application of racially neutral policies." The Supreme Court disagreed that "foreseeability" alone was sufficient for a *prima facie* case of intentional discrimination and sufficient to shift the burden to defendants to offer a racially neutral explanation. However, the Court also believed that foreseeability of consequences "is one type of quite relevant evidence of racially discriminatory purpose" and could show a failure to eradicate the consequences of discriminatory conduct.[591]

For Dayton, Ohio schools, in spite of the Supreme Court's caution for using *foreseeability of consequences*, the Court recognized that faculty and school assignments, school zones and where new schools were built, established segregative intent. The Court noted the school "Board's total failure to fulfill its affirmative duty— and indeed its conduct resulting in increased segregation—to trace the current, systemwide segregation back to the purposefully dual system of the 1950s and to the subsequent acts of intentional discrimination."

In 1913, Woodrow Wilson, a Virginian by birth, of the League of Nations fame and Nobel Prize winner, permitted and endorsed the segregation of blacks (separate toilets, lunchrooms and workspaces) beginning with the Department of the Treasury and the Post Office. His reasoning was that segregation was begun "as much in the interest of the most influential negroes I know, and with the idea that the friction, or rather discontent and uneasiness, which had prevailed in many of the departments would thereby be removed. It is as far as possible from being a movement against the negroes" and "by pitting certain bureaus and sections of the service in the charge of negroes we are rendering them safe in their possession of office and less likely to be discriminated against."[592] Wilson might have truly believed that his reasoning was benevolent and correct. However, the belief in the benevolence of an action does not negate invidious intent and the consequences thereof.

---

[591]Dayton Board of Education v. Brinkman, 443 U.S. 526 (1979
[592]In letter to Oswald Garrison Villard, July 23, 1913, from The Papers of Woodrow Wilson (Arthur S. Link, Ed.), Vol. 28, Princeton, N.J., Princeton New Jersey Press, 1978, p. 65.

Following *Brown*, the intent to discriminate was often masked by benevolent motive. In 1958, pursuant to Senator Larry Byrd's plan of massive resistance, four black students were denied admission to the all-white Stratford Junior High School in Arlington, Virginia because "the transfers could not be justified under sound educational principles" and the admission of the students to the all-white school "would be discouraging and possibly emotionally disturbing." In other words, the students "will no longer be among the leaders" and thus have problems adapting.[593] In 1959 the four black students were admitted to Stratford Junior High which became the first secondary school in Virginia to desegregate. Desegregation was, in the end, the only sound educational principle.

The differential application of the definition of intellectual disability is what binds black children who are disproportionately placed in EMR-type classes and black adults who are denied Atkins relief and disproportionately sentenced to death. In 1886 as Jim Crow laws became an integral part of State constitutions in the South, the Supreme Court was especially concerned not only with the law but the application of the law. In 1986 in Yick Wo v. Hopkins the Court explained that "Though the law itself be fair on its face, and impartial in appearance, yet, if it is applied and administered by public authority with an evil eye and an unequal hand, so as practically to make unjust and illegal discriminations between persons in similar circumstances, material to their rights, the denial of equal justice is still within the prohibition of the constitution."[594] This is the essence of intellectual disability when parsed through law and statute. Professional definitions beget statute which is then applied "with an evil eye and an unequal hand."

For both black adults seeking Atkins relief and black children disproportionally deemed intellectually disabled or treated as such, invidious intent might exist but it is a very elusive existence.

---

[593]Thompson v. County School Board of Arlington, 166 F. Supp. 529 (1958)
[594]Yick Wo v. Hopkins, 118 U.S. 356 (1886)

Attempts to show a constitutional violation based on the disproportionate placement of black children has been, for the most part, woefully unsuccessful. In Larry P. v. Riles in California, in 1979, the District Court judge believed that "that the placement mechanisms for E.M.R. classes operated with a discriminatory effect that effectively foreclosed a disproportionate number of black children from any meaningful education." The court found that Larry P. had made a prima facie case based on the use (or misuse) of IQ tests, developmental history, adaptive behavior and the resulting disproportionate impact. The burden then shifted to the State to show that EMR classes were an educational necessity. The State asserted that EMR classes were a benefit, low IQ was the result of poor nutrition and lack of medical services or socioeconomic factors, and that the low IQ of black children accurately reflected actual subaverage intellectual performance.

In 1984 the appellate court agreed State officials were found to have discriminated against black children, but "the amended majority opinion holds that although the discriminatory effects analysis suffices to establish a violation, intentional discrimination under the equal protection clause requires more than a showing of the pervasiveness of discriminatory effect.'"[595] As explained in Washington v. Davis invidious intent must be, to some extent, a motive for using a test which had a disparate impact on the selection of police officers in the District of Columbia.[596]

For Larry P. the appellate court decided defendants had violated State statutes, provisions of the Education for All Handicapped Children Act, and Title VI of the Civil Rights Act of 1964 which applies to programs receiving Federal financial assistance. Because intentionality was not proven, the Federal violation of the equal protection clause of the 14th Amendment was dismissed. Also, "A finding of purposeful, intentional discrimination by Wilson Riles, a respected black educator of national reputation, is

---

[595]Title VI of the Equal Rights Act of 1964 stipulates that "No person in the United States shall, on the ground of race, color, or national origin, be excluded from participation in, be denied the benefits of, or be subjected to discrimination under any program or activity receiving federal financial assistance."

[596]Washington v. Davis, 426 U.S. 229 (1976)

clearly contrary to the record. That he did so by deliberately and improperly placing black children, by means of invalid and discriminatory IQ tests into 'dead-end' E.M.R. classes, simply does not comport with the realities of this case or his oath as Superintendent of Schools."[597]

As it is, in many death penalty cases a constitutional claim is difficult to prove because statute and judicial guidance further entangles motive and law. States have generally adopted the professional definitions of intellectual disability in statute, then re-interpret intellectual disability in a way never envisioned by professionals (who developed the definitions), and resort to a plain language interpretation of the statute which often ignores the nuanced interpretation of intellectual disability intended by professionals. Age of onset was never intended as a strict criterion to limit those who met the criteria for intellectual disability; most professionals acknowledge that IQ cannot be subjected to a strict interpretation; and adaptive behavior requires a thoughtful analysis of criteria across environments and time periods rather than a stereotypical portrait of what someone with an intellectual disability can or cannot do.

What exactly motivated Florida courts to require a strict interpretation of IQ when professional guidance cautioned otherwise, while a strict interpretation of IQ was not used for children, is not known. Maybe race had a role, or maybe the intent was to eliminate race by invoking a strict statutory standard, or that Atkins claims needed to be reduced to a bright-line to simplify and expedite the processing of claims. There are occasions, albeit very few, when invidious intent can be shown but establishing proof is a slippery slope for a defendant to climb.

McCleskey v. Kemp

Contrary to how statistics were used in *Larry P.* in California most courts are cautious when interpreting statistical data., especially when determining invidious intent. A case in point is that of

---

[597]Larry P. v. Riles, 793 F.2d 969 (1984)

Warren McCleskey who was executed on September 25, 1991. McCleskey, black, was sentenced to death for the murder of a white police officer, Frank Schlatt, during a robbery of the Dixie Furniture store in 1978 with three others. McCleskey's counsel attempted to provide evidence via a study (the "Baldus" study) showing racial bias from indictment to sentencing. The United States Court of Appeals understood the difference between cause, effect and statistics by explaining that "The usefulness of statistics obviously depends upon what is attempted to be proved by them. Statistics readily show disparate impact but do not prove intentional discrimination. Where intent and motivation must be proved, the statistics have even less utility."[598] In *Larry P.* racial bias was readily documented but constitutional invidious intent it was not. A of invidious intent by statistical analysis requires a pattern so overwhelming and so completely improbable that a "clear pattern" rarely emerges. In Hernandez v. Texas statistical data showing racial bias was overwhelming and acknowledges but most statistical analyses do not meet the *taxes credulity test* cited in *Hernandez*.

In 1987 the Supreme Court considered the statistics for McCleskey's appeal which showed that the imposition of the death penalty was given in 22 percent of the cases when the defendant was black and the victim was white, in 8 percent of the cases when both defendant and victim were white, and in 1 percent of the cases when defendant and victim were black. Based on Death Penalty Information Center database data 38 percent of black executions, for the 496 referenced, occurred when the victim was black and 62 percent when the victim was white; for the 832 cited for white offender data, 4 percent occurred when the victim black and 96 percent when the victim was white.[599]

The statistics showing racial disproportionality in lynchings, prosecutors seeking the death penalty, juror selection, the victim's race, exonerations, failed Atkins claims, death row and executions, all triangulate toward "an evil eye and unequal hand." When the

---

[598]McCleskey v. Kemp (Warden), United States Court of Appeals for the Eleventh Circuit, 753 F.2d 877
[599]https://deathpenaltyinfo.org/executions/execution-database

death penalty is sought more when the victim is white and the offender black, the cause might be traced to a long-ago racially discriminatory intent where slavery begot Jim Crow laws, and Jim Crow laws begot other forms of discrimination which begot environmental and educational deprivations. The end result of this racial history is then manifested in increased crime and a death penalty that weighs more heavily on blacks than whites. Racial intent is muddied by history.

Racial bias in jury selection seems almost too obvious, yet one can only speculate, apart from incriminating notes of juror forms, whether the striking of black jurors is racially motivated. During the heyday of lynchings the overwhelming mob mentally would have been on the side of righteousness and good deeds, but there is little doubt about the degree of racial invidious intent. For McCleskey the Supreme Court reasoned that racial bias on the part of specific decision makers must be shown and that overall statistics were insufficient to prove discriminatory intent. The Court explained that "The Constitution does not require that a State eliminate any demonstrable disparity that correlates with a potentially irrelevant factor in order to operate a criminal justice system that includes capital punishment. As we have stated specifically in the context of capital punishment, the Constitution does not place 'totally unrealistic conditions on its use.'"

Duane Edward Buck

The use of statistics works both ways so that a statistical pattern does not prove invidious intent, nor does a pattern of criminality for a racial group prove a defendant more dangerous and thus more eligible for the death penalty. Duane Edward Buck was sentenced to death in Texas for the murder of Debra Gardner Kenneth Butler in 1995. After his arrest, he was very "upbeat" about the murder commenting "the bitch got what she deserved." During the sentencing phase the defense expert considered the statistical data showing that race was a factor in the future dangerousness of a defendant and the expert's report "ultimately concluded that Buck was unlikely to be a future danger." The expert also explained that "Buck was statistically more likely to act violently because he is black." One of the reasons why the Supreme Court remanded the case was ineffective counsel because "No competent defense attorney would introduce evidence that his client is liable to be a future danger because of his race."[600] The Court observed that the expert's "testimony appealed to a powerful racial stereotype and might well have been valued by jurors as the opinion of a medical expert bearing the court's imprimatur." Harsh words for a claim involving the often used, but infrequently successful, ineffective counsel claim.

The Court concluded that the admission of this racial data during sentencing resulted in Buck being "sentenced to death in part because of his race. This is a disturbing departure from the basic premise that our criminal law punishes people for what they do, not who they are. That it concerned race amplifies the problem because relying on race to impose a criminal sanction 'poisons public confidence' in the judicial process." The court then rejected that ineffective counsel claim was *de minimis* (too trivial to consider) and remanded the case. Following the Court's decision Buck agreed to a sentence of life plus two additional 60 year terms and is eligible for parole in 2057.

William Henry Furman

On June 2, 1967, Louis Monge was executed (gas chamber) for the 1963 murders of his wife and three of his 10 children in Denver, Colorado. Following the Monge execution, a six year unofficial moratorium existed during which the Supreme Court considered the constitutionality of the death penalty. In Furman v. Georgia, in 1972, the opinion was that the death penalty was "wantonly and so freakishly imposed" and therefore violated the Eighth and Fourteenth Amendment because "it was inflicted in a small number of the total possible cases and primarily against certain minority groups."[601]

---

[600]Buck v. Davis, decided February 22, 2017
[601]Furman v. Georgia, 408 U.S. 238, 1972

In a fractured 5-4 decision, where each Justice had a unique interpretation of the constitutionality of the death penalty, Justice Stewart captured the overall tone of the majority by observing that the three petitioners comprising *Furman* were "among a capriciously selected random handful upon whom the sentence of death was imposed" and the constitution "could not tolerate the infliction of a sentence of death under legal systems which permitted this unique penalty to be so wantonly and so freakishly imposed, but that it was unnecessary to reach the ultimate question whether the infliction of the death penalty was constitutionally impermissible in all circumstances."

Justice Douglas found that selecting minorities for execution was just as unusual and cruel as more barbaric forms of punishment: "The words 'cruel and unusual' certainly include penalties that are barbaric. But the words, at least when read in light of the English proscription against selective and irregular use of penalties, suggest that it is 'cruel and unusual' to apply the death penalty— or any other penalty— selectively to minorities whose numbers are few, who are outcasts of society, and who are unpopular, but whom society is willing to see suffer though it would not countenance general application of the same penalty across the board."

The *Furman* decision was about race just as much as it was about cruel and unusual punishment. More precisely, the overall conclusion in *Furman* was that the disproportionate application of the death penalty, which targeted minorities, or "outcasts of society," was cruel and unusual. The Court was acutely aware of racial discrimination because "It would seem to be incontestable that the death penalty inflicted on one defendant is 'unusual' if it discriminates against him by reason of his race, religion, wealth, social position, or class, or if it is imposed under a procedure that gives room for the play of such prejudices." Justice Stewart expressed his concern that "my concurring Brothers have demonstrated that, if any basis can be discerned for the selection of these few to be sentenced to die, it is the constitutionally impermissible basis of race."

William Henry Furman, a 26 year-old black, shot and killed a 29 year-old William Micke, white and a father of five children, in Savannah, Georgia during the course of a break-in and robbery. Before his trial, the Georgia Central State Hospital concluded that he was mentally retarded with psychotic episodes. The other two petitioners (Elmer Branch in Texas and Lucious Jackson in Georgia) were both sentenced to death after having been convicted of raping white women. Branch was "found to be a borderline mental deficient and well below the average IQ of Texas prison inmates" while "Jackson was of average education and average intelligence, that he was not an imbecile, or schizophrenic, or psychotic, that his traits were the product of environmental influences, and that he was competent to stand trial."

If a State does not acknowledge a "clear pattern" of racial intent regarding the history rape and the death penalty for blacks when the victim is white, there seems little hope that the State would acknowledge racial bias for Atkins claimants. In *Furman* the Supreme Court explained that the death penalty was often imposed on black more than white defendants, especially when the victims were white. Prison terms were for the white and wealthy Loebs and Leopolds, and the death penalty for the black, the poor and poorly educated. For Lucious Jackson, in 1969, the Supreme Court of Georgia came to the conclusion that "there was no evidence to support the contention that 'there exists a discriminatory pattern whereby the death penalty is consistently imposed upon Negro defendants convicted of raping white women.'" In Georgia between 1930 and 1953 there were 307 executions in Georgia and of these 253 (82.4 percent were black. During this period there were 46 executions for rape alone and of these 44 or 95.7 percent were black. Between 1954 (at the time of the Brown decision) and the execution of Howard Booker (black) for robbery to the execution of J.W. Pugh (white) in 1964 for murder the Georgia had executed 62 offenders of whom 48 (or 77.4 percent were black). During this time frame 14 were executed for rape alone and of these 12 or 85.7 percent were black.[602] Following the last execution in 1964, Georgia had no executions until 1983.

The two white executions for rape alone in Georgia (1954-1964) were the result of Federal and not State prosecution. George and Michael Krull (white) were sentenced and executed by the Federal government for the kidnapping (a Federal crime) and rape of a woman from Chattanooga, Tennessee in Chickamauga National Park. The victim was transported to Georgia (and thus the Federal jurisdiction) and sentenced to death. The brothers were executed by the Federal government on August 21, 1957 in the Georgia. The electric chair which was rented. Michael Krull was reported to have said "It was all prejudice. When your local people commit rape they get just 10 or 20 years." If you were white and local, this is fairly accurate; if you were black, execution was the more likely outcome.

If the "exclusion for the mentally retarded is appropriate" because "only most deserving of execution are put to death," the problem is not a single tactic or strategy by States but unrelenting efforts to ignore, thwart, or limit the Supreme Court's death penalty jurisprudence that capital punishment is for a narrow category of offenders. This is exactly what States did following Brown v. Board of Education in 1954, what States do by stigmatizing and segregating a disproportionate number of black children as having intellectual disabilities, and what States have always done to disproportionality sentence black defendants to execution.

Troy Leon Gregg

Racism is inherent in every aspect of death penalty jurisprudence. There is one notable exception and that is when the Supreme Court decided that execution was constitutional by selecting cases which seemed to avoid all traces of racial bias. In Gregg v. Georgia two black offenders were spared the death penalty and three white offenders not. Following *Furman* in 1972 and the re-installment of the death penalty in Gregg v. Georgia on July 2,

---

[602]Espy, M. Watt, and John Ortiz Smykla. Executions in the United States, 1608-2002: The ESPY File . ICPSR08451-v5. Ann Arbor, MI: Inter-university Consortium for Political and Social Research

1976, States developed guidelines for imposing the death penalty which the Supreme Court deemed constitutional. Of five cases decided on July 2, 1976, three involved white defendants (Troy Gregg in Georgia, Jerry Lane Jurek in Texas and Charles William Proffitt in Florida). The Court affirmed the death penalty in each of these cases.

The concerns raised in *Furman* were addressed in Georgia by a bifurcated proceeding in which the sentencing authority guidelines for the imposition of the death penalty, and for identifying specific aggravating and mitigating factors. A death sentence also required the jury to focus on the crime (e.g., "was it committed in the course of another capital felony?") and the defendant (e.g., "His emotional state at the time of the crime"). As an additional safeguard, all death sentences entailed an automatic appeal to the Georgia Supreme Court which would determine whether the sentence was the result of "passion or prejudice" and whether the sentence was proportionate to the crime. Georgia, at least in the eyes of the Supreme Court in 1976, overcame the wantonness and freakiness of the death penalty described in *Furman* by requiring a consideration of all the evidence during the sentencing phase of a bifurcated trial, by providing jury guidelines, by considering the proportionality of the sentence to the crime, and by an automatic appeal process.[603]

For the two black defendants in *Gregg* the Court decided the procedures for imposing the death penalty were unconstitutional because North Carolina and Louisiana replaced "discretionary jury sentencing in capital cases with mandatory death sentences." For James Tyrone Woodson the Court said that "The North Carolina statute impermissibly treats all persons convicted of a designated offense not as uniquely individual human beings, but as members of a faceless, undifferentiated mass to be subjected to the blind infliction of the death penalty." Woodson was eventually paroled in 1993. For Stanislaus Roberts, in Louisiana, the Court rejected his death sentence because the procedure "not only lacks standards to guide the jury in selecting among first-degree murderers, but it plainly invites the jurors to disregard their oaths

---

[603]O.C.G.A. 17-10-35(c) (2010)

and choose a verdict for a lesser offense whenever they feel the death penalty is inappropriate."

Although none of the five of the July 2, 1976 cases were executed Troy Leon Gregg would have if not for an improbable sequence of events. In 1973, Gregg and Floyd Allen were given a ride while hitchhiking in Florida. At a rest stop in Georgia, Gregg robbed Fred Simmons and Bob Moore and murdered each which, according to Gregg, was the result of self-defense.[604] In 1974, Gregg was convicted of two counts armed robbery and murder and sentenced to death. Gregg's stay on death row was short. He escaped from prison in 1980, the night before his execution, but to no avail. He was beaten to death that night in a barroom fight.

The other two white defendants in *Gregg* (Jerry Lane Jurek and Charles William Proffitt) were also sentenced to death. Jurek, white, strangled 10-year old Wendy Adams in 1973 in Cuero, Texas. In 1974, after deliberating less than one hour, the jury sentenced Jurek to death. In 1982 Jurek was granted a retrial because of how his confessions were obtained and, tangentially, because of low intellectual ability. Before the trial concluded, Jurek reached a plea and was sentenced to life. Because of time served, he was eligible for parole in 1981 but all parole requests have been denied. His next parole review is scheduled for September, 2020.

For Charles Proffitt, in 1974, the judge agreed with the jury's advisory recommendation and a death sentence was imposed for the murder (stabbing) of wrestling Coach Joel Medgebow in Tampa, Florida. In 1987 the Supreme Court of Florida decided that Proffitt's crime did not warrant the death penalty, his death sentence was vacated, and he was sentenced to life without the possibility of parole for 25 years. He died in prison in 2012 of natural causes.

For the three white offenders in *Gregg* the procedures for the death penalty were deemed constitutional but not for the two black offenders. This could be a matter of fortuity or, possibly, the

---

[604]Gregg v. Georgia, 428 U.S. 153 (1976)

five cases were selected to dispel any notion of racial bias when reinstating the death penalty. All data suggests that race is inextricably conjoined with the imposition of the death penalty, but the decision in *Gregg* to permit executions has nary a hint of racism (for the most part). The odd effect of *Gregg* is that crimes by white offenders resulted in the re-introduction of the death penalty whereby a disproportionate number of black offenders would eventually be executed.

Brown v. Board of Education

In Brown v. Board of Education the Supreme Court declared "the plaintiffs and others similarly situated for whom the actions have been brought are, by reason of the segregation complained of, deprived of the equal protection of the laws guaranteed by the Fourteenth Amendment."[605] One year later, in Brown II, the Court issued the poorly named "all deliberate speed" mandate which became a license to use whatever strategy possible, some downright idiotic, to avoid, delay or minimize desegregation.[606] If one strategy failed to maintain segregation another quickly appeared and the litany included depriving funds to desegregated schools, funding private schools, using the National Guard by the peace-loving Orval Faubus in 1957 Little Rock, using State troopers to "preserve the peace...and maintain domestic tranquility" in Tuskegee, Alabama by George Wallace, school closings—Little Rock Central High was closed for one year and prince Edward County Schools in Virginia remained closed for five years to avoid desegregation— tax concessions, retirement benefits for private school teachers, segregation academies, teacher flight, student flight, white flight aided by mortgage discrimination, teacher assignments, student assignments, racially slanted transfer policies, Freedom of Choice plans (not much freedom but very patriotic), neighborhood school policies used in conjunction with discriminatory school boundaries, new school construction, portable classrooms, associating segregated schools with housing projects, maintaining inferior segregated schools,

---

[605]Brown v. Board of Education, 347 U.S. 483
[606]Brown v. Board of Education, 349 U.S. 294 (1955)

extracurricular and transportation segregation, non-faculty hiring, tracking, segregation because of "sound educational principles,"[607] IQ testing to justify all sorts of deprivations from tracking to segregated placements, Educable Mental Retardation to stigmatize and "help" children by providing a segregated and inferior education, and the usual retaliation, intimidation, economic reprisals, interminable litigation—a desegregation suit begun in Macon County, Alabama, in 1963[608] was settled when the system was declared unitary in 2006[609]— re-segregation of schools, and "secession" where a smaller, more wealthy and white segment of the community breaks off from the public school system to form its own school district.

Brown did not end desegregation; *Atkins* did not end the execution of the intellectually disabled. For Atkins claims the strategies are just as persistent as the efforts by States to obviate *Brown*: a bright-line of 70, then an even more insidious bright-line of 75 where in Oklahoma "any" score above 75 disqualifies an Atkins claim, misplacing scores, disbelieving scores, ignoring scores, stating IQ scores lack "credibility" because of malingering or lack of motivation, raising IQ scores for dubious reasons, (IQ is appropriate for segregating children but racially biased for adults in Atkins claims}, dismissing the most probative IQ scores of Atkins claimants in childhood, using current cutoff criteria for interpreting historical scores, creating a new concept of intelligence where a subjective analysis of "street smarts" is considered relevant, ignoring prior determination of intellectual disability, requiring proof of intellectual disability as a child and as an adult, or requiring proof of intellectual disability in childhood and at the time of the crime, emphasizing the importance of adaptive behavior while on death row, ignoring the ADA and a record of disability, re-defining adaptive behavior, resorting to

---

[607]Thompson v. County School Board of Arlington, 166 F. Supp. 529 (1958)
[608]Lee v. Macon County Board of Education, Alabama, 221 F. Supp. 297 (1963)
[609]Lee v. Macon County Board of Education, District Court of the United States for the
Middle District of Alabama, Eastern Division, Case 3:70-cv-00846-MHT-DRB, Filed 05/22/06

stereotypes of intellectual disability to evaluate adaptive behavior (e.g., the ability to read or graduate from high school), not using standardized assessments of adaptive behavior, disbelieving standardized assessments of adaptive behavior, adaptive deficits caused by prison, the ability to adapt to death row, using Briseno-type factors to supplant professional criteria, ignoring or misinterpreting the age of onset criterion, and re-defining each prong of the definition of intellectual disability so that claims can be rejected on multiple counts. The list is surely partial and just as surely never-ending.

The Supreme Court based its 2002 Atkins decision on the Eighth Amendment but States have turned this reasoning upside down by asserting a unique Eighth Amendment standard for defendants seeking relief under Atkins. In *Hall* the Supreme Court explained that the Eighth Amendment is a reaffirmation of a duty, guided by evolving standards of decency, to respect the dignity of man. The essence of both *Atkins* and *Hall* is to pay fidelity to the Eighth Amendment, for even the most heinous crimes, by providing lesser culpability for someone with diminished intellectual capacity. States have met this "duty" by first incorporating the professional definition of intellectual disability into statute and/or judicial interpretation, and then ignoring the underlying professional this definitional basis by asserting that the Eighth Amendment requires a strict interpretation, misinterpretation, or re-interpretation of intellectual disability.

States often make a dichotomy between intellectual disability for social purposes and the death penalty. To achieve this end, the Eighth Amendment is parsed to demand a strict interpretation of the death penalty. In Texas "the ultimate issue of whether this person is, in fact, mentally retarded for purposes of the Eighth Amendment ban on excessive punishment is one for the finder of fact, based upon all of the evidence and determinations of credibility."[610] The Texas court in 2004 regarded the professional definitions used by mental health professionals as broadly defined "to provide an adequate safety net for those who are at the margin

---

[610]Court Of Criminal Appeals of Texas, *Ex parte* Briseno, 135 S.W.3d 1, 3 (Tex. Crim. App. 2004)

and might well become mentally-unimpaired citizens if given additional social services support." The court "believed that the determination of intellectual disability needed to be explicated "through an as-of-yet undetermined process." By creating criteria that center on the capital offense, the court by-passed the essence of the professional definitions of intellectual disability in a failed attempt to assist in defining mental retardation by considering additional "evidentiary factors." In Texas these newly anointed "mentally-unimpaired citizens" were more than suitable for execution.

States are able to discount or completely disregard a record of intellectual disability by asserting that although a defendant might have had an intellectual disability at one time, the defendant is no longer intellectually impaired because of appropriate services. This might seem a sensible approach but in fact this is based on a misguided concept of intellectual disability; that is, if a person who is truly intellectually disabled is able to able to "adapt," the person never was or, at the very least, no longer impaired. This reasoning negates and trivializes efforts to provide appropriate services for persons who are truly intellectually disabled such that the reasons for lesser culpability cited by the Supreme Court (e.g., the " ability to understand and process information, to learn from experience, to engage in logical reasoning, or to control impulses," etc) are diminished; a person with supports might be able to develop adaptive skills but this does not signify that this person no longer has "the diminished ability to understand and process information." If educational services have been appropriate and successful, many children are better able to maximize cognitive ability and to adapt and become productive citizens. The decision by a State that a child is intellectually impaired should be made with great consideration. The consequences are great for a child in terms of educational opportunity, and the consequences should be just as great for the State should this individual seek lesser culpability as an adult.

Intellectual disability is not a singular concept defined by selected and current skills but rather a concept entangled in developmental and childhood data, environment, prior assessments and determinations, educational services and placements, and the array of IQ and other assessments common to most Atkins claims. For children who have been misclassified as intellectually disabled, the resulting curriculum denies educational opportunity, results in unwarranted stigmatization and some degree of segregation (or a very large degree of segregation). To ignore a prior classification of intellectual disability as a child by asserting that this determination was in error ignores the reality and dire educational consequences of misclassification. For a child who has been misclassified, there are consequences; for a State that is responsible for the misclassification, intentionally or not, there are also consequences—especially when this record of intellectual disability should be a determining factor to show that an offender is intellectually disabled and not eligible for the death penalty.

States have extensive regulations for determining intellectual disability for children in comparison to the vague (at best) or nonexistent guidelines used by judge or jury. For a black defendant who was identified as having an intellectual disability as a child, the resulting segregation from the general school curriculum and school population, whether intentional or not, should provide the most salient evidence and the foundation for a claim of intellectual disability. For children who had not been identified as having an intellectual but could have or should have, the resulting lack of services can hardly be used to justify the contention that there was no record of intellectual disability before age of onset. This argument amounts to using segregation (which includes inferior resources and services in black schools) to reason an Atkins claimant is not intellectually disabled because there was no identification before age of onset (because of segregation and discrimination). Again, segregation and discrimination are used to condone segregation, and is exactly what was done on Washington, D.C. in 1966 in Hobson v. Hansen where the effects of segregation were used to re-segregate under the guise of educational benevolence (i.e. a more genteel form of segregation).[611]

---

[611]Hobson v. Hansen, 252 F. Supp. 4 (1966), 269 F. Supp. 401 (1967) and 327 F. Supp. 844 (1971)

Race is used to segregate and stigmatize; race is used to deny services (e.g., compare the disparate racial data for children with severe and mild intellectual disabilities); race is a factor in seeking the death penalty; and race is a factor when denying Atkins claims. Freddie Lee Hall was probably not provided services as a child in the 1950s because he was black and the inferior and segregated education that was provided was all that many black children could expect. By a twist of logic, this segregated and inferior education is then used to show that, as an adult, Hall had no record of intellectual disability as a child. Racism as a child becomes an argument for racism as an adult. Freddie Lee Hall was not provided necessary and appropriate educational services as a child (because of race) therefore he would be eligible for execution as an adult because there was no record of services. Hall was subjected to this "plain language" interpretation of the law for almost 40 years on death row before the Supreme Court of Florida decided that his intellectual disability warranted lesser culpability.[612]

The guile of States to undermine *Atkins* and the Eighth and Fourteenth Amendments will be tested by courts just as a seemingly unending series of strategies were used to undermine *Brown* in 1954. In *Moore* the Supreme Court made clear that States do not have "unfettered discretion" when resolving Atkins claims and for Bonny James Moore, sentenced to death in Texas for the murder of a store clerk, the use of the "*Briseno* pervasively infected" the decision by the Court of Criminal Appeals of Texas.[613] The Black African American alone population in Texas (2018) was 12.7 percent, yet Texas accounts for more black executions (207 of 571 executions) than the overall number of executions in any other State (Virginia and Oklahoma both have 1113 overall executions). Time will tell how *Atkins* claims will be resolved in Texas without the Briseno factors or a more subtle version of this judicial guidance. The decision that Briseno factors cannot be used is easily circumvented by offering Briseno type evidence showing a defendant is not intellectually disabled while duly refraining from any mention of *Briseno*. Florida did not need the

---

[612]Hall v. State of Florida, SC10-1335, September 8, 2016
[613]Moore v. Texas, Supreme Court of the United States, March 28, 2017.

Briseno factors to deny most Atkins claims and a judge/jury need only to believe that the prosecutor's evidence was more credible than the defendants. Of course, whether that belief is flavored by race is near impossible to determine other than from the overwhelming evidence and historical pattern of racism tainting all areas relating to the death penalty.

For all defendants who have been provided services as a child for intellectual disability, black or white, States readily contend that a defendant was never really intellectually disabled and that the identification and services were the result of the benevolence of the State to meet the social needs of children. The end result is that an idiosyncratic, narrow-minded and overly punctilious interpretation of professional definitions is used to negate a record of disability, all credible evidence of disability, and all State actions that contributed to impaired cognitive and adaptive skills. If a child was not really intellectual disabled as a child, the resulting classification would certainly deprive the child of an appropriate education during the "developmental period," and contribute to deficient skills required by IQ tests, and impairment in maturation, learning and social adjustment cited by Heber in 1959 when the current definition of intellectual disability was first conceptualized.[614] If the child was correctly identified as a child, an appropriate education might well maximize adaptive skills but this is testimony of the services provided and not an undoing of intellectual disability of lesser culpability as an adult.

For Atkins claimants who have been identified as mentally retarded/intellectually disabled as a child, the ADA should provide protection against the death penalty as an adult; for children who should have been identified, Atkins should provide the same protection; for children who have been inappropriately identified as having an intellectual disability as a child, this "record" of intellectual disability should prohibit the imposition of the death penalty. The ADA is not a loophole but an acknowledgement of the fact that if a child was, should have been, or was incorrectly

---

[614]Heber, Rick, A Manual on Terminology and Classification in Mental Retardation, Monograph Supplement, American Journal of Mental Deficiency (2nd ed.), 1959 and 1961

identified as having an intellectual disability, subsequent State actions, or inactions, cannot be ignored. Stigmatizing and segregating children because of race and/or environment is a cruel and unusual educational strategy; not providing an appropriate education is cruel and unusual; and misclassifying a child as having an intellectual disability is truly an onerous level of cruel and unusual punishment, especially when the motive for classification is racially invidious. Intellectual disability is not defined by three criteria but all that is used to determine a child has an intellectual disability (including racism) and all that is done, or not done, to meet individual needs.

All the strategies to minimize the need for lesser culpability is accomplished under the guise of the Eighth Amendment which requires, so the theory goes, a less than benevolent interpretation for rendering capital punishment. What the Supreme Court said in Snyder v. Louisiana[615] in 2008 should apply to all Atkins claims. In *Snyder* the Court required that "all of the circumstances that bear upon the issue of racial animosity must be consulted." This requirement certainly includes the self-serving, often preposterous interpretations of intellectual disability where giving differential weights to the three primary elements of intellectual disability is the common practice.

A most unenviable task is to provide a fair interpretation of intellectual disability "by protecting even those convicted of heinous crimes, the Eighth Amendment reaffirms the duty of the government to respect the dignity of all persons."[616] If, as is often the case, the heinousness of a crime influences, either directly or indirectly, the determination of intellectual disability, the protection provided by Atkins can be subverted. As indicated by capital punishment for rape prior to *Coker* in 1977, the interpretation of the heinousness of a crime is often influenced by race; that is, for rape when the offender is black and the victim white, capital punishment was deemed suitable...but generally not when the offender was white regardless of the race of the victim.

---

[615]Snyder v. Louisiana, 552 U.S. 472 (2008)
[616]Roper v. Simmons, 543 U.S. 551 (2005)

The task of ignoring the heinousness of a crime, especially involving torture, children, police officers, etc. when determining intellectual disability is simply impossible for some courts or juries to overcome. The Supreme Court realized that (in *Atkins*) a defense showing of mental retardation might actually enhance the possibility of the death penalty rather than serving as a mitigating factor. This is why a determination of intellectual disability must be made apart from the crime so that no matter how deserving the death penalty might seem to be, the determination of intellectual disability must be consistent and even-handed.

The idiosyncratic interpretation of intellectual disability in Atkins claims might be the product of an inherent error in the use of a definition of mental retardation/intellectual disability, a definition that was primarily designed for children. The professional definitions were centerpiece for interpreting mental retardation in *Atkins* and also, as noted by the Supreme Court, as providing the basis for standards adopted by States. The Court in *Hall* in 2014 suggested that there could be an alternative definition of intellectual disability but none has been offered by States other than the re-interpretation/misinterpretation of existing professional definitions and, of course, additional evidentiary factors such as those offered by in Texas in Ex Parte Briseno. Texas was clever not to use the term "definition" and used "some other" factors to assist when considering evidence of mental retardation. Texas and other States have a history of providing "some other" factors for interpreting professional definitions, but States are not likely to explicitly create a new definition because such an effort would be subject to careful scrutiny. The various techniques for ignoring or misinterpreting IQ, a fair consideration of adaptive behavior and age of onset, or however a State might create a new definition of intellectual disability, would become fair game for courts and professionals.

The definition of intellectual disability could be modified for the purpose of *Atkins* but the essential three-prong definition has provided guidance for the Supreme Court and States. In *Ex parte* Briseno the court asked the rhetorical question "Is there, and should there be, a 'mental retardation' bright-line exemption from our state's maximum statutory punishment?" The court then explained that "we decline to answer that normative question without significantly greater assistance from the citizenry acting through its Legislature." What the Texas court decided was that the professional definition was insufficient for determining lesser culpability and that this court had the knowledge, perspicacity and insight to know what additional factors, based on a subjective analysis and stereotypic interpretation, should be incorporated to define intellectual disability for the purpose of the Eighth Amendment. All these strategies to minimize the need for lesser culpability is accomplished under the Eighth Amendment which requires, so the theory goes, a less than benevolent interpretation for rendering capital punishment. The Supreme Court speaks of legislative, professional and national "consensus" but surely a consensus of Texas citizens, who seem comfortable with being the all-time leader in executions, might not be the most appropriate group for determining what is or is not cruel and unusual punishment.[617]

The Briseno factors are not entirely without merit, especially if there is no history of intellectual disability and IQ scores are used which are subject to misinterpretation, malingering and tainted by racism. Professionals could address these issues by providing a definition that would take into account the ADA, the importance of criteria before age of onset, prioritize to some extent the elements listed for adaptive behavior, and expand the criteria for adaptive behavior that would accommodate some issues raised in *Briseno*. As the case may be, professionals have opted to leave the interpretation of the basic definition to lawyers who are often as ill-informed as judges, prosecutors and juries. This has resulted in an interpretation of intellectual disability that is often void of history and the inclusion of all relevant data. There is minimal discussion, and often no discussion, of childhood data, the meaning and use of IQ scores, racism and IQ testing, the ADA, special education classification, or the rules and regulations governing the determination of intellectual disability for children or adults.

---

[617]Moore v. Texas, Supreme Court of the United States, March 28, 2017.

In some instances, Atkins claims have become little more than a battle of stereotypes by the defense and State. The ease for interpreting data to reinforce either the defense or a State's concept of adaptive behavior illustrates the conundrum presented by the Briseno factors where the ability to "hide facts or lie effectively in his own or others' interests" is regarded as a strength by the prosecution but a deficit by defense: for the State this trait shows cunning but for the defense this is interpreted as a lack of responsibility. For Ricky R. Chase in Mississippi "his behavior when he entered the courtroom during the hearing and his behavior in the halls outside the courtroom prior to the hearing" was used to show that he did not have deficits in adaptive behavior. [618] Just as unconvincing the defense asserted that Chase did have impairments in adaptive behavior because he did not have a bank account, had a child out of wedlock, and "not understanding the degree of his culpability" was "an adaptive deficit."

What is offered in Atkins proceedings is cherry-picked hodge-podge of evidence to promote the position of defense or prosecution. All of this is bolstered by experts whose position for or against a determination of intellectual disability is easily predicted by whoever, defense or prosecution, is providing compensation. The defense provides low IQ scores, the prosecution asserts IQ scores lack credibility; the defense suggests deficits in adaptive behavior based on anecdotal data, the State asserts no deficits based on similar data but obviously contrary; the defense shows intellectual disability before age of onset, the prosecution demands a more recent determination (or a determination before age of onset and after). The contradictory yet predictable expert testimony in *Atkins* claims should be sufficient for showing that a fair enforcement of *Atkins* is a difficult if not impossible task. The only way to incorporate the adversarial process in Atkins claims is to have a common ground for defense and prosecution to examine all relevant evidence pertaining to intellectual disability.

---

[618]Chase v. Mississippi, Supreme Court of Mississippi, Brief of Appellee, NO. 2013-CA-01089-SCT, Attorney General of Mississippi, 2014

In *Arlington* the Supreme Court observed that "Substantive departures too may be relevant, particularly if the factors usually considered important by the decisionmaker strongly favor a decision contrary to the one reached." Atkins claims are replete with "substantive departures" of a fair and objective determination of intellectual disability. The re-interpretation of the definition of intellectual disability has allowed States to dismiss "factors usually considered important by the decisionmaker" by creating factors that reach a contrary decision and the denial of Atkins relief. Prime examples of this are the Briseno-type factors, stereotypes of adaptive behavior, bright line IQ cutoff scores (both 70 and 75), and ignoring age of onset (or not when that is beneficial to the State).

Even after *Atkins* in 2002 a slight-of-hand is used to interpret the criteria for intellectual disability as a *Ford*-like claim where all the evidence, especially adaptive behavior, is used to show mental competence rather than intellectual disability. The standard is not the criteria for intellectual disability but a lesser standard whereby the ultimate criterion is weather the defendant has a sufficient degree of mental ability to commit a murder. Aside from the criteria required for intellectual disability there is an underlying theme that if someone who is mentally competent, no matter the level of intellectual disability, understands the reason for trial, sounds competent and understands his or her degree of criminality, is suitable for imposing the death penalty. This goes beyond a "substantive departure" of the accepted definition of intellectual disability and supports a more State-friendly definition that is confounded by the heinousness of the crime, confusion concerning mental competence and mental ability, and idiosyncratic criteria used by both State and defense for interpreting intellectual disability.

In spite of the 2014 *Hall* decision the IQ criterion is a mere formality to ignore, no matter the score(s), or easily discounted. The decision provided the Court with an opportunity to pay homage to the Eighth Amendment "which reaffirms the duty of the government to respect the dignity of all persons" and to announce that "No legitimate penological purpose is served by executing the intellectually disabled." The ultimate decision in *Hall* relies on a murky interpretation of the standard error of measurement and ignores the importance of IQ testing during childhood, multiple IQ scores, different tests, different standardizations, malingering, even a token mention of research relating to intellectual disability and the death penalty, varied interpretations of IQ scores, the relative importance of various adaptive behavior criteria, and an agreed upon protocol for measuring adaptive behavior.

When considering a previous determination of intellectual disability, an IQ cutoff is meaningless in comparison to how IQ was used and, even more importantly, the record or should-have-been record of mental retardation/EMR/intellectual disability. The fact that the current IQ cutoff, firmly established by the Supreme Court, is now 75 has little bearing on how IQ was used for a particular Atkins claimant as a child, especially when States routinely classified children with IQ scores above 75 or even above 80 as having an intellectual impairment.

Amidst the complexity of data that should be associated with every Atkins claim, the history of racism associated with IQ testing and classification should not be overlooked. States are more than willing to acknowledge racism when considering IQ scores of an Atkins claimant as a child by explaining that scores might have been deflated because of cultural factors or environment, but there is considerable silence when explaining why these same individuals were stigmatized as children, denied educational opportunity, and then blossomed into unimpaired offenders ready and able for execution.

Ignoring a previous determination of intellectual disability, no matter the correctness of this determination, is a misinterpretation of the underlying purpose of the ADA. If a State has correctly identified a child as meeting the definition of intellectual disability and, as a result, provided an appropriate education, the benefits of this education in the form of increased academic help, the development independent living skills, etc. is then used to show that the individual is no longer intellectually disabled. On the other hand, if a child was incorrectly identified, that IQ was above the cutoff value, that there was no indication of impaired adaptive skills, and the child was nonetheless identified as having an intellectual disability, the child must live with that determination and the State as well. For children who have been misclassified as intellectually disabled, and so educated, to say many years later that this prior determination was a mistake does not undo the segregation and denial of educational opportunity, much less the intellectual/educational harm caused by asserting intellectual impairment, that occurred as a result of this prior determination. A history of intellectual disability is not undone by whim of judge or jury and certainly not when a defendant seeks lesser culpability during capital murder sentencing.

The idea that someone, defense counsel, prosecutor, judge or jury can determine if an individual has a "mild" intellectual disability is a difficult task at best, especially for an adult. An IQ score does not set a limit on what an individual can achieve or the ability to read, write, work, have a checking account etc; nor are IQ and adaptive behavior easily separated from motivation, environment, educational opportunity and the long and sordid history of segregation and discrimination. A school district can declassify a child before age 21 but this does not change the reality of the child's education as someone who was identified as having significantly subaverage general intellectual functioning. For Freddie Lee Hall there was evidence from teacher reports that he was mentally retarded and required special services, yet many years later the State off-handily dismissed clear evidence of mental retardation as a child. As stated by Justice Perry in a 2012 dissenting opinion "Hall is a poster child for mental retardation claims because the record here clearly demonstrates that Hall is mentally retarded. The fact that our statutory standard does not agree only serves to illustrate a flaw in the statute."[619]

The Supreme Court has undertaken the task of dealing with the various strategies to undermine *Atkins* on a piecemeal basis. The Court could provide general guidelines for achieving the constitutional mandate in Atkins. For example, the Court could explain that a determination of intellectual disability as a child, in keeping with the ADA, is tantamount to intellectual disability for the purposes of *Atkins*, that IQ scores prior to the capital crime are

---

[619]Hall v. Florida, 109 So. 3d 704, 2012

particularly relevant, that the cutoff for IQ should be high to ensure that other relevant evidence is not excluded, that one IQ score should not invalidate all other IQ scores, that academic functioning should be given special weight when considering adaptive behavior, that the Briseno factors can be relevant but that specific traits such as the ability to plan and forethought should not be determined solely by the crime itself but by carefully examining all relevant data, age of onset should not be a bright-line to exclude intellectual disability-type functioning, a determination of intellectual disability does not necessitate a dual finding before and after age of onset, that performance on death row, and similar re-interpretations of the definition of intellectual disability, is not exemplary of adaptive behavior, and that intellectual disability should not be reduced to stereotype (e.g., the ability to read, drive a car, have a job, etc.).

Overall, the mandate required by *Atkins* seems beyond the ability of States to enforce much less develop a scheme that considers a thoughtful analysis of childhood development, the ADA, measured intelligence, and adaptive behavior. In that this basic task is often ignored or minimized, there is little likelihood that States will consider the complex issue of race, why a child might not have been identified as having an intellectual disability, or why a disability other than intellectual disability might meet the Supreme Court's reasoning for lesser culpability when imposing the death penalty.

To the seemingly endless list of strategies and techniques for obviating the Atkins mandate, there is the underlying factor of racism that lurks about the intent of judges, prosecutors, experts, and jurors, all of whom are mostly white. Maybe this problem is beyond consideration, and this underlying racism cannot be considered or much less addressed. Maybe in the future this will be solved so that the death penalty will not weigh more heavily on blacks than whites, and that race will have no part in the selection of jurors, the decision by prosecutors to seek the death penalty, or by judges to impose the death penalty, or by courts to interpret Atkins in the most unfettered ways. Maybe the task for objectively applying a process for determining intellectual disabilities can be held apart from the crime or, more importantly, the heinousness of the crime. Maybe States can develop a mechanism that can, as much as possible, determine intellectual disability apart from racism, stereotype, judicial expertise and the heinousness of a murder. Maybe all this might or could happen. But it does not happen now, and there is no reason to expect that race will ever be considered apart from all matters relating to the death penalty.

The misapplication of *Atkins* is no different than the misapplication of the death penalty in general, only more obvious. The hypocrisy of disproportionately identifying a defendant as child as having an intellectual disability and then re-interpreting the definition of intellectual disabilities to deny Atkins relief is great. The Atkins mandate is, as was the case for the death penalty decades prior in *Furman*, wantonly and freakishly applied.[620] The disinclination and apparent inability of States to develop a consistent and fair framework for abiding by *Atkins* runs afoul of the Constitution and the narrowing jurisprudence sought by the Supreme Court. As it is, States cannot or will not provide a fair process for Atkins claims, and the processes that are provided by States are idiosyncratic, disingenuous, and unabashedly contort the concept of intellectual disability. The application of *Atkins* is plainly discretionary, haphazard, and discriminatory, exactly the status of the death penalty in 1972 when the Supreme Court decided that "the imposition and carrying out of the death penalty in these cases constitute cruel and unusual punishment in violation of the Eighth and Fourteenth Amendments."

The Supreme Court in *Gregg* offered that States provide "guidance regarding the factors about the crime and the defendant that the State, representing organized society, deems particularly relevant to the sentencing decision." Atkins should require guidance concerning the historical basis for intellectual disabilities, the commonly accepted use of the definitions of intellectual disability, the role of all pertinent regulations and laws, and the complex issue of race in every aspect of the judicial process. Until that happens, until the Supreme Court can conclude, as it did in *Hall* in 2014, that States do not have "unfettered discretion to define the

---

[620]Furman v. Georgia, 408 U.S. 238, 1972

full scope of the constitutional protection" in resolving Atkins claims, there should be a moratorium on Atkins claims and, as a consequence, in consideration of the disproportionate number of blacks on death row, and the manner in which States deny Atkins claims, there should be a moratorium on all executions.

How peculiar that all these things, these lynchings, segregation and discrimination, prosecutor and court decision-making, juror selection, the race of victims, sentencing and judges, Jim Crow laws, mild intellectual disabilities, death row, executions, exonerations, all come together in a swirl of idiosyncratic Atkins relief. We can do better; for black children and black defendants we generally do not.

9 781698 442297